WILDERNESS DEFENDER

WILDERNESS DEFENDER

Horace M. Albright and Conservation

DONALD C. SWAIN

UNIVERSITY OF CHICAGO PRESS · CHICAGO & LONDON

Standard Book Number: 226–78292–1
Library of Congress Catalog Card Number: 70–93057
The University of Chicago Press, Chicago 60637
The University of Chicago Press, Ltd., London

26844 7
6.05.70

To my Parents

LA

Contents

Preface

I met Horace Albright, figuratively speaking, quite by accident in the spring of 1960. He was a name on a piece of paper. I was at the National Archives in Washington making a study of the conservation policies of the federal government during the 1920s. In the course of my research, I read dozens of Albright's letters in the files of the National Park Service—he participated in nearly every phase of its program—and encountered his name in a number of other correspondence collections. He was, I discovered, a remarkably effective bureau chief. He had connections with many of the high-ranking conservationists and politicians in Washington, and he seemed to have an intuitive political shrewdness that enabled him to obtain most of what he wanted from his friends in the executive agencies and in Congress. He interested me primarily because of his creative achievements as an administrator-politician. Moreover, he was an advocate of wilderness preservation and a follower of both John Muir and Stephen T. Mather, whose concepts of conservation had already aroused my curiosity.

By the time I had completed my research in the archives, I had documented the fact that Albright was one of the leading spokesmen for aesthetic conservation in the federal establishment during the 1920s and 1930s, particularly during the Hoover administration and the first hundred days of the New Deal. It occurred to me that by studying Albright's career one might throw new light on the institutional history of the National Park Service, which he helped found, and on the history of the conservation movement in the United States. I scrawled a note to myself to this effect for future reference.

It was precisely four years later that I made up my mind to undertake a full-scale biography of Albright. By then I was aware of his reputation as one of the nation's leading conservationists. I knew that, in addition to his central role in shaping the national park system, he had collaborated in the establishment of the Civilian Conservation Corps, the restoration of Colonial Williamsburg, and the founding of Resources for the Future. I knew that he was one of the key figures in the protracted and bitter Jackson Hole controversy, one of the most remarkable conservation fights of the twentieth century. I had studied the eight-hundred-page transcript of his "Reminiscences" at the Oral History Research Office in Columbia University and had learned that he had a large and informative collection of personal papers to which I could gain unrestricted access. Moreover, I had met him in person and talked to him at length about national park affairs in the 1920s. By carefully checking his statements against the documentary evidence in my files, I demonstrated to my own satisfaction that his recollections were reliable and, in fact, remarkably accurate.

Shortly after I started to work on the biography, Howard H. Hays, one of Albright's oldest friends, gave me fair warning that I had "a tarpon on the line." He was unquestionably right. Albright had two separate and successful careers—one as a government official, the other as an executive in the mining industry. He participated actively in a wide range of conservation organizations, often serving as an elected officer or as a member of the board of directors. A compulsive letter writer, he corresponded with politicians, businessmen, conservationists, and professional men from coast to coast, collecting their opinions on vital issues and reflecting the trend of the times. He was an enormously energetic man, with diverse interests and the inclination to indulge most of them. Certain aspects of his life and career would obviously have to be left out of the biography. Exactly what was to be omitted became a matter of balance and judgment. Lack of advice on this point was not one of my problems.

I determined to make Albright's activities as a conservationist the central, unifying theme of the book. Bureaucrat or businessman, he always remained passionately devoted to the goal of conserving natural resources, especially natural beauty. The decision to concentrate on Albright's conservation work meant that I could give his business career only minimal treatment. Two other organizational decisions significantly shaped the book and helped me keep its length within reasonable limits. First, I resolved to emphasize the early years of Albright's life, for these were his most important years; in my view, nothing he ever did in his life was more creative than his pioneer work as a national park administrator and policy maker. Second, I decided to focus on Albright himself rather than on the institutions and enterprises with which he was identified. In other words, I would avoid, as much as possible, turning the biography into a history of the National Park Service, or the American conservation movement, or the United States Potash Company, of which Albright was the chief executive officer for more than two decades. These decisions appear as plausible and defensible at the conclusion of the project as they did at the beginning.

So many people helped me at various stages of my research and writing that it would be tedious to list all of them. Nevertheless, I am grateful to them all. Philip C. Brooks, director of the Harry S. Truman Library, and Phillip Lagerquist, Harry Clark, and Willie Harriford, of the Truman Library staff, gave me valuable assistance during my trips to Independence. Dwight M. Miller, the archivist at the Herbert Hoover Library, helped make my brief stay in West Branch both pleasant and productive. I owe a large debt of gratitude to Stanley Brown, Roy Wilgus, Helen Finneran, and Robert Kvasnicka, of the National Archives, who patiently and skillfully guided me to the materials I needed. Elmo R. Richardson and Samuel P. Hays gave me the benefit of their comments on chapter 9, which they read and criticized in an earlier form as part of a scholarly panel at a meeting of historians. Morgan B. Sherwood, my friend and colleague, read the entire manuscript, casting a critical eye on the organization and writing style and offering many valuable suggestions. My wife, Lavinia Lesh Swain, listened to my ideas, read and reread every chapter, and winked at my idiosyncrasies during the long writing process.

Oscar L. Chapman, Newton B. Drury, George L. Mauger,

Loye Miller, Gladys Jones Jewett, and many others kindly permitted me to interview them. Horace Albright and Grace Albright patiently endured long hours of my questioning. In the end, it was probably inevitable that my interpretation of events would diverge somewhat from the interpretations suggested to me in some of the interviews. It could hardly be expected that my perceptions would coincide with those of Albright's close friends. Nor would they coincide with Albright's self-image. Happily, there was a minimum of difficulty on this count. Any errors of fact or interpretation that appear in the biography are exclusively my own.

The following individuals generously granted me permission to quote from their personal papers or from the letters of their relatives: Clinton P. Anderson, Oscar L. Chapman, Huntley Child, Beverly S. Clendenin, Newton B. Drury, Melville Bell Grosvenor, Jane D. Ickes, Arthur Krock, Graeme Lorimer, Bertha Mather McPherson, Frank E. Mason (representing Allan Hoover), Fairfield Osborn, Herman Phleger, Laurance S. Rockefeller, Alice Shankland, and Conrad L. Wirth. Horace Albright was especially generous in allowing me to quote extensively from his personal correspondence.

Grants from the Committee on Research of the University of California, Davis, enabled me to travel to Washington, Independence, West Branch, Carlsbad, and Los Angeles. A timely sabbatical leave allowed me to finish the manuscript approximately on schedule.

WILDERNESS DEFENDER

1

Beginning in Bishop

Angling northward from the desert fringes of Los Angeles to the snow-capped peaks of Yosemite National Park, the Owens Valley of California boasts some of the finest mountain scenery in North America. Along the western edge of the valley, the High Sierra forms an enormous granite wall, thrusting up almost vertically to an altitude of fourteen thousand feet. Great ice-hewn precipices reach down toward the floor of the valley, holding in their granite beds "a thread of brook, the small sapphire gems of alpine lake, bronze dots of pine, and here and there a fine enamelling of snow." The jagged summit of Mount Whitney, the plunging canyons of the Kings River, and the soaring redwoods of Sequoia are only a few miles away. Along the eastern edge of the valley, the Inyo and White mountains climb to a height of more than two and a half miles, their rounded, brown slopes contrasting vividly with the angular, gray Sierra. Near the top of the White Mountains stand the gnarled and grotesque bristlecone pines, probably the oldest living things on earth. This is an extraordinarily varied and beautiful country. Caves, craters, lava beds, and lakes rim the valley to the north, and beyond the Inyo Mountains to the east stretch "leagues and leagues of lifeless desert." A boy growing up here would almost surely develop a profound respect for the wonders of nature. Horace Marden Albright was born and raised in Bishop, California, a small town cradled at the northern end of the Owens Valley.[1]

1. The quotations are from Clarence King, *Mountaineering in the Sierra Nevada* (New York: Charles Scribner's Sons, 1926), p. 343, reprinted by permission.

3

In those days Bishop was a quaint little town with scarcely three hundred residents. It was the hub of a splendid agricultural region, where wheat, corn, fruit, livestock, and many other farm products could be grown profitably. While it would be stretching a point to call it a bustling town, the inhabitants prided themselves on being busy and self-reliant, and they held an optimistic view of their community's future. The land in that part of the valley was extremely fertile. An abundant supply of water for irrigation streamed down from the mountains on both sides of town. Cattle thrived on the accommodating pastures, and groves of fruit trees dotted the countryside in all directions. Tall Lombardy poplars, locusts, and cottonwoods lined the streets of the town, breaking the wind and giving shade in the hot summer months. It was a pleasant place to live.

Not the least of Bishop's attractions was that Dr. W. H. George, a respected old physician, practiced there. His reputation had spread throughout the Owens Valley, and it was commonplace for women in that vicinity to come to Bishop so that "Doc" George could deliver their babies. In January 1890 Mary Albright came to town to await the birth of her child. She and her husband, George L. Albright, made their home in Candelaria, Nevada, a little mining town about seventy-five miles to the north, where the Northern Belle and a half dozen other mines produced a steady flow of silver. Like most of the Nevada mining camps, Candelaria was a primitive place. It consisted of a tiny business district and two or three tributary trails along which the small wood and stone houses huddled for protection against the wind. The town had an abundance of saloons, but many of the bare essentials of life, including reliable medical care, were simply not available. Fortunately for those who needed a doctor, getting to Bishop was a relatively simple matter. The narrow-gauge Carson and Colorado Railroad, snaking its way over Montgomery Pass and into the Owens Valley, could make the journey in only a day. Mary Albright had her baby in Bishop on January 6, 1890, and then convalesced at her sister's ranch just south of town. The robust little boy was christened Horace Marden in honor of his grandfather. As soon as the weather warmed, Mrs. Albright took her son and went back to Candelaria to be with her husband.[2]

Horace's father worked in Candelaria until 1893, earning a reasonably good living as a carpenter and engineer at the Northern Belle mine. He installed heavy machinery and built mine shafts. He and an enterprising friend, Christian Brevoort Zabriskie, served as Candelaria's only undertakers. In those days being an undertaker involved little more than constructing an appropriate pine box. George Albright, a soft-hearted, naturally sympathetic man, soon had a reputation for being "pleasant to have around at a funeral." His partnership with Chris Zabriskie produced the unforgettable slogan: "Albright and Zabriskie, A to Z. You kick the bucket and we'll do the rest."[3]

Then came the disastrous depression of 1893 that wrenched the silver-mining country into a state of economic chaos. As the price of silver skidded to its lowest level in decades, the mines began to close and Candelaria was doomed. In the fall of 1893, with the depression deepening, George Albright took his family to Bishop and set himself up as a contractor, mill operator, and part-time undertaker. A ghost town in the Nevada foothills, crumbling and forgotten, now marks the place where Horace Albright spent the first years of his life. All of his childhood memories were to be of Bishop. His values and character were to be molded by the mountains and the people of the Owens Valley.[4]

In the familiar pattern of small American towns, Bishop had its Main Street, a thoroughfare that bisected the village from north to south. The hotels, the business houses, the saloons, and the livery stables clustered along this avenue. The Bishop Creek Hotel stood near the center of town offering rooms for twenty-five to fifty cents a night. Next door was the Pioneer Saloon,

2. *Inyo Register*, Jan. 9, 1890, and Jan. 23, 1890; interviews with Horace M. Albright (hereafter abbreviated HMA), Jan. 11, 1964, and June 25, 1964.

3. Quotation from Robert Shankland, *Steve Mather of the National Parks*, p. 34.

4. *Inyo Register*, Oct. 12, 1893; interview with HMA, June 25, 1964.

featuring "liquors and cigars of the best quality." Just down the street was Mark's and Cohn's Emporium, where one could purchase ladies' black stockings for ten cents a pair or seven pounds of coffee for a dollar. Leece and Watterson's Hardware stood on the corner of Academy Avenue and Main Street, displaying a complete line of guns, tools, and farm machinery. There was an apothecary shop, specializing in patent medicines and other remedies, including "Mrs. Winslow's Soothing Syrup," an all-purpose nostrum that "soothes the child, softens the gums, allays all pain, gulates the bowels, and is the best known remedy for diarrhea."[5]

One of the town's major distinctions was its newspaper, the *Inyo Register*, which was published weekly by the Chalfant family. No bit of news was too insignificant to find its way into the "Taboose" column (a taboose is a succulent desert plant) and no demon too ferocious to be attacked on the front page. This extraordinary little newspaper printed first-rate historical sketches of the West and constantly pointed out the loveliness of nature and the need for conserving natural resources.[6]

At the south end of Main Street a small Chinatown had sprung up. About two dozen Chinese families, clad in Oriental costumes and speaking native dialects, made their homes there. The Chinese men, who had once worked in the silver mines to the north, did odd jobs around town and made themselves generally inconspicuous. Hard feelings existed between the whites and the Chinese in Bishop. "That Chinaman who plays three kinds of musical instruments several times daily in the business part of town," the *Register* one day observed, "doesn't realize how much he monkeys with 'Melican' forbearance."[7]

George Albright established his new business across Main Street and a little to the north of Chinatown. In an attempt to capitalize on his own mechanical skill, he concentrated at first on his planing and feed mill. An old, wood-burning steam engine

5. For information about Bishop see *Inyo Register*, 1890–1900; the quotations are from the *Register*, Jan. 9, 1890, and Jan. 23, 1890; my descriptions of Bishop and vicinity are based in part on my own observations of the Owens Valley.

6. *Inyo Register*, 1890–1908, passim.

7. Ibid., Aug. 16, 1900; interview with HMA, July 24, 1964.

provided the rotary power and a rough board-structure of fairly large dimensions covered the grindstones that were used primarily to process grain. He prepared oats, wheat, and barley for livestock feed and was the only man in the vicinity who made cornmeal. The mill also processed salt which had been collected in Saline Valley, a parched region southeast of Bishop. One of Horace's first jobs was putting freshly milled salt into five- and ten-pound bags and marking them for sale.[8]

As time passed, George Albright began to expand his operations. A successful contractor and builder, he erected many of the largest structures in Bishop, including rambling Victorian-style houses, austere churches, and the modern up-to-date Wildasinn Hall, where concerts, plays, and community dances were held. Because of the increasing demand for his undertaking services, he built a small funeral parlor that fronted on Main Street, and by 1900 he was prosperous enough to purchase a large horsedrawn hearse, "the first genuine hearse to be brought into the county," the *Register* proudly announced.[9]

George Albright had very little time to spend with his family in those days, for he was one of the busiest men in Bishop. He worked long hours tending to his business enterprises. In his spare time he participated enthusiastically in many lodge activities. A native of Canada, he had trekked west in 1873 to work on the Comstock Lode. His formal education had ended abruptly at the sixth grade, which was unfortunate, because he had a good mind and an extraordinary memory. His fraternal brothers always put him in charge of ritual indoctrinations because of his remarkable ability to recall obscure names and dates. Except in 1896, when he backed Bryan, he consistently voted for Republicans throughout his life, and he himself held office several times as a Republican. During the 1880s he represented Esmeralda County in the Nevada state legislature. In 1902 the citizens of Bishop elected him to the town's first board of trustees.[10]

8. Interview with HMA, Jan. 11, 1964.
9. *Inyo Register*, July 26, 1900.
10. Interview with A. A. Brierly, June 22, 1964; *Inyo Register*, Nov. 8, 1900; *Mementos of Bishop, California*, p. 15.

Horace enjoyed a comparatively carefree boyhood in Bishop. The yard of the Albright home on Academy Avenue was sprawling and rustic. An irrigation stream ran through the property. There were big cottonwoods and willows to climb. Apples, peaches, cherries, and plums ripened in the sun; vegetables grew in the garden. Most of the time Horace had the run of the town. His inseparable companion during these early years was a mongrel dog named Jess. One of the familiar sights in Bishop in 1895 was Horace Albright in a two-wheeled cart being pulled by his awkward black dog.[11]

In 1896, the year of William McKinley's election, Horace entered the Bishop public school, a modest institution, occupying a boxlike two-story building about two blocks from the Albright residence. Three teachers did all of the teaching, dividing the pupils roughly according to age. From the beginning, Horace demonstrated that he was an intelligent and conscientious boy. His third-grade teacher gave him an inscribed copy of *Black Beauty* as a reward for excelling in penmanship. His name appeared on the "roll of honor" for the intermediate department of Bishop School in both 1899 and 1900. In future years his marks would not always be so high, but he remained a quick, hard-working, and intelligent student whose academic achievements were consistently above average.[12]

By the time the Spanish-American War had come and gone, Horace was ten years old, a sturdy, active youngster who loved the out-of-doors. Considering the close proximity of the High Sierra, it was curious that he had never gone on a camping trip. In the summer of 1900, George Albright decided to give his boys (there were now three Albright brothers) a taste of the mountains.[13]

Shortly after school recessed, the Albrights and a few friends made their way to the Ten Big Trees campground on Bishop Creek, about fifteen miles from town. Splendid Jeffrey pines

11. Interview with Blanche Chalfant Wheeler, June 24, 1964.
12. "Possible Contents or Prospectus," n.d., and third-grade report card, HMA Papers; *Inyo Register*, Nov. 2, 1899, and Mar. 8, 1900.
13. *Inyo Register*, July 19, 1900.

surrounded the camp site. Aspen, birch, alder, willow, and juniper grew in profusion along the edges of the stream. And straight ahead loomed the massive gray face of Mount Humphreys. It was here that Horace first experienced the thrill of camping in the open. His father instructed him in the intricacies of catching trout. His mother helped him identify the colorful birds. She took him to open places in the woods to point out the beauty of the mountains. Soon his parents turned him loose to fish and hike wherever he wanted. After about a month, the family returned to Bishop, but Horace recounted the highlights and adventures of that camping trip again and again until they were burned permanently into his memory.[14]

The next summer George Albright took his eldest son on a fishing trip to Mammoth Lakes, a scenic spot about forty miles north of Bishop. Horace caught his limit of trout and, as an added treat, was allowed to explore the dilapidated and abandoned mining camp at Mammoth City. On this and several future trips to Mammoth, Horace became well acquainted with R. L. P. Bigelow, the congenial forest ranger there, who often invited the young man to ride with him on his inspection trips through the vast Sierra Forest Reserve. On one of these rides Horace crossed into Yosemite National Park for the first time.[15]

As a boy, Horace enjoyed the comradeship of these outings with his father, but, in the day-to-day process of growing up, it was his mother who exerted the crucial influence on his emerging ideas and personality. Mary Marden Albright was a kindly, outgoing, imperturbable woman who demonstrated a remarkable strength of character at important junctures in the life of her family. She had grown up in the silver-mining towns of California and Nevada and deeply regretted the brawling, primitive environment of her early years. She consciously aspired for her children to escape the peculiar confinement of the mining country. Consequently, her greatest desire was to see her sons well

14. Interview with HMA, Jan. 11, 1964; this account is based in part on my own observations in and around the Ten Big Trees campground.

15. Interview with HMA, Mar. 23, 1964.

educated. She worked tirelessly to instill in each of them her devotion to the ideal of self-improvement through education, and
she campaigned single-mindedly for the establishment of a high
school in Bishop. The fact that Horace eventually did go to high
school and to the University of California may be attributed
largely to his mother's determination and perseverance.

Mary Albright was herself an educated person, having studied
for three years at Napa Collegiate Institute, a school that later
became part of the College of the Pacific. She respected good
books, and on every possible occasion she supplied Horace
with reading material. At first she gave him adventure stories
by the widely read British author, G. A. Henty. Then, as her son
grew older, she introduced him to poetry and to the works of
Charles Dickens and James Fenimore Cooper. The most prized
book in Horace's library was a leatherbound copy of *Poems by
Henry Wadsworth Longfellow* that his mother gave him on his
tenth birthday. But music was Mary Albright's special joy. During the 1890s she took great pride in the ornately carved organ
that stood in her living room. She played it often, singing and
pumping the foot pedals with gusto.[16]

Horace's mother went through life mindful of appearances
and extremely sensitive to her neighbors' opinions. She took
pains to instruct her boys in proper manners. Religion, as a
measure of refinement and respectability, was so important to
her that she helped organize a Presbyterian congregation in
town and later saw to it that her children attended services every
Sunday. She became an avid member of the Women's Improvement Club, an organization that took the lead in planning civic
affairs. She was a personable, hard-working, honest, upward-
striving, civic-minded woman, who imbued her oldest son with
most of her own values and personal standards. Horace did not
realize until many years later how remarkable it was that she
could have husbanded her respect for education, her love of

16. Copies of Henty, Dickens, Cooper, and Longfellow in HMA
Papers; for information on Napa Collegiate Institute see D. Rockwell
Hunt, *History of the College of the Pacific 1851–1951.*

good books, and her devotion to music through all those years in an uncultured, semifrontier environment.[17]

One of the high points of Horace's youth came in 1903 when he journeyed out of the Owens Valley for the first time. His mother had been ill that winter and the family doctor thought she ought to go to San Francisco for special treatment. As the eldest son in the family, Horace was assigned to accompany her. He would go as far as Sacramento, then he would head north to Shasta to spend the summer with his grandfather, while his mother completed the trip to San Francisco. He was thirteen years old.[18]

Horace and his mother left in April, just after school closed for the summer. The narrow-gauge Carson and Colorado Railroad carried them north from Bishop, climbing up the White Mountains and into Nevada. Transferring to the broad-gauge Virginia and Truckee Railroad, the two travelers continued to Reno and then dropped down the Sierra slope into California. It took three days and two nights to reach Sacramento, where Mrs. Albright prudently decided they should rest for a day.[19]

The next morning the boy from the Owens Valley roamed through the streets of Sacramento. He had never seen a city. After lunch, he boarded another train, which carried him up the Sacramento Valley into northern California. At a rustic station in the mountains, his grandfather Marden met him with a buckboard. Together they rode for several miles through the dense forests along Mears Creek, arriving finally at the site of the old man's logging camp. That summer, Horace rode horseback and went fishing. He got to know the lumberjacks and tried his hand at various jobs around the logging camp. Later, he had the thrill of fighting a forest fire.[20]

Horace also delighted in spending long hours with his grandfather, whom he idolized. The old man had originally journeyed

17. Interview with HMA, Mar. 23, 1964.
18. "Summer of 1903," n.d., HMA Papers.
19. *Inyo Register*, Apr. 30, 1903; "Summer of 1903."
20. Interview with HMA, Mar. 23, 1964; "Summer of 1903."

from Maine to San Francisco via Nicaragua in 1851, attracted
by the news of the fabulous gold discoveries in California. He
had worked for many years in the mining country and then had
entered the lumber business. A superlative storyteller, he took
pleasure in regaling his wide-eyed grandson with tales of the
gold-mining days in California. He also took pains to explain the
careless and wasteful logging practices that were common in the
lumber business. "Before the summer was over, I was regretting
the forestry practices as much as this old patriarch did," Horace
later wrote. "He was making a conservationist out of me."
Toward the end of the summer, Grandfather Marden took his
namesake on a long buckboard trip to see Mount Shasta, the
towering giant of the upper Sacramento Valley. It was an incomparable view with "meadow, forest, and grand icy summit
harmoniously blending" in one sublime picture. Horace never
forgot the pleasure of that moment. One of the ironies of his life
was that the foundations of his conservation philosophy, emphasizing preservationism and aestheticism, were laid by an old
man who devoted the major part of his life to the ruthless exploitation of natural resources.[21]

Horace was almost a month late getting back to school that
fall. He found himself a little behind in spelling and arithmetic,
but he was quite a star around town because of his extensive
travels. Only a handful of the other children in Bishop had ever
ventured more than a few miles from home. His parents decided
to enroll him in the Riverside School about five miles north of
town. Mrs. Albright knew that the teacher at this one-room
school was especially talented, and she thought Horace would
benefit by the change. He encouraged the idea because he would
then have an excuse to ride horseback to school every day.[22]

Horace grew up quickly after the summer of 1903. To earn
spending money, he chopped huge piles of piñon pine for fifty
cents a cord. He also began working for his father as a shingler,

---

21. "Summer of 1903"; description of Mount Shasta from John Muir,
Steep Trails (Boston and New York: Houghton Mifflin Company,
1918), pp. 30–31, reprinted by permission.
22. *Inyo Register*, Oct. 8, 1903, and June 23, 1904.

a tedious occupation that required relatively small and nimble fingers. He looked forward to the lively parties and dances in Bishop and especially out in Round Valley, where the Jones sisters lived. It was a long, fifteen-mile ride to Round Valley, but Horace seldom minded, for the parties there were always happy affairs that lasted until dawn. One of the Jones sisters can still remember Horace shouting as the Victrola came on: "Better turn that down, Gladys, or I'll dance right off this rafter."[23]

Bishop Union High School had existed for only three years and had still not been accredited when Horace enrolled as a freshman in 1904. Its classes met haphazardly at first in a single, cramped room and in the second-floor hallway of the grade-school building. Two overworked teachers handled all of the instruction. The students, a number of whom were boarders from the outlying regions of the county, all took the same basic courses: four years of history, English, and Latin, and two years of mathematics and natural science. Horace ranked second in the school in the comprehensive examinations given at the end of his sophomore year and was cited for "perfect attendance."[24]

In September 1906 Horace enrolled for his third year of high school in Stockton, California. Mrs. Albright had continued to worry about Bishop High School's lack of accreditation, so she wrote to her old friend Clara Cross, whom she had known in Candelaria, to inquire if arrangements could be made for Horace to attend school in Stockton. Mrs. Cross replied that Horace would be welcome to stay at her house if he would agree to take care of "the lawn and garden," tend to the "feeding, currying, and exercise of the horse," and "bring in the fire wood." He did his chores and worked especially hard on his studies during the autumn and winter of 1906. He had committed himself to take the West Point examinations in the spring, and he was a more dedicated student than ever.[25]

For more than three years Horace had bedeviled his father

23. Interview with Gladys Jones Jewett, June 22, 1964.
24. *Inyo Register*, May 10, 1906.
25. "Albright and the University of California," n.d., pp. 1–3, HMA Papers.

and mother about the possibility of an appointment to West Point. He got himself a copy of *Three Roads to a Commission* by W. P. Burnham and pored over the small volume. He wrote repeatedly to the War Department and to the president, requesting an appointment. He badgered Congressman S. C. Smith of California so persistently that the distinguished gentleman, obviously astonished by the flood of letters from his young constituent, at last wrote to confess that he admired the young man's "pluck and determination." After a great deal of personal effort and an assist from his father, Horace won a first-alternate appointment to the Military Academy, which meant that he could take the competitive examinations, and in case the principal appointee failed, he would receive the appointment. On April 30, 1907, Horace boarded a small river boat and made the overnight trip down the San Joaquin River from Stockton to San Francisco, fully prepared to earn his coveted billet at the academy. San Francisco still lay in ruins from the disastrous earthquake of 1906. Horace was "aghast" when he saw the widespread destruction. Each morning and evening during the three days of examination he walked four miles from the old Sierra Hotel to the Presidio, where the tests were held. A few weeks later, he received official notification that he had passed the tests, but so had the principal appointee. That ingloriously ended Horace's dream of a military career.[26]

After completing the West Point tests, Horace crossed the bay to Berkeley to visit Ben F. Edwards, whom the Albright family had known in the mining country, and to take a tour of the campus of the University of California. The beauty of the campus and the academic atmosphere immediately appealed to him. He decided on the spot that he would go to Berkeley for his

26. W. P. Burnham, *Three Roads to a Commission;* Military Secretary to HMA, Apr. 14, 1906, George C. Perkens to HMA, Mar. 24, 1906, Frank P. Flint to HMA, Mar. 24, 1906, S. C. Smith to HMA, Apr. 13, 1906, and certificate of alternate appointment to West Point, Jan. 14, 1907, HMA Papers; "Albright and the University of California," pp. 3–4.

college education if his attempt to get into the Military Academy failed.[27]

Horace returned to Bishop for his senior year in high school, after his mother received assurances that the local school would at last win accreditation. Bishop High School had now moved into the old two-story Methodist Academy building, just across the street from the Albright residence, a coincidence that gave Horace certain distinct advantages. One of his schoolmates remembers him spending most of his spare time hanging over nearby front fences talking to the girls who boarded in the neighborhood.[28]

By the time of his senior year in high school, Horace had already become an inveterate joiner, a characteristic that became more and more pronounced as the years passed. He served as president of the newly organized Young Men's Christian Association. He was head of the "Excelsiors," a small literary study group, and he later worked as school editor, with responsibility for writing an occasional column about high-school activities for the Bishop newspaper. He participated in organized debates and helped raise funds for the school by producing amateur stage shows. He was so caught up in the enthusiasm of the prohibition movement that he became a leading member of the Independent Order of Good Templars, a temperance organization whose initials, IOGT, the cynics sneered, really stood for "I Often Get Tight."[29]

For most of the fall term of 1907, Horace averaged more than 90 percent in all of his subjects. He knew by then that he would be attending the University of California, and he meant to prepare himself. Accreditation had not been forthcoming for

27. Interview with HMA, Mar. 23, 1964; "Albright and the University of California," p. 4.

28. *Inyo Register*, Aug. 29, 1907; interview with Mary Watterson Gorman, June 22, 1964; "Albright and the University of California," pp. 4–6.

29. *Inyo Register*, Oct. 3, 1907, Nov. 7, 1907, and Nov. 28, 1907; interview with HMA, July 24, 1964.

Bishop High School, and he would have to enter the university on probation.[30]

Horace's retentive mind and his personal determination easily carried him through high school. He was earnest, serious, unsophisticated, and highly motivated. He meant to succeed and, without being blatant about it, harbored a modest ambition to build a better world. "We as young people," he wrote early in 1908, "are eager to build strong characters. We want to lay hold and cherish the best things in life and eliminate those things that are detrimental." Time-honored American middle-class standards and values, which exalted honesty, sobriety, thriftiness, hard work, and determination to succeed, had been deeply ingrained in him. As he launched into his graduation oration entitled "Opportunity," he sounded remarkably like a character out of Horatio Alger. "The successful ones," he proclaimed, "are those who make the best of the occasions that offer."[31]

The familiar narrow-gauge train carried Horace out of the Owens Valley toward Berkeley in August 1908. He moved into Flora Berger's boardinghouse on Walnut Street in Berkeley and quickly adjusted to the routine of a college student. The university, which was about a mile away, seemed even more fascinating than he had remembered. The main part of the campus opened off Telegraph Avenue, a busy thoroughfare crowded with houses and business establishments. Entering the campus from the south and moving straight ahead, he could see the white granite walls of California Hall, one of the university's principal classroom buildings. To the right, up a gentle slope, North and South halls rose like Victorian courthouses, their red brick walls partly covered with green and brown vines. Groves of tall eucalyptus trees and stands of arching live oaks could be seen near the faculty club and along Strawberry Creek, which ran just inside the southern border of the campus. The massive Greek Theatre, where plays and concerts and distinguished speakers appeared,

30. Interview with Mary Watterson Gorman, June 22, 1964; *Inyo Register*, Nov. 21, 1907.
31. Quotations from *Inyo Register*, Jan. 23, 1908, and May 28, 1908.

had recently been constructed at the base of the Berkeley hills. Across the bay lay San Francisco, sparkling like a string of diamonds in the evening twilight. Berkeley was a tremendously exciting and sophisticated place compared to Bishop, and Horace felt great pangs of insecurity and anxiety at first. "I was as green a freshman as ever came off the 'tall uncut,' " he later confessed.[32]

Horace registered for a full load of courses in the College of Commerce. The university had accepted him with the understanding that his first semester's grades would have to be good enough to warrant his remaining. He also took a job with Mason-McDuffie, a real estate firm in Berkeley, "digging post holes and erecting billboards." As his calluses thickened, he developed a lasting hatred of billboards. At various times from 1908 to 1912 Horace washed dishes, clerked in a bookstore, recorded grades in the registrar's office, tutored other students, and took on numerous one-shot jobs. His father gave him twenty-five dollars a month in 1908 and 1909, but the rest of the time he was essentially on his own. His classmates considered him "studious," "quiet," and "serious," especially during his freshman year.[33]

By February 1909 Horace had begun to widen the circle of his friends. He kept in touch with Beverly S. Clendenin, whom he had met on the train to Berkeley. He got to know Earl ("Pinky") Warren, the future chief justice, a raw-boned and popular fellow who had a loud, hearty laugh and was well known for his prowess with the coeds. He became well acquainted with Ray M. Gidney, of Santa Barbara, whom he coached in algebra and geometry in exchange for lessons in typing and shorthand. Horace sometimes chatted with Newton B. Drury, who excelled as a debater and had an enviable record as a campus politician.

32. "List of Expenses for 1908," and U.C. library card for 1908–9, HMA Papers; *Blue and Gold* (U.C. yearbook, 1909); HMA, "Reminiscing," *The Deller* 3 (July 1929): 26; Beverly S. Clendenin to the author, Sept. 2, 1965.

33. U.C. report cards for 1908–13, HMA Papers; "Albright and the University of California," pp. 9–12; Ray M. Gidney to the author, Sept. 9, 1965.

Thomas J. Ledwich, a prelaw student, and Tracy Storer, who spent most of his time in the zoology laboratory, also became his friends. In future years Albright stayed in contact with all of these men as they distinguished themselves in their own professions.[34]

He joined the Del Rey Club, a local fraternity, in the spring of 1909. The fact that he was an unusually knowledgeable card player accounted for much of his early popularity in the organization. In the fall of 1909 he decided to move into the clubhouse, which stood conveniently close to the campus and offered board and room for twenty-five dollars a month, the same low price Mrs. Berger charged. He soon pulled out of the card games for fear that his grades would suffer. In fact, he became a leading "reformer" in the club. In April 1910, with the annual ritual of electing officers approaching, he was nominated to run for vice-president and house manager on a "dry" ticket. He won by the slender margin of one vote, but that was enough. Backed by other reformers, he outlawed beer busts except on weekends and drastically cut down on the number of card games. Horace continued to serve as house manager for the next two years, collecting all fees, paying the bills, and ringing in "a dance or two with punch and music" each semester. It was excellent training for a future national park administrator. His success as house manager was the first real indication of his ability as an organizer and administrator. His zealous crusading against beer busts and card playing indicated that he still had not lost his determination to "eliminate those things that are detrimental" to the development of strong character. More important was the fact that as house manager he received free room and board and thus eased the pressure of supporting himself in college.[35]

Horace went back to Bishop for the summer of 1909 and worked for his father, doing odd jobs and carpentry. Mr. Al-

34. Ballot for election, Class of 1912, HMA Papers; interview with Newton B. Drury, Sept. 22, 1965; interview with John Quinn, Dec. 19, 1965; Thomas J. Ledwich to the author, Sept. 22, 1965; Clendenin to the author, Sept. 2, 1965; Gidney to the author, Sept. 9, 1965.

35. HMA, "Reminiscing," p. 27; list of Del Rey bank balances on back of blank check [1911], HMA Papers; "Albright and the University of California," pp. 14, 16–17, 27–28, 33.

bright hoped that at least one of his sons would elect to stay in Bishop and go into business with him. Without informing his father, Horace had already decided against a career in engineering or contracting, and he had long since concluded that he wanted no part of the undertaking business. Under the circumstances, a gentle confrontation between father and son was probably inevitable. The decisive moment came when Bill Slee, an old blacksmith in Bishop, suddenly died, and Mr. Albright asked his son to help prepare the corpse for burial. This was an entirely reasonable request, one that Horace had been expecting and passionately dreading for weeks. "I just could not bring myself to do it," he remembered. After procrastinating for as long as possible, he finished the job, but he made no attempt to conceal his profound distaste. After that, it was clearly understood that the eldest Albright boy would not be joining his father. In August Horace returned to Berkeley to continue his education. Except for brief family visits, he never went back to the Owens Valley.[36]

During his freshman and sophomore years, Horace sampled a wide variety of subjects, including Latin, Spanish, mathematics, history, and literature. He was fascinated by Professor Thomas H. Reed's political science classes, which concentrated on state and local government. He enjoyed economics, a field in which he showed early promise. But as time went on, he gravitated more and more toward the law. In his junior year, he began taking jurisprudence courses, and by his senior year, he was spending most of his time at Boalt Hall, the university's law school. He made up his mind to specialize in land and mining law. In spite of his thorough commitment to a legal career, he made some of his most useful personal contacts in the economics department. Professor Adolph C. Miller, the chairman, urged him to undertake advanced study in economics and later gave him a readership to help him make it through graduate school.[37]

Unlike most of his friends, Horace spent long hours drilling

36. Interview with HMA, Mar. 23, 1964; "Albright and the University of California," pp. 15–16.

37. U.C. report cards, 1908–13; U.C. class schedule cards, 1908–12, HMA Papers; "Albright and the University of California," p. 55.

with the University Cadets (the forerunner of the ROTC) as he worked his way up from private to first sergeant to second lieutenant and then to captain of Company D. He stood a good chance of being selected colonel of the regiment in his senior year until the mumps put him out of the running. In 1910 he signed on with the Coast Artillery unit of the California National Guard so that he could learn how to fire the huge guns that protected the Golden Gate. He still had a strong interest in the army.[38]

More than anything else, the appearance of Woodrow Wilson and Theodore Roosevelt on the Berkeley campus in 1911 sparked Horace's interest in politics. Wilson and Roosevelt, personifying the reform impulse that was then sweeping the United States, elaborated on the need for "progressive" reform, urging the students to take a vigorous stand in behalf of economic and political changes. Above all, the progressives hoped to curb the power of the monopolies or trusts and to take politics out of the hands of the bosses. A wave of progressivism engulfed the Berkeley campus, and many students, including Horace, got wrapped up in politics for the first time. In the spring of 1911 Horace helped get Newton Drury elected president of the student body. At about the same time he became an avid member of the "League of the Republic," a student organization dedicated to the proposition that the "only salvation of democracy" lay in "the active interest of college men in politics." The league often met with Professor Reed to discuss the political issues of the day, and it took a militant stand in favor of clean government by providing "at least 100 men," with Horace among them, to watch the polls in San Francisco during the municipal elections of 1911, in which the reformers of the city completed their victory over the remnants of "Boss" Ruef's once-powerful political machine. "We were all reformers in those days," Horace later recalled.[39]

38. Lt. William H. Mallett to HMA, Mar. 7, 1910, HMA Papers; San Francisco *Call*, Feb. 28, 1912.
39. *Blue and Gold* (1913), p. 153; San Francisco *Call*, Mar. 24, 1911; San Francisco *Chronicle*, Mar. 24, 1911; interview with Newton

Horace had a strong personal attachment to Teddy Roosevelt, partly because of the Republican tradition of his own family, but also because he had been lucky enough to shake Roosevelt's hand at the Greek Theatre in March 1911. Even so, he decided to back Wilson in 1912 on the theory that Roosevelt could not possibly win. He intended to cast his first vote in a national election, he explained, "for a winner." During the election campaign that fall, he worked so hard for the Democrats that he earned the right to sit on the platform with William Jennings Bryan at a giant political rally in San Francisco's Dreamland Rink just before the election. It was clear that he was already "hooked" on politics.[40]

After receiving his bachelor's degree in May 1912, Horace chose to remain in Berkeley to study law. To save money, since he could no longer be the Del Rey house manager, he moved in with his mother, who was now renting a home in Berkeley. Because of a weak heart, Mrs. Albright had been advised to spend most of her time away from the high altitude of Bishop. Horace supported himself during the 1912–13 school year by working as a reader for Professor Miller. His duties included typing letters, running errands, taking attendance in Miller's classes, grading examinations, tutoring the slower students, and generally making himself useful, for which he received a salary of about fifty dollars a month. In the spring semester, he was pressed into service as an emergency replacement for a young section leader who contracted tuberculosis. By the end of that year, Horace had acquired a basic knowledge of economic theory and demonstrated that he had some potential as a teacher.[41]

Perhaps the most exacting task Horace faced during his first year in graduate school was to get along with Professor Miller,

B. Drury, Sept. 22, 1965; "Albright and the University of California," pp. 58–59; for information about the progressive reformers in San Francisco, see Walton E. Bean, *Boss Ruef's San Francisco*, pp. 287–316.

40. "Albright and the University of California," pp. 58–59.

41. *Blue and Gold* (1914), p. 233; invitation to reception from Prof. William Carey Jones, May 8, 1913, grade sheets for Economics 107 and Economics 1B (1912–13), and C. H. Rieber to HMA, May 15, 1913, HMA Papers.

a wealthy man who rode around town in a black Duryea limousine, complete with a uniformed chauffeur. He had a national reputation as an expert in banking and finance, but his monumental disdain for his administrative duties as head of the economics department often made him seem sloppy and poorly organized. Few, if any, of the graduate students in economics cared to work for him, for he was reputed to be irascible and hard to get along with. But Horace needed money and did the professor's bidding with a minimum of back talk. Miller soon came to respect Horace's quiet versatility and general competence and become accustomed to working with him. Then, quite unexpectedly, in the spring of 1913, Miller received a letter from his friend Franklin K. Lane, who had recently been named Wilson's Secretary of the Interior, offering him the position of Assistant to the Secretary. After a trip to Washington to talk to Lane, Miller accepted the job. It was only natural that he should think of taking Horace with him as an assistant. Lane had apparently assured Miller that a clerk's position would be available for the young man. In April 1913, Miller asked Horace to consider going to Washington with him.[42]

Horace was genuinely reluctant to leave Berkeley, for he now felt very much at home in law school. Tom Ledwich and Beverly Clendenin, his buddies from undergraduate days, had also entered law school, and the three of them studied well together. Moreover, Horace enjoyed his classes. He especially liked Alexander M. Kidd, who taught criminal law, and William E. Colby, who taught mining law. Colby, a partner of the well-known mining lawyer Curtis Lindley, was secretary of the Sierra Club and a close associate of John Muir. In the fall of 1912 Colby took Horace to a Sierra Club meeting and introduced him to Muir, the grand old patriarch of the aesthetic conservation movement, who died only a little more than a year later. Common interests in mountain scenery and mining law drew Albright and Colby together. They remained friends for many years. Another reason

42. Grade sheets for Economics 107 and Economics 1B; "Albright and the University of California," pp. 55, 63–64; *New York Times*, May 1, 1913.

for Horace's reluctance to leave Berkeley was that he had recently been offered an appointment as assistant in economics for the 1913–14 academic year, at an annual salary of five hundred dollars; for the first time in his student career he would have no financial worries. A further cause for hesitation was the fact that Horace did not want to leave California, where he fully intended to practice law. But Miller kept after him, explaining in detail the advantages to a young attorney of a sojourn in Washington, and guaranteeing him a salary of one hundred dollars a month. Later Miller offered to advance Horace enough money for the trip to Washington and, as a further enticement, promised to give him his recently outgrown full-dress suit in an effort to insure that the young man would not feel embarrassed in Washington's high society. Horace accepted Miller's offer, declined the assistantship in economics, and prepared to leave for Washington as soon as the semester ended.[43]

One of the last things Horace did before leaving Berkeley was to say goodbye to Grace Noble, whom he had admired, mostly from afar, for more than two years. The couple had originally met as sophomores—both were members of the class of 1912. They got to know each other during their senior year, and "ran in the same crowd" in 1912 and 1913. They continued their courtship by mail after Horace left for Washington.[44]

It would be difficult to exaggerate the importance of the university in shaping Horace's adult life. It changed him from a relatively naïve mountain boy to a reasonably self-confident and well-informed adult. It broadened his mind, sharpened his intellect, propelled him into a new and sophisticated world, provided him with valuable personal contacts, and introduced him to his future wife. In short, the university became the means by which Horace Albright escaped the confinement and parochialism of

43. Ledwich to the author, Sept. 22, 1965; Clendenin to the author, Sept. 2, 1965; V. H. Henderson to HMA, Apr. 8, 1913, HMA Papers; "Albright and the University of California," p. 64.

44. Grace Albright, "Horace Marden Albright: Man with a Sense of History," *The Aglaia* 52 (Winter 1958): 20; HMA to Grace Marian Noble [June 1913], HMA Papers; "Albright and the University of California," pp. 19–21; interview with Grace Albright, July 24, 1964.

the Owens Valley. Although the picturesque little town of Bishop, bracketed by tall mountains and surrounded by lush green meadows, would remain a fond memory, Horace had a compelling curiosity about the world beyond the mountains. The Owens Valley could no longer contain him. Mary Albright's high aspirations for her eldest son had been realized.

2

Young Man Goes to Washington

It was still early in the morning and the streets were nearly deserted when the Pennsylvania's overnight train from Chicago edged into Washington's Union Station on May 31, 1913. Albright stepped off the train and walked quickly down the platform. He decided to check his two bags at the station and eat breakfast there. Then, armed with a newly purchased guidebook and map of the city, he set out to find the Patent Office Building where Secretary of the Interior Franklin K. Lane made his headquarters.[1]

Stepping outside for the first time, Albright got his initial glimpse of Washington's skyline. He discovered to his great delight that the white-domed Capitol was only a block or two away and that the Senate Office Building, which he quickly identified by means of his map, stood even closer to the station. He walked off briskly in the direction of downtown Washington, hoping to get to the Patent Office Building by about eight o'clock. He had gone nearly a mile before it occurred to him that after more than three days on the train he needed to clean himself up a little before reporting for work. He found a tailor's shop and, though it was still early, persuaded the proprietor to press the suit and "sponge off any spots he found and do it quickly." While the obliging tailor worked, Albright sat in his underwear with a rug thrown over his lap for the sake of modesty. Thus refreshed, he proceeded to the Secretary's office to introduce himself.[2]

1. "Two Semicentennial Anniversaries," May 31, 1963, HMA Papers.
2. Interview with HMA, Mar. 26, 1964; "Two Semicentennial Anniversaries."

Herbert A. Meyer, Lane's private secretary, greeted Albright cordially and introduced him around the office. He was informed that his official title would be "Confidential Clerk to the Secretary" and that his salary would be $1,600 a year. Having expected an income of only $1,200, he was flabbergasted by his good fortune. He learned that he would be a non–civil service employee—which meant that he could be discharged for reasons of politics—but he had no objections. He intended to stay in Washington for only a year and then return to California to finish law school. Later that afternoon he rented a room at the YMCA for $16 a month and for an additional $30 a month arranged to take his meals at Mrs. Travis's boarding house on G Street.[3]

Washington was a "lovely town" in those days, Albright remembered. The streets were wide, still largely uncluttered by automobiles, and not yet crowded with people. Picturesque horse-drawn Victorias provided transportation for cabinet members and other government officials as they made their way around the city. The ornate State Department Building stood just west of the White House, but there were no government offices beyond this point. A distinctly southern atmosphere, heightened by the presence of a large Negro population, added to the fascination that Albright felt.[4]

He quickly fell into the routine of his new job. Miller, who was one of Lane's old college chums, had received special orders from the Secretary to take charge of the national parks and give them the unified administration they had always lacked. From the very beginning, then, Albright's work required him to deal with national park affairs. But Miller had jurisdiction over much more than just the national parks. He had "general supervision" over the Bureau of Education, the eleemosynary institutions, the territories of Hawaii and Alaska, and a staff of departmental inspectors. He was also assigned to handle all "legislative matters

---

3. HMA, "Reminiscences," (Oral History Research Office, Columbia University), pp. 1–2, 23–25; "Two Semicentennial Anniversaries."
4. Constance McLaughlin Green, *Washington: Capital City 1879–1950*, pp. 132–46; HMA, "Reminiscences," pp. 27b–27e.

in connection with the constructive policies of the Department."
As Miller's administrative assistant, Albright had to familiarize himself with all of these areas.[5]

Miller never developed much zeal for his role as a general
supervisor, and he assigned nearly all matters of detail to Albright, who performed with steady competence as an administrator. In the summer of 1913, Lane and Miller left on a tour
of the western parks, including Yellowstone, Glacier, Yosemite,
and Mount Rainier. The tour must have inspired Miller, who returned to Washington intent upon stirring up congressional interest in the idea of establishing a bureau of national parks. Unfortunately, he got nowhere. In the meantime, as a recognized
expert in matters of banking and finance, he became deeply involved in drafting the Federal Reserve Act and in promoting
its passage through Congress. For better or worse, Albright was
left as a free lance "to take care of affairs that came across Dr.
Miller's desk the best way I could." Within a comparatively
short time, he mastered the department's rules of procedure and
became adept at referring matters to the proper men in the department. W. B. Acker, an experienced attorney on the Secretary's staff, gave the young man advice and assistance when
necessary. As time passed, Albright handled more and more of
Miller's routine duties.[6]

Supervision of the corps of inspectors, a job that fell to Albright by default, gave him virtually unlimited access to the hierarchy of the Department of the Interior. He found it necessary to
keep in constant touch with the bureau directors because his pool
of inspectors served as troubleshooters and investigators for all
the operating agencies of the department. Thus, while still a very
young man, Albright had the opportunity to become well acquainted with all of the bureau chiefs and most of the high-
ranking officers of the department. Moreover, his job gave him
a breadth of experience and an inside knowledge of departmental affairs that no other young man in the department could
match. During his first months in Washington, Albright took

5. *New York Times*, May 1, 1913; HMA, "Reminiscences," pp. 1–9.
6. HMA, "Reminiscences," p. 8.

particular delight in swapping stories with one of the senior Interior inspectors, Major James McLaughlin, an aging specialist in Indian affairs, who had acted as custodian for Sitting Bull and his braves after their bloody encounter with Custer at the battle of the Little Big Horn.[7]

Albright also had an opportunity to rub shoulders with Secretary Lane. Lane's distinctive physical appearance clearly set him apart from his subordinates. He was short and a little pudgy. His round face, pink complexion, and completely bald head made him look like a benign fat-man. Actually, he was far from benign. He directed the affairs of the Department of the Interior with forcefulness and efficiency. But he operated largely without the benefit of a well-conceived conservation philosophy. One of the first decisions he made after coming into office in 1913 was in favor of San Francisco's plan to construct a reservoir in the Hetch Hetchy Valley of Yosemite National Park.

Hetch Hetchy was a deep, glacier-carved gorge, through which the Tuolumne River flowed. Its natural features—precipitous granite walls, misty waterfalls, massive domes, and spires—closely resembled those in the highly touted Yosemite Valley. Some observers pronounced Hetch Hetchy even more beautiful than the Yosemite. About 1900 the city of San Francisco, needing a domestic water supply, applied to the federal government for permission to construct a reservoir in Hetch Hetchy. The fact that the project would seriously damage a great national park did not worry Mayor James D. Phelan and the other local politicians who originated the scheme. But it concerned John Muir and his followers, who quickly rallied to the defense of Hetch Hetchy. In a surprising show of strength, Muir and his men successfully blocked congressional action on the application for more than a decade. Then Lane, former city attorney of San Francisco, became the Secretary of the Interior; his endorsement of the Hetch Hetchy authorization act helped push it through Congress and insured that Wilson would sign it. Muir's admirers thereafter referred contemptuously to the "Hetch

7. HMA, "Reminiscences," p. 3; interview with HMA, Mar. 26, 1964.

Hetchy steal" and branded Lane as an enemy of conservation.[8]
These blanket denunciations of Lane were both inaccurate
and unwarranted, for the Secretary reacted positively in behalf
of the national parks throughout most of his administration. In
fact, by the time the Hetch Hetchy Act became law, he had
already taken steps to strengthen and improve the administration of the parks. It was under his aegis that the National Park
Service came into existence in 1916. A fundamental ambivalence
in matters of conservation policy persisted throughout his seven
years in office, but, with the exception of Hetch Hetchy, the
national parks generally benefited from his actions. Albright
found himself developing a sincere admiration for Lane, although he regretted the outcome of the Hetch Hetchy controversy.[9]

Albright performed various clerical duties for the Secretary.
Sometimes, though not often, he would be asked to work as
Lane's private secretary. While serving in this capacity one day
early in 1914, Albright noticed a "debonair fellow" come into
the office, carrying "a derby hat and a cane." The visitor announced with a bemused smile that as a bona fide member of the
"Franklin Club" he had a right to see Secretary Franklin K.
Lane. Having no appointment, Assistant Secretary of the Navy
Franklin D. Roosevelt waited for almost an hour, and, while
waiting, he chatted congenially with Albright. The two men
would meet again in the 1930s. This casual contact with a future
president and dozens of similar personal contacts made during
these early years in Washington proved invaluable to Albright.
He scribbled notes to himself about the men he met and often
made an effort to keep in touch with them. By working in the
Secretary's office, he accumulated a remarkable fund of information about the Department of the Interior and acquainted

8. Elmo R. Richardson, "The Struggle for the Valley: California's
Hetch Hetchy Controversy, 1905–1913," *California Historical Society
Quarterly* 38 (Sept. 1959) : 249–58; HMA, "Reminiscences," pp. 27f–
32; Roderick Nash, *Wilderness and the American Mind*, pp. 161–81.
9. For a scholarly appraisal of Lane's career see Keith W. Olsen,
"Franklin K. Lane: A Biography," (Ph.D. diss., University of Wisconsin, 1962).

himself with many of the most influential men in Washington.[10]

Albright soon found that it was possible to meet congressmen and other government officials on his own initiative. George W. Norris, the crusading senator from Nebraska, came to the YMCA regularly to swim and to work out in the gym. Albright often talked with him there. He got to know Addison T. Smith, of Idaho, a stubby little man of immense warmth and gentle spirit, who later remained his friend in spite of many official disagreements over national park policy. He met Carl Hayden, the jug-eared congressman from Arizona, with whom he later collaborated on important park matters, especially the establishment of Grand Canyon National Park. He also came to know Huston Thompson, Wilson's Assistant Attorney General who taught a Sunday school class at the Church of the Covenant (now the National Presbyterian Church). Albright was one of the faithful participants in the class.[11]

John E. Raker, of California, was probably the first congressman he got to know well. About three weeks after his arrival in Washington, Albright went to Capitol Hill, hoping to wangle a ticket to the joint session of Congress scheduled for that afternoon, so he could watch Woodrow Wilson make his second precedent-shattering personal appearance before Congress. The president was to deliver a special message on the need for banking and currency reform. "There is such a great demand for seats in the galleries of the House," the *New York Times* reported, "that thousands of people . . . will be disappointed." To avoid "the crush" each congressman and senator received only one ticket, and the doorkeepers had "imperative orders" to keep unauthorized persons out of the Capitol building. Albright remembered that his father had become acquainted with Congressman Raker through the Odd Fellows Lodge in California. On the basis of this rather tenuous personal connection, Albright

10. HMA, "Reminiscences," pp. 15–21; for characteristic examples of his name collecting see diaries for 1921, 1925, and 1928, HMA Papers.

11. HMA, "Reminiscences," pp. 27f, 511–15; interview with HMA, Mar. 26, 1964.

went to Raker's office and inquired about the possibility of obtaining a ticket to the joint session.[12]

The congressman explained personally that he had given his only ticket to his wife, but he evidently felt sorry for the young man from California who seemed so eager and intensely interested in politics. As the hour of twelve approached, Raker decided that he was going to try to smuggle Albright onto the floor of the House. The plan called for Albright to walk, head down, at the congressman's side and for them to launch into an apparently profound political conversation just as they reached the entrance to the House chamber. The scheme worked to perfection. They sailed past the doorkeeper and quickly lost themselves in the crowd. Albright thus had the superb thrill of mingling shoulder to shoulder with the great public figures of the nation. It was an unforgettable first visit to the Hill.[13]

Albright had arrived in Washington just as the progressive movement reached its peak, a coincidence of timing that reinforced his own commitment to progressive goals and methods. Utilization of the power of the central government to solve the pressing problems of the nation, as Wilson seemed to be advocating, and dependence upon experts and planners at the bureaucratic level to improve government efficiency were progressive concepts that Albright readily accepted and carried with him through most of his life. He considered government service a creative enterprise, and he was happy at the prospect of being able to contribute toward the goal of improving government efficiency.

The longer Albright remained in the nation's capital, the more he liked his job and the more he enjoyed the excitement of politics. He had not forgotten his plans, however, for a law career in California. In the time-honored pattern of ambitious, young government employees, he decided to try to finish his law degree in night school. He enrolled at Georgetown University Law

---

12. *New York Times*, June 23, 1913; see also HMA, "Reminiscences," pp. 9–10.
13. HMA, "Reminiscences," pp. 10–13.

School in the fall of 1913. After his evening classes, he would customarily take the streetcar to the Library of Congress for two hours of study. Characteristically, he drew up a weekly schedule that allotted each minute of the evening hours to some particular task. Always meticulous as a youngster, he was becoming increasingly methodical and well organized as an adult. The habit of drawing up schedules and efficiently allocating his efforts became a necessity later as his administrative duties proliferated. The winter of 1913–14 seemed like a "long pull" to Albright, but he persevered and finally received his LL.B. degree in June 1914.[14]

For relaxation Albright liked nothing better than walking in the country. On Sunday afternoons he and his friends would hike along the Chesapeake and Ohio Canal to Great Falls, Maryland, exploring the forests and examining the banks of the Potomac River, which was only a stone's throw from the canal. Occasionally he would walk along the outskirts of Washington looking for the remains of the old Civil War fortifications that once ringed the city. The outlines of trenches and gun emplacements were still clearly discernible, although often obscured by a dense overgrowth of trees. He had a limited social life. His one active organizational affiliation during his first year in Washington was the University of California Alumni Association of the District of Columbia. He was elected its vice-president in 1914.[15]

In the spring of that year, Albright found himself in a completely new situation in the Department of the Interior as a result of President Wilson's appointment of Miller to the Federal Reserve Board. The professor asked his young assistant to go along with him. But Albright refused to leave the Interior Department, where he felt at ease and hoped to gain experience in land law. Before severing his official connections with Miller,

14. "Georgetown University School of Law, Exercises for Fourth Year Class, 1913–1914," report cards from law school 1913–14, and weekly schedule [1914], HMA Papers; HMA, "Reminiscences," pp. 27a–27b.

15. HMA, "Reminiscences," pp. 27d–27f; clipping [1914] from the *Inyo Register*, HMA Papers.

Albright suggested Ray M. Gidney, whom he had known at the university, as his own replacement. Gidney got the job as Miller's assistant and thus began a distinguished career in the Federal Reserve System.. He later became president of the Federal Reserve Bank of Cleveland and comptroller of the currency.[16]

In the meantime, Albright had received a promising job offer from California. "Would you consider position Judge Lindley's office," William E. Colby wired. "Good experience. Opportunity for hard work. Salary only fifty dollars a month. Thought Miller change might cause you return here." This was Albright's chance to get back to San Francisco and to affiliate himself with an old, established law firm. He nearly accepted the offer, but Lane countered by giving him a small promotion and by promising that he would be assigned some legal work for the department. "I want to do some special law work here," Albright wired Colby in reply, "and as Secretary Lane has given me a good position in his office I think I had better not leave Washington just yet. Will take bar examination June eighteenth."[17]

Albright spent a month systematically reviewing the major points of law he had learned since 1911. On June 18 he wrote out his examination; he passed nicely and by the fall of 1914 had been admitted to the bar in the District of Columbia. Understandably, a long year of physical and mental exertion had drained his energy. He had a month's vacation coming, and he decided to take a trip to California, starting in mid-July.[18]

In Los Angeles, Albright held a reunion with Beverly Clendenin, who informed him that the California bar examination was to be given in a day or two. Albright impetuously decided to sign up for it. He had not looked at the California Code for more than a year. But it was to be an oral test, which made him hope he might be lucky. A stern-faced appellate judge administered the examination, going around the room and from man

16. Arthur S. Link, *Wilson: The New Freedom*, pp. 451–52; Ray M. Gidney to the author, Sept. 9, 1965; Edward Duffy (HMA's roommate, 1913–14) to HMA, Nov. 30, 1965, HMA Papers.
17. Telegrams, William E. Colby to HMA, May 18, 1914, and HMA to Colby, May 18, 1914, HMA Papers.
18. Interview with HMA, Mar. 26, 1964.

to man, posing legal questions. Candidates to Albright's right and left were queried on points of California law, but time after time the judge asked him questions about common law or constitutional law. Albright passed the test with flying colors and laughed all the way back to the train.[19]

He stopped next in Bishop, where he spent several days with his parents and renewed acquaintances with some of his boyhood friends. Then he went on to Berkeley for a visit with Grace, with whom he had been corresponding for more than a year. It was a memorable week. A few days after Albright's departure for Washington, the local newspaper reported that Miss Grace Noble, "one of the prominent members of the post-university set," had announced her engagement to "Horace Marden Albright, secretary to Franklin K. Lane, Secretary of the Interior." The wedding would take place in about a year.[20]

Albright plunged back into his job in the Secretary's office with vigor and enthusiasm. The off-year elections of 1914 were approaching, and the Secretary wanted to be kept abreast of the latest political developments in the West. Albright's assignment was to survey and analyze the political situation in California and the other western states. He spent long hours in the Library of Congress, browsing through western newspapers and magazines and writing succinct political reports for Lane. He made it a point to get to know the staff of the congressmen and senators from the Pacific coast region. His list of influential acquaintances grew longer and longer as he took on more responsibility in the office of the Secretary. By the end of 1914 he was on very friendly terms with George Otis Smith, director of the United States Geological Survey, and Clay Tallman, commissioner of the General Land Office. These two men would make valuable friends when Albright was established in a law practice and had cases dealing with mineral deposits or land holdings on the public domain.

19. Ibid.
20. "Dacie" to Albright [1914], HMA Papers; "Albright and the University of California"; interview with Grace Albright, July 24, 1964; interview with HMA, Mar. 26, 1964; unidentified newspaper clipping announcing the engagement, HMA Papers.

About ten days before Christmas, Lane called Albright to his office and introduced him to Stephen T. Mather, a Chicago businessman, who had been invited to become the new Assistant to the Secretary. The vacancy caused by Miller's resignation still needed to be filled, but because of the nominal salary and the magnitude of the problems that the Assistant to the Secretary would have to face, especially in the national parks, Lane had difficulty finding a replacement. At the time President Wilson appointed Miller to the Federal Reserve Board, he had advised Lane to go out and "find another millionaire with an itch for public service."[21]

In tapping Mather for the job, Lane was following Wilson's advice to the letter. Mather definitely had a yen to undertake public service. Moreover, he had all the qualifications, including personal wealth, to serve in Miller's stead. He could trace his family tree all the way back to Richard Mather of seventeenth-century Puritan fame. But Steve Mather was not himself a New Englander. He had been raised and educated in California. While attending the University of California, he had counted both Adolph C. Miller and Franklin K. Lane among his friends. After graduating from the university in 1887, he went to New York and got a job as a reporter for Dana's New York *Sun*. Five years later he abandoned journalism to enter the borax business, in which he eventually made a modest fortune. By 1914 he stood at the very pinnacle of success, a self-made millionaire and philanthropist, forty-seven years old, an enomously personable, energetic, and hard-driving man, who was a trifle restless and on the lookout for new worlds to conquer.[22]

Mather's credentials as a nature lover and national park enthusiast were authentic and impeccable. An avid part-time mountain climber and an active member of the Sierra Club, he knew the wilderness and admired the national parks concept, although the lackadaisical administration he had observed in several of the parks troubled him. In the summer of 1914, while

21. Shankland, *Steve Mather*, p. 7.
22. Ibid., pp. 7–8.

camping in Sequoia and Yosemite, he found conditions so deplorable that he dashed off a letter of protest to Lane, who responded by inviting him to take over the administration of the parks. At first Mather hesitated, but he agreed to come to Washington for exploratory talks. He was intrigued by the challenge that the parks represented, but as a freewheeling activist his mind boggled at the prospect of having to cope with the red tape of government work. Lane introduced Albright as the man best qualified to steer Mather through the red tape and keep him "out of trouble."[23]

Having made his pitch, the Secretary encouraged Mather and Albright to sit down together for a chat. It was a cold and rainy day in Washington, and a fire crackled in the fireplace, warming Lane's spacious office. The young man explained that he had already made plans to go back to California in about six months, and so did not wish to make any long-range commitments. But as Mather began to talk about the parks and to speculate about the great things that might be accomplished in the cause of wilderness preservation, Albright felt himself weakening. "I couldn't resist him," he later confessed. Mather stated that he would consider accepting the job if Albright would consider staying on to help him. Before the conversation ended, Albright had been partially won over. While he made no binding commitments, he indicated that he would probably remain through the summer if Mather took the job. Mather accepted Lane's offer a few days later, and the team of Mather and Albright went to work in January 1915. Neither Albright nor the national parks would ever be the same.[24]

Albright entertained no thought of staying with Mather for more than a few months. In fact, on January 14, 1915, a month after his first conversation with Mather, Albright agreed to set up a law practice with Beverly Clendenin in Los Angeles, "by September at the very latest," but "August first would be better

23. Ibid., pp. 8–9; see also John Ise, *Our National Park Policy: A Critical History*, pp. 193–94.
24. Shankland, *Steve Mather*, pp. 9–10; interview with HMA, Mar. 26, 1964.

still." He also began angling for a position at Occidental College, teaching economics, "one hour a day" to help "pay expenses for awhile." In the meantime, however, working with Mather promised to be an exciting adventure.[25]

25. HMA to Beverly S. Clendenin, Jan. 14, 1915, HMA Papers.

3

Along Came Steve Mather

Mather's prodigious energy and his capacity for fast action astonished almost everybody—congressmen, senators, cabinet officers, and conservationists alike. "I am now acting as private secretary to Hon. S. T. Mather," Albright wrote to his family late in January, and "I am busy every moment of the day." In taking over Miller's duties, Mather had inherited the job of supervising the Bureau of Education, the eleemosynary institutions, the territories of Hawaii and Alaska, and the department's investigative staff, as well as the national parks. But from the beginning, he devoted most of his time and creative energy to the parks. He carefully formulated his objectives, allowing himself a maximum of one year to reorganize national park administration, persuade Congress to establish a national parks bureau, publicize the scenic wonders of the national park system, and handpick a capable staff of park administrators to carry on in the future. Mather intended to pull out of the "national park game" in January 1916. Albright still planned to leave in the summer of 1915. Under the circumstances, a breakneck pace was inevitable.[1]

For more than forty years the national parks had been administrative stepchildren within the federal establishment. They were individually operated and maintained, with little or no pol-

Portions of this chapter appeared, in slightly different form, in *Wisconsin Magazine of History* 50 (Autumn 1967): 4–17. Reprinted by permission.

1. Quotation from HMA to H. Marden, Jan. 23, 1915, HMA Papers.

icy coordination between the various units. Moreover, the lines of administrative and operational responsibility had become badly blurred as a result of decades of sloppy management. While the Department of the Interior held legal jurisdiction over all the national parks, the War Department had long controlled Yellowstone, Sequoia, General Grant, and Yosemite by means of the army detachments assigned to patrol their boundaries and maintain their primitive road systems. These parks received indifferent and often pitifully inadequate supervision. Eight other parks, including Mount Rainier, Crater Lake, Mesa Verde, and Glacier, all under the direct administration of the Interior Department, received little more than custodial care. There was no effective national park policy, only a haphazard, day-to-day administrative arrangement that served no constructive conservation purpose.[2]

The national parks, which were located mostly in the Far West, and which contained some of the best mountain scenery in the world, had been perennially neglected because neither the leaders of Congress nor the leading conservation policy makers in the executive branch of the federal government had any real interest in preserving natural beauty. Headed by Gifford Pinchot, the chief of the United States Forest Service and a close friend of President Theodore Roosevelt, the utilitarian conservationists were at the height of their power and influence during the progressive era. Glorifying scientific efficiency and technical expertise, they advocated giant multiple-purpose development programs that provided for the full and efficient utilization of timber, grass lands, irrigation sites, mineral deposits, and hydroelectric power. Their elaborate plans almost always downgraded aesthetic considerations. A proposal to construct a "useful" irrigation dam in a mountain gorge, for example, invariably took precedence over a proposal to preserve the gorge itself for scenic enjoyment or recreational use. The aesthetic conservationists, who disagreed with the dominant

2. *Annual Report of the Department of the Interior* 1 (1910) : 443–501, 505–98; *Annual Report of the Secretary of the Interior* (1910), pp. 55–67.

utilitarian point of view, were accused of being muddleheaded
and hopelessly impractical.[3]

A small band of park enthusiasts and aesthetic conservationists had been trying for more than ten years to obtain congressional approval for a bureau to oversee national park affairs. J.
Horace McFarland, the agile and ubiquitous president of the
American Civic Association, had taken the lead in this effort
and had inaugurated a so-called national park lobby. He had
ably defended the concept of preserving natural beauty while
outnumbered and surrounded by Pinchot's militant supporters
at the White House Governors' Conference on Conservation in
1908. Almost single-handedly he had cajoled President William
Howard Taft and Secretary of the Interior Richard A. Ballinger
into supporting the idea of a national parks bureau. Ballinger's
successors, Walter L. Fisher and Franklin K. Lane, also backed
the proposed national park service. Senator Reed Smoot and
Congressmen John F. Lacey, Frederick C. Stevens, William
Kent, and John E. Raker repeatedly threw national park service
bills into the congressional hopper, but to no avail.[4]

The Pinchot clique, accusing McFarland, Muir, and the other
national park advocates of peddling "sentimental nonsense,"
posed a formidable obstacle. Eventually the Forest Service
wheeled its influential lobby into the fight against the proposed
park bureau, suggesting that the Forest Service rather than a
new federal agency should administer the national parks. In the
meantime, the explosive Hetch Hetchy controversy further

3. Samuel P. Hays, *Conservation and the Gospel of Efficiency: The
Progressive Conservation Movement, 1890–1920*, pp. 1–174, 261–76;
Donald C. Swain, *Federal Conservation Policy, 1921–1933*, pp. 1–5, 169;
James L. Penick, Jr., *Progressive Politics and Conservation: The Bal-
linger-Pinchot Affair* analyzes Pinchot's attitudes and administrative
style.

4. *Proceedings of a Conference of Governors in the White House,
Washington, D.C.*, May 13–15, 1908, pp. 153–57; Hans Huth, *Nature
and the American*, pp. 183–88; J. Horace McFarland to Robert Sterling
Yard, Sept. 13, 1922, and R. B. Watrous to McFarland, Sept. 15, 1922,
National Archives (hereafter abbreviated NA), Records of the National
Park Service (hereafter abbreviated NPS), gen. admin.; Ise, *Our Na-
tional Park Policy*, pp. 185–90.

polarized the conservation movement, dividing it more clearly than ever into two camps, the utilitarian, or practical, conservationists versus the aesthetic, or nature-loving, conservationists. Mather did not realize the depth of this schism until he began to learn his way around Washington. With Congressman John J. Fitzgerald, chairman of the House Appropriations Committee, jealously guarding the purse strings, Congress seemed in no mood to give in to the anti-Pinchot forces led by McFarland. The park enthusiasts still faced a tough political fight to get a National Park Service Act through Congress.[5]

In the absence of legislation, Fisher and Lane, successive Interior Secretaries, had resorted to administrative devices in an attempt to put the national parks on a solid footing. Starting about 1911, W. B. Acker, an assistant attorney in the Office of the Secretary, devoted a small fraction of his time to park affairs, and though handicapped by lack of money, lack of time, and a shortage of clerical help, his enlightened efforts represented the first step in the unification of national parks administration. In 1913, Lane upgraded park supervision and coordination to the Assistant Secretarial level and brought Miller into the department to take charge of the parks. Two years later, Lane made his most important contribution to the cause of natural beauty by naming Mather as the man to replace Miller.[6]

Park enthusiasts and aesthetic conservationists were enormously pleased when Lane announced that Mather would take charge of the national parks. "The appointment of Mr. Stephen T. Mather . . . is epoch-making," wrote Enos A. Mills, a longtime champion of Rocky Mountain scenery, in April 1915. "He will bring" to the parks "that which they have not yet had—a strong, sympathetic, and constructive administration." Economy-minded members of Congress applauded Mather's early announcement that he would "do all that lies in my power to es-

5. The quotation is from Amos Pinchot, "The Hetch Hetchy Fight," copy in Gifford Pinchot Papers, box 1856; Hays, *Conservation and the Gospel of Efficiency*, pp. 195–98.

6. Jenks Cameron, *The National Park Service: Its History, Activities, and Organization*, Service Monographs of the U.S. Government, no. 11, pp. 33–50; Ise, *Our National Park Policy*, pp. 187–88.

tablish a thorough business administration in these great national playgrounds."[7]

Mather's first impulse was to launch a publicity campaign to persuade more Americans to spend their vacations in the West —in Yellowstone, Yosemite, Glacier, or one of the new park reservations, like Rocky Mountain National Park in Colorado. The war in Europe threatened to curtail or entirely end pleasure trips to Europe, and accordingly, the nation's railroads had already launched a gigantic advertising campaign with the patriotic theme "See America First." Mather was enough of a promoter and opportunist to realize that the wartime dislocation of European travel represented a rare chance for the national parks to expand their operations and win new friends. "What an opportunity this will be," he exclaimed, "to break down provincialism!" But he would require help. He needed a writer and public relations man, someone who could be trusted, to originate a stream of publicity designed to acquaint the American people with the unsurpassed mountain scenery and natural beauty of the national parks.[8]

Mather knew just the man. He went to New York City and persuaded Robert Sterling Yard, one of his old cronies from the New York *Sun*, formerly editor of *The Century* magazine and the Sunday New York *Herald*, to become publicity director for the parks. Albright skillfully handled the mechanics of Yard's appointment. Nominally, Yard was employed by the United States Geological Survey, but, by advance agreement, the U.S.G.S. detailed him to Mather, who paid Yard's $5,000 salary out of his own pocket. This arrangement, though unorthodox, was perfectly legal, and it gave Yard the status of a government official. Albright then found him a comfortable office in the Bureau of Mines building, only two blocks away, and hired a woman who seemed "to come very near possessing" the quali-

7. Enos A. Mills, "Warden of the Nation's Mountain Scenery," *Review of Reviews* 51 (Apr. 1915): 428; Stephen T. Mather to Dr. [————] Shaw, Mar. 6, 1915, in *Review of Reviews* 51 (Apr. 1915): 429.
8. Shankland, *Steve Mather*, p. 8.

fications Yard wanted in a stenographer. Bob Yard, an avid believer in wilderness preservation, thus began his long association with the national parks. It was only a matter of time until a steady flow of articles about the parks, written in his lucid, enthusiastic prose style, began to appear in the big eastern newspapers and magazines. Mather's extraordinary publicity campaign in behalf of the national parks had started, with Yard now a full "member of the team." He was "thoroughly imbued, as are all of us," Albright remarked after Yard had been in Washington for about a month, "with Mr. Mather's splendid enthusiasm."[9]

Mather's next impulse was to get to know the men who were then running the parks. He called a conference in Berkeley in March 1915 and ordered all the park superintendents to be there. He invited most of the concessionaires, or "concessioners" as Mather and Albright called them, who operated business franchises in the national parks, and he asked a number of the Interior Department officials who had worked with the parks or who were especially interested in the parks to be his guests. Making the trip west from Washington were Mather, Yard, Albright, W. B. Acker, Robert B. Marshall and Guy E. Mitchell of the United States Geological Survey, Colonel L. M. Brett, acting superintendent of Yellowstone, and a few technical experts from outside the department. Marshall and Mitchell, both geographers, had already rendered valuable assistance to Mather, who planned to take full advantage of their interest in the parks. In Chicago Mather made arrangements for a special Pullman car, which bore the hybrid name of "Calzona," for the trip to California. "There were conferences day and night," Albright recalled, all the way to the Pacific coast. Mather dazzled the members of the party with high-powered intensity, as he set out systematically to educate himself about the parks. The party was largely drained of ideas and energy by the time it reached Berkeley. Albright, whose orders called for him "to render such stenographic or other assistance" as he could for Mather,

9. HMA, "Robert Sterling Yard" (MS), pp. 2–4, HMA to R. S. Yard, Mar. 24, 1915, and HMA to Mrs. Stephen T. Mather, Mar. 29, 1915, HMA Papers.

absorbed a great deal of new and useful knowledge about the parks.[10]

The Berkeley conference convened on March 11, 1915. Mark Daniels, who, as general superintendent and landscape engineer of the parks, normally headquartered in San Francisco, joined the group. Congressmen Denver S. Church, of Fresno, and J. Arthur Elston, of Berkeley, arrived. Representatives of the automobile clubs and the railroads, a healthy contingent from the Sierra Club, and nearly all of the park superintendents were there. The group gathered for two days on the University of California campus, holding wide-ranging discussions about the parks. It was abundantly clear that most of the superintendents had been appointed for political reasons and that, as a group, they lacked both the ability and the zeal for effective national park work. The conferees slept at the Sigma Chi fraternity house, which the college boys had vacated out of deference to Mather, who was one of their most illustrious and well-heeled alumni. The third day's agenda called for a ceremonial visit to the Panama-Pacific Exposition in San Francisco. Most of the national park group went to the Union Pacific pavilion as guests of the railroad and watched in fascination while "a mechanically controlled geyser" gave an "excellent imitation of . . . Old Faithful." Earlier, on their way to lunch, the delegates walked past an exhibition that featured "bathing girls" in "abbreviated suits" doing the swan dive and basking in the sun. Thoroughly indoctrinated in the subtleties of appreciating unadorned natural beauty, a number of the national park men lingered to watch the shapely divers. Mather dispatched his trustworthy young assistant to round up the stragglers and get them back in time for the afternoon session.[11]

Mather's Washington contingent returned to the East via Salt Lake City, Denver, and Chicago. All along the way, they talked

10. HMA, "Robert Sterling Yard," p. 4; Franklin K. Lane to HMA, Feb. 27, 1915, HMA Papers.

11. *Proceedings, Third National Parks Conference*, Berkeley, Mar. 11–13, 1915; Shankland, *Steve Mather*, pp. 60–63; San Francisco *Chronicle*, Mar. 10, 1915, and Mar. 13, 1915; HMA, "Robert Sterling Yard," pp. 4–5.

to "governors, mayors, civic leaders, mountain club officers, and good roads proponents" to whom they preached the "economic importance of the tourist business" and with whom they mapped the strategy for a projected national parks publicity campaign. Editors and publishers received Mather's special attention. His object was to make friends and win converts to the idea that, if properly promoted and advertised, the parks would attract "tourist gold" to the West. Mather hoped that local editors and chambers of commerce would include the parks in their own promotional campaigns and that enthusiastic boosterism on the local level would help to "sell" the parks. It was on this trip that Mather's administrative style crystallized. Once a supersalesman for Twenty Mule Team borax, and later for his own Sterling Brand borax, he had decided that shrewd salesmanship would also work for the parks. A glad-hander and a promoter by nature, he became an indefatigable and exceptionally effective salesman for America's "great national playgrounds." Albright, hardly a glad-hander himself, watched Mather operate. Within a short time, Albright would himself become a smooth and persuasive public relations man for the national parks, although he ordinarily used a softer sell than Mather. In the aftermath of the Berkeley conference, it was Albright who made the gracious gesture of sending a gift to the boys in the Sigma Chi house to express appreciation for their hospitality. The gift was "an enlarged picture of Secretary Mather, framed in redwood from the Muir Woods."[12]

Back on the job in Washington, Albright felt for the first time the full force of Mather's persuasive powers, as the talented borax salesman attempted to persuade him to stay in Washington for another year. "Mr. Mather says he cannot fill my place," Albright hurriedly wired Grace. "Will give me two hundred dollars per month if I stay until March first next. What do you think best?" "Think advisable you accept," Grace replied. "Too

12. HMA, "Robert Sterling Yard," p. 5; HMA to Leslie Albright, June 10, 1915, HMA Papers; Mather often used the phrase "great national playgrounds," see "National Parks on a Business Basis," *Review of Reviews* 51 (Apr. 1915) : 429.

favorable an opportunity to refuse. Can decide question of wedding later, whether this year or next."[13]

Mather next set out to make himself known to the most influential men in Washington. Here Albright could be helpful in a creative way. Only a few days after Mather arrived in town, Albright made arrangements for him to meet Huston Thompson, the Assistant Attorney General, who quickly became one of Mather's greatest admirers and ablest allies. Albright also introduced his boss to his friends in Congress. Very soon Mather knew many members of both houses, including John E. Raker, William Kent, Carl Hayden, Louis C. Cramton, Edward T. Taylor, James R. Mann, Addison T. Smith, Reed Smoot, and George Norris.[14]

Mather's promotional schemes multiplied at a remarkable rate during the first half of 1915. Drawing upon his personal contacts in eastern newspaper circles, he set out to broaden his acquaintances among both newspaper and magazine editors. George Horace Lorimer, editor of the *Saturday Evening Post,* C. V. Van Anda, managing editor of the *New York Times,* and Arthur Brisbane, of the Hearst chain, soon became genuine national park boosters and began publishing enthusiastic articles about the parks. Another one of Mather's early publicity schemes, undoubtedly his most successful, came in July of that year, when he invited a distinguished group of legislators, conservationists, writers, publishers, and lecturers to be his guests on a memorable camping trip through the High Sierra. He called on Bob Marshall, of the Geological Survey, who had helped survey both Sequoia and Yosemite and was intimately acquainted with the Sierra country, to plan the trip, and he assigned Albright to help in making the arrangements. The object would be to show the distinguished gentlemen a good time while thoroughly imbuing them with the mystique of the national parks and persuading

13. Telegram, HMA to Grace Noble, Apr. 12, 1915, and telegram, Noble to HMA, Apr. 12, 1915, HMA Papers.

14. HMA to Huston Thompson, Feb. 23, 1915, and Thompson to HMA, Feb. 27, 1915, HMA Papers; interview with HMA, Mar. 26, 1964.

them to throw their weight behind the establishment of a National Park Service.[15]

The planning phase of the trip moved swiftly. Marshall stitched together a superb itinerary which began at the Giant Forest on the edge of Sequoia Park and included stops at Redwood Meadow, Mineral King, Junction Meadows, Funston Meadows, Crabtree Meadows, Mount Whitney, Horseshoe Meadows, and then down the east side of the Sierra into the Owens Valley. Albright assumed responsibility for planning the remainder of the trip from the little town of Lone Pine northward to Yosemite Park. He tentatively arranged an overnight stop in Bishop, then a drive north to Leevining, and into the park via the scenic Tioga Road, a privately owned mining road that Mather and a few wealthy friends had recently purchased and given to the Interior Department.[16]

The prospect of playing host to such an illustrious group of men caught the imagination of the citizens of Bishop, who foresaw great benefits for the future development of the Owens Valley growing out of this trip. Albright wrote letter after letter to W. A. Chalfant, the editor of the *Inyo Register*, and to W. G. Scott, executive secretary of the Inyo Good Roads Club, drumming up interest in the Mather party and working out tentative schedules. He also tried to convince his old friends that they should make a more concerted effort to meet their quota in a drive to reimburse Mather for the cost of the Tioga Road. At one point he indulged in a rather heavy-handed attempt to coerce the leading citizens of Bishop into stepping up their fund-raising campaign, thus revealing both his youthful inexperience and a slightly inflated estimation of his own importance. After emphasizing "what a tremendously powerful advertisement" it would be to have Mather's party pass through the Owens Valley, Albright pointedly remarked that he "was not going to make arrangements . . . for this end of the journey until after I have

15. Shankland, *Steve Mather*, pp. 83–99, 181–82; HMA to W. G. Scott, June 12, 1915, HMA Papers.
16. HMA to Scott, Mar. 29, 1915, and June 12, 1915, HMA Papers.

learned definitely what Inyo [County] has done in this matter of the Tioga purchase." Chalfant and others finally convinced Albright that it was "a mistake to suppose the Inyo people to be indifferent" about the Tioga Road. In the end, Albright arranged for the Mather party to proceed up the Owens Valley and spend the night in Bishop.[17]

The party assembled in Visalia, California, "the gateway to Sequoia," on July 14, 1915, amid fanfare and excitement so great that the local papers temporarily shunted aside their articles about the war in Europe and Carranza's success in Mexico in favor of stories about the "Big Men" from Washington who planned to visit the "wonders" of the Sierra. Although last-minute cancellations by Congressmen Denver Church and Swagar Sherley pared down Mather's original guest list, the party still contained an impressive line-up of "Big Men," including Henry Fairfield Osborn, eminent scientist and head of the American Museum of Natural History, Emerson Hough, big-name writer and self-styled nature lover, Frederick H. Gillett, ranking Republican on the House Appropriations Committee and a future Speaker of the House, Gilbert H. Grosvenor, world traveler and editor of *National Geographic*, E. O. McCormick, vice-president of the Southern Pacific Railroad, Peter Clark Macfarlane, popular novelist and magazine writer, W. F. McClure, state engineer of California, Burton Holmes, one of the foremost professional lecturers in the country, Clyde L. Seavey, of the California State Board of Control, and Ben M. Maddox, owner and publisher of the Visalia *Times* and the *Tulare County Times*. Other guests were Henry Floy, Mather's brother-in-law, F. B. Johnstone, a Chicago attorney, Samuel E. Simmons, a physician, and Frank Depew, Holmes's camera man and assistant. Mather, Marshall, Daniels, and Albright rounded out the party. The first evening a few prominent Visalians hosted a "very delightful Spanish banquet" in Pablo Parlors, at which Mather had "some

17. HMA to Scott, Mar. 29, 1915, and June 12, 1915, HMA to W. A. Chalfant, June 10, 1915, Chalfant to Albright, June 22, 1915, Fred M. Hess to HMA, June 22, 1915, and HMA to Hess, July 2, 1915, HMA Papers.

interesting things to say concerning park development" and the efforts that were "being made by Interior Department officials to popularize the national parks." Early the next morning the Mather party departed by automobile for the Giant Forest in the High Sierra.[18]

The first breath-taking glimpse of the towering sequoias and the rock-strewn Sierra ridges gave promise of an unforgettable trip. With the stately redwoods standing guard, the campers ate "an excellent dinner" prepared by Tie Sing, the remarkable trail cook who accompanied the party to tend to the gentlemen's culinary needs. Mather had spared no expense in outfitting his guests. Each man had a new sleeping bag and air mattress which combined to make a "classy and perfectly comfortable" wilderness bed. There were horses to carry the men and mules to carry the supplies, which included a bountiful stock of fresh fruit, fresh eggs, and other delicacies. The first night in the mountains Albright ingratiated himself with Emerson Hough by inflating the mattress for him. Hough was a crusty and outspoken man, whose tirades as well as his writings had made him famous, but he was on good behavior during this trek through the mountains. Whenever possible he would steal away to catch a few trout or to rest. He thoroughly enjoyed himself and later remarked that it was "rare" to find "so wholly congenial a party." Gilbert Grosvenor, who had never seen the High Sierra, insisted on bedding down that first night in the duff at the base of a redwood tree.[19]

On the morning of July 17 the party moved out into the wilderness, traveling easily and in deluxe style. The route Marshall had picked carried them to the headwaters of the East Fork of the Kaweah River, then across the eleven-thousand-foot Franklin Pass into the Kern River watershed, down Rattlesnake Creek to Funston Meadow, up the Kern River, then to the summit of

18. Visalia *Morning Delta,* July 14–17, 1915; *Tulare County Times,* July 15, 1915; HMA, "The Mather Mountain Party," *Westways* 56 (June 1964) : 24.

19. Letter from Ben M. Maddox, in *Tulare County Times,* July 22, 1915; Emerson Hough to Maddox, in *Tulare County Times,* Aug. 5, 1915; Albright, "The Mather Mountain Party of 1915" (MS), HMA Papers; Shankland, *Steve Mather,* p. 71.

Mount Whitney, and out of the mountains at Lone Pine. The party decreased by two when Holmes and Macfarlane decided they did not want to continue after Mineral King, but the rest of the group stayed with it. On the way to Junction Meadows, the party stopped long enough to christen "Gillett Hot Springs" in honor of the congressman from Massachusetts, who had gone there "the previous afternoon to take a bath in the hot water." Tie Sing's dinners furnished the perfect ending to every day. As camp was pitched, he would construct a dining table, usually out of logs, then, as one member of the party expressed it, "a linen table cloth shows up and there are real napkins for everybody." Tie Sing would put together his two collapsible stoves, and calmly prepare, as at Whitney Meadow, "soup, lettuce salad, fried chicken, venison and gravy, potatoes, hot rolls, apple pie, cheese, tea and coffee." The box lunches he served on the trail were equally substantial. Several members of the party, "who expected to reduce their weight on the trip," expressed their soulful but unconvincing disappointment.[20]

As the youngest member of the party, Albright fell heir to many extra duties, such as pitching tents, setting up camp, and inflating air mattresses. Moreover, he was the only man present who could keep up with the indefatigable Mather, who usually demanded company as he rushed off to climb a canyon wall or explore a new trail after the others, slowed by fatigue, had decided it was time to sit by the fire and rest. Out on the trail all hands nicknamed Albright "Bishop" (after his home town), while they affectionately referred to Grosvenor as "the Tenderfoot." The hearty travelers climbed to the summit of Mount Whitney, descending in a fierce hail and rain storm. Ten days after leaving the Giant Forest, the Mather party emerged from the mountains, saddle-sore and tired, at Lone Pine.[21]

Before breaking camp in the Giant Forest, Albright had written to Guy P. Doyle, a physician in Bishop and president of the Inyo Good Roads Club, that Mather and his "prominent" guests

20. Letter from Maddox, in *Tulare County Times*, Aug. 5, 1915.
21. Henry Fairfield Osborn to Maddox, n.d., in *Tulare County Times*, Aug. 5, 1915; see also HMA, "The Mather Mountain Party," p. 25.

would arrive in Lone Pine about noon on July 27. The trail party was precisely on time, "ready for a change of transportation" from horseback to automobile. Dr. Doyle's group provided the cars, and Bishop's leading citizens turned out to greet their distinguished visitors. After luncheon in Lone Pine, the group drove north through the little towns of Independence and Big Pine, arriving in Bishop in time for dinner. "A bomb salute welcomed their arrival." An informal reception at the Piñon Club, featuring a "projectoscope," which showed Sierra scenery, and an exhibit of photographs by A. A. Forbes, capped the day. After the reception, the guests met with a few "business people" and then retired early at the homes of Bishop residents who had volunteered to entertain them.[22]

The next morning the townspeople of Bishop outdid themselves by treating the Mather party to a magnificent trout breakfast served in an open meadow at the base of the tall Sierra. "The table was alongside a big stream," one member of the party wrote, describing the scene, "and was decorated with a profusion of wild flowers." The trout were displayed on a canvas near the fire, "where they could be inspected before they were cooked." The bill of fare included, in addition to trout, "cantaloupes, tomatoes, hot biscuits, Inyo honey, [and] surpassing coffee." Henry Fairfield Osborn announced that "the trout breakfast alone was almost worth" the trip from New York. After breakfast the members of the party climbed into their automobiles and began the last stage of the scenic but tiring journey to Yosemite, driving north to Leevining and connecting there with the Tioga Road. On the long climb to Tioga Pass, Albright rode in an open Studebaker touring car. E. O. McCormick sat in the front seat next to the driver, and Emerson Hough occupied the rear seat next to Albright. The precariously narrow road and uninhibited driving of Will L. Smith, a Bishop merchant, left the three travelers petrified with fear. Albright remembered the driver "rising in his seat" to point out especially beautiful vistas, "but never stopping the car." Every time the

22. *Inyo Register*, July 22, 1915, and July 29, 1915.

driver stood up, Albright wrenched open the back door and put his foot "on the running board," ready to leap "when the car went over the cliff." Hough cowered beside him muttering, "Damn this scenery-lovin' S.O.B." McCormick was too frightened to say a word. At the summit there was a brief ceremony dedicating the Tioga Road to public use, after which the party drove on to Tuolumne Meadows in Yosemite Park to rendezvous with the Sierra Club, which was having its annual outing. The party broke up the next day, July 29, after having reached the Yosemite Valley itself.[23]

This two-week tour of the mountains had far-reaching results for Mather, Albright, and the national parks. It convinced Grosvenor, Osborn, Hough, and to a lesser extent Holmes and MacFarlane—all men who could do yeoman duty in publicizing the parks—that getting a National Park Service Act through Congress was absolutely imperative. Furthermore, they agreed to support the expansion of Sequoia Park to include the canyons of the Kings River and Kern River. This country "is too big for any man or men to own," Hough later wrote. "It belongs to humanity, as it is, unchanged and never to know change." Congressman Gillett, a powerful figure on the Appropriations Committee, gained a very favorable impression of the national parks and began a warm friendship with Mather and Albright. Over the next few years, he extended much-needed political support to the National Park Service. As far as Mather and Albright were concerned, the trip infected them with a new enthusiasm for the national parks cause and gave them the solid satisfaction of knowing that their first big promotional effort had been a splendid success. The young man, in particular, came away with a new feeling of excitement and commitment to conservation goals. He was becoming more deeply involved in his job than he had anticipated in April 1915 when he had agreed to stay with Mather for twelve months.[24]

23. Maddox letter, *Tulare County Times*, Aug. 5, 1915; *Inyo Register*, July 29, 1915, and Aug. 5, 1915; the description of the hair-raising ride and the quotations are from HMA, "The Mather Mountain Party of 1915," pp. 6–7.

24. Quotation from Hough to Maddox, n.d., in *Tulare County Times*, Aug. 5, 1915.

After the mountain party broke up, Mather and Albright left on an inspection tour of the national parks. E. O. McCormick invited them to ride with him in his private car as far as Seattle. The three old trail buddies stopped at Crater Lake and Medford, Oregon, where they talked parks to the local businessmen and where they learned about an innocent-looking, seemingly nonalcoholic drink called a "Rogue River Rhapsody." The weather was terribly hot, and Albright, an avowed temperence advocate, had a towering thirst by the time they reached Medford. After downing several tall glasses of punch in quick succession and beginning to feel a little dizzy, he sensed that the punch was not really so innocent after all. In his ignorance, it seemed, he had overimbibed a fruity, delicious punch made mostly from applejack. And so had Mather and McCormick. The three men, slurring their words and staggering slightly, walked back to the train and fell into bed. Albright preached prohibition more fervently than ever after that.[25]

The tour continued to Seattle and Mount Rainier, and then to Denver for the dedication of Rocky Mountain National Park, a ceremonial occasion that Enos A. Mills had arranged. Mills generally had the reputation of being "the father of Rocky Mountain Park." He was a noted outdoorsman, writer, and lecturer, who made an unpredictable friend and a formidable enemy. From Denver, Mather and Albright turned north to Yellowstone and then to Glacier, where they spent three days crossing the continental divide in the face of the first heavy snowstorm of the autumn. They headed back to Washington during the third week of September, more convinced than ever that a way had to be found to replace the political appointees then holding down most of the park superintendencies. Moreover, the parks needed roads and tourist facilities, or "development," as Mather usually phrased it, much to the discomfort of the purists who later asserted that the national parks should be preserved untouched and relatively undeveloped. Mather held that the parks were "for the people." To deny them good roads or comfortable lodgings, he argued, was both unwise and unreasonable.

25. Assistant Secretary of the Interior to HMA, June 30, 1915, HMA Papers; interview with HMA, Mar. 26, 1964.

Neither he nor Albright ever considered their recurrent campaigns to increase the number of park visitors and accelerate park development at odds with the urge, which they shared in full measure, to preserve the extraordinary beauty of the parks. The political facts of life in 1915 and 1916 demanded simply that the parks be "used." Unless and until the American people started flocking to the national park reservations, Congress would refuse to appropriate adequate funds for the administration and protection of the parks.[26]

In the autumn of 1915 the volume of Mather's and Albright's correspondence rapidly increased, for they made it a policy to keep in touch with virtually all of the people they met on their camping and inspection trips. Mather's relationship with Grosvenor was especially warm. To help publicize the parks, the *National Geographic,* Grosvenor decided, would devote an entire issue to "A Tribute to the Scenic Grandeur and Unsurpassed Natural Resources of Our Own Country." Albright worked with Grosvenor and John Oliver LaGorce, assistant editor of the *National Geographic,* in gathering pictures and preparing copy for the magazine. LaGorce invited Albright to put his "fine Italian quill into operation" in future issues of the magazine, but Albright demurred. "My own Italian quill will not be sharpened while yours is in working order," he wrote, "besides I could not write a story" even if "hanging was . . . the penalty . . . for failure." Emerson Hough, who wrote for the *Saturday Evening Post,* took a great interest in the young man immediately after the Mather mountain party, offering to entertain him in Chicago and asking him to run various errands in Washington. When Hough sent him a batch of pictures taken during the 1915 mountain trip, Albright warmly replied: "I can't very well express my appreciation of your kindness . . . but perhaps I shall have

26. *Rocky Mountain News,* Sept. 5, 1915; Shankland, *Steve Mather,* pp. 74–82; this philosophy of park management ran throughout the *Annual Report of the Director of the National Park Service* (1917), which was the first annual report of the NPS, see pp. 10–20 (hereafter cited as *Annual Report, NPS*) ; see also HMA, "Reminiscences," pp. 67–69.

a chance to blow your bed up next year if we happen to be out in the mountains together."[27]

Late in November 1915, Albright and Mather sat down in Washington to take stock of what they had accomplished in the past year. It was astonishing how quickly the twelve months had passed. They were proud of what they had achieved in the way of publicizing the parks, but they felt dismayed and disappointed that so much remained to be done. After a long discussion they agreed to stay on for another year, with the expectation of obtaining a National Park Service Act from Congress and getting a national parks bureau firmly established. During that first busy year Mather developed a deep fatherly affection for Albright, but, more important, he steadily increased his admiration for the young man's administrative ability. Albright more than proved his worth as a valuable and versatile assistant. He could always be counted on, Mather knew, to work out the practical details of policy and to have at his fingertips an array of facts and figures about the parks. Mather clearly reigned as the leader and dominant member of the twosome, but Albright contributed creatively to Mather's success, and the more so as time went by."[28]

There can be no doubt that Mather exerted an enormous influence on Albright, shaping his values, enriching his youthful perspective, and holding out a vision of public service that was almost irresistible. Mather's civic-mindedness and dedication to the concept of preserving natural beauty, squarely in the John Muir tradition, also had a great appeal to Albright, whose family background and boyhood in the Owens Valley made him susceptible to Mather's conservation philosophy and his special brand of activism. After deciding to remain with the Interior Department for another year, Mather named Robert B. Marshall, whom he had tentatively selected as the first director of the proposed Park Service, to the job of superintendent of National Parks. Mark Daniels had recently resigned to return full time

27. John Oliver LaGorce to HMA, Oct. 6, 1915, and Nov. 4, 1915, HMA to LaGorce, Nov. 4, 1915, and HMA to Emerson Hough, Oct. 7, 1915, HMA Papers.
28. Shankland, *Steve Mather*, p. 83.

to his work as a landscape architect. With the coming of the new year, it was hoped, the time would be ripe for a new attempt to push through a bill creating a national parks bureau. In the meantime, Mather and his assistant would have time to relax over the holidays.[29]

Standing stiffly in the formal dress suit that Professor Miller had given him two years before, Albright married Grace Noble in Berkeley on December 23, 1915. The couple remained in Berkeley until after Christmas and then traveled to Washington, with a brief stopover at the Grand Canyon. Albright entertained his bride on the long train ride back to Washington by reading aloud from the *Guide Book of the Western United States,* explaining in tedious detail all of the geological formations they passed. "It's a wonder she stuck with me," he later admitted.[30]

Early in 1916, Mather launched an all-out drive for legislation to establish a national parks bureau and, of course, Albright became deeply involved. Yard had worked at a man-killing pace through the summer and fall of 1915, writing articles, collecting materials about the parks, and issuing an endless stream of publicity releases. The Sixty-fourth Congress was better informed about the national parks than any previous Congress, thanks to his publicity work and Mather's unstinting public relations efforts. Now began the task of drafting a suitable bill. Mather, Acker, Albright, Marshall, and Yard, from the Interior Department, and John Raker, William Kent, Huston Thompson, J. Horace McFarland, Frederick Law Olmsted, the renowned landscape architect, and Richard B. Watrous, McFarland's associate in the American Civic Association, met frequently at Yard's Washington apartment and Kent's George-

29. Ise, *Our National Park Policy,* p. 187; Shankland, *Steve Mather,* pp. 83–84; *Annual Report of the Superintendent of National Parks* (1916), pp. 4–5; HMA to William M. Sell, Jr., Dec. 3, 1915, HMA Papers.

30. Berkeley *Gazette,* Dec. 24, 1915; see also San Francisco *Chronicle,* Dec. 21, 1915, and *Inyo Register,* Dec. 30, 1915; *Guide Book of the Western United States,* part C, *The Santa Fe Route,* U.S. Geological Survey Bulletin 613 (Washington, D.C.: Government Printing Office, 1915), copy in HMA Papers.

town home in January and February of 1916. Enos Mills occasionally joined the group. These strategy sessions produced a bill well calculated to please as many members of Congress as possible and, at the same time, insure adequate protection for the parks. Olmstead proposed the wording of the key section. "The service thus established," the bill stated, "shall promote and regulate" the use of the national parks "by such means and measures as conform to the fundamental purpose" of the parks, namely "to conserve the scenery and the natural and historic objects and the wild life therein . . . by such means as will leave them unimpaired for the enjoyment of future generations."[31]

Congressman Raker richly deserved the honor of introducing the bill, having already proposed a number of National Park Service bills. But, for tactical reasons, it was decided that Kent, who was better liked by the floor leaders of the House, should become the bill's official sponsor. Once Kent had formally introduced the bill, a well-timed wave of national parks publicity hit the newsstands. George Horace Lorimer rallied the popular *Saturday Evening Post* to the side of the parks. And Gilbert Grosvenor, just as he had promised, devoted an entire issue of the *National Geographic* to the scenic grandeur of the United States, especially the national parks. Albright saw to it that "copies were on the desks of every member of Congress." Then Yard's magnificent *National Parks Portfolio*, published by Scribner's and paid for mostly by the western railroads, appeared. A handsomely illustrated cloth-bound book covering all of the major parks, it was mailed free of charge to more than a quarter of a million people, carefully selected by volunteers from the General Federation of Women's Clubs and a corps of clerks working under Albright's direction. "It was a job of mammoth proportions," Albright proudly recalled, "to wrap, address, and mail" all those books. Needless to say, every member of Con-

31. HMA, "Robert Sterling Yard," pp. 8–9; Huth, *Nature and the American*, pp. 189–91; the National Park Service Act appears in full in *Annual Report of the Superintendent of National Parks* (1916), pp. 81–82; Shankland, *Steve Mather*, pp. 100–101.

gress received a copy of the *Portfolio.* McFarland promptly threw the American Civic Association into the fight, and William E. Colby mustered the Sierra Club. It was a well-conceived and skillfully executed legislative drive.[32]

The Kent Bill moved out of the House Public Lands Committee on schedule, although its sponsors had to agree to certain changes in order to satisfy Irvine L. Lenroot, of Wisconsin, who insisted that the Washington office of the Park Service should be limited to an expenditure of $19,500 annually for salaries. The bill also included a provision, inserted at the last minute by Kent, who believed it would be beneficial, authorizing the Secretary of the Interior to grant grazing privileges in the national parks. With the valuable assistance of Edward T. Taylor of Colorado, Kent and Raker slipped the bill through the House on July 1. Unfortunately, as the session stretched into the summer, the bill got bogged down in election-year stalling and politicking. The Republican national convention met and nominated Charles Evans Hughes, an associate justice of the Supreme Court, to run for president. Then the Democrats convened and nominated Woodrow Wilson for a second term. Congress remained in session all the while, refusing to adjourn because of its uneasiness over the war in Europe and because of a great deal of unfinished business. Instead of adjourning, Congress simply recessed in fits and starts, according to an elaborate plan approved by the leadership of both houses. Faced with this extraordinary calendar and the innumerable complications it caused, Mather decided that the situation was hopeless. He had already committed himself to a second camping trip in the High Sierra in the hope of converting still another group of prominent men to the national parks cause. He had also arranged to make a special motor tour of Yellowstone Park. So he headed west in July, determined

32. Ise, *Our National Park Policy*, p. 190; *Congressional Record,* 64th Cong., 1st sess. (May 10, 1916), p. 7791; editorial, "National Park Service," *Saturday Evening Post* 188 (Mar. 18, 1916): 26; Herbert Quick, "Handling the Parks," *Saturday Evening Post* 188 (June 24, 1916): 16; G. H. Grosvenor, "The Land of the Best," *National Geographic* 29 (Apr. 1916): 327–430; HMA, "Robert Sterling Yard," p. 10.

to line up support for a new legislative campaign in the second session of the Sixty-fourth Congress, leaving Albright to look after the Kent Bill.[33]

The young man from California proved how persistent and effective he could be, in organizing and overseeing the last push to get the Park Service bill enacted into law. He and Joseph J. Cotter, the assistant superintendent of the National Parks, and the rest of the Park Service lobby, composed largely of McFarland's crew, kept the pressure on key members of Congress. Senator Reed Smoot, of Utah, piloted the Kent Bill through the Senate on August 5, seeing to it that an amendment was passed to strike out the provision authorizing grazing in the parks. Having kept Smoot supplied with all the information he needed, Albright next had to coax the conferees to iron out the differences between the House and Senate versions of the bill, a task that promised to be unusually difficult. It was virtually impossible to get all the conferees together because of the frequent recesses. Albright therefore concentrated on the chairmen of the respective conference committees, Congressman Scott Ferris of Oklahoma and Senator Henry L. Myers of Montana. By sheer persistence, he got them to work out a compromise which he then took around to each individual conferee for approval. In the end, the Senate-House committee agreed to keep the grazing provision in the bill, except that no grazing would be allowed in Yellowstone. On August 15 the Senate approved the conference report. At the last minute, Congressman William H. Stafford of Wisconsin, who opposed the creation of all new bureaus as a matter of principle, attempted to block the bill in the House. Albright, Raker, Kent, and a few other conspirators responded by counting noses. On the afternoon of August 22, Raker requested unanimous consent to consider H.R. 15522, the Kent Bill, and got the conference report adopted by a voice vote in

33. *Congressional Record*, 64th Cong., 1st sess. (May 17, 1916), p. 8221, and (July 1, 1916), p. 10363–65; U.S., Congress, House, Hearings before the Public Lands Committee, "To Establish a National Park Service," 64th Cong., 1st sess. (Apr. 5–6, 1916); HMA, "Robert Sterling Yard," p. 11; HMA to George A. Work, June 10, 1916, HMA Papers; Shankland, *Steve Mather*, pp. 102–3.

spite of Stafford's belated opposition. Assured of a favorable majority, the conspirators cancelled their contingency plans, which called for Stafford to be lured out to the golf course during the debate on the bill.[34]

As a final triumph, Albright persuaded the enrolling clerk at the Capitol to speed the enrolled bill to the White House, where Maurice C. Latta, the White House legislative clerk, agreed to place it before President Wilson for signature on August 25, 1916, three days ahead of schedule. These special arrangements stemmed from Albright's pride in his own achievement and from his flair for the apt, dramatic touch. When Mather came down from the mountains on August 26, after two weeks in the wilderness, a splendid surprise awaited him at Visalia's Palace Hotel. "Park Service bill signed nine o'clock last night," Albright's telegram read, "have pen used by President in signing for you." The National Park Service still keeps Albright's telegram and Wilson's pen as treasured souvenirs.[35]

34. *Congressional Record*, 64th Cong., 1st sess. (Aug. 5, 1916), pp. 12150–52 (Aug. 15, 1916), p. 12632, and (Aug. 22, 1916), pp. 13004–5; Joseph J. Cotter to R. B. Marshall, Aug. 12, 1916, and telegram, HMA to Mather, Aug. 14, 1916, NA, Records of NPS, gen., Supt. and Landscape Engineer; Shankland, *Steve Mather*, p. 103, claims that Stafford "had been enticed out on a golf course by a sly band of crypto-conservationists." Actually, Stafford was on the House floor during the entire final debate on the National Park Service Act, as the *Congressional Record* testified.

35. HMA to Maurice C. Latta, Oct. 24, 1945, NA, Records of NPS, gen., admin., Dir. Albright; in this letter Albright reminisces about those special arrangements; telegram, HMA to Mather, Aug. 26, 1916, photocopy in Shankland, *Steve Mather*, p. 51; HMA to George C. Purdy, Aug. 28, 1916, HMA Papers.

4

Organizing the National Park Service

The elections of 1916 loomed very large to Mather, Albright, and Yard as they looked ahead to the next Congress and the crucially important business of getting an initial appropriation for the National Park Service. Having come to Washington under the auspices of the Wilson administration, Mather's crew hoped that Wilson would be reelected. The Park Service, though authorized by law, still had not been established, and Mather feared that if Hughes won, necessitating a change of administrations, the parks would inevitably suffer. Late in October 1916, Albright and Yard, accompanied by their wives, went to Chicago for a visit at the Mather home, a trip planned to coincide with an inspection tour of the beautiful Indiana Sand Dunes which had been proposed for national park status. After touring the dunes and endorsing the proposed park, the party settled down at Mather's spacious home on Chicago's Dorchester Avenue to await the election results.[1]

The ladies went off to the theater on election night, but the gentlemen adjourned to the University Club, where they made arrangements to receive telegraphic summaries of the early returns. It was a long and dreary evening. With increasing gloom, the men studied the reports of the ballot counting, which seemed to indicate that Hughes would be the next president. "The news that night was a terrific shock to us," Albright wrote, "for we envisioned our Park Service beginning to live and breathe just in time for the Republicans to appoint all the policy-making officials." By the time the women returned from the theater, the men were back home, sadly bemoaning their fate. "I can still see

1. HMA, "Robert Sterling Yard," p. 12.

61

Bob Yard," Albright wrote several years later, "sitting on the front stairs of the Mather home holding his head in his hands and moaning, 'We're lost—everything is lost.' " Three days later, the news from California revived the group's sagging spirits. Wilson had carried the state by the narrow margin of a few thousand votes and had thus won the election. There was an impromptu celebration in Mather's office when the official announcement arrived. Franklin K. Lane would presumably continue as Secretary of the Interior, and the National Park Service, it seemed clear, would become a reality. By the end of November, Mather and Albright were laying plans for a new campaign to publicize the parks and win an appropriation from Congress.[2]

Serious problems confronted the national parks toward the end of 1916 and during the early weeks of 1917. In Yellowstone, the situation was particularly precarious. Mather and Albright had schemed rather shrewdly, they thought, with General Hugh L. Scott, the Army Chief of Staff, to remove the troops from Fort Yellowstone after more than thirty years of patrol duty. Scott readily agreed that the army had outlived its usefulness in the park. The era when the vast Yellowstone preserve needed protection against game poachers and western desperadoes had ended long ago, and, after all, the United States now faced a great national emergency, with war raging in Europe. It seemed more than likely that the troops then assigned to custodial duty in Yellowstone would be needed for purposes of national defense. Mather and Scott worked out a plan for the Interior Department to "take over the guardianship of the park," if the Secretary of War approved. When the Secretary raised no objections, the transfer took place smoothly in October 1916, all of it accomplished by administrative action. Congress had been completely bypassed.[3]

Albright worked out the details of a corollary agreement un-

2. Ibid.; *New York Times*, Nov. 8–12, 1916; Shankland, *Steve Mather*, pp. 107–8.

3. HMA to Marshall, Aug. 28, 1916, Newton D. Baker to Secretary of the Interior, Aug. 19, 1916, and memorandum, Adjutant General to Commanding General, Western Dept., Aug. 24, 1916, NA, Records of NPS, gen., Supt. and Landscape Engineer; Shankland, *Steve Mather*, pp. 104–5; HMA, "Reminiscences," pp. 44–47.

der which Colonel L. M. Brett, the commander of the army detachment in the park, would remain temporarily in charge, and a cadre of experienced noncommissioned officers would be discharged from the army to form the nucleus of a Yellowstone ranger force. The only trouble came from Congressman John J. Fitzgerald, chairman of the House Appropriations Committee, who resented the fact that Congress had not been consulted prior to the removal of the troops. He served notice that he would demand their return during the next fiscal year.[4]

A series of vexing park problems grew out of the increasingly clumsy administration of Robert B. Marshall, whom Mather had handpicked to become the first director of the National Park Service. Marshall had worked closely with Mather for nearly two years. Most recently, he had headed the interim Park Service (composed of staff members borrowed from other agencies), which came into existence when the National Park Service Act was passed in August 1916 but no money was made available to establish the service. There was every reason to expect that Marshall would make an effective National Parks Director. Hardworking, dedicated, knowledgeable about the parks, experienced in Washington circles, he nevertheless lacked the sensitivity and finesse of a first-rate administrator. He offended Congressman Fitzgerald by exhausting appropriations for an urgently needed power plant in Yosemite long before the project was finished. He angered the concessioners in Yellowstone, the managers of the western railroads, and the state officials in Montana and Wyoming, by closing Yellowstone Park ahead of schedule in September because of a threatened railroad strike that failed to materialize. His unintentionally heavy-handed style of correspondence and his sometimes pompous public statements were not well adapted to winning friends for the National Park Service or for the public relations work that Mather emphasized so heavily. Shortly before Christmas 1916 Mather gave Marshall back to the Geological Survey and faced the new year without an interim director.[5]

4. Telegram, HMA to Marshall, Aug. 14, 1916, NA, Records of NPS, Parks gen., Dir.; HMA to L. M. Brett, Sept. 28, 1916, HMA Papers.
5. *Annual Report, NPS* (1917), p. 2; Ise, *Our National Park Policy*,

Potential disaster struck the national parks in January 1917 when Steve Mather suffered a severe nervous breakdown and had to withdraw from the Interior Department for a prolonged period of rest and recuperation. His breakdown occurred in the midst of a National Parks Conference he had organized in Washington for the purpose of publicizing the parks and dramatizing the need for an initial appropriation for the National Park Service. Meeting in the auditorium of the National Museum, the conference was an unqualified success. A distinguished contingent of senators and congressmen attended, led by Frederick H. Gillett, a member of the now famous Mather mountain party of 1915. Secretary Lane, Huston Thompson, Emerson Hough, Enos Mills, J. Horace McFarland, Gilbert Grosvenor, E. O. McCormick, and many other highly placed park enthusiasts, spoke in support of the Park Service. A splendid collection of paintings and sketches of national park scenes, carefully selected by Mather, went on display at the Smithsonian Gallery, drawing further attention to the parks. The strain of arranging the conference, coming on top of three or four tempestuous scenes with Marshall, a donnybrook with Senator Thomas J. Walsh, of Montana, over concessions policies in Yellowstone Park, and two years of man-killing work, threw Mather into a mood of deep despondency. He seemed suddenly to lose all of his self-confidence and self-esteem. The strenuous efforts of his friends to bolster his sagging spirits utterly failed. A few days after the conference ended, Albright telephoned Mrs. Mather, who was visiting her parents in Elizabeth, New Jersey, to tell her what had happened. Following her instructions, he and E. O. Mc-Cormick quietly took Mather to Philadelphia and placed him under the care of Dr. T. A. Weisenburg, a specialist in nervous disorders. By nightfall Mather had been admitted to a private sanitarium in Devon, Pennsylvania, a few miles outside of Philadelphia.[6]

---

p. 195; Shankland, *Steve Mather*, pp. 106–7.

6. *National Parks Conference in New National Museum, Washington, D.C.,* Jan. 2–6, 1917; Shankland, *Steve Mather*, pp. 108–10.

This was not the first time Mather had suffered a mental collapse. In 1903, following a long period of overwork and stress in the borax business, he had manifested the same symptoms and had required prolonged psychiatric care. Two months after the 1917 breakdown, the doctor described Mather as "very much depressed" and "fearful," with "no confidence in himself." And yet, the doctor wrote, "I am confident that he will fully recover." It was mostly a matter of removing him from the source of his anxiety and providing total rest. Dr. Weisenburg directed that Mather be cut off from all contact with the national parks and be separated from his family and friends for more than a month. The original estimate was that he "could not return to business within six months." Meanwhile, Albright agreed to fill in for Mather, taking on the full range of Mather's official duties and responsibilities, including the task of running the parks and the delicate business of getting an appropriation to establish the National Park Service. "My ambition," he wrote to Mrs. Mather late in January, "is to have everything brought up to date and every disagreeable and tiring matter cleaned up by the time he comes back so that he will find it easy to go ahead and run the park system during the summer." "Please do not feel that I am being overworked or overburdened . . . ," he continued. "I am young and strong" and "engaged in a labor of love." As time passed, it became increasingly clear that Mather would be out of commission for many months. In fact, more than a year would pass before he could resume his old responsibilities in the Department of the Interior.[7]

Albright was barely twenty-seven years old when he stepped into Mather's shoes, but he was clearly the best available substitute. He had visited all of the important parks. He had systematically studied Mather's methods and had helped to shape Mather's policies. He already knew the ropes in the department and on Capitol Hill, and he had demonstrated his ability as an

7. Mrs. S. T. Mather to HMA, Jan. 27, 1917, T. H. Weisenburg to Mrs. S. T. Mather, Feb. 16, 1917, Weisenburg to HMA, Feb. 27, 1917, Mar. 20, 1917, Apr. 30, 1917, May 12, 1917, and June 14, 1917, and HMA to Mrs. Mather, Jan. 19, 1917, HMA Papers.

administrator. He was able to draw upon his experience in the Secretary's office and to call upon his influential friends for assistance. Surely no other young man in the department was as well qualified. Working at a frantic pace, he did his own job as well as Mather's and somehow managed to remain unruffled. It was during 1917 and 1918 that Albright finally had an opportunity to demonstrate his full capabilities as an executive. Secretary Lane never regretted his decision to take a chance on Albright while Mather slowly regained his health.

Immediately after Mather's collapse, Albright moved to solidify his own position and to install a new chain of command in the interim Park Service. Bob Yard, many years Albright's senior, apparently jumped to the conclusion that he should take command of Mather's Washington domain. Thoroughly horrified at the prospect of having the impetuous Yard giving orders, Mrs. Mather immediately wrote to Albright imploring him to "hold Mr. Yard in." She made it absolutely clear that Mather wanted Albright to be in charge of the Washington operation, including Yard's office, and that she herself would be "perfectly agreeable" to whatever Albright cared to do as long as he kept a tight rein on things. Accordingly, Albright had a "straightforward talk" with Yard and informed Mrs. Mather that he and his older colleague had "reached an understanding." Henceforth, Albright wrote, Yard was "going to consult with me on everything before taking action. Also, I am going to see all letters that come out of his office which have the remotest chance of bringing results that Mr. Mather would not be pleased with." It is a measure of Albright's deft touch that he did not alienate Yard and that the two men remained on friendly terms throughout this period.[8]

Albright also took charge of Mather's Washington purse strings, receiving periodic bank drafts from Oliver Mitchell, Mather's business manager, and disbursing monthly salary payments of $650 to Yard, $75 to a clerk in Yard's office, and $83.33 to himself. Mather had been augmenting Albright's sal-

8. Mrs. S. T. Mather to HMA, Jan. 17, 1917, and HMA to Mrs. Mather, Jan. 19, 1917, HMA Papers.

ary at this rate since April 1915 when the young man agreed to remain in the government service for at least another year. Mitchell trusted Albright from the start and worked closely with him in managing Mather's affairs, but he distrusted Yard, whose administrative ineptitude was obvious. A few weeks after Mather's collapse, for example, Yard tried to bind his boss to purchase more than $500 worth of beautiful but clearly unneeded slides and in the process thoughtlessly angered a potentially important friend of the parks. At this, Mitchell lost all patience and, in March, recommended "tying a can to Mr. Yard." Albright wrote to Mather and urged him "to give Mr. Yard the year's notice he thinks he should have before the termination of his services." But the young man resolutely refused to fire Yard, who was one of Mather's oldest friends. "You know," he explained to Mitchell, Mather "is very close to Mr. Yard, and it seems to me that no matter what we individually think about retaining him or about the work he is doing we would be taking a chance [of displeasing Mather] if we laid him off." Albright informed Mitchell that "we have simply got to let this matter run along until we get our word from the Chief." His sense of the situation was exactly right. Mather kept Yard on the payroll until 1919 when the National Parks Association was organized and Yard became its executive secretary. Time and again, during 1917 and 1918, Albright reacted precisely as Mather would have reacted, thus saving his mentor a great deal of anguish and demonstrating a well-developed sense of discretion. This was what made Albright so valuable to Mather. The two men increasingly thought alike and reacted in similar ways to similar situations.[9]

After settling matters with Yard and reconciling himself to the fact that Mather would not be able to return to his old job for several months, if ever, Albright turned his attention to the touchy problem of obtaining an appropriation for the National Park Service. "I am going to do as I promised," he pledged, "—remain here through the current year and do all that I can

9. HMA to Oliver Mitchell, Mar. 19, 1917, and June 6, 1917, Mitchell to HMA, Mar. 22, 1917, and May 2, 1917, HMA Papers.

to further" Mather's "principles" and "plans." Getting the
National Park Service permanently established, he knew, would
please Mather immensely. In January he went before the House
Appropriations Subcommittee in charge of Sundry Civil Appropriations to defend his estimates of national parks expenditures
for the 1917–18 fiscal year. John J. Fitzgerald, the fearsome congressman from Brooklyn, chaired the subcommittee, but Frederick H. Gillett, Albright's camping companion, was also a committee member, a circumstance that gave the young man room
for a certain amount of optimism. Albright carefully explained
at the beginning of his testimony that Mather had "suffered a
nervous and physical collapse" and would have to be "away for
an indefinite period," but that Secretary Lane had "designated
me to supervise . . . the administration of the parks in Mr. Mather's absence." Albright then pointed out that he had been
"closely associated with Mr. Mather" for more than two years
and had been "right with him most of the time."[10]

At first, Albright's testimony went smoothly, as he launched
into an explanation of the recently completed reorganization of
Yellowstone's concessions setup. His strategy was to show that
the parks were already being widely used but, more important,
that steps were being taken to increase the amount of public
use. "We are compelling the camp company and the hotel company," he stated, to expand and improve their facilities and
"to tell the people . . . about the possibilities of Yellowstone as a
summer resort." The politics of the situation clearly demanded
that Albright take an unequivocal stand in favor of park development.[11]

As the hearings continued, however, Fitzgerald hurled a bar-
rage of caustic remarks at Albright and launched a spirited attack on the National Park Service. When Albright requested
money for seven clerks, in addition to the five main officers authorized by the act of August 25, 1916—this was to be the entire

10. HMA to Mrs. Mather, Feb. 3, 1917, HMA Papers; U.S., Congress, House, Hearings Before Subcommittee in Charge of Sundry Civil
Appropriation Bill for 1918, "Sundry Civil Bill, 1918," 64th Cong., 2d
sess. (Jan.-Feb. 1917), pp. 760–61.
11. Ibid., p. 421.

complement of the Washington office—Fitzgerald snapped, "Why does every man who has a job in the Government have to have a clerk?" He then growled ominously that prospective office workers in the National Park Service "ought to be employed by a Member of Congress for about six months and they would find out what a day's work is." Albright replied earnestly, "we are not asking for anything more than we deserve. Every one of us down there has worked overtime for a year or more, and on Sundays and holidays."[12]

The fireworks came when Fitzgerald interrogated Albright about the removal of the troops from Yellowstone Park. "How did the soldiers come to be taken out of the park?" the chairman asked. "They were taken out at the behest of the War Department," Albright replied, adding that "for several years" the army had been "endeavoring to get rid of that responsibility." "No," shouted the chairman. "The Interior Department started the effort" to get the troops out. "I know what happened." From that moment on, the hearings degenerated into a brusque cross-examination of Albright and a dollar-by-dollar scrutiny of the proposed parks budget. A request for funds to complete the power plant in Yosemite triggered Fitzgerald's angriest blast. "You were given $150,000 to build this power plant," he raged, "and you proceeded to attempt to build one double the size originally contemplated." When Albright tried to answer, Fitzgerald cut him off and roared: "The trouble with this service is that it does not imagine it is controlled in any way by either the limitation of law or the appropriation. You come before Congress and ask for a specific appropriation for a definite purpose and after you get the money then you proceed to do as you please, regardless of what you have presented here." Albright lamely explained that Marshall, recently resigned, had supervised the power-plant project and was therefore responsible for disregarding the committee's wishes. Now completely on the defensive, he got himself into further difficulty by trying to absolve Mather of all blame.[13]

By the end of his third day before the subcommittee, Albright

12. Ibid., pp. 760–62.
13. Ibid., pp. 763–66, 818–22.

was emotionally exhausted. He had never lost his composure in his long contest with Fitzgerald, but he knew that he had presented the wrong image and feared that the National Park Service would not get the money it needed. The committee "handled me pretty roughly," he later admitted to Mrs. Mather. In a more candid moment, he confided to a friend that he had spent "two miserable days before Fitzgerald of the Appropriations Committee. I like him almost as well as I do smallpox and typhoid fever."[14]

Albright, though humbled and dissatisfied with himself, built a case strong enough to justify an initial appropriation for the Park Service. The Sundry Civil bill passed the House on February 28, with a large cut in appropriations for the Yosemite power plant and a requirement that the troops be restored to Yellowstone. In the upper house, Albright worked with Senator Smoot in an attempt to restore the funds and win approval of the troop withdrawal. Late in April, the Senate passed its version of the Sundry Civil bill, giving Albright and the Park Service lobbyists virtually everything they wanted. As the House and Senate conferees took the bill under advisement, Albright wrote to Gillett expressing hope that the Park Service would "be allowed to finish the [Yosemite] power plant" and the conferees would "not insist that we put the troops back in Yellowstone." He implied that national park administrators, including himself, had learned a hard lesson. "I am going to watch the expenditure of every cent," he pledged, "and I am going to be able to come before the committee next year and show that this year's administration of the park funds has been strictly in accordance with the estimates and with the wishes of the committee." "You will pardon me, I know," he added, "if I let this letter run into a personal appeal to give me a chance to administer the parks without legislative restriction." Gillett promised "to do everything" he could "to ease" his friend's way. At the right moment Albright and Yard issued a special national parks road map and made copies of it available to all members of Congress for distribution

14. HMA to Mrs. Mather, Feb. 3, 1917, and HMA to Mark Daniels, Mar. 19, 1917, HMA Papers.

to constituents. The bill as finally passed included a generous appropriation for Yosemite, but Fitzgerald got his pound of flesh and the troops went back into Yellowstone. The total appropriation for all the parks during the first year of the National Park Service was about half a million dollars. Under the circumstances, this was more than anybody expected.[15]

Albright's work in getting the Park Service appropriation through Congress left him more than a little bruised and considerably chastened. He resolved to establish friendly relations with all the members of the appropriations subcommittees, and he determined not to make the mistake of being overconfident again. Having to bear the "whole burden" of national parks administration, with only a makeshift staff of clerks to assist him, and having to handle all the legislative matters pertaining to the parks required an extraordinary personal effort from Albright. "It took me quite a while to get into the swing of affairs," he admitted to a friend on Capitol Hill, "although everything is going very nicely now."[16]

While Albright placed his major emphasis on obtaining a regular Park Service appropriation for the fiscal year beginning July 1, 1917, he also took the lead in persuading a reluctant Congress to approve a small deficiency appropriation so the Park Service could be promptly organized. Fitzgerald flatly refused to write the new bureau into the House version of the deficiency bill, but Albright won support on the Senate side, where Senators Smoot and Thomas S. Martin pushed through an amendment providing the necessary funds. The deficiency bill, with the Senate amendment still in it, became law on April 17, 1917, a few days after Congress voted to declare war against Germany. Within two weeks, Lane made arrangements for Albright's appointment as assistant director by means of an executive order signed by President Wilson. Mather was slated to

15. HMA to Mrs. Mather, Mar. 1, 1917, HMA to F. H. Gillett, May 2, 1917, Gillett to HMA, May 3, 1917, and HMA to Mather, June 8, 1917, HMA Papers; *Congressional Record*, 65th Cong., 1st sess. (Apr. 4, 1917), pp. 265–85 (Apr. 11, 1917), p. 590, and (June 7, 1917), pp. 3297–3301.

16. HMA to F. H. Gillett, May 2, 1917, HMA Papers.

become director, but until his return, Lane ordered, Albright would be "Acting Director" of the National Park Service.[17]

"I want to continue to pay you the thousand per year," wrote Mather, now obviously recovering, "after you get your new government salary as Assistant Director." By thus boosting Albright's total income to $3,500, Mather greatly increased the probability that Albright would remain with the Park Service. It was perfectly legal to augment official government salaries with personal gifts, and Mather proposed to continue doing so. Albright certainly had no objections, but his dream of practicing law in California persisted. "I, of course, want to do everything I can to help Mr. Mather," he wrote to a lawyer friend in San Francisco, "but I do get awfully anxious sometimes to get into active practice in the West." In March he rejected a feeler from the San Francisco firm of Morrison, Dunne, and Brobeck, explaining that, because of Mather's absence, he "was not in a position . . . to be able to accept." He was attempting to keep up his contacts in the legal profession, but it became increasingly difficult. "It looks like I am getting quite a long ways from the practice of law, doesn't it?" he wistfully observed to William E. Colby of the Sierra Club.[18]

By the first week of May, 1917, the Washington office of the National Park Service had begun to function. A. E. Demaray and Isabelle F. Story, whom Marshall had brought over from the Geological Survey, became two of Albright's most effective and versatile assistants. Frank W. Griffith, formerly of Lane's personal staff, became the chief clerk, and Noble J. Wilt, an expert stenographer and accountant, took charge of Park Service records and bookkeeping. A messenger and five clerks, or stenographers, with Beatrice Ward and Mae Schnurr among them, rounded out the original complement. W. B. Acker, of the Secre-

17. *Annual Report, NPS* (1917), pp. 1–2, 226; *Congressional Record*, 65th Cong., 1st sess. (Apr. 3, 1917), pp. 158–67 (Apr. 6, 1917), pp. 442–47, and (Apr. 16, 1917), pp. 726–27; Executive Order no. 2613, May 9, 1917.

18. Mather to HMA, May 6, 1917, Orrin K. McMurray to HMA, Mar. 10, 1917, Herman Phleger to HMA, Mar. 31, 1917, and HMA to William E. Colby, Apr. 23, 1917, HMA Papers.

tary's office, continued to advise and assist Albright in many ways, although he never became a member of the National Park Service and had to spend almost all of his time on other duties. With this tiny group, Albright set out to coordinate and direct the administration of seventeen national parks and twenty-two national monuments (areas set aside, usually by presidential proclamation, to protect places of historic or scientific significance). His first notable accomplishment as acting bureau chief was to outmaneuver Cato Sells, the commissioner of Indian affairs, in a contest over a choice fourth-floor office location in the Interior Department's new gray-stone building on the corner of 18th and E streets, about two blocks from the White House. After May 1917, when the department occupied the new building, the Park Service enjoyed a superb view of the Potomac River, the Washington Monument, Rawlins Park, and the historic Octagon House, which stood just across the street. The view, Albright claimed, befitted an agency committed to the protection and preservation of beautiful scenery.[19]

Under the best of circumstances, the launching of the National Park Service would have posed difficult problems, but the onset of World War I seriously complicated Albright's task as acting director. A mood of wartime urgency gripped the nation, and in Washington the conduct of routine government business became haphazard and unpredictable at best. The need to win the war inevitably overshadowed all other governmental objectives.[20]

Much to his regret, Albright discovered that the war had made the national parks highly vulnerable to attacks by utilitarians. Secretary Lane himself began to question the policy of keeping the national parks "locked up." Never deeply committed to preservationist goals, and now extremely eager for the Interior Department to make a contribution toward the winning of the

19. *Annual Report, NPS* (1917), pp. 2, 100–102; Shankland, *Steve Mather,* pp. 111–12; interview with HMA, Dec. 21, 1965; HMA, "Reminiscences," pp. 73–76.
20. Charles R. Van Hise, *Conservation and Regulation in the United States During the World War* gives an indication of the kind of "conservation" thinking typical of the Great War.

war, he proposed that the parks be thrown open to grazing. In Yosemite, for example, he wanted "all of the park above the valley" to be made available for sheep pasturage, and Albright had "to fight like a trooper to get him out of the notion." Soon cattlemen in the vicinity of Sequoia, Glacier, and Mount Rainier national parks began demanding the right to graze cattle on the beautiful park meadows. Albright sensed that he could not hold the line much longer. As the pressure for emergency grazing increased, he began searching for a palatable compromise that would keep all sheep out of the parks and admit only a limited number of cattle. (The cattle, he held, would be much less destructive in their grazing habits than sheep.) Lane forced Albright to admit a few head of cattle to the parks as early as June 1917, but the young man successfully forestalled the issuance of large numbers of grazing permits for the remainder of the 1917 park season.[21]

The pressure from cattlemen, sheepmen, and livestock experts working for the Food Administration sharply increased as the war extended into 1918. Newspaper articles appeared in the West, expounding the theme that "wild posies," though beautiful, were hardly "as vital as mutton." Many of the articles castigated Albright for obstructing the war effort. One zealous group of westerners went so far as to suggest that the magnificent Yellowstone elk herd be slaughtered to provide canned meat for the doughboys in France. To head off the invasion of Glacier Park by vast herds of sheep, Albright arranged to lease most of its grazing lands to Walter Hansen, a friend of the park, who quietly promised to graze only a token herd of cattle for the duration of the war. Early in 1918 Albright induced his old college friend, Ralph P. Merritt, now food administrator for California, to prepare a memorandum for Hoover's signature, indicating that there would be no necessity to graze sheep in the National Parks. Earlier, Frederick Walcott, head of the Fisheries Section of the Food Administration, helped Albright subdue the mounting pressure against the strict game laws in the parks by preparing a

21. Mather to HMA, June 1, 1917, HMA Papers; Shankland, *Steve Mather*, pp. 202–6.

similar memorandum de-emphasizing the value of hunting and sport fishing as sources of food.[22]

"As a matter of fact," Albright admitted in the 1920s, "we did permit grazing in most of the parks during the war." But luckily for the National Park Service, the war ended before much damage could be done. One of Albright's most important achievements as acting director was in successfully protecting the national parks from the threat of wartime incursions. The Boone and Crockett Club, the American Civic Association, the Camp Fire Club of America, and the Sierra Club gave him strong support. Huston Thompson, Gilbert Grosvenor, and E. O. McCormick helped in the work of "educating" the members of Congress. There were a number of compromises on grazing, but the parks came out of the war generally unscathed.[23]

The manpower pinch and the military draft dealt the Park Service a severe blow in 1917 and 1918. Since the time of the national parks conference in Berkeley in 1915, Mather had been trying to attract able young men into the "park game." As soon as the war started many of these young men enlisted or were drafted into the army. Albright tried to persuade key people to give up their chance for military glory in favor of staying with the Park Service. "I want to ask you to do your best to strangle that ambition to enter the Engineers' Reserve Corps," he wrote to W. B. Lewis, superintendent of Yosemite. "The Park Service can not spare you now or in the early future, and I take the position that you are serving your country where you are. . . . The Service is just being organized," Albright argued, "and we need conscientious and capable men more than we need even appropriations and legislation these days." Albright himself felt the lure of the military. Eager to enlist, he "went so far as to make out" an application form. He nostalgically recalled his

22. Clipping from *Tacoma News-Ledger*, Nov. 4, 1917, scrapbook, HMA to Emerson Hough, Jan. 14, 1918, Ralph P. Merritt to HMA, May 9, 1918, and May 30, 1918, HMA to Merritt, May 23, 1918, and HMA to Fred M. Hess, Mar. 20, 1918, HMA Papers; telegram, Mather to HMA, July 18, 1918, NA, Records of NPS, gen., admin., Assist. Dir.; *Annual Report, NPS* (1918), pp. 23–25.

23. HMA to Frank J. Taylor, May 10, 1926, HMA Papers.

dreams of going to West Point and his training in the Cadet Corps at Berkeley. But with Mather ill he really had no choice but to remain with the Park Service. "Secretary Lane told me . . . ," he wrote, " that I must not think of going into the military service in any capacity." Albright's first deferment came in December 1917 at the behest of Lane and Mather.[24]

Frustrated in his own military ambitions, Albright found consolation in being able to help some of his friends get into the army. He knew many of the upper-echelon officials of the War Department as a result of his and Mather's scheme to get the army out of Yellowstone. If he needed to, he could pull a few strings in the War Department. When Newton B. Drury, his classmate at the University of California, wrote to ask for assistance in wangling a commission, Albright galloped into action. Drury was a vigorous and energetic man, in the full bloom of good health, but he was of short stature and, by his own admission, "somewhat underweight." He wanted to become "adjutant of an Aerial Squadron" and he was well qualified to hold down that kind of a billet, having served as President Benjamin Ide Wheeler's administrative assistant at the University of California for the past several years. Albright went to the War Department and talked to the officers in charge of "administrative matters in the office of the Chief Signal Officer . . . [and in] the Office of the Surgeon General." These officers agreed to give Drury's case "their personal consideration" and to give Albright an "opportunity to be heard" in Drury's behalf. "I am quite sure . . . that we have your difficulties straightened out," Albright informed his friend. About two weeks later, he triumphantly wired Drury: "Your deficiency waived. Your training school is Ohio State University." There were at least a half dozen episodes like this, with Albright trying his best to expedite his college friends' applications for officer's training.[25]

24. HMA to W. B. Lewis, June 2, 1917, and affidavit requesting deferment, executed by Mather, Dec. 19, 1917, HMA Papers; HMA, "Reminiscences," pp. 42–44.

25. Newton B. Drury to HMA, Dec. 21, 1917, HMA to Drury, Jan. 3, 1918, and telegram, HMA to Drury, Jan. 19, 1918, see also Fritz Grabner to HMA, Sept. 20, 1917, and HMA to Grabner, Sept. 22, 1917, HMA Papers.

In the meantime, Albright was having his troubles with the parks. "Dusty" Lewis decided to pass up the army and stay on as superintendent of Yosemite, thus easing the potential crisis in that important park. In Yellowstone and Glacier, conditions were painfully chaotic. Yellowstone's administrative structure had been undermined by Congressman Fitzgerald's single-minded drive to put the army back into the park and by the maneuverings of the concessioners, who also favored retaining the army. "The removal of the troops from the Yellowstone last fall was a most unfortunate step," Albright ruefully admitted to the park's acting superintendent, Chester A. Lindsley. "To say that the [Appropriations] Committee was mad is putting it very mildly." Albright, too, was mad and "bitterly disappointed" that Fitzgerald felt it necessary "to punish us." There was no choice, he knew, but to order the dismissal of the entire existing ranger force and request that a "detachment of cavalry" be dispatched to take over the rangers' duties. But Albright had clearly not given up the fight to oust the army from the park. He asked for the smallest possible number of troops to be sent back. He ordered Lindsley to establish Park Service headquarters in the largest and finest building in the park "before the soldiers" returned. He determined to keep Lindsley "in charge of the park" during the 1917 season and, if possible, to "keep the Army officers from assuming too much authority." Title to the buildings, horses, and essential utility systems was to remain with the Park Service. "I firmly believe," he told Lindsley, "that we can get the troops out again in a year or two."[26]

As a matter of fact, Albright had already talked to his friends on the House Public Lands Committee about the possibility of a special bill to remove "both the protection and improvement of the park from the War Department." As for the concessioners in the park, he considered them "positively the most obstreperous" group of businessmen he "ever had to deal with." He charged Lindsley with the responsibility for watching them "every minute" to prevent them from taking advantage of the unsettled situation. Finally, in an effort to improve conditions, he promised

26. HMA to C. A. Lindsley, June 10, 1917, HMA Papers.

to inspect the park personally during the summer of 1917. The complex problems of administering this huge "national playground" with its extraordinary geyser basins, breath-taking scenery, and remarkable wildlife population, already seemed to fascinate Albright. He clearly recognized that Yellowstone's difficulties would continue until the Park Service evicted the army and found a top-flight administrator to install as superintendent.[27]

In Glacier the trouble stemmed from the fact that Thomas J. Walsh and Henry L. Myers, the Montana senators, considered the park their private preserve. They continually interfered with its administration and controlled practically all of its staff appointments, dispensing the superintendency and most of the ranger billets on the basis of political patronage. Almost all of the rangers, openly taking their orders from Walsh or Myers instead of the Park Service, were incompetent or lazy. Albright doubted that "any of them" patrolled "a mile beyond their stations." To compound these difficulties, Albright considered Walsh "one of the most cantankerous men" in public life. If Glacier's problems were ever to be solved, the senators' political stranglehold over the park would have to be broken. Albright decided that he would visit Glacier Park as soon as possible.[28]

By June 1917 the relentless pressure of Albright's job had begun to tell. Handling all of the legislative and legal aspects of the National Park Service, fighting off those who wanted to exploit the parks during the wartime emergency, trying to build up a competent staff both in Washington and in the field, acting as general troubleshooter for all of the parks, and tending to many of Mather's personal affairs amounted to a tremendous load for one man to carry. Marshall, of course, was gone. Joe Cotter, Marshall's assistant, had been transferred back to the Secretary's office. Acker no longer had time for Park Service matters. Mather, though now able to give advice on minor problems, had still not returned to Washington. Essentially, Albright was per-

27. Ibid.; *Annual Report, NPS* (1917), pp. 32–33.
28. HMA to George E. Goodwin, May 14, 1917, HMA Papers.

forming the duties previously performed by all of these people. "I think I have been the busiest man in Washington since January first," he wrote to a friend, and none of his colleagues in the Interior Department were inclined to argue the point. As the summer approached, he became so fatigued that he lost his customary optimism and seemed deeply discouraged. "I hope that I shall never spend another year alive," he moaned, "if I have to work like I have been working for the last six months." A few weeks in the field, inspecting conditions in the parks, would be a welcome tonic.[29]

Albright had to talk long and loud to get Secretary Lane's permission to leave Washington on an extended field trip. Finally, he won the Secretary over by arguing that the affairs of the Park Service were in good order, that the appropriations bill had already passed, and that the administrative coordination of the national parks would suffer unless he soon had a chance to inspect most of the parks. Albright and his young wife caught a train for the West late in June. Grace planned to travel with Horace as far as Denver. Then, while he inspected the parks, she would go to Berkeley for a visit with her parents. When the Albrights reached Denver, they climbed off the train thoroughly relaxed and in high spirits, only to discover that Grace's luggage was missing. Albright quickly realized what had happened. "This is the first time I have traveled with my wife," he sheepishly wrote to the passenger agent in Chicago, requesting that Grace's bag be forwarded, "and I went ahead and checked my own trunk through to Denver, but entirely forgot hers. It will be a long time before I live this down."[30]

Albright's inspection trip that summer showed how much he had learned from Steve Mather. The young man handled himself with poise and self-assurance, not only inspecting the parks, but also cultivating friendships with automobile club members, businessmen, newspaper editors, railroad officials, and chambers

29. HMA to Lindsley, June 10, 1917, and HMA to R. A. Kennedy, June 16, 1917, HMA Papers.
30. HMA to Mather, June 2, 1917, and HMA to P. S. Eustis, June 30, 1917, HMA Papers.

of commerce wherever he went. Mather himself could scarcely have done better. Albright received generous press coverage in Denver, where he sounded his central public relations theme for the trip, that "America's participation in the world war" was not going "to lessen the stream of summer travel" in the West. Tourist dollars, he assured his listeners, would continue to roll in because the Park Service had undertaken a vast campaign to promote and publicize the parks. From Denver Albright went directly to Rocky Mountain National Park, where he conferred with Enos Mills and the other businessmen in Estes Park. "I talked to nearly every hotel keeper in town, and everybody else that I could find," he reported to Mather, "and I think I have gotten them to assume a brighter and better attitude."[31]

By the end of June he was on his way to Yellowstone to talk with Chester Lindsley. "Line up all of the matters you want to take up with me, meet me at [West] Yellowstone in your car, and we will go right to work the moment we get alone," he ordered. "I am what they sometimes call a 'speedburner' these days." After about a week, he moved on to Glacier and thence to Mount Rainier, where he was entertained by the "roads and park enthusiasts" of the Seattle area. The failure of the state legislature "to provide funds for the constructing of . . . [access] roads," he proclaimed in a newspaper interview, "has seriously injured the Interior Department's plans for the development of Rainier National Park." A few days later, at Crater Lake Park, near Medford, Oregon, he urged greater "educational" work in behalf of the parks and publicly boosted the idea of a "National Park to Park Highway." Hardly pausing for breath, Albright raced down to Berkeley for a brief reunion with his wife and mother, then proceeded southward to Yosemite, where he was shocked by the poor quality of the public services and the apparent inefficiency of the concessioners. He made a fast trip to Sequoia, then swung back to Yosemite to welcome a party of

31. Clippings from Denver *Times*, June 23, 1917, and *Rocky Mountain News*, June 23, 1917, and June 27, 1917, and HMA to Mather, June 30, 1917, HMA Papers.

high Japanese officials, headed by Ambassador Kikujiro Ishii.[32] On his way back to Washington, Albright joined Douglas White, the passenger-traffic officer of the Union Pacific Railroad, on a side trip into Zion Canyon, then a little-known national monument. He was so enthralled by the canyon's beauty that he promised to publicize the region and try to have it designated as a national park. Two years later, with the help of Senator Smoot, he pushed a bill through Congress authorizing the establishment of Zion National Park, which became one of the jewels of the national park system. In 1917, however, he contented himself with a news release saying that he was "thoroughly convinced of the importance of Zion Canyon as a tourist center." At Mesa Verde Park, in southern Colorado, Albright got to know both the vice-president and the passenger-traffic manager of the Denver and Rio Grande Railroad, and, during an excursion in the vice-president's private car, filled John Steel, a reporter for the *Rocky Mountain News*, "so full of national park enthusiasm that it just naturally ran out of his mouth." Passing through Denver on the last leg of his inspection tour, Albright made headlines in the local papers by predicting that more than "100,000 automobiles" would be touring the national parks "within five years." He arrived back in Washington the last week of September, after having traveled about ten thousand miles. It had been "rush, rush, rush all the time, from morning until late at night," he reported to Secretary Lane. But he was well satisfied with the results. Now for the first time he really comprehended the immense organizational problems that still faced the National Park Service. He had accumulated a valuable new fund of first-hand information about the parks, the superintendents, and the concessioners. And after nearly three months in the mountains, he was psychologically ready to face Washington again. His natural optimism strongly reasserted itself and, in-

32. HMA to Lindsley, June 10, 1917, clippings from Seattle *Times*, July 10, 1917, Tacoma *Tribune*, July 13, 1917, Medford *Sun*, July 25, 1917, San Francisco *Chronicle*, Aug. 8, 1917, and HMA to Joseph Cotter, Aug. 6, 1917, HMA Papers.

credible as it seems, he found himself relishing the prospect of another encounter with Fitzgerald.[33]

Soon after returning to Washington, Albright began thinking about what he wanted to say in the annual report of the director of the National Park Service, which had to be submitted by October 15. Because of his small staff and his own heavy work load, he might justifiably have contemplated a minimal report, covering only the activities of the Park Service from April 17, when it was officially established, to June 30, when the 1917 fiscal year ended. Instead, Albright resolved to make the first annual report of the National Park Service a full-blown and "important" document. In addition to a description of the new bureau's functions, he decided to include extensive statistical data about park use, a brief history of the "national park idea," a summary of legislation bearing on the national parks, and a number of suggestions about what needed to be done to improve the administration of the parks. Noble Wilt helped him by compiling the statistical tables. Arthur Demaray, a talented draftsman, prepared all the maps. Isabelle Story provided all-around editorial and clerical assistance. Grace Albright, eager to help her overburdened husband, spent many hours in the Library of Congress compiling a bibliography of the books and articles on national parks topics published from September 1916 to October 1917. Containing more than three hundred titles, Grace's compilation provided uncontrovertible proof of the effective publicity campaign masterminded by Mather and Albright.[34]

The bulk of the annual report, consisting of 98 printed pages plus 150 pages of supplementary information, was the product of Albright's "fine Italian quill." His earnest, slightly overripe prose style was unmistakable. "We stand now in the light of a new order of things," he wrote, "but as we gaze back from the

33. Clippings from Salt Lake City *Desert Evening News*, Sept. 8, 1917, Salt Lake City *Herald Republican*, Sept. 9, 1917, Denver *Commercial*, Sept. 20, 1917, and HMA to Mather, Sept. 18, 1917, HMA Papers.

34. *Annual Report, NPS* (1917), pp. 100–258, and see Bibliography, pp. 231–44.

threshold of the future to the efforts of the past, accomplishments of large importance gather before us and we recognize in them tremendous influences that will wisely guide us in our onward and upward steps." This was not an era of great annual-report writing in the federal bureaucracy, and therefore Albright may be forgiven for his stylistic lapses. It was the forceful nature of his remarks and the timeliness of his proposals that gave his report its distinction. He strongly advocated "bringing all of the parks and monuments together . . . under a single authority." He suggested that the national monuments "would mean infinitely more to the American people if their funereal surname could be changed." He called for the battlefields at Gettysburg, Vicksburg, Chickamauga, Chattanooga, and Shiloh to be turned over to the National Park Service. He proposed that the coming year was "precisely the time for our government to adopt a policy" of actively encouraging "touring in the United States," a policy "already established in the European nations." He placed great emphasis on the "astonishing increase in the number of cars in the national parks," pointing toward the many new problems that would be created by the onslaught of the automobile. "The appropriations that are now being made for many parks," he pointed out, "are inadequate." He called for the removal of both the Army Engineers and the cavalry detachment from Yellowstone Park, which under present circumstances, he wrote, "may be likened to a great three-headed monster." He stated that not having the Grand Canyon in the National Park system was "almost ridiculous." He suggested that Sequoia Park should be enlarged to include both "the Kings and Kern River gorges and the crest of the Sierra Nevada" and that "part of the Jackson Hole region should be added to Yellowstone National Park." His final urgent request was for funds to continue "roads and trails improvements." Albright's 1917 annual report amounted to a national park manifesto, which established the guidelines for the next decade of Park Service work. Obviously this was the gospel according to Mather, but as interpreted by Horace Albright. The young Californian was intensely proud of that annual report. He sent copies of it to dozens of newspaper editors from coast to coast and to hundreds of national park boosters, many of whom wrote to congratulate him ."The worst that I can say," observed John Oliver LaGorce, associate editor of the *National Geographic*, "is that it reads very much like an issue of the Geographic Magazine."[35]

By November 1, 1917, the end of Albright's acting directorship was in sight. Mather had recovered sufficiently to take a leisurely western trip during the late summer of 1917. Albright had kept in touch with him throughout the year, running up to Devon for frequent visits after the middle of March. Gradually Albright began informing Mather about Park Service business. Dr. Weisenburg agreed that this would be good therapy. But Albright carefully shielded Mather from all but the happiest developments in Washington. Time and again Mather expressed his appreciation to Albright for "all you have been doing for me." Mrs. Mather also felt a great indebtedness to Albright for his unfailing "devotion to Mr. Mather's interests." As the year passed, a bond of close affection developed between the young man and the Mather family, an affection that would play an important part in determining Albright's decisions in the future.[36]

Late in September, Mather came to Washington for a two-day visit, but he carefully stayed away from the office. "He still lacks confidence in himself, has many fears about his health, etc., is quite frequently gloomy and is not capable of sustained mental effort," Dr. Weisenburg wrote to Albright early in October. Still, it would be "an excellent thing for him" to move back to Washington. Albright quickly agreed to make the necessary arrangements, suggesting that Mather could "come over to the office in the morning at 9:30 or 10:00, read his personal mail, dictate replies thereto, handle such official matters as I may deem it wise to present to him, then go away . . . for lunch-

35. Quotations from *Annual Report, NPS* (1917), pp. 3, 5, 7, 9, 18, 97, 98; HMA to Joseph R. Knowland, Dec. 1917, and John Oliver LaGorce to HMA, Jan. 3, 1918, HMA Papers.

36. HMA to Mather, May 29, 1917, Mather to HMA, June 15, 1917, and Mrs. Mather to HMA, Feb. 5, 1917, HMA Papers.

eon at the Cosmos Club or the Capitol." He could "take an automobile ride in the afternoon," then return to the office and "sign his mail" before going out "with Secretary Lane or some friend for dinner." Albright guaranteed that he could "hold to a schedule of this kind" if Mather came back. "I have worked very hard during the past year," he explained to the doctor, "and have got the administration of the National Park Service in such condition that I can handle it without any difficulty, and I can keep Mr. Mather from worrying and fretting over any phases of the work." Mather, Albright emphasized, "doesn't know much more about the details of the Park Service work now than you do, and I don't propose to let him acquaint himself with them." Under this kind of special arrangement, Steve Mather returned to the Interior Department, toward the end of November 1917. He officially assumed the title of director of the National Park Service, and Albright elaborately deferred to him in all matters of protocol. In reality, however, Albright continued to run the bureau, protecting Mather from all but the least taxing and most enjoyable duties. Mather spent much of his time in Chicago. This awkward but necessary administrative compromise continued until late in the spring of 1918, when Mather, at last fully recovered, assumed definite control of the bureau.[37]

During this tedious period of transition, with Mather slowly and cautiously working himself back into good health, Albright handled bureau affairs with exceptional discretion. Over a period of months he gradually relinquished his power, without resentment and without remorse. He was generally satisfied with what he had accomplished in 1917, although he recognized that Mather's reputation and Lane's personal backing had been responsible for much of his success. He had unquestionably enjoyed having bureau chief status, which gave him an entrée to the highest social circles in Washington. He had become accustomed to the

37. Telegram, Mather to HMA, Sept. 26, 1917, T. H. Weisenburg to HMA, Oct. 8, 1917, HMA to Weisenburg, Oct. 10, 1917, and HMA to Jesse B. Agnew, Nov. 26, 1917, HMA Papers; telegrams, HMA to Mather, Nov. 30, 1917, Dec. 1, 1917, Feb. 25, 1918, and May 20, 1918, NA, Records of NPS, Parks gen.

prerogatives and power of bureaucratic leadership, but he was tired. With Mather back on the job, Albright felt considerably relieved. Perhaps he could now relax and find a little more time to spend with his wife.[38]

Above all, in 1917 Albright had demonstrated an extraordinary capacity for getting the important things done. He had pursued a surprisingly strong and independent course, standing up to Secretary Lane at times and blocking the vested interests who wanted to exploit the parks. He felt free to adopt an independent stance on most issues because, bluntly stated, he did not really care if he got fired. "I just didn't give a damn," he later recalled. He had a yen to enlist in the army anyway, and he had never planned to make a career of government service. Moreover, he continued to hold out hope of returning to California to take up the practice of law. In the context of the Interior Department, he was relatively less constrained than most of his counterparts, who wanted to preserve their status within the bureaucracy and were therefore fearful of incurring the wrath of the Secretary and the Assistant Secretaries. Occasionally, one suspects, the young man must have seemed somewhat bumptious to his elders in Washington and in the National Parks. He paid no homage whatsoever to the venerable Harry W. Child, the most powerful and in many ways the most troublesome of the Yellowstone Park concessioners. He gradually fell out with Enos A. Mills, the irascible proprietor of Long's Peak Inn and an influential writer and lecturer, who unjustly accused him of using his official position "to screen the insidious work of the Forest Service."[39]

Mills's motives were hard to calculate. A long-time opponent of the Forest Service, he was apparently offended because Albright chose not to spend more than a few days in Rocky Mountain Park during the summer of 1917, a decision that may have

38. HMA described his first White House reception in his "Reminiscences," pp. 60–61.

39. HMA to Enos A. Mills, June 16, 1917, Mills to HMA, Oct. 31, 1917, and HMA to Mills, Nov. 15, 1917, HMA Papers; interview with HMA, Dec. 20, 1965.

seemed disrespectful to Mills, the self-styled "father of Rocky Mountain National Park." While he certainly had not intended to anger Mills, Albright's later correspondence, attempting to defend his own record from Mills' attack, only added to the difficulty. It was probably inevitable that Mills and the Park Service would become permanently estranged, but the fact remains that it happened while Albright was acting director. One or two park superintendents bridled at Albright's preoccupation with problems in Washington. "Are you aware," one of them wrote, "that it was three or four months before I received a communication from the [Washington] office except the pay check?" Irritated and somewhat miffed, this superintendent went on to point out that "there is not the cooperation with the Washington office which could and rightfully should exist." Considering the large number of problems he faced and the small staff he had at his disposal, Albright made precious few mistakes. He had reason to be proud of his record in 1917.[40]

Shortly after Thanksgiving 1917, Albright heard the best news of the year. Congressman Fitzgerald had announced his intention to resign from the House of Representatives. "The 'Gentleman from New York,' who has been standing in the way of our Yellowstone plans," he gleefully wrote to Lindsley, "will be the 'Gentleman in New York' . . . after the first of the year." Albright had continued his quiet campaign to get the troops out of Yellowstone. In September, he had begun buttonholing his friends on Capitol Hill, arguing that for the sake of national defense the soldiers ought to be released from nonessential park patrols for combat duty in France. Fitzgerald's unexpected resignation, which came in December, suddenly removed the only man who was fundamentally committed to opposing the Park Service on this issue. The army's two-hundred-man cavalry detachment moved out of Yellowstone Park at the end of the 1917–18 fiscal year, but not the Army Engineers, who jealously maintained control of all road repair work in the park. The engineers knew a few political tricks of their own, it seemed, and they tem-

40. Quotations from C. G. Smith to HMA, Dec. 9, 1917, HMA Papers.

porarily thwarted Albright's efforts to have them evicted. "I hope that I may never run across another body of men," he observed to Mather, "that I dislike as much as the Engineer Corps of the Army."[41]

The Great War, still a bloody stalemate, commanded more and more of everybody's attention as 1918 began. The dough-boys in France found themselves heavily involved in the fighting for the first time. Bernard Baruch, as chief of the War Industries Board, wielded an enormous influence over the American econ-omy, allocating scarce materials and coordinating all industrial production. Herbert Hoover's voluntary food conservation pro-gram moved into high gear, changing the eating habits of an entire generation of Americans and providing a large exportable surplus of agricultural products. The railroads, telegraph lines, and cable facilities had already come under rigid governmental control. Operating with an unparalleled amount of personal power, and skillfully manipulating public opinion, Woodrow Wilson, champion of the New Freedom and of progressivism, transformed the war into yet another Wilsonian crusade—"a war to end all wars," "a war to make the world safe for democ-racy." "These are stirring times back here," Albright observed in mid-1917. "Everybody who can come to Washington now-adays . . . is here, and here to stay. Certainly it is the most inter-esting place in the world right now." The exhilarating wartime atmosphere of the nation's capital obviously enthralled him. "I would almost rather live on bread and water here," he added, "than live in luxury some place else." In the spring of 1918, after months of overwork, Albright came down with a mild case of the measles. Capturing the mood of the war years almost perfectly, one of his California friends sent him a note, chiding him for having contracted "such an unpatriotic disease as German Mea-sles; out here we call them the 'Liberty Measles.' "[42]

41. Franklin K. Lane to Secretary of War, Sept. 25, 1917, HMA to Lindsley, Dec. 4, 1917, J. H. Carroll to HMA, Oct. 16, 1917, and HMA to Mather, Oct. 17, 1917, HMA Papers.
42. HMA to Mark Daniels, May 1, 1917, HMA to Jesse B. Agnew, Oct. 20, 1917, and F. J. Chamberlain to HMA, Mar. 14, 1918, HMA Papers.

With Mather finally back full time, Albright found himself in a position to think about joining the army once again. He still hoped to get into the fighting, but, Grace was now "in a pregnant condition" and "in a very delicate state of health." The family doctor prepared an affidavit swearing that Grace was "utterly unable to support herself by work of any kind, or even to contribute to her support," and Albright decided to request another deferment, which his draft board granted him in June 1918.[43]

The year and a half from January 1917 to June 1918 tested Albright's mettle in any number of ways, and he repeatedly demonstrated his competence. His primary goal was to get the Park Service started and to keep it alive until Mather returned. He performed skillfully as acting director, carrying on and expanding Mather's program. He never conceived of himself as an innovator or as a pioneer in Park Service policy making. And yet, he shaped basic park policies because certain essential decisions simply had to be made before Mather's return. By May 1918 Albright had organized and articulated a set of policy objectives, derived mainly from Mather's ideas, to guide the infant Park Service. Announced officially in the form of a letter from Lane to Mather, dated May 13, 1918, these policy objectives have remained the core of national park administration ever since. Albright's foremost guideline, as stated in Lane's much-quoted letter, was that "the national parks must be maintained in absolutely unimpaired form for the use of future generations." This above all was the concept that had guided Albright as acting director. His clear-cut aestheticism, reflecting his Owens Valley background as well as Mather's influence, and his sincere devotion to the ideal of preserving nature's loveliness, crystallized during 1917. Included in Lane's letter was another one of Albright's main guidelines, namely, that the parks must be made available for the "use, observation, health and pleasure of the people." Over the years, the problem of reconciling these

43. Affidavits from HMA and Dr. Louis Mackall requesting deferment, June 28, 1918, HMA Papers.

two fundamentally incompatible objectives would cause the National Park Service more than a little anguish.[44]

Having had an extraordinary chance to influence the National Park Service in its earliest, formative stages, and having poured every ounce of his energy into its well-being, Albright found his loyalties and career motivation shifting more and more toward the parks. He had not intended to stay with the Park Service more than a few years, but as he himself recognized, the probability of his remaining in the Interior Department increased with every month. If he ever hoped to get back to California he would have to make his move soon.

44. HMA, memorandum for the files, Sept. 19, 1917, HMA Papers; Franklin K. Lane to Mather, May 13, 1918, NA, Records of NPS, gen., misc.

5

Young Man Leaves Washington

Through the summer and fall of 1918 Albright relaxed and fell
back into his accustomed role as Mather's chief assistant. After
more than a year as acting director, he found that he could perform his duties with casual competence. He was under less
pressure than before, but his relationship to Mather had changed.
Judged in terms of administrative effectiveness and ability to
get things done on Capitol Hill, the two men were now practically
on a par, although Mather's affable personality and his lavish
style of entertaining put him in a class by himself as a public
relations expert. More and more Albright became Mather's troubleshooter, concentrating on the most vexatious administrative
problems and remaining in close touch with the committees of
Congress on national park matters. By the summer of 1918, the
young man was functioning more nearly as an associate director
than assistant director. He had become indispensable to both
Mather and the National Park Service.

There was more than enough work to keep Albright busy
during that summer and fall. Lassen, Mount McKinley, and Hawaii national parks, having recently been created, needed funds
to begin operations. An arbitrary $10,000 limitation on appro-
priations for Rocky Mountain National Park, insisted upon by
economy-minded members of the House, still needed to be
removed. A publicity campaign to win support for the proposed
extension of Sequoia and to bring the Grand Canyon into the
national park system had to be coordinated and directed.
Above all, now that Fitzgerald no longer graced the House of
Representatives, a bill could be ramrodded through Congress to

authorize the removal of the troops from Yellowstone. On June 10, 1918, in a Sundry Civil Appropriations Act, Congress went through the formality of approving the abandonment of Fort Yellowstone and turning the park over to the exclusive jurisdiction of the National Park Service. A few months later, the Army Engineers pulled out of Yellowstone and Crater Lake national parks, thus relinquishing their last outposts in Mather's domain. This was a crucial breakthrough for the National Park Service, which no longer had to share the administration of the parks with another agency or department. "You can bet I am walking on five feet of air . . . ," Albright wrote to his friend Howard H. Hays. "I am so proud [of the appropriations bill] that I would be inclined to make even you sit out in the office and wait awhile before getting into my private sanctum sanctorum."[1]

Albright and Howard Hays had known each other since 1915, when they met for the first time in Yellowstone Park. In those days, Hays worked for Wylie's camps and staging company in Yellowstone, scheduling railroad tours in and out of the park and coordinating the company's advertising program. He was imaginative and witty, a young businessman who had a way with words and a feeling for public relations. He got along famously with Mather and Albright. In 1917, shortly before the war started, Hays left Yellowstone to become manager of a tourist bureau sponsored jointly by the Union Pacific and the Chicago and Northwestern railroads. In this job he cooperated closely with Albright in 1917 and 1918 in promoting the "See America First" campaign, designed to wean easterners away from Europe and educate them about the matchless scenery in the West, especially in the national parks. With the strong backing of Mather and Albright, Hays later took charge of the National Parks and Monuments Division of Western Lines Service Bureau in the United States Railroad Administration and

1. *Congressional Record*, 65th Cong., 2d sess. (June 15, 1918), p. 7866 (June 29, 1918), p. 8508, and (June 29, 1918), p. 8457; HMA to Howard H. Hays, June 14, 1918, HMA Papers; telegram, HMA to Mather, June 10, 1918, NA, Records of NPS, Parks gen., Dir.

immediately made plans for an all-out national parks publicity campaign in the postwar period.[2]

In the fall of 1918, Hays's outfit edited and published "a series of national park booklets" which "became at once the most powerful inducement to travel in the parks since the publication of the National Parks Portfolio." It was Albright and Hays who had earlier come up with the idea for a "travel division" in the National Park Service, which, in cooperation with the Railroad Administration's Service Bureau, would be able "to meet the competition" of European tourism in the postwar period. They argued that tariff protection for the "dyestuff industry of the United States" would come "as a matter of course," and "aid to our potash producers will doubtless be granted," but "what protection will the great resorts of this country have from the greatest campaign for tourist travel in foreign lands that will ever have been waged?" The answer, they suggested, was "none." There was an urgent need for a national parks travel bureau "to protect" the domestic travel industry. Couching their objectives in the language of the businessman, they attempted to capitalize on the Republican-inspired postwar demand for an increase in the protective tariff. Surprisingly enough, the argument fell on deaf ears. The Park Service never received enough money to establish a full-fledged travel bureau, but it did allocate more and more time and effort to publicizing the parks. The harmonious collaboration between Albright and Hays, which began during Albright's eighteen-month term as acting director, would continue into the 1920s and be particularly important in Yellowstone Park.[3]

2. HMA to Hays, June 16, 1917, HMA to J. H. Carroll, Jan. 2, 1918, and Hays to HMA, June 12, 1918, and Dec. 17, 1918, HMA Papers.
3. HMA to Carroll, Jan. 2, 1918, HMA Papers; *Annual Report, NPS* (1919), pp. 12–13 (1917), pp. 9–10; Hazen H. Hunkins, "Department of Tours—1917, Bureau of Service, National Parks and Resorts—1920," mimeographed (Mar. 1, 1963); and "The Organization and Wartime Activities of the Chicago Bureau of Service National Parks and Monuments of the United States Railroad Administration, 1918–1920," mimeographed (Mar. 1, 1962), copies in HMA Papers.

The hot controversy with Enos Mills, another legacy of Albright's acting directorship, lingered on through 1918 in spite of Albright's best efforts to pacify the older man. Mills's wrath seemed to know no limits. He was more than ever convinced that Albright had "sold out to the Forest Service" because of the delay in getting rid of the $10,000 limitation on appropriations for Rocky Mountain National Park and because of the alleged reluctance of the Park Service to study the Mount Evans area of Colorado as a possible national park site. In fact, Albright had been working hard to get more money for Rocky Mountain Park. Whether Mills liked it or not, the Mount Evans region lay squarely in the middle of a national forest reserve. Any plan contemplating the addition of the Mount Evans region to Rocky Mountain National Park, however attractive the proposal might appear to national park enthusiasts, had to be approached with the utmost tact and finesse because of the complicated interagency relationships involved. Angry and suspicious, Mills soon lost his patience. He wrote to Secretary Lane late in May 1918, charging that Albright was "a menace to the entire cause of the National Parks." Lane swiftly came to Albright's defense, describing him to Mills as a "conscientious and indefatigable worker in every phase of Interior Department activity looking to the advancement of the parks, including a very successful part in acquainting Congress with their needs." But the Secretary's letter failed to quiet Mills. A few weeks later, he told A. E. Demaray, of the Park Service, in front of a number of witnesses, that Albright was a "crook," who had "sold out to the Forest Service" to further "his own cheap political interests." Moreover, Mills shouted, Albright had "abandoned the principles of the national parks."[4]

These charges were completely unfounded, which was bad enough, but the slashing personal attacks that accompanied the charges were more than Albright could bear silently. He drafted an indignant letter to Mills in which he passionately denied the

4. Enos A. Mills to Lane, May 25, 1918, Lane to Mills, July 22, 1918, A. E. Demaray to HMA, Aug. 10, 1918, and Aug. 13, 1918, and Demaray to Mather, Oct. 8, 1918, HMA Papers.

charges. "It would be undignified for me to protest too much in my own favor," he wrote, "except to say that in sincerity and faithfulness of effort and in sheer love of the parks . . . I shall not yield to you nor any man." Albright had made plans to inspect the Mount Evans region in October, and he apparently had decided "to have it out" with Mills on that trip. At the last minute, however, he made up his mind to ignore Mills, and the indignant letter was never posted; the drafting of it had been therapy enough for Albright, who sensed that an expression of confidence from Mather would be a far more influential retort under the circumstances. Mather had a lengthy conference with Secretary Lane and then wrote Mills a blunt and hardhitting letter, defending Albright on every count. "Mr. Albright's record is as clean as a hound's tooth," Mather stated, "and in and out of season, he has given of himself without stint to the exacting duties of his office, carrying a particularly heavy burden during the period when my own illness threw everything on his shoulders." The charges made against Albright, Mather continued, "are not even worth discussing." He explained that he was "sorry to write such a letter as this" to a respected conservationist, "but I simply will not stand by in silence and have slanderous statements of this kind go by without a protest." Albright found Mather's letter "very gratifying."[5]

This was the first of a series of clashes between Albright and certain old-time park boosters, usually with vested interests in one particular park, who objected to his behind-the-scenes maneuverings to achieve Park Service goals. Albright characteristically preferred to settle administrative problems or conflicts of interest in private, on a man-to-man basis, rather than in the heat of public debate, although he could hold his own at most public meetings. In the true Mather tradition, he constantly attempted to avoid bad publicity and to reduce factionalism among Park Service supporters. He sometimes took vigorous

5. HMA to Mills (n.d., never mailed), Mather to HMA, Oct. 10, 1918, Mather to Mills, Oct. 11, 1918, and HMA to Howard Hays, Oct. 25, 1918, HMA Papers; Mather to Henry S. Graves, Dec. 10, 1918, NA, Records of NPS, Parks gen., Dir.

action to modify or suppress unflattering news stories and to "manage" the news. He viewed this as the proper function of a public official, for the essence of creative leadership, he believed, was to persuade a frequently apathetic and sometimes recalcitrant public to do what would be wise and beneficial in the long run. Enos Mills contended, on the other hand, that "there must be no 'politics' in the National Parks" and that the "Park Service must take the public" into its confidence and "make no 'secret moves.'" Albright's methods of leadership, especially his propensity to operate behind the scenes and, if necessary, in secret, would open him to criticism in future years. But his motives were generally above reproach. His one objective was to protect and expand the national parks so that future generations of Americans would have free access to magnificent and unspoiled examples of natural beauty.[6]

Mather's letter reached Mills not long after Albright arrived in Colorado to make a survey of the Mount Evans area and to inspect Rocky Mountain National Park. While in the park, he "utterly ignored Mills," who fumed and waited in vain to be contacted. "He had never had a Government officer go into the park before," Albright gleefully observed, "and refrain from seeking his advice." "Of course," Albright wrote to Hays, "I am done with the fellow, unless he comes around with an apology." The controversy with Mills had now largely spent itself. Within a fairly short time, Mills died, tangible evidence, a few partisans argued, that any attempt to oppose the National Park Service increased the probability of one's early death or, at the very least, brought down the wrath of God Almighty.[7]

Albright's report on the Mount Evans region contained a large amount of pertinent information about the area's scenic and recreational values. He investigated every road into the area and spent a number of warm October days tramping up and down its valleys and mountain slopes. He concluded that the

6. Mills's accusations quoted in Demaray to Mather, Oct. 8, 1918, HMA Papers.
7. HMA to Hays, Oct. 25, 1918, HMA Papers; telegram, Mather to HMA, Sept. 25, 1918, NA, Records of NPS, Parks gen., Dir.

region was "eminently fit" for national park status and that it ought to be "made a part of" Rocky Mountain National Park. Mount Evans itself, he pointed out, lay only "35 miles in an air line from the capitol of the State of Colorado" and only about 33 miles from the "southern boundary of the Rocky Mountain National Park." He carefully emphasized that, as far as he could ascertain, "the lands in this proposed park area have no commercial value." He also explained that the Mount Evans region amounted to "only eight percent" of the huge Pike National Forest, administered, of course, by the Forest Service. He urged "early action" on legislation to create the proposed park.[8]

Pressure on the Park Service to bring the Mount Evans region into the national park system increased steadily. The members of the Denver Mountain Parks Commission, composed of prominent businessmen in Colorado, wanted the new park developed as soon as possible, because they recognized that Denver's economy would probably benefit. These men would not be put off, and their persistence finally exposed the bitter rivalry that had developed between the Park Service and the Forest Service. Once the uncontested leader of the national conservation movement, the Forest Service found itself increasingly on the defensive after 1917. One of its greatest worries was that the aggressive young Park Service would attempt to take control of all federal recreation areas, including vast stretches of the national forests.[9]

The fearfulness of Pinchot's old bureau was well warranted, for the Park Service was on the move. "The time has come," Albright wrote to the Denver Mountain Parks Commission in December 1918, "when the choice must be made between the

8. HMA, "Report on the Proposed Mount Evans Addition to Rocky Mountain National Park," Dec. 5, 1918, *Municipal Facts Monthly* 2 (Aug. 1919) : 3–17; George E. Goodwin to HMA, Aug. 28, 1918, Mather to HMA, Oct. 10, 1918, F. W. Griffin to HMA, Oct. 14, 1918, and HMA to Hays, Oct. 25, 1918, HMA Papers.

9. HMA to Fred R. Ross, Dec. 31, 1918, HMA Papers; Henry S. Graves, "A Crisis in National Recreation," *American Forestry* 26 (July 1920) : 391–400; W. B. Greeley to W. F. Bade, Feb. 28, 1921, NA, Records of the Forest Service, Forester's file.

Forest Service and the Park Service in matters relating to recreation. The development of tourist travel and the encouragement of the use of the mountains for recreation is the National Park Service field." Mather made a series of equally strong statements. The forestry bureau, led by Henry S. Graves, mustered its powerful lobby and successfully staved off the Park Service bid for control of the Mount Evans region, which soon became a well-publicized Forest Service recreational area. But the rivalry between these two hard-driving federal agencies persisted throughout the 1920s, with the Park Service prevailing about as often as not. This heated bureaucratic clash was basically an extension of earlier differences between the utilitarian and aesthetic wings of the conservation movement. Albright took a leading part in marshaling the Park Service forces, privately denouncing the "monstrous recreation campaign" of the Forest Service and working diligently with Mather to expand the influence of the Park Service. Shocked by the open aggressiveness of Mather's bureau, the Forest Service suddenly and unexpectedly embraced the idea of wilderness preservation. Among other things, Mather and Albright deserve credit for goading the Forest Service into recognizing the validity of the concept of preserving natural beauty, once described by Pinchot as "sentimental nonsense."[10]

Instead of returning to Washington from Denver, Albright went to San Francisco, where he planned to make his headquarters for the next four months, lobbying for the extension of Sequoia Park, attempting to get a state-built all-year road into Yosemite, and awaiting the birth of his first child in February 1919.[11]

His plans exploded only a few days after his arrival in Berkeley when Secretary Lane directed him to return at once to Washington. "Don't let Mather know I wired you," Lane ordered, "but send him a wire saying that you must come home

10. HMA to Ross, Dec. 31, 1918, HMA Papers; telegram, HMA to Mather, May 14, 1919, NA, Records of NPS, Parks gen., Dir.; Swain, *Federal Conservation Policy*, pp. 134–38.
11. Interview with HMA, July 24, 1964.

to consult with him." Albright caught the first train for Washington, not knowing what to expect. "My chief has suffered a recurrence of the nervous trouble of last year," he telegraphed Grace soon after reaching Washington. Mather would have to be temporarily eased out of the directorship, and Albright would have to step in for an indefinite period. Mather's trouble this time was a tendency toward megalomania rather than acute depression. The Park Service director now considered himself infallible. He adopted a caustic and overbearing attitude toward his co-workers in the Park Service. His schemes for influencing important congressmen, grandly conceived and executed even under normal circumstances, had mushroomed enormously. He announced that he was dispatching $500 checks to politicians who were friendly to the national parks to help defray campaign expenses incurred in the 1918 elections, and he was personally prepared to go on the hustings to help a few favored candidates. As a civil service officer, of course, he was barred from all such activities. He organized a useless and hopelessly childish "school" for employees of the National Park Service. He impetuously and illegally "confiscated" Harry Child's hotel and transportation properties in Yellowstone Park. Mather would simply brook no interference from his subordinates.[12]

When Albright arrived in Washington and finally made an effort to put a halt to these ill-conceived adventures, Mather informed him that he was "fired." Albright ignored his mentor's remarks, maneuvered him aboard a Chicago-bound train, and returned him to his family. In Chicago, Albright and Harold F. White, Mather's friend and attorney, managed to calm the high-strung director and persuade him to take an extended rest. Within a few days, Albright was back in Washington, and Mather was on his way to visit Henry Fairfield Osborn at the secluded Osborn Castle estate on the Hudson River. Albright then quietly made arrangements for Mather to spend three weeks

12. Telegram, Lane to HMA, Oct. 27, 1918, telegram, HMA to Grace Albright [Nov. 1, 1918], and telegrams, HMA to W. B. Lewis, Nov. 6, 1918, and Nov. 7, 1918, HMA Papers; Shankland, *Steve Mather*, pp. 163–65.

at Hot Springs, Arkansas, in the company of a small group of close friends. Rest and relaxation worked wonders for Mather. "He has clearly escaped prostration similar to that of last year," Albright wrote to "Dusty" Lewis. By the middle of December, Mather had apparently recovered. "There has been a most flattering change in his attitude toward you," Harold White informed Albright, "and he cannot say enough of what you have done." As a safety precaution, Albright insisted that Mather take a long restful trip to California before returning to Washington. Meanwhile, the young man worked overtime preparing for the annual appropriations hearings and mending his bureau's political fences. Mather had not paid enough attention to the congressional committees in the last two months.[13]

The remarkable aspect of Albright's second acting directorship, as in 1917, was the extent to which he reflected Mather's standards and administrative philosophy. "We are going to try to run things on a business basis," Albright admonished one Park Service employee in December 1918, "and show that just because a bureau is in the Government" it does not mean that a larger work force will be required than "on the outside under similar circumstances." He was happy and proud, he contended, that "we are getting a tremendous amount of satisfactory work done in the national parks . . . with a very low overhead." The efforts of Mather and Albright to put the National Park Service on a "business basis" foreshadowed the trend of government administration in the 1920s and clearly revealed their personal commitment to the business ethic. Because of the businesslike goals and methods Mather and Albright infused into the National Park Service, it was in a position to flourish and expand during the "New Era" of the 1920s.[14]

13. Telegram, Hays to HMA, Nov. 14, 1918, telegram, Mather to John Oliver LaGorce, Nov. 21, 1918, and telegram, Harold F. White to HMA, Dec. 14, 1918, HMA Papers; Shankland, *Steve Mather*, pp. 163–65; telegram, Mather to HMA, Nov. 25, 1918, and telegrams, HMA to Mather, Dec. 11, 1918, and Dec. 26, 1918, NA, Records of NPS, Parks gen., Dir.

14. HMA to George E. Goodwin, Dec. 24, 1918, HMA Papers; Swain, *Federal Conservation Policy*, pp. 41–42.

By January 12, 1919, Mather felt well enough to resume his responsibilities as director, and Albright went back to California to be with Grace, whose confinement was near. He commuted daily by ferry from Berkeley to San Francisco, where he had a desk in the office of the United States Public Health Service in the Call-Bulletin building. He also made frequent trips to Sacramento, the California capital, to lobby for a bill removing the last vestiges of the state's authority over Yosemite, Sequoia and General Grant parks. California had previously maintained police authority in these areas. The bill passed on April 15, 1919, thanks to Albright's hard work and to his good fortune in having a friend from university days, Charles Kasch, in the state assembly. On February 2, 1919, Grace gave birth to a baby boy, who was immediately named Robert Mather, in honor of the director of the Park Service.[15]

Mather and Albright had been angling for the extension of Sequoia for more than three years, but the Mineral King region, the canyons of the Kern and Kings rivers, and the high country around Mount Whitney, through which the Mather mountain party had passed in 1915, still remained outside the park boundaries. Powerful economic interests opposed the planned extension. Cattle and sheep grazers protested that they would lose valuable summer range lands. Sportsmen's organizations and shooting clubs did not want some of their favorite hunting and fishing places to be off-limits inside the national park. Certain business syndicates, including the city of Los Angeles, were interested in developing power and water resources inside the proposed park zone. Predictably enough, the Forest Service, in charge of the disputed territory, refused to endorse any Park Service scheme that would remove another large area from a national forest. Albright set out to lobby in favor of the expansion of Sequoia. In cooperation with Frederic Bade and William Colby, of the Sierra Club, he issued appeals to the press in San

15. Telegrams, HMA to Director of NPS, Jan. 15, 1919, Jan. 16, 1919, and Mar. 5, 1919, NA, Records of NPS, Director's Office File, Albright; HMA, "Reminiscences," p. 102; HMA to Hays, Feb. 17, 1919, HMA Papers; interview with HMA, July 16, 1965.

Francisco to help preserve this "scenic territory unsurpassed in the world." In Fresno, he faced a hostile audience of "senators, congressmen, attorneys, Army officers, and representatives of chambers of commerce and civic organizations" to preach his preservationist gospel. It was "one of the most heated debates that have ever been heard here," the Fresno *Republican* observed. To calm the fears of Fresno businessmen, Albright rang in Mather's "tourist gold" theme and explained pragmatically that Lane, Mather, and he himself were all "native Californians" and "we are for making California the most beautiful tourist spot on the American continent." He traveled to the town of Visalia, the self-designated "gateway to Sequoia," to combat local opposition to the expansion. "We wish that every citizen opposed to the enlargement of Sequoia National Park . . . could have heard Horace M. Albright," the Visalia *Delta* editorialized. "We are firmly of the opinion that nine out of ten would have come out of the encounter boosting for the larger park, for Mr. Albright has a vision, is armed with facts, and as a native of Inyo County has an unbounded enthusiasm for California's mountain wonderlands." Albright became so enthusiastic in his speech making in Visalia that he had to be "admonished" that he had only ten minutes to catch his train. It was "necessary then for the honor guest . . . to cease speaking," the newspaper reported.[16]

At Mather's urging, the Park Service attempted to capitalize on the public demand for a national memorial to Theodore Roosevelt, who died on January 6, 1919, by proposing that Sequoia Park be enlarged and renamed "Roosevelt National Park" in honor of the late president. Albright readily confessed that "we were much more interested in getting what we wanted in the way of a great park in California . . . than we were in memorializing Theodore Roosevelt, much as we were devoted to his memory." California's Senator James D. Phelan cooperated by getting the United States Senate to pass a bill enlarging and renaming Sequoia in Roosevelt's honor, but Congressman Denver S. Church unexpectedly bottled up the bill in the House. The

16. San Francisco *Chronicle*, Feb. 10, 1919; clippings from Fresno *Republican*, Feb. 19, 1919, and Feb. 20, 1919, HMA Papers; Visalia *Times*, Mar. 3, 1919; Visalia *Delta*, Mar. 4, 1919.

Park Service failed in its efforts to extend Sequoia Park in 1919, but Albright made a strong showing in California, and he refused to give up. The groundwork had been laid for a later, successful attempt to bring the superbly beautiful mountain zones to the north and east of Sequoia into the national park system.[17]

While in San Francisco, Albright had ample opportunity to reestablish his contacts with Morrison, Dunne, and Brobeck, the law firm that had approached him in 1917. Late in February, after his friend Herman Phleger interceded in his behalf, the firm made him a second offer. Albright now had to make up his mind whether to remain in government work or resign as he had been saying he wanted to since 1913. It was a hard decision. Finally, on March 9, 1919, Albright informed Mather of his intention to resign from the Park Service. "It will not be difficult now," he wrote, "for you to work without me, and it seems that now is the time for me to form new connections in the West if I am ever to take this step. I am going to ask you therefore to let me go on July 1st, or as soon thereafter as you can find someone to fill my place." He cited salary considerations, professional interest, and family responsibilities as his main reasons. He explained that he "had no ambition to become director" and that he owed it to his wife and son "to undertake other means of earning a livelihood." Albright assured his chief that he would remain "passionately devoted" to the national parks. His decision to resign was final, he said. "I really am more devoted to the Park Service today than I have ever been in the past," he wrote to a friend a few days later, "and the idea of severing my connection with Mr. Mather is most distasteful to me." But he simply could not afford to pass up a second opportunity to join this respected San Francisco law firm. "I have firmly determined that I would rather live out here on $150 per month," he stated "than be an administrative officer of the Washington end of the Park Service at $10,000 per year."[18]

17. San Francisco *Chronicle*, Feb. 10, 1919; HMA, "Reminiscences," pp. 100–101.
18. HMA to Mather, Mar. 9, 1919, Harold F. White to HMA, Feb. 28, 1919, and HMA to White, Mar. 14, 1919, HMA Papers.

Mather's immediate response was to implore Albright to reconsider and to ask him, as a personal favor, to return to Washington temporarily to head the Park Service while the director accompanied Secretary Lane to Hawaii to inspect Hawaii National Park. Mather wanted to keep Albright in the Park Service. His request was clearly designed as a stalling action to give him enough time to come up with a seductive counter offer that would change the young man's mind. Because of his affection for Mather and his loyalty to the Park Service, Albright agreed to fill in for Mather in Washington so the important inspection trip would not have to be cancelled. But he made it clear that he intended to resign in the summer. Mather made every effort to accommodate him. "The dear, good soul," Albright noted affectionately, "how I dislike even the thought of cutting away from my close associations with him."[19]

With Harold White acting as a good-natured intermediary, Mather and Albright shadowboxed for a time about what it might take to keep Albright in the Service. It became more and more obvious to all concerned that the answer was the superintendency of Yellowstone Park. Albright had recently informed White that "the Yellowstone place is the only thing that could possibly hold me after July 1st." Unfortunately, Mather had already offered the Yellowstone appointment to Emerson Hough in a misguided display of comradeship during the fall of 1918. Hough was, of course, a renowned writer and a great friend of Yellowstone, but he was certainly no administrator. After the offer had been duly made, "a half dozen people," including Howard Hays and Harry Child, told Mather that he would make the greatest "mistake of his career if he put Hough into any position in the Park Service." The old gentleman was too opinionated and tactless. Without consulting Mather, Albright took it upon himself to dissuade Hough from accepting, by explaining the dis-

19. White to HMA, Feb. 28, 1919, and HMA to White, Mar. 14, 1919, HMA Papers; HMA, "Reminiscences," pp. 102–3; telegrams, Mather to HMA, Feb. 26, 1919, and Mar. 4, 1919, and telegrams, HMA to Mather, Mar. 1, 1919, and Mar. 10, 1919, NA, Records of NPS, Director's Office File, Albright.

advantages of the Yellowstone job and telling him that "he would lose his identity as a writer" and would "be required to remain in the park most of the year." Hough's interest rapidly cooled. Later, after Albright himself expressed an interest in the superintendency, Mather let the news slip out to Hough, a conversational lapse that put the young man in a difficult and highly embarrassing personal dilemma. "It seems to me," Albright complained to White, "that I stand about in the position of a d--- liar in Mr. Hough's estimation." Albright could not possibly accept the Yellowstone superintendency until things were squared with Hough. Delicate negotiations followed between Mather and Hough with the result that the writer gracefully bowed out of the contest, making way for Albright. Toward the end of March, Mather wired Albright that a "solution satisfactory" to all parties could be "worked out." The offer of the superintendency came when Albright returned to Washington about April 1. He would have two months to think about it while Mather was in Hawaii.[20]

Taking over as superintendent of Yellowstone Park would have certain definite advantages for Albright. For one thing, he would get out of the Washington office, in which he felt increasingly uncomfortable and confined. It would move him back to the rugged mountain country where he felt at home, and it would presumably allow him to spend more time with his family, since there would be less need for him to travel in the summer months. The huge park, at that time one of the most famous tourist attractions of the world, was the oldest and most prestigious single unit in the national park system. With the army now out of the Yellowstone, Albright would face the challenge of being the first Park Service man to administer the day-to-day operations of this mammoth preserve, larger in territory than the states of Delaware and Rhode Island combined. A compe-

20. Harold F. White to HMA, Feb. 28, 1919, HMA to White, Mar. 14, 1919, and telegram, Mather to HMA, Mar. 27, 1919, HMA Papers; HMA, "Reminiscences," pp. 102–3, 109; telegram, Mather to HMA, Mar. 11, 1919, and telegram, Mather to HMA, Mar. 27, 1919, HMA Papers; HMA, to Griffith, Apr. 3, 1919, NA, Records of NPS, Director's Office File, Albright.

tent staff would have to be recruited and organized. The roads would have to be improved to face the onslaught of the automobile, and the concessioners would have to be brought into line if facilities were to be provided for the expected upsurge in the total number of visitors to the park after the war. The utility systems, especially water and sanitation, would have to be improved and expanded. The job of protecting and managing the park's matchless collection of big game animals, including elk, grizzlies, mountain sheep, black bear, deer, buffalo, and moose would offer a special challenge. On top of all this, liaison with state and local governments in Wyoming, Montana, and Idaho would have to be established. Albright knew that Mather would continue to use him as his chief troubleshooter and would count on him to come to Washington in the winter months to help with the annual appropriations hearings, but for most of the year he would be on his own in the West.[21]

The job seemed demanding and appealing from Albright's point of view. It would provide a stimulating change of pace, and it offered, among other things, a substantial financial boost. Albright's new salary would be $3,600 per year plus a house and an official car for his exclusive use in Yellowstone. Congress had recently declared it illegal for government employees to have their salaries increased by private donations, and therefore Albright's annual income would have dropped back to $2,500 on July 1 had he remained assistant director. His genuine affection for Mather, who was, Albright admitted, "the one man that I am mighty nearly as fond of as I am my own parents," was the final ingredient in his decision. "I just couldn't let him down," he later recalled. Albright decided to take the job.[22]

Mather sailed for Hawaii on April 10, 1919, and Albright, once again separated from his family, settled down in Washington to run the Park Service. Most of Albright's work that spring

21. HMA, "Reminiscences," pp. 102–10.
22. The Reference Service Branch of the Federal Records Center, St. Louis, Mo., furnished me with complete information about Albright's salary and job descriptions, from 1913 to 1933, see M. D. Davis to the author, Dec. 10, 1965; HMA, "Reminiscences," pp. 102–10.

consisted of humdrum administrative duties. The Mount Evans region of Colorado continued to cause him trouble. The Forest Service adamantly refused to turn the area over to the National Park Service, and Albright, though he tried, could not mollify the Colorado businessmen, who accused the Park Service leadership of stalling on the proposed extension of Rocky Mountain Park. The Grand Canyon had become a national park in February 1919 with the help of Congressman Hayden, who worked energetically in behalf of the authorization act. Albright now had to make a number of policy decisions about how the park should be developed and by whom. He followed through on long-standing agreements with the Santa Fe Railroad and the Fred Harvey Company to expand overnight accommodations on the south rim of the canyon. Realizing that an awesome thirty-mile mule-back trip was the only available means of crossing the canyon, and believing that commercial "aeroplanes" had only a limited future in the park, Albright also tentatively approved a plan submitted by George K. Davol, a San Francisco engineer, for the construction of a cableway across the canyon. According to the plan, cable cars would make the crossing on four giant spans, beginning from a point near El Tovar on the south rim. Construction could be completed, apparently, with a minimum of disturbance to the natural features of the canyon, using giant natural buttes to anchor the cables. Albright's position was that the unforgettable view one could obtain by taking a cable car from rim to rim would more than compensate for any aesthetic damage, and it might ultimately reduce the pressure to build a road into the canyon. "The Secretary is heartily in favor of granting this permit," he reported to Mather, and "Mr. Yard and I are quite enthusiastic about it."[23]

23. Mather to Gilbert Grosvenor, Mar. 18, 1919, HMA to White, Mar. 14, 1919, telegram, HMA to Mather, May 14, 1919, and HMA to Mather, May 14, 1919, HMA Papers; for an example of the publicity campaign the Forest Service undertook at this time to boost the recreational use of the national forests, see Sacramento *Bee*, Mar. 29, 1919, and S. Riley to Metropolitan Consulate, New York, N.Y., May 5, 1919, HMA Papers; HMA to Mather, May 21, 1919, quoted in Shankland, *Steve Mather*, p. 207.

Fortunately for the Grand Canyon, Mather strenuously objected to the entire concept of the cableway, which he believed
would seriously intrude on the natural beauty of the park, and
he vetoed the project. This was one of the rare occasions when
Albright's impulses as an administrator and conservationist ran
counter to Mather's. The differing views of the two men arose
out of the subtleties of trying to maintain the parks "in absolutely unimpaired form" while at the same time making them
available for the "use, observation, health, and pleasure of the
people." Albright occasionally placed a higher value on giving
the public access to nature's splendors than Mather did. In the
case of the cableway, Mather was unquestionably right, and his
steadfast refusal to allow obtrusive mechanical contrivances to
be constructed in the parks set a precedent that Albright himself later carried on and defended. The episode demonstrated
that Albright needed Mather's guidance on important policy
decisions. The young man still had a few things to learn from
his mentor.[24]

As the weather turned hot in Washington early in June, Albright began making preparations to move his family from
Berkeley to Yellowstone Park. Because of the usual rush to get
the Park Service appropriations bill through Congress, he could
not take up his new duties until after July 1, although his change
in status from assistant director to park superintendent had become official on June 10, 1919, the day the park opened for
the season. Arno B. Cammerer, formerly executive secretary
of the Fine Arts Commission in Washington, replaced Albright
as assistant director. He would handle the routine administrative
work of the bureau, and he would presumably be able to fill in
for Mather if the need arose. Albright would coordinate all
of the field activities of the National Park Service in addition to
being Yellowstone's superintendent. In the next decade, Albright

24. Quotations from Lane to Mather, May 13, 1918, NA, Records of
NPS, gen., misc.; Shankland, *Steve Mather*, p. 207; it should perhaps
be noted that in recent years landscape architects and planners, some in
the NPS, have seriously considered whether cableways should be used
where road construction would badly disfigure beautiful natural features.

worked closely with Cammerer and came to admire his steady, if unspectacular, performance. Cammerer moved into the inner circle of "Mather men" almost from the start, generating great enthusiasm for his job and developing a boundless admiration for the national parks. With Albright's departure from Washington, the Park Service staff lost a little of its youthful verve, but Albright left with a clear conscience, knowing that he had stayed on the job longer than anybody had expected and confident that Cammerer could fill his shoes.[25]

25. M. D. Davis to the author, Dec. 10, 1965; Grace Albright, "Horace Marden Albright: Man with a Sense of History," p. 20; H. W. Child to HMA, June 10, 1919, HMA Papers; *Annual Report, NPS* (1919), p. 44.

6

The "Duke" of Yellowstone

Albright reached Yellowstone about the tenth of July and moved his family into the great stone house that had formerly been the home of the commandant of Fort Yellowstone. The park's enormous size at first awed him. Yellowstone contained 2,142,720 acres, or 3,348 square miles, a magnificent expanse of territory that included tall mountains, bubbling mudpots, vast pine forests, jewellike lakes, large and untouched wilderness regions, hissing geysers, rugged gorges, spectacular waterfalls, and an unrivaled wildlife population. Inside the park there were about three hundred miles of roads—approximately the same total as now—all of which had been built originally by the army, and every mile of which was in need of some improvement. The main road system, forming a giant figure eight connecting the principal features of the park, stretched approximately 125 miles; 100 miles of this road had to be sprinkled twice a day to keep down the dust. Within the park there were about twenty road-maintenance stations and roughly the same number of ranger stations, mainly along the loop road and at the park entrances, but also in remote areas. Machine shops, storage warehouses, automobile and electric repair facilities, even a blacksmith shop had to be maintained. A large and weather-vulnerable telephone system had to be kept functioning. A contingent of skilled workmen and unskilled laborers had to be recruited every season, as did a competent summer force of rangers. Depending upon appropriations, Albright's seasonal staff often reached three hundred and up. His permanent, year-around staff was considerably smaller, ranging from fifty to one hundred. The concessions system, too, needed attention. There were five hotels, a permanent camping system, a photographic concession, gift shops, food stores, and transportation lines from Cody, West Yellowstone, and Gardiner.

All of this and more—the concessioners, the rangers, the summer workers, the road system, the patrol stations, the maintenance men, the headquarters staff, and even the families of park employees—Albright had to oversee. Staying on top of his multifaceted job and keeping himself informed about the complex administrative problems of this large park would tax his executive ingenuity. It took many hours of his time just to drive from place to place within Yellowstone.

Albright's first task was to establish himself as head man of the park. His immediate predecessor had been Colonel L. M. Brett, a distinguished army officer. Chester Lindsley, acting superintendent since September 1916 and now assistant superintendent, was Albright's elder by many years. "I felt so desperately young," Albright later recalled, ". . . among all those people who were older." He "just prayed to be 30 years old." To complicate matters, Albright looked even younger than his twenty-nine years. On his numerous trips into the field, he resorted to wearing eyeglasses not only because of his "anxiety to see animal life" but also because they helped to make him look older. There was really no need for him to be so sensitive about his age. The local people knew him for his five previous visits to the park and respected him because he had served as acting director. From the start, he had the reputation of being a boy wonder.[1]

For years the army had assigned housing in Yellowstone on the basis of rank rather than need, with the officers occupying the largest and finest houses regardless of the size of their families. Acting superintendent Lindsley had instituted the same system for the park's civilian employees as soon as the army departed in 1918, assigning the biggest houses to the white-collar workers. Albright dug into this problem before the end of his first

1. HMA, "Reminiscences," pp. 111–12.

summer in the park and "worked out a complete re-arrangement of housing." Moreover, he put every dollar he could squeeze out of his tight budget into fixing up the long-neglected smaller houses. He began "moving the families around to suit their needs, without reference to who they were." His successful administration of Yellowstone Park grew largely out of the harmonious relationship that emerged between himself as superintendent and the park employees. Chester Lindsley, his assistant superintendent, Sam T. Woodring, the chief ranger, Joe Joffe, his secretary, Leroy Hill, his finance man, and Arthur Burney, the chief engineer, among others, gave him invaluable assistance. Albright demanded a high level of performance from his staff, but he always protected their interests and gave his personal attention to their problems. The rangers, in particular, reciprocated with a dauntless loyalty for their chief and an uncommon amount of dedication.[2]

Yellowstone had a record-breaking season in 1919, the first summer after World War I. The camp grounds and hotels literally bulged with people in July and August and the rush of automobiles was, for those days, truly remarkable. During August, Albright proudly noted in his monthly report that "there was scarcely a state in the union that did not send one or more private automobiles filled with happy sight-seers." More than sixty thousand people visited the park before the season ended, almost tripling the 1918 total. Albright's reaction was to cheer long and hard, for he knew that increased park use, as gauged by the sharply rising visitor totals, was the key to larger appropriations for the National Park Service. But intensified park utilization inevitably complicated the problems of administration. Soon after his arrival in the park, the waitresses at Old Faithful Inn went out on strike. The drivers of the Yellowstone Park Transportation Company began ignoring the park's speed limits and, when Albright ordered "drastic action against the offending employees," they retaliated by hanging "crepe on the front of their

2. HMA, "Reminiscences," pp. 112–16; interview with E. T. Scoyen, Dec. 19, 1965; for examples of loyalty see Sam T. Woodring's correspondence with HMA, HMA Papers.

cars" and proceeding "at such a slow rate of speed" that the incoming tourists missed their evening meal. "Next year," Albright announced, "I propose to take the drivers in hand on the opening date of the season and give them to understand that they must obey the rules and regulations." Under the prevailing conditions, with nationwide strikes threatening and a pervasive postwar restlessness affecting many American workers, it was extremely difficult "to keep any of the employees contented," he wrote to Mather. When a series of forest fires occurred, Albright mustered his road maintenance crews and reported "with considerable satisfaction" that they "loyally fought fire without demanding increases in wages which they might have obtained from us in the face of the impending disaster to our forests." Albright spent a good deal of his time in the summer of 1919, and throughout the 1920s, keeping the concessioners in line and trying to insure that the tourists got reliable service.[3]

Other areas of Yellowstone's administration begged for attention. There was no adequate sewage disposal system, and as a result, the water supply was in constant danger of contamination. The state highways approaching the park, as well as the roads inside the giant Yellowstone preserve, were disreputable —veritable quagmires in the early summer and dangerous dust wallows later on. Above all, since the military superintendents had never troubled themselves to stay in close contact with the the nearby communities, the park's local image needed to be refurbished. Albright established cordial relations with the business leaders in Cody, West Yellowstone, Gardiner, Livingston, and Bozeman, the cities bordering the park to the north, east, and west. But in the incomparably beautiful Jackson Hole region, directly to the south, he had less success.[4]

For more than three years, Mather and Albright had dreamed of adding the Grand Teton Mountains and part of the scenic

3. "Yellowstone Monthly Report," mimeographed (July 1919), pp. 1–2, 15 (Aug. 1919), pp. 3–4 (Sept. 1919), p. 8, copies in HMA Papers.
4. "Yellowstone Monthly Report" (Aug. 1919), p. 24, HMA to Charles J. Belden, July 16, 1919, HMA Papers; HMA, "Reminiscences," pp. 117–18.

Jackson Hole region to Yellowstone Park. The Tetons, rising abruptly along the fault line a few miles south of Yellowstone, are one of the most distinctive mountain ranges in the world. Jagged and ice-hewn, much like the High Sierra, these peaks surpass even the Swiss Alps in the grandeur of their natural setting. Juxtaposed against the high-rising Tetons is Jackson Hole, a stretch of rolling green meadows and flatlands running to the northeast toward Yellowstone, forming a spectacular valley similar in many ways to the Owens Valley of California.[5]

Albright first visited Jackson Hole in July 1916, on an inspection trip with Mather, Huston Thompson, and Alexander T. Vogelsang, First Assistant Secretary of the Interior. They drove south from Yellowstone to Moran and spent the night with Ben Sheffield, a well-known hunter and guide who operated a small cabin camp near Jackson Lake Dam. The party "was entranced by the Teton Range" and realized that "here was one of America's greatest scenic areas." From that day on, "it seemed inevitable" to Mather and Albright that "this region must become a park." In the winter of 1916–17, they began formulating plans for an extension of Yellowstone to the south to include both the Tetons and Jackson Hole. Albright discussed the project "from time to time" with Congressman Frank Mondell and Senator Francis E. Warren, of Wyoming, both of whom believed that "the region was fit primarily for recreation." Their only apparent concern was that elk hunting—Jackson Hole was also a magnificent natural elk range—should not be entirely eliminated.[6]

Albright visited Jackson Hole again in the summer of 1918 and continued to work with Congressman Mondell in framing legislation to incorporate the Tetons and Jackson Hole into the

5. *Annual Report, NPS* (1919), pp. 47–48; HMA to Wilford Neilson, Apr. 5, 1933, in U.S., Congress, House, Hearings Before a Subcommittee of the Committee on Public Lands, "Enlarging Grand Teton National Park in Wyoming," 75th Cong., 3rd sess. (Aug. 1938), pp. 5–20 (hereafter cited as HMA to Neilson, in 1938 Hearings); the letter is also published in *Mr. John D. Rockefeller, Jr.'s Proposed Gift of Land for the National Park System in Wyoming*, pp. 1–6.

6. HMA to J. A. Brecksons (sec. to Senator Warren), Oct. 6, 1917, and HMA to Emerson Hough, Oct. 27, 1917, HMA Papers; *Annual Report, NPS* (1919), pp. 47–48; HMA to Neilson, in 1938 Hearings.

national park system. They worked out a number of compromises on boundary lines and grazing rights to protect the handful of ranchers who grazed cattle in the national forests around Jackson Hole. Their preliminary agreement, embodied in a draft bill, called for the Teton Mountains and the hilly lands north of Buffalo Fork to be included in Yellowstone Park. Mondell threw the bill into the Congressional hopper and got it approved by the House in February 1919. Unexpectedly, Senator John F. Nugent of Idaho, the state that bordered the Tetons on the west, blocked the bill in the Senate in the mistaken notion that the proposed park extension would deprive the ranchers in his state of valuable sheep ranges. In the meantime, opposition began to appear in the Jackson Hole country, with the dude ranchers and cattlemen taking the lead in speaking out against the Park Service plan. In the spring of 1919 the Wyoming state legislature passed a resolution protesting the proposed extension of Yellowstone's borders. This was where the matter stood when Albright took over as superintendent of Yellowstone.[7]

On his way to the park in July 1919, Albright stopped in Cheyenne, Wyoming, to pay his respects to Governor Robert D. Carey. Over a pleasant evening meal the two men discussed "the tourist business as it related to Wyoming." The governor, like virtually all western politicians of that era, believed that good roads were the key to economic progress in his state. He left the distinct impression with Albright, perhaps unintentionally, that he would favor the development of the Teton region and endorse a National Park Service campaign to attract tourists to the area. About a month later, when Carey took a vacation trip to Yellowstone, he casually informed Albright of a public meeting in Jackson at which the proposed park extension would be discussed. Albright decided to attend. Clay Tallman, the commissioner of the General Land Office, who also happened to be in the park, and Howard Hays accompanied him.[8]

7. HMA to Neilson, in 1938 Hearings.
8. HMA to Clay Tallman, Oct. 13, 1919, HMA to D. S. Spencer, Oct. 21, 1919, and Walter B. Sheppard to Editor, New York *Evening Post*, Sept. 18, 1919 (copy), HMA Papers.

It was a night that the new superintendent would long remember. Nearly a hundred angry local citizens turned out to badger Albright, who was quite unprepared for this show of hostility. Having no advance opportunity to gauge the sentiment of the crowd, he spoke in favor of development, resting his case on the well-rehearsed Park Service pitch for opening up the area to tourists. He promised that the roads into the valley would be improved and maintained at high standards, presuming erroneously that the citizens of Jackson Hole would find his proposals irresistible. This was a critical, and in the end tragic, miscalculation, as Albright quickly realized.[9]

The outspoken dude ranchers, led by Struthers Burt and Horace Carncross, operators of the Bar B-C ranch, chorused unanimously that they did not want their valley "opened up." They ardently desired to keep it rustic and unspoiled. Ironically, Albright's primary purpose was almost exactly the same, to preserve the natural beauty of the area and protect it from commercialization. His proposals for roads and his emphasis on tourists had been deliberately designed to win local support for a preservationist scheme that he feared would not endear itself to the rugged individualists of Wyoming. In those days, westerners habitually accused the federal resouce agencies of wanting to impede the West's rightful economic development. In fact, the cattlemen of Wyoming adopted this argument later on in the Jackson Hole controversy. But at the start Albright affronted the dude ranchers and old-time cattlemen who despised the idea of "outsiders" flocking into the valley. His efforts to retract his statements came to nothing because the Park Service had already prepared a map (to be published in the 1919 *Annual Report*) containing a tentative plan for a road over Two Ocean Pass into Jackson Hole. "How many times later," Albright recalled, "we wished that map had never seen the light of day."[10]

The proposed road appeared on the map as a public relations

9. HMA to Neilson, in 1938 Hearings.
10. Sheppard to Editor, New York *Evening Post*, Sept. 18, 1919; Struthers Burt, "A Certain Mountain Chief," *Scribner's Magazine* 35 (June 1929) : 626; HMA to Neilson, in 1938 Hearings; *Annual Report, NPS* (1919), p. 48.

gambit, and nothing more. The Park Service had never officially approved the project, but the ranchers refused to accept this explanation. Albright was "almost hooted off the platform by the enraged citizens." Clay Tallman, who attempted to defend Albright, received identical treatment. As the evening continued, the debate became more and more heated. The Park Service took a severe tongue lashing from the cattlemen, who were worried about their grazing rights. Much to Albright's disgust, the Forest Service representatives refused to support him, and Governor Carey abandoned his previous position in favor of development. When the session adjourned some time after midnight, Albright turned over his hotel room to Carey because the governor had not been able to obtain accommodations. Rancher Frank L. Peterson finally offered the embattled Yellowstone superintendent a place to sleep and remarked that it was like "taking Jess Willard home." This was an apt description, for Jack Dempsey had recently flattened Willard in the prize ring.[11]

The meeting at Jackson, Albright claimed, "was not a representative gathering." The small farmers living inside the proposed extension zone "were not invited to be present and did not have a hearing before the Governor." Big cattlemen and others "who are constitutionally opposed to [land] reservations of any kind and Government control of any kind" dominated the affair. He vowed to return to Jackson Hole and continue the fight. Thus began one of the greatest conservation battles of the twentieth century, a controversy that would rage for more than thirty years, involving sensational charges and countercharges, congressional investigations, and brutal political maneuvering, but which, in time, would result in the addition of the Grand Teton Mountains and the choicest part of Jackson Hole to the national park system. Albright limped back to Yellowstone and concentrated on other problems for the rest of the season.[12]

11. HMA to Neilson, in 1938 Hearings; U.S., Congress, House, Hearings Before a Subcommittee of the Committee on Public Lands, "To Abolish the Jackson Hole National Monument," 78th Cong., 1st sess. (May-June 1943), p. 299.
12. "Yellowstone Monthly Report" (Aug. 1919), pp. 16–17; Burt, "A Certain Mountain Chief," p. 626.

Mather called upon Albright that summer for a number of
special assignments, which came on top of his work as superintendent. Albright took charge of preparing the budget estimates
for all the parks for the 1920–21 fiscal year, and he began a
study of concessions policies in Mount Rainier Park. When Secretary Lane ordered Mather to rush to Glacier Park to investigate complaints about the concessioners, Mather delegated the
job to Albright, who reported that the trouble stemmed from a
"general lack of push and energy" on the part of the park administrators and concessioners. He noted that the "rangers have
loafed about the hotels in some instances," and that a forest fire,
which probably could have been contained, had swept through a
part of the beautiful Two Medicine Valley. The fact that the
damage occurred just outside the park did not lessen Albright's
indignation. "It was a horrible sight," he reported, "and it just
about broke my heart when I first visited it." The Park Service
still had a long way to go in bringing the administration of Glacier Park up to the desired standards, but having Albright close
enough to run up there for consultations several times a year
promised to speed up the improvement process. Cammerer's
success as the new assistant director also augered well for the
future. Bob Yard reported from Washington that Cammerer
"has got everybody together" in the Park Service office. "They
all like him. I think he is the very man we were dreaming about
—the man to solve the office problem and take its troubles off
ST's [Mather's] hands."[13]

The aspect of the superintendent's job that Albright enjoyed
above all was entertaining distinguished guests and showing
them around the park. As a tour guide and wildlife interpreter he
had few peers. Even before becoming superintendent, he had
begun studying the history of Yellowstone and had started collecting books about the plants and animals of the region. He
could recite endless facts and figures about the park. He could

13. HMA to Mather, Aug. 13, 1919, telegram, A. B. Cammerer to
Mather, Aug. 22, 1919, telegram, Mather to HMA, Aug. 23, 1919, NA,
Records of NPS, Parks gen., Dir.; HMA to William F. Bade, Sept. 2,
1919, and Yard to HMA [Oct. 1919], HMA Papers.

explain the mysterious workings of geysers and warm springs and identify most of the birds and mammals in the vicinity. He delighted in using his memory to entertain his guests and win friends for the National Park Service whenever he had the time to do so. He gave Huston Thompson the deluxe tour in August. About two weeks later a party of fourteen state governors, having attended a governors' conference in Salt Lake City, adjourned to the park where Albright outdid himself playing host. Governor John G. Townsend of Delaware soon discovered that the Yellowstone preserve was considerably larger than his own state, and he unhesitatingly moved that Albright be made an honorary member of the conference for that year. At the conclusion of their sojourn in the park, the governors expressed high esteem for both Albright and the National Park Service.[14]

A widely heralded Brooklyn *Eagle* tour also came to Yellowstone that summer, with H. V. Kaltenborn, then a young newspaper man, in command. Albright met the carefree travelers in Denver. After a brief stop in Rocky Mountain Park, they pushed on to Cheyenne to see Frontier Days, the city's renowned western festival. Next they motored through Yellowstone, stopping at Old Faithful, Lake Yellowstone, the Grand Canyon of the Yellowstone, and Mammoth Hot Springs, near which Albright had his headquarters. Then they caught the train north to Glacier Park, where the Blackfoot Indians, on whom Kaltenborn planned to bestow a generous gift of cash, met the train in full battle dress and put on a "terrific series of dances" for the tourists. The high point of the ceremony came when Chief Two Guns White Calf, assisted by Fish Wolf Robe, made Kaltenborn an honorary member of the tribe, christened him "Mountain Chief," and adorned him with a regal headdress. Kaltenborn dug into his pocket and after some frantic searching gave Fish Wolf Robe a ceremonial gift in return. While the tom-toms beat rhythmically, the enthusiastic journalist joined the Indians in the dance, prancing until he neared exhaustion, not knowing that protocol required the braves to keep dancing until he, the hon-

14. "Yellowstone Monthly Report" (Aug. 1919), pp. 21–22; HMA, "Reminiscences," pp. 125–26; HMA to Neilson, in 1938 Hearings.

ored guest, signaled the end. Later that evening, Kaltenborn confessed to Albright that the only thing he could find to give Fish Wolf Robe was his prized Swiss watch, one that chimed "to tell time in the dark, and showed the moon phases." The next morning, Albright bought the watch back from the Indian for fifteen dollars and presented it to Kaltenborn. The journalist remained a firm admirer of both Albright and the National Park Service for the next forty years, although in his autobiography, *Fifty Fabulous Years,* he quietly omitted the story about the watch, an act of discretion that Albright never let him live down.[15]

With the late September snows the Yellowstone season came to an end, and Albright could survey his first summer as superintendent. Most of all, he was delighted to be back in the West. "I am tremendously interested in the work I am doing in Yellowstone National Park," he wrote to a friend in Washington, "and of course I have enough of my old duties to perform to keep up my interest in the whole park system." The unanimous verdict was that Albright had succeeded in his first hectic Yellowstone season. His old friend Beverly Clendenin wrote from Salt Lake City to say that he had heard that Albright was doing "excellent work" and that "what you are doing is really of a constructive nature with a definite theory behind it." The Sierra Club offered its congratulations via William F. Bade, and Albright proudly responded that he hoped above all to please "my fellow members of the Sierra Club." He had only two minor regrets as the snow began to fly. One was that he had not been able to complete the task of reorganizing the park's administrative structure to reflect his own distinctive ideas. "To say that I have accomplished only about half of what I intended to do," he wrote to Jack LaGorce in October, "is speaking with extreme caution and in a most conservative vein." His other regret was that he had

15. HMA to C. S. Hill, July 5, 1919, H. V. Kaltenborn to HMA, Oct. 1, 1919, and HMA to Kaltenborn, Oct. 14, 1919, HMA Papers; telegrams, Mather to HMA, June 27, 1919, HMA to Mather, July 10, 1919, and Aug. 1, 1919, NA, Records of NPS, Yellowstone, Admin. Supt.; HMA, "Reminiscences," pp. 122–25; H. V. Kaltenborn, *Fifty Fabulous Years, 1900–1950: A Personal Review,* pp. 105–7.

been unsuccessful in his efforts to shake the title of assistant director. "Somebody persists in calling me acting director or assistant director or some other kind of director all the time," he ruefully observed, "while I am now a mere superintendent."[16]

It was clear beyond any doubt that Albright was no "mere superintendent." By the middle of November, after attending a conference in Denver, he found himself back in Washington helping Mather administer all of the parks. He performed capably before the Appropriations Committee. Later, he joined Mather in a whirlwind campaign to obtain a deficiency appropriation and also to raise money from wealthy friends to buy hay for the Yellowstone elk, who were in danger of starving or being exterminated by hunters because heavy snows had driven the animals out of the park toward the northern plains. A series of heart-rending wildlife photographs Grace had taken earlier in the fall tremendously impressed the Appropriations Committee and received wide publication in the press. "I have worked the picture game to the limit," Albright wrote to Lindsley, "and with the greatest success. I have got so many pictures out now that I do not know where they all are, and almost every day I see them bobbing up in some publication." The money came through in time to help save the remnants of the once magnificent herd and thus preserve the breeding stock for future years. But the gravest crisis facing the Yellowstone in the winter of 1919–20 had nothing to do with the elk but concerned water and reclamation.[17]

A searing drought had hit eastern Idaho in 1919, and as the farmers and ranchers of that state pondered the acute water shortage they turned toward Yellowstone in an urgent search

16. HMA to A. B. C. Dohrmann, Oct. 25, 1919, Clendenin to HMA, Sept. 5, 1919, HMA to William F. Bade, Sept. 2, 1919, HMA to John Oliver LaGorce, Oct. 16, 1919, and HMA to LeRoy Jeffers, Sept. 6, 1919, HMA Papers; interview with Mrs. E. T. Scoyen, Dec. 19, 1965.

17. HMA to Arthur Chapman, Oct. 13, 1919, HMA to H. V. Kaltenborn, Oct. 13, 1919, HMA to Emerson Hough, Nov. 8, 1919, and Dec. 11, 1919, HMA to C. A. Lindsley, Dec. 19, 1919, and Jan. 27, 1919, and telegram, HMA to Lindsley, Feb. 21, 1920, HMA Papers; "Yellowstone Monthly Report" (Oct. 1919), pp. 17–18.

for new reservoir sites. The fact that Yellowstone Park enjoyed unique legal protection against commercial incursions from neighboring states did not stop the political leaders of Idaho, who now proposed that storage reservoirs be built in the southwest corner of the park, especially in the Falls and Bechler rivers. The Reclamation Service, noting that "the contour map of the Geological Survey . . . shows the character of the country to be swampy," gave the project its powerful endorsement. Even Secretary Lane, who was eager to assist homesteading veterans of World War I, approved the idea. "I thoroughly sympathize with the desire of the Idaho people to secure use of the waters within the park for the irrigation of their lands," he wrote to the sponsor of the bill, Congressman Addison T. Smith, "where such use would improve the park instead of injuring it, as would appear to be the case here." Mather and Albright were utterly appalled at the prospect of a part of Yellowstone being sacrificed to the utilitarian demands of a few hundred farmers. Having once established a precedent for entering a national park, they theorized, the reclamation and irrigation developers would undoubtedly encroach on other parks. There would be no stopping them. Almost overnight the Falls-Bechler scheme assumed a lofty symbolic significance. "Is there not some place in this great Nation of ours where lakes can be preserved in their natural state," Mather asked in his 1919 *Annual Report,* "where we and all generations to follow us can enjoy the beauty and charm of mountain waters in the midst of primeval forests?" If Yellowstone were not to be "spared from the hand of commercialism," what hope could the people entertain "for the preservation of any scenic features of the mountains in the interest of posterity?"[18]

Mather and Albright bent every effort to change Lane's mind. They coaxed and argued. Invoking the memory of the "Hetch Hetchy steal" of 1913, they unofficially but effectively brought

18. U.S., Congress, House, Hearing Before the Committee on Public Lands, "Irrigation Easements, Yellowstone Park," 66th Cong., 2d sess. (Mar. 20, 1920), p. 5; Franklin K. Lane to Addison T. Smith, Feb. 3, 1920, in U.S., Congress, House, Hearing Before the Committee on Rules, "Rule for H. R. 12466. . . ," 66th Cong., 2d sess. (May 25, 1920), p. 4; *Annual Report, NPS* (1919), p. 49.

the aesthetic conservationists into the fight. All the lobbying resources of J. Horace McFarland and the American Civic Association, the Sierra Club, the Boone and Crocket Club, and the National Parks Association (now directed by Bob Yard) could not sway Lane, who ordered the Park Service to prepare a favorable report on the Smith bill. When gentle persuasion failed, the director and his assistant resorted to stalling. Instead of preparing the report as directed, Mather suddenly found that he had to leave town on urgent personal business. Albright inexplicably "lost" key documents and correspondence files which were needed to prepare the report. Earlier he had quietly obstructed the work of an official survey party that came to Yellowstone to study the Falls-Bechler region.[19]

In February, before the hearings on the Smith bill had even begun, Mather and Albright regretfully decided that they would resign rather than support the Secretary's position. But the need for their resignations never arose. Secretary Lane unexpectedly bowed out of the cabinet, reportedly because of poor health and an accumulation of minor disagreements with the White House. He was replaced by John Barton Payne, who dramatically reversed Lane's stand on allowing irrigation works to be built in Yellowstone. Although the Senate had already approved the Smith bill, the Park Service, with Payne's forceful assistance, blocked the legislation in the House. Not only had Yellowstone been saved but a valuable precedent had been established. Later, when Senator Walsh introduced legislation to dam Lake Yellowstone and siphon off water for irrigation projects in Montana, it was relatively easy for the Park Service to block passage of the bill. Albright was very proud of his role in protecting one of the great wilderness areas of the United States. Essentially undisturbed by civilization, the remote watersheds of the Yellowstone would remain the domain of the moose and the deer, the bison and the grizzly.[20]

As luck and a certain amount of harmless scheming would

19. HMA to Emerson Hough, Nov. 29, 1919 and Dec. 11, 1919, and George Bird Grinnell to Mather, Dec. 1, 1919, HMA Papers; HMA, "Reminiscences," pp. 78–82.

20. Shankland, *Steve Mather*, pp. 212–14.

have it, the Albrights had an opportunity to go to Hawaii in the spring of 1920. There were legal problems to be settled in connection with the new Hawaii National Park, and Albright was the logical man to undertake the job. After reaching the islands, he and Grace spent a week on Oahu and then sailed to the "Big Island," or Hawaii, to inspect the park, which encompassed both the volcanic slopes of Mauna Loa and the spectacular Kilauea crater, which was in the midst of a fiery eruption. Albright's mission was specifically to dispose of "the matter of rights of way, private holdings, etc. which are responsible for the delay in getting a really adequate appropriation for the park." To add to his official stature and facilitate his work in Hawaii, Albright was named the "field assistant to the Director," a promotion that meant practically nothing. Not until autumn did he receive a pay increase, to $4,000 per annum, to go with his new title.[21]

"The Hawaii National Park is a world-beater," Albright wrote to Emerson Hough. "The volcano is easily the sensation of all the parks, and it is only one of a hundred different features." During his brief stay in the islands, Albright sold Mather's park philosophy to businessmen and chambers of commerce, helped plan the development of the park's first tourist facilities, emphasized the possibilities of Park Service research in volcanology, and smoothed out the last legal difficulties that impeded the development of the Hawaiian preserve, thus leaving his mark on still another segment of the national park system.[22]

Back in Yellowstone, Albright fell into his accustomed administrative routine and began the perpetual round of entertaining that his job demanded. John Barton Payne, the new Secretary of the Interior, received special attention, because Albright wanted to impress upon him the need for protecting Yellowstone against future encroachment by irrigation projects. The new Secretary responded warmly, and Albright developed a very high regard

21. HMA to Lindsley, Jan. 27, 1920, itinerary for March and April 1920, Edna M. Peltz to HMA, May 7, 1920, HMA to Hawaii Promotion Committee, Jan. 24, 1920, Mather to HMA, Mar. 5, 1920, and A. T. Vogelsang to HMA, Mar. 8, 1920, HMA Papers.
22. HMA to Hough, May 15, 1920, HMA Papers.

for the man. "I wish he could be Secretary of the Interior for the rest of his life," Albright wrote to a colleague. Payne followed through on an earlier promise to get the national parks exempted from the provisions of the Water Power Act of 1920, which had originally authorized the Federal Power Commission to grant permits for the construction of hydroelectric power projects in the nation's navigable streams and their tributaries, even in the national park system.[23]

Soon after the Secretary's party left, Congressman James W. Good, chairman of the House Appropriations Committee, accompanied by a number of his fellow committee members, including James F. Byrnes, descended on Albright, who spent an entire week guiding them around the park. The Congressmen were obviously happy with what they saw. "Personally, I am at a loss to understand how you are able to keep up so perfect an organization," Good later wrote Albright. By the time the season ended, Albright had entertained, among others, George Horace Lorimer, influential editor of the *Saturday Evening Post*, Congressman and Mrs. Mondell of Wyoming, writers Hal G. Evarts and Elizabeth Frazer, Emerson Hough and his wife, Bob Yard, and Christian Zabriskie, his father's old partner, now a mining-company executive. In addition to administering the park, he began writing parts of the annual report of the National Park Service, a time-consuming job Mather gladly delegated to him.[24]

Although Congressman Good had pronounced the park's organization "perfect," Albright was well aware of the many improvements that still needed to be made. The ranger force needed to be upgraded. The services provided by the concessioners had to be improved and expanded. The road-maintenance

23. Telegrams, HMA to Mather, May 31, 1920, and June 1, 1920, NA, Records of NPS, Yellowstone admin., Supt.; HMA to Mather, Apr. 26, 1920, and May 31, 1920, telegram, William Noble to HMA, May 31, 1920, telegram, Grace Albright to HMA, June 6, 1920, and HMA to D. B. Trefethen, Aug. 7, 1920, HMA Papers; *Inyo Register*, June 3, 1920; Shankland, *Steve Mather*, p. 214.

24. James W. Good to HMA, Aug. 1, 1920, HMA to Mather, June 25, 1920, and Isabelle F. Story to HMA, July 22, 1920, HMA Papers; "Yellowstone Monthly Report" (July 1920), pp. 26–32.

program had to be modernized. The water and sewage disposal systems required further overhauling to provide at least minimal public health protection in a heavily used park. And Albright's public relations efforts would have to be doubled and redoubled to win the support of the surrounding communities. To accomplish these things would require increased appropriations from Congress and continued, hard-driving leadership from the young superintendent.

Albright knew precisely what had to be done to upgrade the park's ranger force. He would have to set higher standards in recruiting and training, and he would have "to get out into the park" as often as possible to see that his orders were followed and to demonstrate his personal commitment to better park management. Each season he traveled about ten thousand miles, visiting ranger stations, inspecting roads, and systematically covering the huge park from boundary to boundary. "He can do more in a day and be at more places than most men," an admiring journalist wrote after observing Albright in action. "The speed laws in the national parks are very strict, but Albright breaks them. If he didn't break them, he couldn't do what he does." The rangers never knew where he would turn up next. E. T. Scoyen, later associate director of the National Park Service but then a young ranger in Yellowstone, reported that one morning he climbed out of bed about dawn to go trout fishing with a friend. No sooner had he washed his face and pulled out his tackle box than "along came the long chauffeur driven car that Albright used." The ubiquitous park superintendent was out inspecting. He stopped for a chat and before leaving wrote in his pocket notebook that Scoyen was up and at his station at an extraordinarily early hour. "I always thought that was the beginning of my happy relationship with Horace," Scoyen later recalled with a wink. "The point is," Scoyen continued, "Albright was up and had driven thirty-one miles [from park headquarters] by six o'clock." This kind of unpredictable inspection schedule served to keep the rangers on their toes. He constantly admonished his assistant superintendent, Chester A. Lindsley, and his dependable chief ranger, Sam T. Woodring, to be on the lookout for "slackers" and incompetents, who were "not the kind of men we want to keep in our permanent force."[25]

A form letter sent to all applicants for Yellowstone ranger positions summarized the qualities Albright looked for in his employees. The letter began with a brusque refutation of the idea that "the ranger is a sort of sinecure with nothing resembling hard work to perform . . . and [with] very frequent trips about the park and innumerable dances and other diversions to occupy one's leisure hours." These conceptions of the duties of a ranger, according to Albright, were "just as untrue as it is possible for them to be." Albright explained that he preferred "men of 25 to 30 years of age" who were "mature in appearance." In his view a ranger was "primarily a policeman," and therefore he wanted large men, "big in frame, tall, and of average weight." Above all—this was given special emphasis in the letter—a ranger "*must have a pleasing personality.*" He must be "tactful, diplomatic, and courteous." "If you are not possessed of such characteristics," Albright stated, "please don't apply." He added that he looked for men with "experience in the out-of-doors in riding, camping, woodcraft, fighting fires and similar activities." The salary was only $100 a month, and the ranger had to pay for his own meals, buy his own uniform, and "bring his own bed." Many of them brought their own horses. Albright closed his letter by observing that "you have perhaps believed Government jobs to be 'soft' and 'easy.' Most of them are not, and certainly there are no such jobs in the National Park Service. The ranger's job is especially hard. . . . Apply if you are qualified. Otherwise, please plan to visit the Yellowstone National Park as a tourist." By being highly selective about the men he hired, and by drumming into them the need for courtesy and versatility, Albright slowly improved the level of performance of his Yellowstone staff. Once satisfied with his men's capabilities and loyalties, he gave them his unqualified support and backing, taking pains to get to know each individual. By 1923 he had vastly improved

25. HMA to Lindsley, Jan. 4, 1920, HMA Papers; Burt, "A Certain Mountain Chief," pp. 625–26; interview with E. T. Scoyen, Dec. 19, 1965; HMA Diary, June 20–30, 1921.

the efficiency of his men and had noticeably raised their morale. Almost all of his rangers were now imbued with the enthusiasm and esprit that clearly set the National Park Service apart from most other government agencies.[26]

Not only did Albright constantly patrol the park roads in the summertime, but he also packed into the wilderness in the off-season in an effort to familiarize himself with every square mile of the park's vast territory. A quarter of a century had passed since a Yellowstone superintendent had undertaken a two-hundred-mile pack trip, as Albright did in late September and early October 1920. The trip was important for two main reasons. By averaging twenty-five miles a day and by penetrating a large area of wilderness, he established himself as a rugged outdoorsman and gained the admiration of his permanent ranger force. But, more important, he acquainted himself with the southwest portion of the park—the part Idaho farmers still hoped to lop off for irrigation purposes. Accompanied by a ranger who knew the country, Albright rode south from Lake Yellowstone to the park boundary line, camping along the way at the Thorofare and Fox Creek patrol stations. From this high ground he could see the Tetons "garbed in snow from top to bottom," presenting "the most wonderful spectacle of mountain scenery" he had "ever seen." He then crossed the continental divide and moved into the Falls-Bechler basin which was, as he noted in his report, "not at all as described by . . . the Reclamation Service." "Instead of being a swamp, it is mostly covered with a fine forest growth of rather large conifers." The Bechler canyon, located to the west of the Falls River, contained "great waterfalls and cascades" and "lava cliffs that rise above the bed of the stream" as well as "numerous waterfalls not mentioned on the map. This confirms my suspicion that the topographers who made the map [referred to by the Reclamation Service] did not go through the canyon." Soon after returning to civilization, Albright made arrangements for his friends in the United States Geological Survey to restudy this portion of the park so that the territory

26. Form letter, HMA to ———, n.d., HMA to A. B. Cammerer, Nov. 29, 1923, HMA Papers; Yellowstone monthly reports (1920–24).

would not be designated "swampy" on future contour maps. Albright's dedication to aesthetic values and his sheer love of natural beauty permeated his official report of his adventure. "I shall never forget the thrill that I experienced," he wrote, "when I realized that I was standing in the midst of more wild country than exists anywhere else in the United States." His report effectively countered every claim made by the irrigationists, and it provided essential ammunition for the Park Service in its fight to protect Yellowstone. Although intended only for internal use in the National Park Service, the report's scope, sensitivity, and descriptive power vividly recalled some of the best nineteenth-century journals of exploration.[27]

Seeing the Tetons, in all their glistening beauty, from inside Yellowstone reinforced Albright's determination to extend the park's boundary to the south. "I know now," he proclaimed, "that with the Tetons and the headwaters of the Yellowstone added to the park, it will stand far above any other national park" in terms of "natural phenomena" and because of its "wild, rugged, beautiful scenery."[28]

The public furor over Jackson Hole died down to some extent in the early twenties, but Albright kept working, staying in touch with Carey and W. B. Ross, Cary's successor in the Wyoming governor's chair, as well as with Congressman Mondell. He quietly converted both Struthers Burt and Horace Carncross to his side, convincing them that they could "all work towards a common end," namely the preservation of Jackson Hole's matchless beauty. As a result of Albright's adroit salesmanship, George Horace Lorimer, of the *Saturday Evening Post*, departed from Mammoth Springs in 1920 claiming that "the best part of Yellowstone Park is not yet in the park" and pledging that he would take up the fight "in a series of editorials I am writing." The Boone and Crocket Club volunteered to help. Nevertheless,

27. Telegram, HMA to Director of NPS, Sept. 29, 1920, NA, Records of NPS, Yellowstone admin., Supt.; HMA to Director of NPS, Oct. 16, 1920, in "Yellowstone Monthly Report" (Oct. 1920).

28. HMA to Director of NPS, Oct. 16, 1920, in "Yellowstone Monthly Report" (Oct. 1920).

the stalemate continued, with the Jackson Hole cattlemen now leading the opposition.[29]

By 1924, the proposed extension of Yellowstone seemed hopelessly snarled in factionalism and bogged down in a ritualistic debate between those who glorified the principle of local control and those who held that the national interest should be preeminent. Albright had not given up the fight, but he fell back more and more on behind-the-scenes maneuvering. Convinced that the Jackson Hole country would someday be national park land and that recreation in its many forms rather than ranching offered the key to the region's economic future, he was prepared to guide the people of Jackson Hole into doing what was best. In the long run, he was perfectly right about the future of the area. But there were those who contended that a federal official, especially an appointed officer, no matter how enlightened his position, should never force his will on the public. The stage was now set for Albright's most controversial action, in which he secretly initiated a scheme to bring the Jackson Hotel region into the national park system. It was his style of operating that would cause the trouble rather than his ultimate goal, which was to prevent the commercialization of Jackson Hole.[30]

In the meantime, Albright's bold administrative approach paid off in his battles with Harry Child. Since 1901, Child had operated a string of five hotels and a transportation franchise in Yellowstone. He had thrived during the pre-1916 era, when the army left the concessioners almost completely to their own devices. After 1916, when Mather and Albright sought to consolidate and regulate business operations in Yellowstone, Child refused to cooperate. He managed to survive a massive reorganization of the park's franchise holders in 1918, but he would not recognize the superintendent's authority to oversee his com-

29. HMA to F. W. Mondell, Oct. 31, 1920, Struthers Burt to R. S. Yard, Apr. 19, 1920, G. H. Lorimer to HMA, Aug. 18, 1920, George Bird Grinnell to HMA, Dec. 1, 1919, James R. Brooks to HMA [1920], and HMA to F. P. Farquhar, Oct. 14, 1922, HMA Papers; "Yellowstone Monthly Report" (July 1924).

30. See Ise, *Our National Park Policy*, pp. 490–508 for a summary of the controversy.

pany's affairs. He was a persuasive and hard-fighting westerner who had amassed a small fortune as a businessman and who boasted the friendship of Theodore Roosevelt and Warren G. Harding. Child thoroughly resented Albright's early attempts to regulate his business affairs in Yellowstone, even though the Park Service had both the legal right and the duty to insure fair and dependable service to the public. Child's consistent policy was to put as little capital into his franchise as possible and to take out the maximum profit each season. His hotel and eating facilities were overcrowded and badly in need of repair. His transportation company had too few buses to give reliable service. He was accustomed to cutting thousands of cords of firewood in the forests near his hotels, without obtaining a permit and without making any payment to the government. His employees carried out a systematic and unregulated program of "market fishing" (catching fish to feed to the customers), which annually provided thousands of free trout for his hotel dining tables.[31]

Soon after Albright took over as superintendent he prohibited all market fishing in the park and took steps to "force the company" to cut only "dead and down timber." He also kept after Child to improve and expand his hotel facilities. By the summer of 1920, the contest between Albright and Child had reached serious proportions. After Harding won the Republican presidential nomination in June 1920, the testy concessioner began making veiled threats about what would happen after the election. "He has openly boasted that there will be a change in things next year," Albright reported to Mather, "and only yesterday his assistant, Mr. [W. M.] Nichols, made this statement . . . that 'There is just about a fifty-fifty chance of Albright's being superintendent next year if Harding is elected.' " But Albright kept pushing, formally requesting Child to do a large amount of construction and to purchase a number of new buses. He also wrote an exhaustive report to Washington about Child's violations of Park Service directives. "My idea in writing this

31. HMA to Mather, Oct. 21, 1920, HMA to Director of NPS, Oct. 21, 1920, HMA Papers; *Annual Report, NPS* (1919), pp. 45–46; Shankland, *Steve Mather*, pp. 120–26.

report," he stated, "is that should, by any chance, I not be in charge of the park after this year, my observations and findings on the operations of these companies may be useful to the Service in perhaps more than one connection."[32]

After the election of 1920, which propelled Harding into the White House, Albright prepared for the worst. But the gruff and unpredictable Child surprised everybody by pushing through a joint resolution in the Montana state legislature requesting the Republican administration to retain his presumed enemies, Mather and Albright, as director and superintendent respectively. Evidently he had been bluffing, hoping to force Albright to back off. The truth was that he valued the young man's energetic leadership and considered him an asset to the park. Since Child showed no real willingness to acknowledge the authority of the Park Service, Albright continued his single-minded drive to curb the obstreperous concessioner. His most ingenious and telling move came in December 1921, when he suggested that if Child's "soulless corporation" wanted to work on a "strictly commercial basis" then he too was going to adopt commercial standards and "by heaven, you will pay for everything you get from us." Driving the administrative dagger home, he listed a few of the charges that would be levied, and he pointedly observed, "We pay for everything we get at rates to be approved by the Director and you pay for everything you get, also at rates to be approved by the Director." The level of cooperation rose perceptibly after that. By 1923 Albright had won his contest with Child, who grudgingly but nevertheless effectively recognized the park superintendent's authority. In October 1923, for example, Albright and Child had a disagreement over equipment purchases for the 1924 season. Child wanted to buy thirty new buses while Albright thought sixty should be purchased by November 1. "Today, Oct. 31st," Albright crowed to a newspaperman acquaintance, "I received a letter advising

32. HMA to Mather, Oct. 21, 1920, HMA to Director of NPS, Oct. 21, 1920, HMA to Cammerer, Oct. 4, 1922, and HMA to Hough, Sept. 2, 1919, HMA Papers; "Yellowstone Monthly Report" (Aug. 1922); HMA, "Reminiscences," pp. 141–42.

me that 60 have been ordered. This was a satisfactory compromise for me."[33]

Albright had practically no trouble with the other major concessioners in the park, Jack E. Haynes, who ran the photographic concession, George Whittaker, Charles Hamilton, Elizabeth Trischman, and Anna Pryor, who operated the stores, and Howard Hays, who had bought out the Yellowstone Park Camping Company in July 1919. Hays provided relatively inexpensive facilities for the thousands of campers who came to the park—mostly by rail in those early days. Moreover, he served as Albright's sounding board and confidential adviser on administrative problems. "You know a fellow who is running a proposition as big as this needs a little checking now and then," Albright candidly admitted, "and I used to talk over many of my most perplexing problems with Howard, and he took an interest in them." Unfortunately, Hays became seriously ill in 1924 and had to dispose of his Yellowstone interests.[34]

The fact that Harry Child was awarded the camps franchise when Hays bowed out (this left all of the hotels, lodges, camps, and buses in Child's hands) demonstrated very clearly that Albright and the "soulless corporation" had made their peace by the summer of 1924. Service to the tourists improved consistently throughout the twenties, as Child and Albright worked together, hammering out the final guidelines of a policy of "regulated monopoly" in Yellowstone. Mather and Albright always operated on the theory that since Congress refused to appropriate enough money to develop the parks the only alternative was to turn to private capital, making each park a well-regulated business preserve for a single franchise holder. By 1924, the policy of regulated monopoly, which was firmly rooted in the ideas of Theodore Roosevelt's New Nationalism, an ideology that had deeply influenced both Mather and Albright, was a

33. HMA to W. M. Nichols, Dec. 12, 1921, and HMA to Harry Frantz, Oct. 31, 1923, HMA Papers; HMA, "Reminiscences," pp. 142–142a.

34. HMA to Walter C. White, Dec. 29, 1919, Howard Hays to HMA, Apr. 10, 1920, HMA to Mather, Oct. 21, 1920, and HMA to White, June 3, 1924, HMA Papers.

reality in Yellowstone Park. Some of the other parks had always operated on a monopoly basis. Soon all of the park units would adopt the same pattern.[35]

It was entirely predictable that Albright, after serving a long apprenticeship under Mather, would continue to place heavy emphasis on public relations. On his countless inspection trips around the park, he would often stop to talk to visitors, swapping stories with them, telling them about the features of the park, and asking them if they had any complaints about the rangers or the concessioners. When he spotted a deer or a female bear with her cubs, he would sometimes climb out of his car and flag down approaching buses to make sure the tourists saw the wildlife. At other times, Albright would collect a group of tourists and ask them to close their eyes. Then he would lead them to a beautiful but inconspicuous nearby vista "and have them open their eyes and just shock them." He had his rangers trained to do the same thing. "We loved that," he readily admitted. In the cool evenings he would walk into a crowded campground, stir up a fire, and regale the campers with stories about the history of Yellowstone Park. This type of unabashed boosterism would be considered undignified and wholly unnecessary by most park superintendents today, because the parks now bulge with hundreds of thousands of visitors. In the 1920s Albright saw nothing wrong with "selling" the park to the customers and urging them to come back next year. It was all part of his and Mather's strategy to increase Park Service appropriations by increasing park usage. "We never had any trouble getting along with the tourists," Albright proudly recalled. His affable personality and his unpretentious style made him popular with the people who came to the park.[36]

Moreover, he continued his efforts to build good will in Wyoming, Montana, and Idaho. He made annual trips to the capitals of these states in order to keep up with the latest political developments. He spent as much time as he could in Livingston,

35. Shankland, *Steve Mather*, pp. 114–27.
36. HMA, "Reminiscences," pp. 241–45; HMA and Frank J. Taylor, *"Oh Ranger!" A Book About the National Parks*, pp. 26–27.

Gardiner, and Cody, invariably making a special effort to meet the local editors and publishers and to get to know the railroad men in these towns. His web of personal contacts spread all the way to Denver and Cheyenne. He became so well known in Livingston that the city's Rotary Club made him an honorary member and published a special edition of "Mammoth Lies," an occasional newspaper, devoted exclusively to a good-natured lampooning of both Albright and Yellowstone. In its one serious column, the newspaper urged: "May the kindly feeling and shoulder-to-shoulder team work that have prevailed in the past between Livingston and Superintendent Horace be continued, for after all we are engaged in a common work." Cliché-ridden as it was, this statement revealed the proportions of Albright's success in Livingston.[37]

The meeting at which he received his honorary Rotary membership "developed into an ovation" for the guest of honor, according to a story in the Livingston *Enterprise*. One notices immediately that when it suited his purposes Albright could adopt the style and rhetoric of a classic Rotarian, although he normally avoided practical jokes and backslapping. It was simply part of his job as he conceived it, and there was no doubt about his effectiveness in winning friends for the park.[38]

When writers and newspaper men, like Kaltenborn, Hough, Hal Evarts, and Frank J. Taylor, came to the park, Albright always gave them the full treatment, and in return received very generous coverage in the press. In 1922, for example, Taylor wrote a series of feature stories for the Scripps-McRae syndicate on the park's spectacular Centennial Geyser and about "Horace M. Albright, the youthful, exuberant, enthusiastic superintendent of America's first national park," who "talks, thinks, dreams and lives Yellowstone." It would be difficult, Hough wrote in an amusing *Saturday Evening Post* article in 1920, "to find a

37. HMA to Arthur Chapman, Oct. 13, 1919, C. Watt Brandon to HMA, July 2, 1923, HMA to Mather, Oct. 3, 1922, and "Mammoth Lies" (issued "Now and Then By Irresponsibles of the Livingston Rotary Club"), HMA Papers.
38. "Mammoth Lies"; clipping from Livingston *Enterprise*, n.d., HMA Papers.

more long-suffering man" than Albright. "During the open season on superintendents, some three months in duration, he does not sleep at all. For one month after the first snowfall he digs a hole beneath a rock, somewhere above the timberline, and falls into a torpor, using no food for thirty days. Then he goes to Washington to meet the Director of Parks, after which he gets no more sleep until next fall. It is this perpetual insomnia which gives the park superintendent his haunted look."[39]

Although Albright's public relations record was, from the point of view of the Park Service, extraordinarily good, he occasionally suffered a costly reversal in his promotional work. His initial maneuvers in Jackson, Wyoming, for the extension of Yellowstone, left impressions that were extremely difficult to erase. But his most traumatic setback came in the winter of 1921–22 when Emerson Hough suddenly turned on him in an editorial published in the *Saturday Evening Post*. Hough had a passion for trout fishing. His persuasive argument that the trout streams in Yellowstone were rapidly being depleted had impelled Albright to crack down on market fishing and "to do something in the way of restocking the streams" during his first summer as superintendent. Hough and his wife spent much of the 1920 season in Yellowstone, living with the Albrights and sharing their table while he worked on a novel, *The Covered Wagon*, which later became a best seller. "During the summer, Mr. Hough quarreled with me a lot," Albright noted, "because I mentioned the number of people that were coming into and enjoying Yellowstone. He said we made a great mistake in the National Park Service in measuring the success of the season by the number of people that we had visiting the national parks, that rather we should be boastful of visitors only when they were declining in numbers." In the summer of 1921 the Houghs returned to Yellowstone but stayed in a house borrowed from Harry Child. Albright extended them every possible courtesy, arranging fishing trips, allowing his secretary to type some of

39. Clipping from Philadelphia *Ledger*, May 7, 1922, scrapbook, HMA Papers; Emerson Hough, "Maw's Vacation," *Saturday Evening Post* 193 (Oct. 16, 1920) : 63.

Hough's dictation, and giving the writer unrestricted access to park records.[40]

In September 1921, following a trout luncheon for two hundred railroad men at one of Hays's camps, Hough loudly accused Albright of not rigorously enforcing the ban on market fishing in the park. Albright investigated the matter and found that, while Hays had perhaps violated the spirit of the rules by allowing his employees to catch trout for his guests, no one individual had exceeded his legal daily limit. After a quiet talk with Hays, Albright considered the incident closed. But Hough, angry and resentful, left Yellowstone muttering that Albright had treacherously "double-crossed" him. The old man had a reputation for being irascible and for falling into prolonged grouches. Albright assumed that Hough would soon snap out of it. Hays had not consulted Albright about his plans for the luncheon. "I was wholly innocent in the matter," Albright wrote later, "and really it did not amount to anything anyway, but Hough upbraided me for what he called partiality to Hays, and demanded that I punish him." The unexpected *Post* editorial appeared in January 1922 and it bore Hough's imprint.[41]

"The violator of the law," the *Post* editorialized, "who escapes punishment in a national park goes home ripe for further contempt of all game laws. His offense runs on, it grows. So also does the offense of any official who winks at violations of his own regulations." The editorial carefully mentioned no names, but Albright knew immediately that he was the "official" the *Post* had in mind. His outraged reaction led him to dispatch a torrent of indignant letters and telegrams to the East. "Emerson Hough's editorial in this week's Saturday Evening Post," he wired Mather, "was criminally unjust and unfair . . . and will result in great embarrassment to me as Superintendent of Yellowstone Park unless it is counteracted. . . . I feel this very keenly and bit-

40. HMA to Hough, Sept. 2, 1919, HMA to Mather, Jan. 10, 1922, and Hough to R. S. Yard, Dec. 23, 1921, HMA Papers.
41. HMA to Mather, Jan. 12, 1922, and HMA to C. C. Adams, Jan. 23, 1922, HMA Papers; "Shall Our Game Join the Dodo?" *Saturday Evening Post* 194 (Jan. 21, 1922) : 22.

terly. . . . If any part of the editorial as it affects my administration is found to be true, my resignation is ready." In his rage, Albright had jumped to the conclusion that all of his conservationist friends would read the editorial and identify him as the culprit. He wrote to John Burnham, of the American Game Protective Association, George Bird Grinnell, editor of *Field and Stream,* and to a dozen other well-known conservationists asking them "to suspend" judgment until he had an "opportunity to relate the circumstances surrounding the preparation of this editorial." As it turned out, Albright had jumped to the wrong conclusion. The editorial aroused virtually no interest in the East.[42]

As reassuring telegrams and letters began to flow in from Mather, Cammerer, LaGorce, Grinnell, Yard, Burt, and a number of high officials in the Interior Department, Albright's anger began to fade. "I hope that you will not let that dyspeptic editorial worry you," wired Gilbert Grosvenor. "Your unselfish and devoted service on behalf of our national parks is appreciated by your multitude of friends, who wish you continued success and happiness." The editorial, "fell so flat" in the East, Yard reported, "that you can afford to ignore it in toto." Mather assured his protégé that he was "thoroughly out of patience with Hough's insinuations and innuendoes" and that he planned to discuss the matter with Lorimer, "whose house guest I will be next Monday." Lorimer wrote Albright a friendly letter to explain that nothing personal was intended in the editorial. After a few days of petulence, the young man realized that he had grossly overreacted. "I was about the maddest man on the Pacific coast when I first read the editorial," Albright confessed, "and in my fury I wrote some letters to Mr. Mather that I now wish I had put away until I cooled down." For the first time in his career he had completely lost his sense of proportion. He not only resented Hough's dogmatic attitude, but also "Lorimer's action in permitting the editorial to be published" and his imagined betrayal "by disloyal men in my own organiza-

42. "Shall Our Game Join the Dodo?"; telegram, HMA to Mather, Jan. 21, 1922, HMA to John Burham, Jan. 19, 1922, and HMA to George Bird Grinnell, Jan. 19, 1922, HMA Papers.

tion." Most of all, he resented Hough's blatant ingratitude. "If the grouchy devil had not . . . been so ungrateful," Albright confided to LaGorce, "I probably could have kept better control of my temper. Anyway, he has stabbed the hand that has been feeding him—tried to amputate it, in fact—so it is not unlikely that he will find upon future visits to the park that he will negotiate on a strict commercial basis for service in the way of meals, lodging, fishing trips, etc."[43]

In many respects, the Hough embroglio resembled Albright's controversy with Enos Mills. In the end, the issues were almost the same. Albright was branded by Hough as a "theorist" and a contemptible "politician," constantly compromising and maneuvering to avoid unpleasantness and unfavorable publicity. Most of all, Hough disliked Albright's zeal for boosting the total number of park visitors every year and catering to automobiles. In fact, as the 1920s progressed an increasing number of conservation purists, especially in the Sierra Club and the Seattle Mountaineers, organizations dedicated to the preservation of wilderness areas, questioned the wisdom of packing the parks with visitors and allowing automobiles to "ruin" the natural atmosphere. After an encounter between Albright and the Mountaineers in 1923 over the issue of enforcing the rules in Mount Rainier Park, one of the participants in the discussion wrote that Albright had said much about "the exercise of a wise discretion by the individual park superintendent. My impression was that the [Interior] Department believes in a government of men rather than a government of laws.[44]

As in his previous controversies, it was Albright's style of operating, which usually emphasized flexibility and pragmatic solutions rather than the open confrontation of issues, that got him

43. Telegram, Mather to HMA, Jan. 23, 1922, telegram, Grosvenor to HMA, Jan. 28, 1922, telegram, John Oliver LaGorce to HMA, Jan. 24, 1922, telegram, George Bird Grinnell to HMA, Feb. 6, 1922, telegram, HMA to Yard, Jan. 28, 1922, telegram, HMA to E. C. Finney, Jan. 31, 1922, telegram, HMA to LaGorce, Feb. 9, 1922, and telegram, Lorimer to HMA, Jan. 27, 1922, HMA Papers.

44. Hough to L. T. Meyer, Feb. 18, 1922, and George E. Wright to William E. Colby, Mar. 22, 1923, HMA Papers.

into difficulty. His primary goal, which was to strengthen the National Park Service and thus to provide a strong institutional framework for the preservation of natural beauty, was unquestionably sound. Within a few days the crisis over Hough's accusations passed, but Albright had clearly demonstrated that he was capable of fierce pride and thundering anger, and that he had become a trifle thin-skinned since leaving Washington. The *Saturday Evening Post* more than redeeemed itself in 1925 by publishing an affectionate and flattering character sketch by Kenneth Roberts entitled, "Grand Duke Horace of Yellowstone," ruler of a territory "some four times larger than the Grand Duchy of Luxemburg."[45]

One possible cause of Albright's burst of temper in early 1922 was the tension and lack of sleep inevitably connected with the arrival of a new baby, a daughter named Marian, born on December 21, 1921 in Berkeley, where the Albright family spent the winter. Grace and the new baby arrived home from the hospital only two weeks before Hough's editorial appeared.[46]

Moving back to Yellowstone in the summer of 1922, Albright settled into the hectic but enjoyable routine of being both superintendent of the park and field assistant to the director. For the next two years, nothing out of the ordinary occurred to disturb his tranquility. He worked hard at improving, but not expanding, the existing road system in the park, experimenting with motorized road maintenance and snow-removal methods. With the help of Jack Haynes he established a small but interesting museum. In cooperation with ranger naturalists Milton P. Skinner and Edmund J. Sawyer he stook steps to initiate a nature-guide program in the park, patterned after the successful Yosemite program that California Professors Harold C. Bryant and Loye H. Miller had originated. Accompanied by Sam Woodring, Albright pushed into the wild northwest section of the park on another extended pack trip, emerging ten days later to pro-

45. "Grand Duke Horace of Yellowstone," *Saturday Evening Post* 197 (Apr. 18, 1925) : 58.
46. HMA to Cammerer, Jan. 5, 1922, and Cammerer to HMA, Dec. 27, 1921, HMA Papers.

claim that "it would be unwise, if not disastrous," for a road to be "built through the Gallatin Mountains." Following the recommendations of the United States Public Health Service, he supervised the construction of sewage disposal systems in the upper geyser basin and at Lake Yellowstone. He contracted for a physician to practice in the park. As the need arose, he traveled to the other western parks, carrying out numerous troubleshooting assignments for Mather. And every winter he went back to Washington to defend the bureau's budget requests before Congress. Frequently dashing to New York, Boston, and Philadelphia, he became a lecturer, specializing in illustrated talks on Yellowstone wildlife. In addition to everything else, he found himself deeply involved in the internal affairs of the Boone and Crocket Club and the Save-the-Redwoods League, whose executive secretary was Newton B. Drury. His chief interest and constant delight remained Yellowstone National Park, to which he gave his most creative energy, although, as he candidly confessed, he was "inclined to have not less than 500 irons in the fire at once."[47]

Yellowstone was the National Park Service in microcosm during the 1920s, reflecting the problems of the national park system as a whole. From 1919 to 1923, Albright concentrated on solving these problems. He recruited first-rate young men to work in the park, and he imbued them with the Park Service mystique. He imposed his authority on the concessioners, but he did so without personally alienating them. He insisted that the tourists receive courteous treatment and decent accommodations. He instituted new educational programs in the park. He placed great emphasis on public relations, concentrating on the people who visited the park as well as the business leaders of the surrounding communities. He took steps to modernize the roads, to improve sewage disposal methods, and to upgrade

47. "Yellowstone Monthly Report" (June 1922), pp. 22–24 (July 1922), pp. 16–18 (Oct. 1923), pp. 13–14 (May 1924), p. 29 (June 1924), pp. 19–21 (July 1924), pp. 20–21; John C. Merriam to HMA, Aug. 25, 1919, Drury to HMA, July 12, 1920, HMA to Drury, July 25, 1920, Drury to HMA, Mar. 28, 1922, and HMA to M. P. Skinner, Feb. 17, 1920, and Feb. 23, 1921, HMA Papers.

health facilities. His success as an administrator not only made Yellowstone a showplace among the national parks, but also contributed to the satisfactory solution of similar problems in other parks. Yellowstone became a training ground for the future leaders of the National Park Service and a proving ground for the bureau's policies. The park's annual visitor count pushed above the 130,000 mark during the 1923 season. Appropriations for Yellowstone, while not as high as he had hoped, were up significantly. "I am damned proud of this lay-out," Albright wrote to Cammerer in the fall of 1923, "and make no bones about it."[48]

48. HMA to Cammerer, Nov. 29, 1923, HMA Papers.

7

Bears, Princes, and Presidents

Making the transition from the Wilson administration to the
Harding administration in 1921 posed no serious problems for
the hierarchy of the National Park Service, although Mather
and Albright approached the impending changes in the Interior
Department with genuine trepidation. Albert B. Fall, a storytelling, poker-playing, big-dealing westerner, one of Harding's
Senate cronies, was slated to become the new Secretary of the
Interior. "Naturally we are in a pretty uncertain state of mind
just now," Albright wrote to Lorimer in February 1921. He
apparently feared that all Park Service jobs, which had not
yet been blanketed under civil service, would soon be filled
with political appointees and that Mather's own position might
be in jeopardy. Working quietly with Congressman J. A. Elston
of California, and with a few well-known conservationists and
journalists, Albright attempted to bolster Mather's position as
the Republicans took office in March. "The main thing to emphasize," Albright explained to Edmund Seymour, president of
the American Bison Society, who had agreed to buttonhole Fall,
"is that the National Park Service is a semitechnical bureau
made up of men who know and love the national parks and who
are working for the Government primarily because they are interested in the parks . . . rather than because of the salaries that
the jobs pay." It would be "particularly important," Albright
pointed out, "to emphasize what Director Mather has done and
how exceedingly important it is that he be retained." During his
first week in office, Secretary Fall received dozens of letters supporting Mather, and a flock of editorials appeared in print,

suggesting that Mather be continued in office. Fall was obviously impressed. "Everything seems to be in fine shape," Elston informed Albright, "although [Mather] ought to play the game with Fall the same way that he played it with Lane," allowing for some "give and take." Not until the end of March did Albright relax. "Had short but interesting conference with Secretary this afternoon," Mather wired his assistant on March 30, 1921. "Attitude very favorable and expressed much interest. No intention of making radical changes." Albright's own position, as well as Mather's, now seemed secure.[1]

Toward the end of the 1921 summer season, Mather persuaded Fall to accompany him on a tour of the entire national park system. As the two men progressed from Rocky Mountain Park to Mesa Verde to Zion Canyon, Mather subjected Fall to a constant and remarkably effective stream of park propaganda. In southern California, Harry Chandler, publisher of the Los Angeles *Times,* and other successful businessmen extolled the virtues of the National Park Service. In San Francisco and Seattle the same thing happened, as park enthusiasts and Mather's friends rallied unanimously behind him. Above all, as Mather had anticipated, the national parks sold themselves to the new Secretary.[2]

The high point of the tour came in Yellowstone, where Albright was primed and ready to entertain the jovial, gregarious Fall. The Secretary's party spent a week in the park, making overnight stops at Old Faithful, Lake Yellowstone, the Grand Canyon of Yellowstone, and Mammoth Springs. Albright casually steered Fall down to the Jackson Hole and Teton country, observing in a matter-of-fact way that this scenic area would soon be in the park system. On the road back to Lake Yellowstone, he pointed out the loveliness of the Falls-Bechler region. Two days later, with Fall proudly demonstrating his skill as a horse-

1. HMA to G. H. Lorimer, Feb. 8, 1921, HMA to Edward Seymour, Feb. 7, 1921, Seymour to HMA, Feb. 8, 1921, J. A. Elston to HMA, Mar. 5, 1921, and telegram, Mather to HMA, Mar. 30, 1921, quoted in HMA to W. B. Lewis, Mar. 31, 1921, HMA Papers.
2. Shankland, *Steve Mather,* pp. 217–21.

man, the party pushed into the wild Absaroka range, bedding down in the forest at night and observing wildlife conditions during the daylight hours. Albright and his Yellowstone rangers were pleasantly surprised by the cordiality and generosity of the new Secretary and his wife. Albright's favorite anecdote in the autumn of 1921 was about Mrs. Fall's pitching in with the cooking at the Snake River ranger station and teaching the rangers "how to make doughnuts, using a simple recipe that can be employed at all times of the year" and under the primitive conditions of a trail camp.[3]

The Secretary's party left Yellowstone with warm feelings toward the National Park Service. Unmistakable proof that Mather and Albright had made a favorable impression came in the next session of Congress when Fall opposed a series of proposed reclamation projects to be built in Yellowstone. Albright knew perfectly well that the Secretary's sympathy and friendship, no matter how satisfying and rewarding, were no substitute for a thoroughgoing commitment to conservation goals, but they were better than nothing. While Fall had no clear understanding of the need for conservation—he continued to believe in the rapid and relatively unregulated development of the West's natural resources—he generally supported the National Park Service during his years as Secretary. His timely backing of the parks, Albright suggested forty years later, was "one of the phases of Fall's career that someday ought to be written up."[4]

Evidently Mather and Albright convinced Secretary Fall of the economic advantages of the national parks to a degree that exceeded their expectations. During the early months of 1922, Fall unexpectedly proposed the establishment of an "All-Year National Park" in New Mexico, in the vicinity of his own ranch. His idea, as he explained it to Cammerer, was to set up "another class of parks," attractively located but of less scenic grandeur

3. HMA to E. C. Finney, Oct. 23, 1921, HMA Papers; park circular no. 26, Nov. 14, 1921, attached to "Yellowstone Monthly Report" (Nov. 1921); Livingston *Enterprise*, Sept. 8, 1921.
4. Shankland, *Steve Mather*, pp. 218–21; Ise, *Our National Park Policy*, pp. 296–97, 314–16; HMA, "Reminiscences," p. 91.

than Yellowstone, Yosemite, and most of the other existing national parks, by picking up "scattered pieces of the public domain here and there . . . wherever there was a fine piece of scenery." He contended that among the existing parks "the Hot Springs and Platt were really not National Parks in the larger sense" and that therefore his scheme was not necessarily a departure from the established Park Service pattern. Fall's description of Hot Springs and Platt admittedly hit the mark, but what really worried Mather and Albright was the fact that the Secretary planned to sanction hunting, grazing, mineral prospecting, lumbering, and reservoir construction inside the proposed all-year park, a policy that would establish the very precedent that the Mather men had fought desperately to avert in Yellowstone. Mather dutifully went with Fall to inspect the proposed New Mexico park site, an area that swung in a disjointed horseshoe around the Secretary's personal land holdings. "I don't see how the thing is workable at all," Mather wrote to Albright, indicating that he planned to oppose the scheme. Albright himself stalled when Fall asked him to tour the suggested park territory.[5]

Relying heavily upon his standing as an ex-senator, Fall quickly pushed a bill through the Senate authorizing the all-year park. Meanwhile, the Park Service leadership remained officially silent as required by departmental protocol. Knowing full well that Mather's bureau was united against the proposed park, Fall took personal command of the drive to get his bill passed by the House. He charitably refused to order Mather to support him. J. Horace McFarland, George Bird Grinnell, and Bob Yard led the open opposition to the bill, while the Park Service contributed tacit but telling behind-the-scenes opposition. The bill died in the House, with Congressman Carl Hayden taking a prominent part in its burial. Albright admired the way Fall handled himself in this episode. The Secretary pressed relentlessly for his own bill, yet he refrained from taking any action that would have required the Park Service hierarchy, including

5. Cammerer to HMA, July 22, 1922, Mather to HMA, May 8, 1922, and HMA to Mather, May 16, 1922, HMA Papers.

the field assistant to the director, to resign. Albright repaid Fall's political courtesy later in the decade by refusing to believe that Senator Walsh's Teapot Dome investigation amounted to anything more than a questionable political maneuver. Past experience had conditioned him to be suspicious of Walsh's political motives.[6]

Fall resigned from the cabinet in 1923 to return to his New Mexico ranch, where he planned to retire. There was no scandal or dishonor immediately connected with his resignation, although Walsh doggedly continued his investigation into Fall's policies and actions as Secretary. Early in 1924, the senator uncovered circumstantial evidence that Fall had conspired to lease the underground Naval Oil Reserves, at Teapot Dome in Wyoming and Elk Hills in California, to Harry F. Sinclair and Edward L. Doheny in return for $400,000 in "loans." It soon became apparent, moreover, that Fall had lied in his testimony before the investigating committee in a misguided attempt to protect his friends and cover up for the Republican party in an election year. As the scandal deepened Albright privately defended Fall, refusing to believe that the former Secretary was guilty of malfeasance in office and continuing to suspect the political motives of the men investigating Fall.[7]

Indeed, recent scholarly studies have tended to confirm that Fall was to some degree a victim of circumstances. His decision to lease the naval oil reserves probably came as a result of his overriding conviction that the West should rapidly develop its own natural resources, and not because of any money that changed hands. The Pinchot conservationists wanted Fall censured because his policies posed a real threat to their own conservation philosophy, which had been largely implemented on the public domain. In this respect, the Teapot Dome scandal was reminiscent of the Ballinger-Pinchot controversy of 1910 in

6. Cammerer to HMA, July 22, 1922, and HMA to E. C. Finney, May 24, 1922, HMA Papers; U.S., Congress, House, Hearing Before the Committee on Indian Affairs, "Mescolero National Park Project," 67th Cong., 4th sess. (Dec. 14, 1922, and Jan. 11 and 12, 1923), pp. 45–95.
7. HMA to E. C. Finney, May 24, 1922, HMA Papers.

which the Pinchot clique charged a previous Secretary of the Interior with corruption because he rejected their guidelines for the administration of the public domain. Albright naturally tended to take sides against the Pinchot clique because of his respect for Fall and because of his own conservation philosophy, which spurned the emphatic utilitarianism of Pinchot's disciples.[8]

On the basis of the same incriminating legal evidence, Fall was convicted of accepting bribes but both Doheny and Sinclair, the men who allegedly gave him the tainted money, were acquitted. Albright maintained that Fall, though admittedly not a conservationist, had served creditably as Secretary of the Interior. From time to time in the 1930s and early 1940s, Albright visited the ill and impoverished Fall, who spent his last years in a veterans' hospital in Texas.[9]

An unheralded reason for Fall's leniency toward the National Park Service during the political fight over the proposed all-year park was the fact that Mather, whom Fall held in high esteem, suffered another nervous collapse shortly after returning from his trip to New Mexico in the spring of 1922. Remorseful and worried by the prospect of being forced to establish a park that did not measure up to his high standards, and fatigued after another long period of strain, he became gloomy and deeply despondent in the same pattern as occurred in 1917. This time Cammerer, as the assistant director in Washington, had to handle Mather's affairs. He persuaded his chief to go to Darien, Connecticut, where the Mathers maintained a summer home, for a period of extended rest. Within a few days Mather placed himself in a sanitarium and called in a psychiatrist, hoping that by obtaining early treatment he could avoid the prolonged

8. David Hodges Stratton, "Albert B. Fall and the Teapot Dome Affair" (Ph. D. diss., University of Colorado, 1955), pp. 509–15; Burl Noggle, *Teapot Dome: Oil and Politics in the 1920's,* pp. vii–ix, 200–215; J. Leonard Bates, *The Origins of Teapot Dome: Progressives, Parties, and Petroleum, 1909–1921,* pp. 236–44; see also Penick, *Progressive Politics and Conservation.*

9. Shankland, *Steve Mather,* pp. 217–22; interview with HMA, July 24, 1964.

mental anguish he had endured in 1903 and 1917. But the illness ran precisely the same course it had in the two previous attacks. He found it nearly impossible to make decisions or articulate his ideas. He worried obsessively about his personal financial affairs. His recovery would take at least six months and there would inevitably follow a period of uncertainty about whether he should continue as director.[10]

Even before his 1922 attack, Mather had begun to talk about retiring. Now his wife initiated an all-out effort to induce him to quit, for she believed that his condition resulted largely from overwork in the Park Service. Mather expended a prodigious amount of energy in everything he did, whether it was business, national park affairs, or simply vacationing. Forcing him to retire would have served no therapeutic purpose. On the contrary, encouraging him to look forward to resuming his work in the National Park Service proved to be a powerful stimulus toward his recovery. To Albright's immense relief, Mather, exuberant and in excellent health, returned to the directorship in January 1923. Albright would have come under intense pressure to take over as director had Mather made up his mind to resign. Vastly preferring to remain in Yellowstone, the young man had firmly resolved to refuse the Park Service directorship, if proffered. In the meantime, Cammerer stood in for Mather, serving as the acting director from May 1922 to January 1923.[11]

Mather showed his gratitude to Albright and Cammerer a few months after returning to Washington by giving each of them a sizable block of common stock in his reorganized borax company. His object was to keep his two main assistants happy and solvent in government service. Unfortunately for all concerned, Mather's company soon stopped paying dividends and by the

10. Cammerer to HMA, July 2, 1922, Oliver Mitchell to Cammerer, July 14, 1922, and Mitchell to HMA, July 14, 1922, HMA Papers.
11. Cammerer to HMA, July 2, 1922, Mitchell to HMA, July 14, 1922, HMA to Cammerer, Sept. 4, 1922, and Oct. 22, 1922, J. O. LaGorce to HMA, Oct. 5, 1922, Lorimer to HMA, Oct. 16, 1922, HMA to Frances Farquhar, Oct. 14, 1922, William F. Bade to HMA, Aug. 8, 1922, and HMA to Bade, Nov. 3, 1922, HMA Papers.

late 1920s was in serious financial difficulties, its ore deposits having been largely depleted.[12]

As the Harding administration matured, reflecting the nation's feverish search for "normalcy" and stability, Albright found the new mood of the federal establishment surprisingly congenial. While still professing a sincere admiration for Woodrow Wilson, he felt entirely at ease in the business-dominated Republican ascendancy of the 1920s. His entrepreneurial instincts came into play increasingly as time passed and as he continued to observe Mather in action. Quietly and cautiously, he began purchasing a few shares of preferred stock in nonspeculative public utilities corporations, such as Pacific Gas and Electric and the Montana Power Company. The fact that the power companies in which he invested were not renowned for their devotion to the ideals and objectives of aesthetic conservation never seemed to trouble him.[13]

Not only as an individual but also as a government administrator, Albright adapted himself easily to the changing times. His normal impulse was to strive for an accommodation with all individuals and groups voicing criticism of the national parks. But this was not the way he reacted to the Ku Klux Klan, which became powerful in rural districts near Yellowstone in the early 1920s. He let the organization know in no uncertain terms that he would brook no interference with his administration of the park. He "flatly refused" to join the Klan himself, although certain local businessmen pressured him to do so. He rejected the Klan's demand that all Roman Catholics on the park staff be fired, and threatened instead to dismiss any of his employees who associated themselves with the Klan. In only one enterprise, namely, enforcing the prohibition laws, did Albright cooperate with the Klan—and this was to his own advantage. In Montana the only subject that aroused the Klan as much or more than anti-Catholicism was the crusade against the demon rum. As

12. HMA to Cammerer, Sept. 24, 1923, and HMA to C. A. Zabriskie, Nov. 29, 1923, HMA Papers; Shankland, *Steve Mather*, pp. 166–67.

13. HMA to W. E. Creed, Mar. 2, 1926, J. P. Thomas to HMA, Aug. 23, 1927, HMA Papers.

the chief federal officer in the Yellowstone preserve, Albright was responsible for enforcing the law and setting an example for everybody else by abstaining from the use of intoxicants. Pragmatically facing up to the gigantic proportions of the enforcement problem in Yellowstone, Albright accepted all the help he could get, including an occasional assist from the Klan, in curbing the flow of illegal liquor into the park. "As in other parts of the country," he observed, "the use of intoxicants in violation of the federal laws is becoming more and more apparent every day, but this is a matter that is extremely hard to regulate." In a majority of cases, he pointed out, "the law does not seem to be backed by public sentiment." By resorting to threats and coercion the Klan got rid of a number of bootleggers around Yellowstone. Albright also worked closely with the United States prohibition agents in Wyoming and Montana, cooperating in intermittent raids on the towns closest to the park and seizing secret caches of "pure poison." Even so, a fair amount of intoxicating liquor got into the park's blood stream, with its effects "occasionally noted among our own employees." Albright had no trouble setting a noble example for his park rangers, for he had been a temperance advocate since boyhood.[14]

By the middle of the 1920s, the day-to-day administrative routine at Yellowstone Park had fallen into a smooth pattern, with Albright's staff and all the park employees working harmoniously to give the public first-rate service. Yellowstone's reputation, not only as an extraordinary exhibition of natural phenomena but also as a pleasant place to spend a vacation, spread across the country. In June of 1923, when the itinerary for President Harding's trip to the West Coast and Alaska was publicly announced, it seemed appropriate that the presidential party planned to stop for two days at Yellowstone Park. Colonel Edmund W. ("Bill") Starling, head of the White House detail of the Secret Service, came to the park about two weeks ahead of Harding to confer with Albright about appropriate security

14. HMA, "Reminiscences," pp. 144–45; HMA Diary, July 30, 1921; "Yellowstone Monthly Report" (Apr. 1921, June 1922, June 1927, and Aug. 1927).

measures. The two men agreed that all traffic in the immediate vicinity of the president would be halted while he moved from place to place and that the tourists should be kept under strict control. Both Secret Service men and park rangers would guard Harding during the one night he was to spend in the park.[15]

The president's special train pulled into Gardiner, Montana, at six o'clock in the morning, June 30, 1923, carrying a party of seventy-two people, including Henry C. Wallace, the Secretary of Agriculture, Hubert Work, the new Secretary of the Interior, and approximately three dozen newsmen. Albright stepped aboard the train to meet the president, emerging at half-past seven to guide the Hardings to a waiting motorcade. Harding was ceremoniously "escorted through the entrance arch by a mounted guard of eleven rangers," as motion picture cameras "duly recorded" the event. This was a big moment for the National Park Service. Not since the days of Theodore Roosevelt had a president visited one of the national parks.[16]

Harding's party saw the standard sights in Yellowstone, with Albright personally leading the way. They toured Mammoth Springs, the Upper Geyser Basin, the Lake area, and both rims of Yellowstone Canyon. They viewed the Teton Mountains from afar (spontaneously the president announced his support for the park extension plan), and they watched Old Faithful geyser erupt. The day ended at Old Faithful Inn, where the president and his wife spent the night. The highlight of the next day came at the fish hatchery near Lake Yellowstone when two black bears (thoughtfully cornered in advance by the Park Service) romped down out of a tree in front of the bemused president, who then playfully fed the animals and posed for news photographers. An hour or two before sunset, Harding's party entrained again at Gardiner. The president capped the day by making a short, extemporaneous speech to a crowd gathered at the depot in Liv-

15. "Yellowstone Monthly Report" (June 1923), pp. 31–32, and attached park circular no. 47, June 26, 1923; HMA, "Reminiscences," pp. 149–50.

16. "Yellowstone Monthly Report" (June 1923), p. 31; HMA, "Reminiscences," p. 151; the arch through which Harding passed was dedicated in 1903 by President Theodore Roosevelt.

ingston, Montana, about sixty miles north of the park. Mixed liberally with his sonorous platitudes about God and Nature were references to the "great Yellowstone National Park" and to a "mother grouse" and her "little grouse chicks." Harding's brief visit to the park generated more column inches of publicity about Yellowstone and the Tetons than any other event during Albright's tenure as superintendent.[17]

About a month after Harding's departure from Yellowstone, a telephone call from the Associated Press informed Albright of the president's death in San Francisco. Albright could not entirely suppress his feelings of regret that the Park Service would not be able to capitalize on having inoculated the president of the United States with an enthusiasm for the national parks.[18]

Although the Park Service lost a potential friend when Harding died, it acquired an extraordinary new benefactor in the summer of 1924 when John D. Rockefeller, Jr., visited Yellowstone and went away wondering how he might assist the superintendent in enhancing and preserving the park's natural beauty. He had previously purchased several parcels of land for Acadia National Park in Maine, but this trip marked his full entry into national park philanthropy. The Washington office of the Park Service advised Albright that Rockefeller would arrive in Yellowstone in July, but his instructions stated emphatically that he was to insure quiet and privacy for the celebrated philanthropist and "not to present any park problems" to him. Albright scrupulously obeyed these instructions. He went to Gardiner to meet Rockefeller, whose party included his three older sons, John, Nelson, and Laurance, ages eighteen, sixteen, and fourteen. After searching vainly for a private railroad car, which he

17. "Yellowstone Monthly Report" (June 1923), pp. 32–33; clipping from Hutchinson, Kansas *News*, July 2, 1923, HMA Papers; HMA, "Reminiscences," pp. 151–58; quotations from Warren G. Harding, *Speeches and Addresses of Warren G. Harding ... Delivered during the Course of His Tour from Washington, D.C., to Alaska ...*, pp. 224–28.
18. "Yellowstone Monthly Report" (Aug. 1923), pp. 21–22 and attached park circular no. 51, Aug. 10, 1923; HMA, "Reminiscences," pp. 158–59.

assumed the family would be using, Albright found the Rockefellers disembarking from a regular Pullman. John was metic-
ulously recording a tip he had just given the porter, and Nelson
and Laurance were helping to carry everybody's baggage across
the platform and into the waiting buses. The party was traveling
under the name Davison. Albright drove Rockefeller to park
headquarters in his official car, but the boys rode in the buses
with the other passengers.[19]

Once inside the park, Albright made certain that the "Davison's" reservations were in order and then left the family completely alone. They toured the park for three days and quietly
departed via Cody, Wyoming. This was the beginning of a
cordial and remarkably productive friendship between Albright
and Rockefeller.[20]

Approximately a month after his departure, Rockefeller wrote
to Albright thanking him for his courtesy and inquiring about
why the roadsides in the park were so terribly cluttered with old
logs and dead brush. Albright explained that the unsightly lit-
tering had occurred when the roads were originally constructed.
The Park Service, he added "had been very unhappy about
those roadsides for years and had tried to get money from Congress to clear them up" but to no avail. Rockefeller responded
by suggesting the possibility of undertaking an experimental
project to determine the cost per mile of clearing up the debris,
and he offered to foot the bill. In September 1924 the work
began, "under instructions from a wealthy friend of Yellowstone
National Park." The pilot cleanup project, on a stretch of road
between Mammoth Springs and Norris Geyser Basin, demonstrated both the soundness and the aesthetic value of Rockefeller's plan. Over the next four years, the anonymous "wealthy
friend" provided the money for a systematic cleanup of all the
major roads in the park. At the same time, Albright wheedled
funds from Congress to finance the removal of the park's telephone lines from along the roadsides to new, well-hidden loca-

19. "Yellowstone Monthly Report" (July 1924), p. 42; HMA, "Reminiscences," pp. 212–19.
20. HMA, "Reminiscences," pp. 212–19.

tions in the forests. The results were so dramatic and aesthetically pleasing that Congress eventually appropriated money for roadside cleanups in several other parks, and the National Park Service henceforth included the cost of debris disposal as a legitimate part of its construction estimates for all new roads in the national parks. Rockefeller also contributed generously toward the construction of museums in Yellowstone, one of Albright's pet educational projects. In all of his early dealings with Rockefeller, Albright displayed independence of mind, administrative ingenuity, and absolute reliability. Rockefeller soon came to respect his young friend's judgment and integrity.[21]

The Rockefeller family returned to Yellowstone Park for a twelve-day vacation in July 1926, and this time Albright spent several days with them, guiding them around the park and arranging for a special camping trip to Grasshopper Glacier. Mrs. Rockefeller and the three younger sons in the family, Laurance, Winthrop, and David, rounded out the party. Albright showed them the progress already being made in cleaning up the cluttered roadsides in the park. Then he took them down to the Jackson Hole country and spent two days showing them the valley. There was no doubt about the purpose of the trip, although Albright initially avoided talking about his hopes for the region. The first afternoon he took Mr. and Mrs. Rockefeller to a hillside above Jackson Lake and sat with them for more than two hours as the sun moved behind the Teton range and cast a long shadow across Jackson Hole. It was a magnificent sight, with wild moose feeding contentedly in the marshes near the lake. The following morning, under a superbly clear sky and bright sun, the party drove along the road from Moran to Jack-

21. "Yellowstone Monthly Report" (Sept. 1924), p. 13, and (June 1925), p. 21; Rockefeller to HMA, Oct. 16, 1924, and Sept. 16, 1926, "Annual Report for Yellowstone National Park, 1928," p. 215, HMA Papers; HMA, "Reminiscences," pp. 219–22, 234–36; *Annual Report, NPS* (1925), p. 19 (1926), p. 17; Raymond B. Fosdick, *John D. Rockefeller, Jr.: A Portrait*, pp. 308–9; Michael Frome, "Portrait of a Conserver," *Westways* 56 (Oct. 1964) : 27 (© 1964, by the Automobile Club of Southern California), all quotations from this work are reprinted by permission.

son, skirting Jenny Lake and getting a close-up view of the Teton range. The scenery "made a profound impression on my guests," Albright later recalled, but a dilapidated gasoline station, a tawdry dance hall, and a cluster of nondescript cabins along the road "horrified" the Rockefellers, who expressed their dismay that "this glorious country was rapidly being marred" by tasteless and obnoxious commercial development. Albright explained that all of these "unsightly structures" stood "on private holdings" and that the prospect was for more of them to be constructed as an increasing number of tourists came into the area. A grotesque configuration of telephone poles rose between the road and the mountains, destroying the view. Rockefeller asked how much money it would take to buy up these properties. Albright replied that he did not know but that he would find out and send the information to Rockefeller's headquarters in New York in the fall. On the way back to Yellowstone that afternoon, Albright steered his guests to a bluff over-looking the Snake River and there told them of his "dream" to "protect and preserve" all of "this sublime valley," a dream that could be realized easily enough, he pointed out, by acquiring the privately owned lands, mostly ranches, north of Jackson and putting them under the jurisdiction of the Park Service or some other federal agency.[22]

Essentially, this was a plan that Burt, Carncross, Richard Winger, Maude Noble, J. R. Jones, Cy Ferrin, and Jack Eynon, all residents of Jackson Hole, had suggested to him in 1923 in the hope that donations could be obtained from private sources to purchase the ranch lands and preserve them from ruinous commercial exploitation. But by 1926 only a few thousand dollars had been raised. Furthermore, two high-powered federal commissions—a special coordinating commission appointed by the President's Outdoor Recreation Committee and the Jackson Hole Elk Commission—had studied various aspects of the

22. "Yellowstone Monthly Report" (July 1926), pp. 22–23; HMA to Cammerer, Aug. 20, 1926, and Rockefeller to HMA, Sept. 16, 1926, HMA Papers; HMA to Neilson, in 1938 Hearings; HMA, "Reminiscences," pp. 223–26.

problem of how best to preserve the unique scenic and wildlife qualities of the Jackson Hole country but had failed to bring the warring factions in Jackson together. By the time of Rockefeller's visit in 1926, Albright had decided that all public boards and commissions were impotent in the face of the powerful vested interests and grass-roots opposition that had developed. He was more than ever determined that Jackson Hole must be saved. The Rockefellers "did not make any comments on the proposal," Albright remembered, "nor did I ask for their support. None of us mentioned the subject again."[23]

The Rockefellers left Yellowstone on July 25, after spending their last evening at the Albright's home. "We are thinking with truest pleasure," Rockefeller wired from Chicago, "of our wonderful visit to the park made doubly enjoyable by your many courtesies and unfailing kindness."[24]

Undoubtedly, the summer of 1926 was Albright's busiest season in Yellowstone. Only two weeks before Rockefeller's arrival, he had entertained Gustaf, the crown prince of Sweden, for a memorable eight-day visit. A great fisherman, an enthusiastic camper, and an avid photographer, the prince found Yellowstone's scenery and wildlife exactly to his liking. Albright took him to Peale Island in Lake Yellowstone, one of the best fishing places in the park, and hiked with him along the beautiful forest trails. On the road to the top of Mount Washburn, Albright pointed out some rare mountain sheep; the prince immediately suggested that they try to obtain a close-up motion picture sequence of the shy creatures. The two men squirmed on their bellies through the rocks for several hundred yards toward the sheep, skinning their elbows and wearing holes in their clothes, but the prince returned triumphantly with his pictures.[25]

The tour of the royal party, which ended in the Jackson Hole country, was a success from every angle. The prince obviously

23. HMA to Neilson, in 1938 Hearings; HMA, "Reminiscences," pp. 226–29, 237–39; HMA to Estelle Schiveley, June 22, 1926, and Rockefeller to HMA, Sept. 16, 1926, HMA Papers.

24. Telegram, Rockefeller to HMA, July 28, 1926, HMA Papers.

25. HMA, "Reminiscences," pp. 173–76.

enjoyed himself, and he developed a warm regard for Albright, whose talents as a fisherman, storyteller, and tour guide were never more skillfully marshaled. Gustaf showed his gratitude a few months later by persuading his father, the king of Sweden, to confer on Albright the Royal Order of the Northern Star, to be held by the United States State Department until the park superintendent retired from government service and could accept the award. From Mather's point of view, the prince's tour was important because it "attracted so much publicity about the park," especially among Scandinavian-Americans, who flocked to Yellowstone "by the thousands" that summer. Albright pronounced his visitor "a royal good fellow" and made him an honorary park ranger.[26]

The founder of the Forest Service, Gifford Pinchot, then governor of Pennsylvania, also spent some time in the park in 1926, following a conference of governors in Cheyenne, Wyoming. "I rounded up some old time foresters" who had served with Pinchot in his Forest Service days, Albright remembered, and got them together for a long talk. The next morning Albright breakfasted with Pinchot and was amused to discover "that this famous fiery Gifford Pinchot," like many another hapless husband, "was not quite boss in his own household." He had enjoyed talking conservation with Albright and the foresters, and he wanted to stay over for another day. But Mrs. Pinchot, a formidable redhead, announced that they were taking "the first bus out of here after breakfast." And so they did, much to Albright's regret. He rather hoped to be able to persuade Pinchot to back the Park Service's plan for Jackson Hole and the Grand Tetons. In future years, Albright had very little contact with Pinchot. The Forest Service, after all, was the enemy, and courtesy could be extended only so far.[27]

26. HMA to F. E. Williamson, July 8, 1926, W. Bostrom to HMA, Nov. 18, 1926, and HMA to Bostrom, Nov. 24, 1926, HMA Papers; "Yellowstone Monthly Report" (July 1926), pp. 21–22; HMA, "Reminiscences," pp. 173–76.

27. Nellie Tayloe Ross to HMA, Sept. 1, 1926, and HMA to Ross, Sept. 21, 1926, HMA Papers; "Yellowstone Monthly Report" (July 1926), p. 23; HMA, "Reminiscences," pp. 165–67.

Had the Pennsylvania governor persuaded his strong-willed wife to let him stay in Yellowstone for another day, Albright would have had no time for proselytizing about Jackson Hole. Disastrous forest fires were raging out of control in Glacier Park, and Albright received an urgent telegram from the Assistant Secretary of the Interior ordering him to Glacier to head up the massive fire-fighting operation just getting under way. "Full authority is given to you to act in the situation," the wire stated. A prolonged drought had turned Glacier into a dangerous tinderbox, and Albright faced a demanding task in bringing the fires under control. He stayed in the park for three weeks, sweating profusely in the heat of the fires, regularly wiring Washington for more money, and commanding an ever-increasing army of skilled and unskilled firemen. "We'd pick them off railroads, riding the freight cars, we'd get them wherever we could. Then we'd look them over to see if they were suitable for fire fighting, load them into trucks and start them out to the fires, and if they were put on the trucks they were put on the payroll." One day Albright was startled to find that he had just signed on "Jesus Christ," a big, swarthy fellow of Mexican origin, as one of his temporary fire fighters. "All right, you're hired," he snapped, "but, Christ, we'd like to have you bring us a little rain."[28]

When Albright returned to Yellowstone in September 1926, he was "almost disappointed" to discover that the park had "run so smoothly" while he was gone. Owing to the "vigilance" of his staff, he informed the director, "conditions in the park were splendid," and there was no doubt that "the whole place was well operated throughout the month." In high spirits once again, he took the oath as "Assistant Director of the National Park Service (Field)," a well-deserved promotion that reflected his expanding responsibilities as coordinator and troubleshooter for all of the western parks. His salary now stood at "$5400 per annum less $400 per annum for quarters." The Secretary of the Interior designated him "ex officio Superintendent of Yellowstone

28. Telegram, John H. Edwards to HMA, July 31, 1926, and HMA to Cammerer, Aug. 20, 1926, HMA Papers; HMA, "Reminiscences," pp. 171–72, 176–78.

National Park," an official subterfuge that allowed him to continue as superintendent in fact. His salary still came out of the Yellowstone budget.[29]

All of this frantic activity during the last part of the 1926 season prevented Albright from getting on with his Jackson Hole scheme. He had simply not had enough time to begin collecting the information that Rockefeller had requested about the value of privately owned lands in the Jackson Hole region. As soon as possible after his return to Yellowstone, Albright asked Richard Winger, one of the men who, in 1923, had helped him draw up the plan that Rockefeller found appealing, to prepare both a map showing the private holdings along the western side of the Snake River and a detailed statement of probable purchase costs, which totaled about $250,000. Albright went to Washington early in November armed with this information. On November 20 he caught the train to New York for a conference with Rockefeller about the Jackson Hole proposal. The philanthropist scanned the map that Albright handed to him and said: "Mr. Albright, you haven't given me what I want." From the beginning, he explained, he had contemplated "an ideal project"—buying up the land on both sides of the Snake River—and therefore he would not be interested in the smaller-scale proposal portrayed on Albright's map. "You can imagine what a shock this was to me," Albright later exclaimed. Colonel Arthur Woods, Rockefeller's executive assistant during the 1920s, loved to describe how Albright "staggered" into his office later that day, "completely overwhelmed" by the fact that he had tried to interest Rockefeller in a $250,000 project and had "accidentally sold him one worth more than a million."[30]

Albright dispatched a message to Winger asking him to send the additional information, and on February 16, 1927, Rockefeller received a new collection of maps and data. "I think I am now in a position," Albright wrote in his cover letter, "to give

29. HMA to Cammerer, Aug. 20, 1926, Hubert Work to HMA, Aug. 9, 1926, and HMA to Secretary of the Interior, Sept. 17, 1926, HMA Papers; "Yellowstone Monthly Report" (Aug. 1926), p. 1.

30. HMA to Neilson, in 1938 Hearings; Rockefeller to HMA, Nov. 17, 1926, and telegram, HMA to Rockefeller, Nov. 19, 1926, HMA Papers; HMA, "Reminiscences," pp. 226–28.

you a definite program of action on the Teton Mountain and Jackson Hole land question." He had carefully consulted Struthers Burt as well as Winger before spelling out his proposals. There were about four hundred landowners in the Jackson Hole, he wrote, holding "a little over 100,000 acres." The total value of the land was "perhaps $1,000,000," but he could "not say what it could be acquired for." He suggested that a dummy "recreation and hunting club" or a "land and cattle company" be established to take control of all land purchases and mask both Rockefeller's identity and his long-range intent, which was to remove the lands from commercial use and turn them over to the National Park Service. At first, Albright suggested, all acquisitions should be confined to the area "west of the Snake River." It was imperative, he warned, that Rockefeller "say nothing, at the present time, about the larger or ultimate plan of acquiring all of the private holdings in the Jackson Hole" because land prices would skyrocket and local opposition would undoubtedly harden if the news leaked out. He said he "had in mind" retaining the Salt Lake City law firm of Fabian and Clendenin, "men of unimpeachable integrity and judgment," to handle the necessary legal transactions. "Mr. Clendenin I have known since childhood," Albright added. "We were classmates in college and closest chums. He and his partner would act in this matter on a very narrow margin of cost." In closing, Albright cautioned Rockefeller about certain hazards that might complicate the project, especially the fact that Congrss would have to enact the "final" administrative policy for the lands in question, "and none may be adopted." He had written at length, he concluded, "not with any idea of trying to urge favorable action but just to give you this big park and wildlife-preserve plan as we have visualized it. I think if it could be consummated, it would go down in history as the greatest conservation project of its kind ever undertaken."[31]

Albright had acted with the best of motives. He had long

31. HMA to John D. Rockefeller, Jr., Feb. 16, 1927, in U.S., Congress, Senate, Hearings Before the Committee on Public Lands and Surveys, "Enlarging Grand Teton National Park in Wyoming," 75th Cong., 3d sess. (Aug. 1938), pp. 106–8.

dreamed of preserving this splendid area for the enjoyment of future generations of Americans, a goal that he and countless others considered noble. His procedural advice to Rockefeller was sound and pragmatic, designed to insure the accomplishment of a recognizably worthy conservation goal. But he had chosen to maneuver covertly. His emphatic statements about the need for secrecy would come back to bedevil him in the 1930s as his old foes in the Jackson Hole conjured up a conspiracy theory, pitting Albright, the federal bureaucracy, and the "tainted" Rockefeller millions against the "common good," a theme which was used effectively to obstruct congressional acceptance of Rockefeller's proposed gift of land to the federal government.[32]

After studying the matter for several days, Rockefeller notified Albright that he had "decided to undertake the project" for two reasons: "First, in order to restore and preserve the valley landscape which formed the foreground and general setting for the Teton Mountains, and, second, to aid in the preservation of the wildlife through elimination of fences and other barriers impeding natural drift to winter range and to provide additional winter feeding grounds" for the elk. Albright paused long enough in his jubilation to put Rockefeller in touch with Fabian and Clendenin in Salt Lake City. On May 26, 1927, Kenneth Chorley, one of Rockefeller's assistants, and Vanderbilt Webb, from Rockefeller's legal staff, met with Harold P. Fabian in Salt Lake City and retained him as their counsel. At the same time Robert E. Miller, a Jackson banker and real estate man, agreed to act as purchasing agent for the Rockefeller group. On July 7, President Calvin Coolidge withdrew from entry virtually all of the unappropriated public lands at the northern end of Jackson Hole, following a quiet conference in Washington at which Chorley explained the purpose of the undertaking to Hubert Work, Secretary of the Interior, and William B. Greeley, chief

32. For examples of the opposition to Albright in Jackson see the statements and newspaper articles printed in U.S., Congress, Senate, Hearings, "Enlarging Grand Teton National Park in Wyoming," pp. 171–73, 232–55.

forester. On August 23, Miller was authorized to begin making purchases, and two days later Fabian organized the Snake River Land Company, a Utah corporation, "solely for the purpose of acquiring and holding temporarily the lands being purchased." Rockefeller earmarked one million dollars for the project.[33]

At this point, neither Fabian nor Miller knew the identity of the man for whom they were acting, but they had been assured that the lands to be purchased would "be devoted to the use and enjoyment of the public." Early in the fall of 1927, after Fabian and Miller had been retained and the Snake River Land Company organized, Albright bowed out. He was "merely kept advised of progress made in land acquisitions."[34]

By late summer 1927, rumors about the purpose of the Snake River Land Company had begun to circulate in the Jackson Hole region, and "the people in Jackson were quite agitated about it." Webb and Chorley then decided that the elected officials of Wyoming, including Governor Frank C. Emerson, Senator John B. Kendrick, Congressman Charles E. Winter, and former Congressman Mondell, should be fully informed about the reasons for the company's purchases. A "round table conference in Washington on the entire Snake River Land Company project" on December 2, 1927, attended by the full Wyoming delegation, seemed to clear the air. Miller started making land purchases in earnest early in 1928. Rockefeller's association with the project was confirmed publicly for the first time in 1930. By 1933, in spite of a loud chorus of opposition led by attorney Milward L. Simpson, cattleman Ben F. Gillette, Senator Robert D. Carey, and the *Grand Teton*, a Jackson newspaper that was relentlessly opposed to the undertaking, the Snake River Land Company had purchased approximately thirty-five thousand acres of land in the Jackson Hole at a total cost of about $1,400,-000. The *Grand Teton's* oft-repeated charge was that the people of Jackson Hole had been secretly "betrayed by Horace M. Al-

33. Harold P. Fabian to Wilford W. Neilson, Apr. 6, 1933, in ibid. (hereafter cited as Fabian to Neilson, in 1938 Hearings), pp. 21–25; HMA to Neilson, in 1938 Hearings.

34. HMA to Neilson, in 1938 Hearings.

bright" into the hands of "Mr. Rockefeller and his interests."
The Jackson Hole country was on the way toward eventual inclusion in the national park system, but more than two decades
of hard political fighting lay ahead before the issue would finally
be resolved.[35]

Throughout the 1920s Albright tried to persuade wealthy
businessmen to take a philanthropic interest in the national
parks. "I don't want you to think that I am trying to get the park
into the hands of Wall Street," he wrote to Mather, "but I believe that it is a fine thing to get rich men . . . spending some of
their wealth in this conservation work." In the fall of 1922 he
approached Thomas Cochran, of J. P. Morgan and Co., with a
proposal to buy up all of the private holdings along Slough
Creek, just north of the park, in an effort to solve a serious problem in wildlife protection in that part of Yellowstone. Joseph
("Frenchy") Duret, a notorious game poacher, owned most of
this land, and he had been a "thorn in the side of the park administration" for many years. Duret was always "watched very
carefully" by Albright's men "during his journeys back and forth
through the park." After a wounded grizzly bear mauled Duret
to death in June 1922, Albright saw a chance to solve one of his
long-standing administrative problems. First, he ingratiated himself to Mrs. Duret by satisfactorily establishing the cause of her
husband's death and by making all the arrangements for Duret's
funeral. Albright then convinced Cochran, who visited Yellowstone in September 1922, to buy out the widow and all other
private owners in the vicinity. The purchase price was "13,000
cash," a fair market price, for 550 acres to be held in common by
Cochran and his silent partners, William Pierson Hamilton and
Solomon R. Guggenheim, who would maintain it as a vacation
retreat and would cooperate fully with the National Park Service
on all administrative matters. Albright and Billie Nichols, of the
Yellowstone Park Hotel and Transportation Companies, handled
the legal transaction free of charge. For the "first time in years

35. Fabian to Neilson, in 1938 Hearings; articles from *Grand Teton*,
May 9, 1933, and May 16, 1933, in 1938 Hearings, pp. 231–55, quotation
from p. 246.

Slough Creek will cease to give us worry in our protection work,"
Albright noted with delight.[36]

In this arrangement and in the Rockefeller purchases in Jackson Hole, Albright had been opportunistic. In both cases, he recognized a problem and moved to solve it by the only means immediately available, private philanthropy. Congress was locked in the grip of an obsessive economy crusade during most of the 1920s. Mather and Albright had to look outside of Washington to find the financial resources to develop the parks and to meet special aesthetic or wildlife needs. Under their leadership, the National Park Service, like few other federal agencies, turned to private philanthropy as a source of supplementary financing. The Park Service had already obtained congressional authorization to accept monetary gifts, many of which, in fact, came from Mather himself. Albright scrupulously observed the requirements of the law, depositing all donated funds in the United States Treasury and then drawing against them. But by accepting the help of eastern millionaires, like Rockefeller and Cochran, he opened himself to the charge of working with "the interests" against the "little men" of the West. In the end, Albright had no regrets. He did what he believed he had to do to achieve his goals as an administrator and conservationist. The idea of a possible conflict of interest—a concept only vaguely defined in the 1920s—never entered his mind. One must attempt to understand Albright's distinctive style of bureaucratic leadership—dynamic, unorthodox, high-minded, flexible, opportunistic, and occasionally impetuous—in order to understand the so-called Mather tradition of Park Service leadership.[37]

The fact that he had confidence in his own ability to protect himself in case of adverse political circumstances further encouraged Albright's administrative freewheeling. In 1925, Senator Ralph H. Cameron of Arizona, one of the leading anticonservation spokesmen in the country, had occasion to find out how

36. HMA to Mather, Oct. 3, 1922, Thomas Cochran to HMA, Nov. 8, 1922, and Dec. 13, 1922, and HMA to Cochran, Dec. 17, 1922, HMA Papers; "Yellowstone Monthly Report" (June 1922 and Sept. 1922).
37. Swain, *Federal Conservation Policy*, pp. 141–42.

skillfully Albright could defend his own interests. Cameron had been badgering the National Park Service since 1919, when Congress originally authorized the Grand Canyon National Park. In the midst of a heated controversy over his asserted mining claims in the Canyon, the senator set out "to get" Mather and Albright, using as his main weapon a Senate-authorized investigation of the administration of the public domain. A subcommittee consisting of Senators Cameron, R. N. Stanfield of Oregon, co-sponsor of the probe, John B. Kendrick of Wyoming, and Tasker L. Oddie of Nevada, arrived at Grand Canyon Park in August and held open hearings. Cameron intimidated the superintendent, J. Ross Eakin, and filled the record with unfounded charges against the Park Service hierarchy. Albright and Yellowstone National Park were next on the schedule, although the Senate investigators had not publicly announced their plans to visit the world-famous park. The general passenger agent for the Union Pacific Railroad, D. S. Spencer, tipped Albright off that the Senate subcommittee was on its way.[38]

Albright barely had time to get to the western entrance of the park before the senators arrived. He greeted them cordially, especially Kendrick and Oddie, whom he knew. Then Kendrick departed for a visit to his home in Wyoming, thus missing the fireworks in Yellowstone. Trailing the Senate subcommittee was a *New York Times* reporter, L. C. Speer, who also took pains to warn Albright about the intentions of Cameron and Stanfield. "Those two birds are out to get you," he whispered. Albright responded by inviting the newspaperman to take a day-long tour of the park to see for himself how well it was being run, and he assigned the park's chief engineer as the journalist's chauffeur and guide. Albright next invited the senators to inspect the park. They declined, although Oddie insisted that they at least visit Old Faithful on their way to Gardiner, where the hearings were to be held. One of the committee's staff of attorneys drove directly to park headquarters, rifled through Albright's desk, and

38. HMA, "Reminiscences," pp. 357–65; Shankland, *Steve Mather,* pp. 225–42.

then proceeded to Gardiner, where he rounded up about a dozen witnesses, all of whom had personal grievances against Albright.[39]

The next day, August 29, the hearings began with extended testimony about Albright's alleged dictatorial and wrong-headed administration of the park. He was charged with extending "special privileges" to "members of the firm of J. P. Morgan & Co." He was accused of allowing the park's buffalo herd to be stampeded "for the benefit of movie producers" during the filming of "The Thundering Herd." One of the witnesses even swore that "the movie picture people ate buffalo steaks while the picture was being filmed." Other witnesses criticized Albright for interfering with the tourist traffic near Gardiner to the detriment of the local merchants and professional guides. He was castigated for discriminating against old-time miners and prospectors in the area. After each witness, Albright dispatched a ranger to park headquarters to bring back pertinent files to be used in rebuttal. Senator Oddie became uneasy over Cameron's tactics, and he quietly came to Albright's assistance, forcing almost all of the witnesses to admit that they had been banned from the park or fired from jobs in the park for violating the rules. "Were you ever convicted of selling liquor" or bootlegging in the park, the Senator asked one man. "No, Sir," the witness replied. "I pleaded guilty."[40]

After lunch Albright took the stand. He had brought together a roomful of friendly witnesses who could be called upon to testify in his behalf if that seemed desirable. He was, by his own admission, "mad clear through," but he successfully controlled his temper. "I have been on trial all morning," he began, "with convicted bootleggers, a quack doctor, a disgruntled ex-road foreman, an ex-ranger with a bad record, and other men with grievances testifying against me through the convenient method of leading questions from a man who assembled this group of

39. HMA, "Reminiscences," pp. 357–65.
40. Quotations from Speer's reports in *New York Times*, Aug. 30, 1925, and Aug. 31, 1925.

malcontents." Albright swiftly ran through the list of previous
witnesses, pointing out that he had fired or brought legal charges
against every one of them. He confronted each specific accusa-
tion, explaining the circumstances and countering the charge.
It was clear that his many appearances before congressional
committees in Washington had taught him how to handle senators' questions. "Not once was he interrupted," Speer reported
in the *Times,* "and when he ended the committee promptly and
without another word adjourned." Senator Cameron had evidently "caught a tartar," Speer pungently observed. Albright's
foresight in having Speer escorted around the park paid off
handsomely in friendly reportage. Two days later the *Times* editorialized that Albright's reply "to the charges made before the
Senate Subcommittee on Public Lands was so conclusive as to
silence completely the witnesses testifying against him." The
Brooklyn *Eagle* and several other big eastern newspapers picked
up the story, giving it front-page coverage.[41]

Albright had reason to be pleased with his performance before
the Cameron subcommittee. "Taking everything into consideration," he wrote a few days after the hearings, "I think that the
investigation by the Senate Public Lands Committee will re-
dound to the benefit of the park. The publicity that came out of
the hearing certainly stirred up the friends of the park and I
have had an avalanche of letters and telegrams commending the
stand I took." George Horace Lorimer, Madison Grant, I. H.
Larom, Secretary of the Interior Hubert Work, and dozens of
other conservationists sent Albright letters of congratulations.
"I was amused and delighted by your testimony before the Congressional Committee," wrote feisty old William T. Hornaday, a
pioneer game conservationist. "The thorough-going and far-
reaching manner in which you mopped the floor of the auditorium with your disgruntled critics and enemies was most ad-

41. *New York Times,* Aug. 31, 1925, and Sept. 2, 1925; U.S., Congress, Senate, Hearings Before the Subcommittee of the Committee
on Public Lands and Surveys, "National Forests and Public Domain,"
69th Cong., 1st sess. (Aug. 29, 1925), pp. 4445–4586; Brooklyn *Eagle,*
Aug. 31, 1925.

mirable and highly edifying. I laughed through sheer joy at the thoroughness of it."[42]

It was decidedly ironic that Albright's wildlife policies came under attack in the 1920s because he consistently placed a high priority on the task of protecting Yellowstone's unrivaled wildlife resources. In the fall and spring of every year he gave his personal attention to the problems of keeping the animals healthy, ordering extensive game counts and authorizing lifecycle studies of selected species. On his pack trips into the wilderness, he took special pains to observe both the number and condition of the wild game he encountered. When a crisis arose involving the park's animals, he acted quickly and forcefully to alleviate the situation. The elk particularly benefited from his efforts. In the winter of 1919–20 he helped to obtain both public funds and private donations to buy hay for the winter-ravaged animals. Two years later he was instrumental in persuading Montana state officials to tighten up their game laws to give the elk greater protection. And he campaigned endlessly against the brutal tooth hunters, who killed the elk solely for the two teeth that could be sold at premium prices to the members of the Benevolent and Protective Order of Elks. After much leg work and talking in Washington, Albright won appropriations from Congress to rebuild the "snowshoe" cabins in the remote parts of Yellowstone to facilitate game patrols during the winter months. His interest in wildlife extended even to the trout in the park's lakes and streams. Year after year he insisted that more fish should be planted in the park "to take care of the demands" of park visitors, and he worked to get the Bureau of Fisheries to expand the fish hatchery it maintained in the park.[43]

42. William T. Hornaday to HMA, Sept. 4, 1925, HMA to Hornaday, Sept. 9, 1925, Lorimer to HMA, Aug. 31, 1925, Madison Grant to HMA, Sept. 1, 1925, and I. H. Larom to HMA, Sept. 4, 1925, HMA Papers; Shankland, *Steve Mather*, p. 240.

43. "Yellowstone Monthly Report" (Apr. 1920), p. 14 (Nov. 1920), pp. 12–13 (Aug. 1921), pp. 12, 17 (Mar. 1922), p. 18 (Aug. 1922), p. 21 (June 1924), pp. 30–31 (Apr. 1927), pp. 7–12, see especially the monthly report for May 1923 for extensive information on Yellowstone wildlife; HMA to Director of NPS, June 7, 1923, and Sam T. Woodring to HMA, Apr. 25, 1925, HMA Papers.

Albright had his own ideas about how and why wildlife should be managed. He believed that wild animals constituted one of the greatest attractions of the park and that visitors to Yellowstone had a right to see wildlife whenever possible. He expanded the so-called Buffalo Corral at Mammoth Springs, where buffaloes, and at various times (never for very long), deer, elk, coyotes, bears, porcupines, and badgers were kept in cages "for the close inspection of tourists" so that "those interested in the park's rich wild life may make close-up studies and photographs of the mammals of this region." Albright believed that the educational and entertainment value of the Buffalo Corral far outweighed its disadvantages. Later in the 1920s he expanded the bear pits near the park's hotels, where every evening the bears gorged themselves on food scraps and garbage from the hotel dining rooms. "The feeding grounds at Old Faithful, Lake, and Canyon are one of the feature attractions at these points," he claimed in 1927. "Seating accommodations have been provided . . . and ranger lectures on the bears and other wild animals of the park are delivered at 7:30 P.M. daily. These talks have been largely attended and many favorable comments have been brought to the attention of this office." The fact that bears groveling in garbage and buffaloes living in enclosures were not really "wild" life did not particularly trouble Albright. This was another instance in which the stated Park Service goal of preserving nature unspoiled conflicted with the legal imperative that the parks should also be "pleasuring grounds" for the people. Albright compromised in favor of the people. A later generation of Park Service leadership, decreeing that wildlife should be observed only in a natural setting, ordered the bear pits and Buffalo Corral removed.[44]

Albright's affection for the impish and comical Yellowstone bears became almost legendary. In his idle moments, the hardworking park superintendent often entertained himself by watching the antics of "Mrs. Murphy," or some other talented "Beg-

44. "Yellowstone Monthly Report" (June 1924), pp. 30–31 (June 1925), p. 32 (July 1925), p. 51 (June 1927), p. 19, with attached park circular no. 6, dated June 1, 1927.

gar bear," followed by a couple of gamboling cubs, "hold up" a string of cars and win a bountiful handout. His monthly reports to Mather contained numerous bear stories, as when an unfortunate cub, evidently in quest of honey, got his head stuck in a hollow tree and had to be sawed free by two compassionate rangers. A compulsive storyteller, Albright naturally collected anecdotes about bears. After his first season or two in the park, he began writing down the best of these stories for the benefit of his children and by 1927 had recorded about two hundred pages of manuscript. Frank Taylor, who had recently forsaken journalism for free-lance writing, discovered Albright's collection of anecdotes. He immediately suggested that the stories be published, and he persuaded Albright to allow him to collaborate on the project. The rough anecdotes were to be expanded and smoothed out by Taylor, who would also add a certain amount of general information about the other national parks in the West. Published originally in 1928 by Stanford University Press, under the title of *"Oh, Ranger!" A Book About the National Parks,* the book went through thirteen printings, with the commercial publishing firm Dodd, Mead and Company handling the details of publication after the second edition. *"Oh, Ranger!"* finally went out of print in 1949.[45]

Albright and Taylor also published an article in the *Saturday Evening Post* in 1928. Albright wrote the article, entitled "The Everlasting Wilderness," but Taylor put it into final shape. Albright was attempting to answer the purists, who were loudly condemning the large road-building program initiated by the National Park Service under Mather's direction. In 1924 Congress had authorized approximately seven million dollars for road construction in the parks, and by 1925 the sound of construction crews echoed through some of the most beautiful scenery in the world. But, in most cases, existing roads were simply

45. The Yellowstone monthly reports for the 1920s are full of bear stories; HMA, "Reminiscences," pp. 270–71; Frank J. Taylor to HMA, Aug. 1, 1927, and HMA to Taylor, Aug. 5, 1927, HMA Papers; HMA Diary, Jan. 29, 1928, and Mar. 15, 1928; HMA and Taylor, *"Oh, Ranger!"*

widened and modernized. This was clearly the case in Yellowstone. And yet the Sierra Club, the Mountaineers, and other similar groups continued to condemn "unnecessary" road building, conjuring up images of the parks being "gridironed" with roads and inundated with people. One wilderness admirer, distressed by the crowded conditions in Yosemite, compared the main intersection in that incomparable valley to "Seventh and Broadway" in Los Angeles. The only difference between the two locations, he claimed, was that there were "trees and no traffic cop in Yosemite Valley," while in the city there were traffic cops and "no trees." The population density was about the same. "The trouble," the man noted, "takes its roots in the Mather regime, and goes deep throughout the entire service."[46]

Albright's article argued that the National Park Service had "attempted to steer a middle course" between those "who want no roads into the parks" and the automobile clubs and chambers of commerce "whose appetites for road building are never appeased." In spite of all the highway construction and the thousands of tourists, he observed, "nine-tenths of Yellowstone is still—and we hope it always will be—an everlasting wilderness."[47]

Another parade of notable visitors passed through Yellowstone in 1927, starting with the arrival of Herbert Hoover, the Secretary of Commerce, whom Albright had known in a cursory way since 1918. Tall and square-faced, Hoover arrived wearing a double-breasted blue serge suit and a high, stiff collar, which he stolidly refused to change. He inspected the fish hatchery run by the Bureau of Fisheries, one of the agencies of the Commerce Department, and he gave Albright the go-ahead to build a new

46. HMA and Frank J. Taylor, "The Everlasting Wilderness," *Saturday Evening Post* 201 (Sept. 29, 1928) : 28; HMA Diary, Jan. 10, 1928, Jan. 11, 1928, Jan. 30, 1928, and Mar. 7, 1928; HMA, "Reminiscences," p. 271; *Annual Report, NPS* (1924), pp. 11–12 and (1925), 17; R. S. Yard to A. D. Beers, Mar. 21, 1925, NA, Records of NPS, gen., admin.; H. I. Curzan to Ray Lyman Wilbur, Jan. 12, 1931, NA, Records of the Office of the Secretary of the Interior, gen., parks, reservations and antiquities.

47. HMA and Taylor, "The Everlasting Wilderness," p. 28.

hatchery (to be financed by a $27,500 gift from William E. Corey of United States Steel). The next morning Hoover joined the crew of the fish hatchery for a ham and egg breakfast and then cruised off with Albright and a couple of men from the hatchery for a day of fishing on Lake Yellowstone. Hoover still wore his blue serge suit, although he donned a pair of leather leggings for this outing. "From the time he arrived," Albright recalled, "the Secretary had not been very communicative." Only after Hoover opened his tackle box and got down to fishing did he abandon his tight-lipped reticence. As he reeled in large cutthroat trout one after the other, he told stories about his fishing trips in other parts of the world.[48]

By the time Hoover ended his two-day stay, Albright was well occupied in preparing for the arrival of Secretary of the Interior Hubert Work and a party of his close friends, including Governor John S. Fisher of Pennsylvania, who planned to vacation in the park. Albright met them at the train and "had them about half way around Yellowstone Park" when he suddenly received word of Coolidge's terse announcement: "I do not choose to run for President in 1928." Work and his friends were dumfounded when Albright told them the news. They immediately began speculating about what Coolidge really meant, even asking Albright to look up the word "choose" in an unabridged dictionary on the chance that it had some obscure, unrecognized meaning. The men later came to the conclusion that regardless of Coolidge's real intentions (which may have been to spark a draft-Coolidge movement) the president would not be in office after March 1929. Work rushed off to see Coolidge, who was vacationing in the Black Hills of South Dakota. Meantime, Hoover announced his intention to run for the Republican nomination.[49]

48. "Yellowstone Monthly Report" (July 1927), pp. 3, 5; HMA, "A Big Bad Year in Yellowstone Park," (MS), pp. 9–10, HMA Papers; HMA, "Reminiscences," p. 182.
49. "Yellowstone Monthly Report" (Aug. 1927), p. 1; HMA, "A Big Bad Year in Yellowstone Park," pp. 10–11; HMA, "Reminscences," pp. 183–89.

Not long after his surprising announcement, the president, his wife, and their son John decided to spend a few days in Yellowstone. Albright conferred extensively with Bill Starling of the Secret Service about security precautions. There was cause for some concern about the president's safety, because Sacco and Vanzetti were to be electrocuted on August 22, the very day Coolidge was to arrive at the park. In a drenching downpour, an honor guard of mounted rangers escorted the president into the park.[50]

Coolidge rested, toured the park, and fished. Hoping to generate publicity in favor of the proposed southward extension, Albright wanted to get the president to visit the Teton country as well as Yellowstone. The superintendent's office prepared a detailed memorandum for the newspaper men traveling with Coolidge, describing the Tetons as the "most beautiful range in America," and pointing out that this area deserved to be removed from the Teton National Forest and placed in the national park system. The Forest Service, the memorandum contended, "is required by law to develop the resources" of the lands it administers, while the Park Service "is required to keep its territory inviolate." At the last minute the president, who tended to get carsick, refused to make the trip to Jackson Hole, but Mrs. Coolidge and their son went anyway. The Tetons were once again featured in the news, thanks to Albright's careful planning.[51]

Coolidge enjoyed the trout fishing most of all. The first day out he stubbornly baited his hook with a worm, as he had always done in Vermont, and had absolutely no success. The next day, against Starling's advice, Albright insisted that Coolidge use a spinner lure, and this time the trout fairly jumped at the presidential hook. At the end of the day, the delighted president

50. HMA to Director of NPS, Aug. 20, 1927, HMA Papers; HMA, "A Big Bad Year in Yellowstone Park," pp. 12–14; HMA, "Reminiscences," pp. 188–90.

51. Memorandum for press representatives regarding the Teton extension to Yellowstone National Park, Aug. 25, 1927, attached to "Yellowstone Monthly Report" (Aug. 1927); HMA to Director of NPS, Aug. 30, 1927, HMA Papers.

thanked Albright for the advice. In the evenings Coolidge stayed in his hotel room and usually went to bed early, but his wife and son attended a series of dances and gala entertainments produced by the college students working in the park during the summer. Late one night, Albright heard a terrific noise on the floor below him in the Old Faithful Inn. He raced down the stairs to see what was happening, only to find John Coolidge playfully wheeling his mother around in a baggage cart. Albright retreated back up the stairs unnoticed, and dutifully recorded that "after a few minutes the fun stopped."[52]

Albright persuaded the president to leave the park via Cody to please the businessmen and civic leaders at the eastern gateway to the park, who wanted to entertain the president if only for fifteen minutes. A particularly rough stretch of road on the way to Cody prompted Coolidge to remark wryly: "Pretty bad road we've been over. . . . Suppose you're hoping to get a new one?" As a matter of fact, though Albright protested that he had no ulterior motives, a personal letter from Mather about ten days earlier had stated the hope that Albright would "have an opportunity to talk" to the President "about our bigger road program."[53]

The excitement of the summer of 1927 served as the capstone to Albright's years as the Yellowstone superintendent. After nine seasons, he felt completely at ease in the superintendency and calmly self-confident about his ability to run the park. "My success here, if I do say so myself," he wrote to Cammerer, "has been of my own making. I have a group of department heads here who like to work for me personally, and they work hard." Not only the headquarters staff but also the park rangers carried out their duties with efficiency and enthusiasm. Even the doughty Harry Child cooperated. Complimentary letters from hundreds

52. HMA, "A Big Bad Year in Yellowstone Park," pp. 14–17, 19–21; HMA to Director of NPS, Aug. 30, 1927, HMA Papers; HMA, "Reminiscences," pp. 191–93, 198–201.
53. HMA, "A Big Bad Year in Yellowstone Park," pp. 17–19; Mather to HMA, Aug. 17, 1927, Reed Smoot to HMA, Oct. 24, 1927, and clipping from *Publisher's Auxiliary*, Sept. 10, 1927, HMA Papers; HMA, "Reminiscences," pp. 193–203.

of satisfied tourists and dozens of junketing politicians attested to the smoothness and proficiency of the men Albright recruited and trained. His performance could hardly have been improved upon.[54]

A number of important personal factors contributed to Albright's success in Yellowstone. He was a "preserver," that is, a conservationist who wished above all to save superlative examples of natural beauty and to protect most forms of wildlife. He managed to convey his preservationist gospel to nearly all of his employees, several of whom admitted that they became "disciples" of both Albright and Mother Nature. At the same time, Albright reacted positively to the presence of tourists. Increasingly gregarious, he enjoyed mingling with the campers and helping them feel the same excitement he felt about Old Faithful or the bears. Moreover, he understood the political advantages of having the parks used. Almost singlehandedly, he framed and rationalized the compromise between preservation and use in Yellowstone. In the eyes of the Yellowstone rangers, the National Park Service was doing the work of the Lord. Strangely enough, the leading citizens of Montana, Idaho, Utah, and even a few in Wyoming agreed. Albright's vast and effective public relations effort must be considered one of the major ingredients in his successful administrative technique.

Albright also left an indelible imprint on the physical development and the educational program of the park. Under his direction, the concessioners expanded hotel and campground facilities. The existing roads were widened and given a modern oil topping, which materially reduced the dust. Only a small amount of new road construction was undertaken, and always with meticulous attention to protecting the scenery. The new museums built with Rockefeller money blended into the park setting in an aesthetically pleasing way. The museums, the nature-guide program, the campfire lectures—all of which are still thriving in Yellowstone—date from Albright's superintendency. In many respects, his work in Yellowstone Park es-

54. Quotation from HMA to Cammerer, Oct. 8, 1926, HMA Papers.

tablished the pattern of administration for all of the larger national parks, a pattern that is basically still followed by the National Park Service.

By 1928, Albright had served a long and demanding apprenticeship. Throughout the 1920s he had continued his winter treks to Washington, assiduously maintaining his political contacts on the Hill, working on the National Park Service budget, and appearing before the House and Senate appropriations committees. As assistant director in the field, he increased his familiarity with all of the parks and expanded the range of his personal experiences in park management. Everywhere he went, he met businessmen, politicians, and civic leaders. By 1928, because of his extensive travels and his position "at the crossroads in Yellowstone," he had hundreds of influential friends and acquaintances. He regularly corresponded with congressmen, senators, business executives, writers, and prominent citizens from every corner of the United States. Thirty-eight years old, hardworking and self-confident, a personification of the Mather tradition, he was well qualified to become the director of the National Park Service, if and when Mather decided to step down.

8

Director of the National Parks

On November 10, 1928, a few days after Hoover's decisive victory at the polls, Albright received the news that Mather, felled by a massive stroke, was critically ill in Chicago. Since 1922, Mather had successfully avoided a recurrence of his disabling nervous condition, but his general health had begun to deteriorate. In the spring of 1927, he suffered a mild heart attack while on a trip to Hawaii, and for a time openly talked of retiring, expressing his wish that Albright should succeed him. A few weeks later, Secretary Work quietly suggested to Albright that he take over all the Park Service field work. Albright refused, unless Mather approved the arrangement, and Mather would not approve it. He was not ready to limit his activities. Ignoring the pleas of his family and physician, Mather plunged ahead with his backbreaking schedule, constantly traveling, giving speeches, and glad-handing as effectively as ever, apparently intent upon demonstrating that his strong constitution had not been impaired. Albright became increasingly concerned about Mather's overexertions and offered to 'take over the Washington work" whenever the time seemed right, "provided everything was agreeable to the Secretary of the Interior." But Mather hung back, painfully reluctant to end his close association with the national parks. His crippling stroke in November 1928 left no doubt about the necessity for his retirement. "He was sitting in a big leather chair near my desk," Harold White sadly wrote to Albright. "Suddenly he stopped speaking in the midst of a sentence" and, after clumsily attempting to relight a cigar, "slumped down in the chair." He lay in a hospital bed for the next six months, practically unable to talk, his left side paralyzed.[1]

As telegrams and letters from Harold White and Oliver Mitchell arrived describing Mather's critical condition, Albright carefully considered what he should do. He was "terribly worried," he confided to White, "particularly about Mr. Mather, and more incidentally about the status of the National Park Service." He asked White to repeat to Mather "the same commitment I made to him last spring," namely that "I am ready to go back" to Washington and "run the National Park Service just as he would like to have it run. I suppose because of my association with him," he added, "I am the best available man for his successor, although I have no illusion of indispensability."[2]

Cammerer and Albright met in Chicago on November 19. From the start, Cammerer insisted that Albright should succeed Mather, although by this time Albright had begun to question the wisdom of his moving back to Washington. It would cost him personally and financially. The next morning, Hubert Work, who had resigned as Secretary of the Interior to manage Hoover's successful presidential campaign, joined Cammerer in urging Albright to take over the directorship. There was nobody else fully prepared to carry on the Mather tradition, Work contended. Moreover, if Albright turned down the appointment there was the possibility that an outsider might be brought in. Albright countered by suggesting that Cammerer could handle the job. When Albright visited Mather's hospital room for the first time, the brutal shock of seeing his chief and dear friend helpless was enough to settle the issue. "Pitiful case," he wrote

1. HMA, "A Big Bad Year in Yellowstone Park," pp. 2–3; Oliver Mitchell to HMA, Nov. 6, 1928, Harold F. White to HMA, Nov. 7, 1928, and HMA to White, Nov. 12, 1928, HMA Papers; Shankland, *Steve Mather*, p. 276.

2. White to HMA, Nov. 7, 1928, HMA to White, Nov. 12, 1928, HMA to Mrs. Mather, Nov. 12, 1928, telegram, Mitchell to HMA, Nov. 15, 1928, and Cammerer to HMA, Nov. 16, 1928, HMA Papers; HMA Diary, Nov. 16, 1928.

in his diary. "Paralyzed. Can't talk or write his ideas. Seems almost hopeless." He soon promised Cammerer and Work that he would "accept the appointment if and when it is tendered to me."[3]

On his own initiative, Albright undertook a modest amount of lobbying in the next few days, attempting to protect the National Park Service and his own interests as well. In Chicago, he talked confidentially to James W. Good, whom observers tabbed as a sure member of Hoover's cabinet, "about helping to keep the directorship in safe hands." He also saw Albert Harris, president of Harris Trust Company and a close friend of the current Secretary of the Interior, Roy O. West, about "keeping park matters in status quo." Ford Harvey, head of the dining car and restaurant chain, and Fred Williamson, president of the Burlington Railroad, promised to help. Then Albright caught the train to New York, where he received the blessings of Nicholas Roosevelt, Kenneth Chorley, and John D. Rockefeller, Jr., all influential friends of the National Park Service. During his brief sojourn in New York, Albright and Chorley spent an afternoon "on the Jackson Hole project."[4]

On November 25, Albright reached Washington ready to meet Secretary West, who had asked him to come in for a talk. West asked Albright to take over as acting director until the first of the year when the situation would presumably be clearer. Albright agreed on condition that he be allowed to spend the holiday season with his family in California. He pointed out that Cammerer could run the Washington office in the meantime. West approved this arrangement and inquired in general terms whether Albright would be willing to undertake the directorship if Mather resigned. Albright replied that he would "accept the appointment" if it were offered. Pausing only long enough to confer with Demaray and Cammerer about the Park Service

3. HMA Diary, Nov. 16–20, 1928; HMA to Yard, Dec. 20, 1928, HMA Papers; HMA, "Reminiscences," pp. 291–93.
4. HMA Diary, Nov. 20–29, 1928.

budget for 1930, on which hearings would soon begin, he hurried back to California in time for Thanksgiving with his family.[5]

Albright fought a constant battle with his conscience during the weeks between Thanksgiving and Christmas of 1928. He was tempted to refuse the directorship. He "hated the thought" of leaving his "beloved West" and, according to his businesslike calculations, accepting the directorship would not improve his financial position. "At the present time," he noted, "my salary and emoluments are approximately equal to the salary of a Director, and living expenses are less than they are in Washington." He had the feeling that once again he was "putting the good of the Service above the immediate personal welfare of myself and my family." And yet, how could he refuse to carry on in the name of the Mather tradition? All the park superintendents demanded that he accept the job. So did the concessioners, the mountain clubs, the members of the Washington office, and most of the national conservation organizations. "Here and there are a few who think the new Director ought to be a rich man," wrote Bob Yard "to travel . . . in the wholesale way Mather did, to entertain trail parties, give fine dinners, and associate generally with men of heavy consequence, conferring a super-financial if not super-social aura on the Service." Yard thought these ideas were pure "bosh." "Mather was Mather. The particular creative thing he did with the Park Service no other could have done at the time, nor will any other need to continue. His money was an unnecessary picturesque part in his personality." Albright readily concurred. "I would only make myself ridiculous if I tried to be another Steve Mather," he observed. "My job as I see it, will be to consolidate our gains, finish up the rounding out of the Park system, go rather heavily into the historical park field, and get such legislation as is necessary to guarantee the future of the system on a sound permanent basis where the power

5. HMA Diary, Nov. 20–29, 1928; HMA to Cammerer, Nov. 26, 1928, and HMA to Yard, Dec. 20, 1928, HMA Papers.

and the personality of the Director may no longer have to be controlling factors in operating the Service."[6]

The transfer of leadership from Mather to Albright was accomplished with a minimum of difficulty. Work and a number of other highly placed politicians lobbied quietly in Washington in behalf of Albright, who soon received word that both Coolidge, the retiring president, and Hoover, the president-elect, had approved his appointment as Mather's successor. Shortly before Christmas, the Secretary of the Interior directed Albright to be in Washington by January 3, 1929, "to take over the active administrative work" of the Park Service. There remained only the formality of Mather's official resignation. Reconciled at last to the necessity of leaving the directorship and happy that Albright had consented to take his place, Mather bowed out of office in time for Albright's swearing in on January 12, 1929. The Mather era had lasted almost precisely fourteen years.[7]

Seldom has an appointed government official been the object of such an outpouring of affection and admiration as Steve Mather on the occasion of his retirement. He received thousands of letters from all over the country. Nearly every major American newspaper and news magazine editorialized about his inspired leadership and solid achievements, not the least of which, many of the editorials agreed, was to recruit and train Horace Albright as his successor. "This means not only that the policies which Mr. Mather developed will be carried on," said the *New York Times,* "but that their execution is entrusted to a man [Albright] who played a large part in framing them." *The Nation* commented enthusiastically that both Albright and Mather "are illustrations of what fine public servants the government can command when politics are banned. The willingness of such men to serve the community for relatively small

6. HMA to Yard, Dec. 20, 1928, Yard to HMA, Dec. 9, 1928, and Jess Nusbaum to HMA, Dec. 1, 1928, HMA Papers.

7. Hubert Work to Roy O. West, Jan. 10, 1929, HMA to Yard, Dec. 20, 1928, and West to HMA, Dec. 17, 1928, HMA Papers; Mather to West, Jan. 8, 1929, and West to Mather, Jan. 11, 1929, NA, Records of NPS, gen., admin., Dir. Mather.

salaries gives us hope that our government bureaus may some-day attain the high standard of the British civil service." "The mantle of Elijah," The Los Angeles *Times* observed, "has fallen on capable shoulders."[8]

Albright inherited a large and varied domain when he became director. There were twenty-one national parks and thirty-three national monuments under his jurisdiction in 1929, including mountains, hot springs, caves, deserts, active volcanoes, geysers, cliff dwellings, and seashores. More than 2,600,000 Americans visited the parks in 1929. Total appropriations, counting funds for road and trail construction, stood at more than $8,750,000, a far cry from the paltry $500,000 allocated to the parks and monuments in 1915. The National Park Service had prospered and grown under Mather's direction. Albright had no intention of allowing the bureau to mark time now that he was its head, although he recognized from the start that an important part of his job would be to protect the gains Mather had made and to bring to a successful culmination a number of plans initiated earlier in the 1920s. "I will do my best to carry out Mr. Mather's policies," he asserted over and over again in his correspondence with Mather's friends and in his replies to the congratulatory telegrams and letters he received after taking office.[9]

It was the busiest season of the year in Washington when Albright moved into the directorship. Congress was rushing toward its mandatory March 4 adjournment date. Having to shepherd the appropriations bill safely through both houses required a large amount of time, and there were a number of pending national park bills that had to be carefully watched. A

8. *New York Times*, Jan. 15, 1929 (© 1929 by the New York Times Company), reprinted by permission; *The Nation*, Jan. 30, 1929; *Los Angeles Times*, Jan. 16, 1929; see also Washington *Post*, Jan. 14, 1929, Boston *Evening Transcript*, Jan. 18, 1929, and *Saturday Evening Post* 201 (Feb. 23, 1929): 24; *Congressional Record*, 70th Cong., 2nd sess. (Jan. 15, 1929), pp. 1734–36; Shankland, *Steve Mather*, pp. 284–86.
9. *Annual Report, NPS* (1929), p. 3; George H. Dern to HMA, Jan. 16, 1929, HMA to Harry Chandler, Feb. 13, 1929, Chauncey J. Hamlin to HMA, Feb. 13, 1929, and HMA to James V. Lloyd, Jan. 15, 1929, NA, Records of NPS, gen., admin., Dir. Albright.

measure extending the northern and eastern boundaries of Yellowstone Park passed on March 1. A bill to establish a Grand Teton National Park, excluding the Jackson Hole region, but encompassing the Tetons themselves, became law on February 26 with the full approval of Senator Kendrick of Wyoming. Albright would have preferred having the Teton region added to Yellowstone Park, as originally proposed, but he deferred to Kendrick's wishes in the hope of pacifying the elected officials of Wyoming, whose wrath he had incurred. The idea behind the bill was to give the state of Wyoming a national park entirely within its own borders. Meanwhile Rockefeller's Snake River Land Company continued to buy real estate in the Jackson Hole country. Albright doubtless anticipated that someday the Grand Teton National Park would be expanded into the larger and more logical scenic unit that he and Rockefeller had envisioned. The enactment of Kendrick's bill, though clearly a compromise, represented a major triumph for Albright, who had been working to bring the Tetons into the national park system since 1919. The new park was opened to the public in July 1929, with Sam T. Woodring, Albright's long-time friend and chief ranger in Yellowstone, as superintendent.[10]

Practically unnoticed in the hubbub over the authorization of the Teton Park were two other important pieces of national park legislation. Buried in the Department of Interior Appropriations Act for 1930 was a provision empowering the National Park Service to use condemnation proceedings to step up its drive to eliminate private holdings in the parks. This, too, was the culmination of a legislative campaign begun nearly a decade before. As a final triumph, Albright got Congress to authorize a small but strategic extension of Yosemite, laying the ground work for still another Rockefeller-Albright collaboration, this time to bring a priceless virgin stand of sugar pines, then being threatened by lumbering operations, into the park. During the last week of February and the first week in March, Albright proudly wrote to Lorimer, "more legislation regarding national

10. *Annual Report, NPS* (1929), pp. 1–4; Ise, *Our National Park Policy*, pp. 328–30.

parks was put through Congress than . . . in any similar time in all our history." In his excitement and enthusiasm, he exaggerated only slightly. Albright had catapulted off to a fast and effective start as director.[11]

A fortnight before Coolidge's term in office expired, Albright received a call from the White House asking him to come over—the president wanted to see him. He was immediately ushered into the president's office and cordially greeted by Coolidge, who then reached into his desk and took out a cigar. After inviting Albright to sit down, the president perched on the edge of his desk, put his feet in his chair, and lighted his cigar. "Want to talk to you about fishing," he said. He was proud of the fact that he had recently learned how to fish with a fly, and he was savoring the thought of doing some more of it after his retirement. "Suppose I went back to Yellowstone," he continued, "and I went out to that Grebe Lake where we were. What kind of flies would a rainbow take?" Albright launched into a spirited discussion of the best lures to use in Yellowstone, and, of course, he urged Coolidge to revisit the park. Then the president's secretary announced that a senator was waiting in the outer office. "Did he have an appointment?" Coolidge grumbled, obviously piqued by having to suspend his daydreams about retirement. Albright quietly excused himself. Unfortunately, Coolidge never did get back to Yellowstone.[12]

Change was in the air in Washington as the day approached for Herbert Hoover's inaugural. Albright had welcomed Hoover's victory at the polls in 1928 and, like many other conservationists, had eagerly looked forward to having him in the White House. Hoover's crusades against waste, his championing of multiple-purpose river-basin planning, and his concern about the regulation of the public domain marked him as a dedicated conservationist. He knew and admired the national parks, especially Yellowstone. There was every reason to believe that

11. *Annual Report, NPS* (1929), pp. 1–2 (1930), pp. 1, 16; HMA to Lorimer, Mar. 8, 1929, NA, Records of NPS, gen., admin., Dir. Albright.
12. HMA, "Reminiscences," pp. 204–6; Coolidge quoted on pp. 205, 206.

Hoover and his prospective Secretary of the Interior, Ray Lyman Wilbur, would retain Albright as director of the National Park Service. But the incoming president let it be known that he intended to make major changes at the cabinet and subcabinet levels, even though he was succeeding a fellow Republican, and Albright felt apprehensive.[13]

Two or three days after Hoover's inauguration, Secretary Wilbur asked for written resignations from all of his assistant secretaries and bureau chiefs. This was a startling and unusual request, which shook the Interior Department from top to bottom. Only those bureau chiefs who were to be retained would have their letters of resignation returned. Albright reacted warily, submitting a carefully phrased letter, reserving his "civil service [retirement] rights and whatever attached to them" after nearly sixteen years of service. Then the inevitable rumors started to circulate. At one point Albright heard on good authority that George Hearst, the eldest son of the influential newspaper publisher, had mounted a vigorous campaign for the directorship of the National Park Service. After nearly a month of suspense, the Secretary called Albright to his office and said: "Here's this resignation of yours—the President wants you to stay."[14]

With his job now assured, Albright began making plans to bring his family to Washington. He decided to have "a modest house" built in the new Spring Valley division of the Wesley Heights section of town. Grace and the children arrived in October, after Albright had completed his summer inspection tour of the parks. The family lived comfortably in Spring Valley for the next four years.[15]

13. HMA, "Reminiscences," pp. 278–80; Swain, *Federal Conservation Policy*, pp. 161–66.

14. HMA, "Reminiscences," pp. 280–89; Ray Lyman Wilbur, *The Memoirs of Ray Lyman Wilbur, 1875–1949*, edited by Edgar E. Robinson and Paul C. Edwards, pp. 409–12; Herbert Hoover, *The Memoirs of Herbert Hoover: The Cabinet and the Presidency, 1920–1933*, pp. 221, 242.

15. HMA to Louis C. Cramton, June 19, 1929, NA, Records of NPS, gen., admin., Dir. Albright.

Albright quickly established a cordial relationship with Secretary Wilbur, who was a physician by training but had been president of Stanford University for many years before his appointment to the cabinet. A tall, large-boned man with a prominent nose and dark, unruly hair, Wilbur enjoyed fishing and camping and had all the impulses of an outdoorsman, but he had to learn about the national parks and about how to function effectively in Washington. As the president of a private university, he had not worried much about elected officials, and he had never gone before a legislature in quest of funds. He therefore had very little conception of how to deal with the members of Congress who controlled his department's purse strings. Politicians found the new Secretary's habit of reading his mail while talking to them particularly annoying. Albright tried to give Wilbur advice about Washington politics, but without much success. "In this administration, Albright," the Secretary would growl, ". . . Congress will look after its business and we'll look after ours." Although not an accomplished political tactician, Wilbur was a thorough, competent administrator.[16]

In his dealings with the National Park Service, the new Secretary was helpful and enthusiastic from the start, largely because Albright handled himself with great skill during the initial stages of the new administration. He prepared a special booklet for the Secretary containing "the principal facts regarding the National Park Service." Then he proposed that Wilbur accompany him on a get-acquainted tour of the major parks. Bouncing over gravel roads in the Secretary's old Buick, the two men inspected Lassen, Crater Lake, and Mount Rainier. Later, traveling mostly by rail, they visited Glacier, Yellowstone, Grand Teton, Zion, Bryce Canyon, and Grand Canyon National Parks. By the time Wilbur returned to Washington, he had developed a genuine respect for the National Park Service and a warm regard for Albright. "In visiting the parks," he reported in his first annual report, "I have found the personnel of this

16. Wilbur, *Memoirs*, pp. 158–225, 403–21; HMA, "Reminiscences," pp. 294–301, Wilbur quoted on p. 295; see the collection of correspondence between Wilbur and HMA in the Hoover Papers.

young and vigorous bureau one of the most valuable contact groups between the Federal Government and the people." In his memoirs, Wilbur later observed that "the thinking of Director Albright was very much like my own." The National Park Service received strong support from the Secretary of the Interior throughout the Hoover administration.[17]

During 1929 Albright operated in a familiar pattern. Not only did he cultivate Wilbur's favor, but he also took pains to insure the continued cooperation of Congressmen Taylor and Cramton, Senators Norbeck, Gillett, and Hayden (the last two having now moved up from the House), and the other congressional friends of the national parks. He maintained excellent relations with Congress throughout his directorship. Hardly a month went by in the summer without Albright's arranging for a congressional committee or an influential senator to visit one or more of the parks. Whenever possible he met them personally. His approach was to let the rugged beauty of the parks and the general competence of the Park Service organization impress the legislators.[18]

Congressman Louis C. Cramton of Michigan, chairman of the subcommittee on Interior Department appropriations, cooperated especially well with Albright. Knowledgeable and well informed, Cramton was inclined to be opinionated and at times arrogant. Albright had known him since the early 1920s and had learned to overlook his outbursts. Thanks to Albright's patience and Cramton's benevolent interest, total appropriations for the National Park Service increased rather sharply after 1929. Defeated for reelection in 1930, Cramton nevertheless influenced Interior Department appropriations through the 1931–32 fiscal year. (The appropriations process runs about eighteen months ahead of the fiscal calendar.) By then the annual budget

17. HMA to Cramton, Mar. 16, 1929, and HMA to Demaray, Apr. 5, 1929, NA, Records of NPS, gen., admin., Dir. Albright; HMA, "Reminiscences," pp. 301-8; *Annual Report of the Secretary of the Interior* (1929), p. 19; Wilbur, *Memoirs*, pp. 431–40, quotation on p. 431, reprinted by permission of the publisher.

18. See NA, Records of NPS, gen., admin., Dir. Albright, for Albright's voluminous correspondence with congressmen.

of the National Park Service stood at more than $12,800,000, an increase of forty-six percent in only three years. This was a remarkable showing in an era of tightfisted Congresses, just after the onset of the Great Depression. Other bureaus in the Interior Department were not so fortunate. In 1931 Albright showed his appreciation to Cramton by helping him get an appointment as special attorney to the Secretary of the Interior.[19]

Albright's success in obtaining money from Congress threw him temporarily into conflict with Secretary Wilbur. Congressional committees, impelled by the deepening depression, had recently finished cutting appropriations for all bureaus in the Interior Department except the Park Service, which escaped with conspicuously fewer cuts than any other bureau. In one category, road construction, Congress appropriated even more money than the Park Service had originally requested. This momentarily angered Wilbur, who blurted to a reporter that the National Parks were "getting too much" money while the other bureaus were "being starved." The story appeared the next day on the front page of the early edition of the Washington *Star*. When Albright read it, he immediately went to see Wilbur, who admitted that he had made the statement criticizing the National Park Service. "We can't run the Department on these appropriations," he fumed. "Men will have to be discharged." Albright pointed out that it was one thing to argue publicly that certain bureaus were being starved, but it was quite another matter to castigate one bureau for receiving too much financial support. The Secretary granted that his statement might have been indiscreet, and he gave Albright permission to try to get the story killed in the late editions of the *Star* and in the next morn-

19. Telegram, Cramton to HMA, Sept. 15, 1930, HMA to H. M. Myers, Oct. 6, 1930, memorandum, Demaray to HMA, June 18, 1931, HMA to Wilbur, Aug. 23, 1932, and HMA to Cramton, Aug. 23, 1932, NA, Records of NPS, gen., admin., Dir. Albright; Cramton to the author, Aug. 23, 1965; *Annual Report, NPS* (1929), p. 31 (1930), p. 34 (1931), p. 34 (1932), p. 31; see also U.S., Congress, House, Hearings Before the Subcommittee on Interior Department Appropriations for Fiscal Year 1931, 71st Cong., 2d sess. (1930) and for Fiscal Year 1932, 71st Cong., 3d sess. (1930).

ing's Washington *Post*. With a few telephone calls, Albright quashed the article. Later, at Wilbur's urging, he went to the Capitol to testify in favor of legislation granting the Secretary of the Interior authority to redistribute approximately 10 percent of the funds originally earmarked for "roads and trails, national parks" to other bureaus in the department. More than $450,000 was eventually transferred from the Park Service to the Geological Survey, the General Land Office, and the Office of Education. Albright's reaction in this case was characteristic, and squarely in the Mather tradition. He regretted the loss of funds for the construction of much-needed roads and trails in the parks, but he regretted the damaging publicity even more.[20]

Albright made the enlargement and professionalization of the National Park Service one of his prime objectives in 1929 and 1930 because he believed that the time had come to put the bureau on a par with the other important federal conservation agencies. The Washington office of the Park Service "is far too small," he informed Wilbur, "and the fact that we have had several men break down physically shows that there is too much to be done by a wholly inadequate force." He argued convincingly for the reclassification of the Park Service as one of the "largest and most important bureaus" in the department, an administrative maneuver designed to secure more employees and better salaries for his agency. The reclassification went through successfully in 1930. Of course, Albright had a personal stake in this change. As the head of one of the "largest and most important bureaus" in the department, he would receive a substantially higher salary, which was a matter of no small importance to him. Unless the bureau's salary scale could be boosted, he maintained, he would have to reduce his outside activities "to such an extent as to perhaps handicap myself in the exercise of my full capabilities, particularly along the lines of public relations." He had no intention of entertaining on the lavish scale of his predecessor. And yet, unavoidably, his social obligations were heavy. One of his close associates seriously

20. HMA, "Reminiscences," pp. 312–14; *Annual Report, NPS* (1932), p. 31.

suggested that the Rockefeller Foundation might be willing to give financial assistance to the director to enable him to operate in the accustomed Mather style. Albright rejected the idea, but he made it clear to Secretaries West and Wilbur that he would require a larger monthly salary than Mather, who had a sizeable outside income and had never bothered much about the amount of his government paychecks. The Secretary's office apparently understood the problem. Albright received a $500 pay increase only four days after becoming director and another $500 promotion approximately six weeks later, raising his pay to $7,500 per annum. After the reclassification of the Park Service, his salary went up to $9,000 where it leveled off. This rapid escalation in pay revealed the fact that both West and Wilbur placed a high value on Albright's services to the Interior Department.[21]

In August 1931, Albright capped his drive to professionalize the Park Service by securing Hoover's signature on an order placing all park superintendents and national monument custodians under the civil service. Mather had previously obtained civil service coverage for the rangers. At last the Park Service was completely removed from the hazards of the spoils system and could look forward to the organizational advantages of systematic recruiting and regular staff promotions. Continually aware of the need to attract able men into the ranks of the Service, Albright was especially proud of having upgraded and strengthened the structure of his bureau.[22]

Fortunately for Albright, the statistics on park use were all in his favor. Congress could be persuaded to give the Park Service greater and greater financial support, and the Secretary of the Interior could be prevailed upon to permit the reclassification of the Service because the data so convincingly demonstrated that the national parks were being used and appreciated

21. HMA to Wilbur, July 8, 1929, HMA Papers; *Annual Report, NPS* (1930), p. 36; HMA to Yard, Dec. 20, 1928, and HMA to Jess Nusbaum, Dec. 1, 1928, HMA Papers; "Memorandum for Division of Accounts" (Jan. 16, 1929), NA, Records of NPS, gen., admin., Dir. Albright; M. D. Davis to the author, Dec. 10, 1965; HMA to Wilbur, Dec. 23, 1930, Hoover Papers, box 1-D/232.
22. *Annual Report, NPS* (1931), p. 2.

by the voters. In the 1931 season more than 3,100,000 people visited the parks, an increase of almost 25 percent since 1928 and an astonishing increase of more than 600 percent since 1917, the year the National Park Service was established. There were fewer visitors in 1932 and 1933 as the Great Depression reached bottom, but even so, the figures remained well above the 1928 level. As both Albright and Mather had sensed more than a decade before, increasing public use of the parks was the key to strengthening and expanding the Park Service program.[23]

The continuity between Mather's administration and Albright's was striking. Like his predecessor, Albright fought to maintain high aesthetic standards as new units were added to the national park system. The Grand Teton, Carlsbad Caverns, and Great Smoky Mountains national parks, all opened to the public during Albright's directorship, would stand comparison with any of the older units in the system. So would Isle Royale and the Everglades, which were proposed for national park status in 1929 and 1930. Albright stepped in to prevent the establishment of a number of obviously inferior new parks. In fact, his first real crisis came in March 1929, when he had to persuade Coolidge to pocket veto a bill authorizing Ouachita National Park in Arkansas, a project championed by the powerful Senator Joseph T. Robinson of that state. Albright later managed to eliminate Sullys Hill National Park in North Dakota, the one clearly substandard unit in the existing national park system. Fully atoning for his favorable recommendation on the proposed Grand Canyon cableway in 1919, he refused to approve a plan, sponsored by Harry Chandler, A. B. C. Dohrmann, and other high-powered California businessmen, to build a tramway to Glacier Point in Yosemite Valley. Albright's close cooperation with Rockefeller, his significant expansion of the major parks, and his continuation of existing concessions policies were other aspects of the Mather-Albright continuity.[24]

23. The statistics are from *Annual Report, NPS* (1917, 1929–33).

24. *Annual Report, NPS* (1929), pp. 3, 9 (1930), pp. 12–13 (1931), p. 6; HMA to Henry Van Dyke, Feb. 3, 1930, Frederick Law Olmstead to HMA, Nov. 25, 1930, "Memorandum for the Secretary from HMA"

Busy as he was with his new duties, Albright took time to dictate long, cheerful letters to Mather, attempting to keep his old friend abreast of the good news about the National Park Service. In May 1929 Mather left the hospital in Chicago and went to Darien, Connecticut, to spend the summer. When his train passed through Washington, the whole Park Service staff turned out to greet the former director, who had begun to make progress in shaking off the effects of his stroke. He had taught himself to walk with the help of a sturdy cane presented to him by his friends in the Park Service, and he could pronounce his words clearly and precisely.[25]

Shortly after the first flurry of snow in the fall of 1929, Mather moved to Brookline, Massachusetts, and undertook an extensive program of physical therapy that presumably would have completed his rehabilitation. But he died quite unexpectedly in January 1930, following a second massive stroke. Albright sadly joined the pilgrimage to the small Episcopal church in New Canaan, Connecticut, for the simple funeral services. He left New Canaan more than ever resolved to protect and inculcate the Mather tradition in the National Park Service. Mather's will, when probated, gave the young man renewed incentive not to forsake his role as torchbearer, for it included a $25,000 bequest to Albright (Cammerer received a similar amount) to help steel him against the seductive appeal of the business world.[26]

Increasingly during his first year as director and especially

(Nov. 11, 1929), and HMA to Kenneth Chorley, May 16, 1932, NA, Records of NPS, gen., admin., Dir. Albright; see also NA, Records of NPS, Director's Office File, Albright, and Kenneth Chorley files for information about Albright's close cooperation with Rockefeller in 1932 and 1933.

25. HMA to Edward Seymour, Nov. 4, 1929, HMA to Adelaide Underwood, Nov. 1, 1929, NA, Records of NPS, gen., admin., Dir. Mather; Robert Mather Albright to Stephen T. Mather, June 29, 1929, HMA Papers.

26. Shankland, *Steve Mather*, pp. 286–87; HMA to Howard Hays, May 2, 1930, NA, Records of NPS, Director's Office File, Albright; clipping from Oakland *Tribune*, Feb. 8, 1930, scrapbook, HMA Papers.

after Mather's death, Albright let his own personality assert itself in matters of administration and policy making. He was too forceful and proud a man to stand indefinitely in Mather's shadow. His directorship took on certain distinctive qualities that set it apart from the Mather years, not in terms of basic park policies, for they continued virtually unchanged, but in terms of style and emphasis. For one thing, there was a new and much-needed administrative orderliness in the internal affairs of the Service. Mather's executive leadership, while generally effective, had been eclectic and frequently haphazard. His was a highly personal kind of administrative technique that sometimes involved an underutilization of subordinate staff members in Washington, an overreliance on Albright, his chief assistant in the field, and a tendency to burden himself with too many details. Under its new director, the Park Service began to function more smoothly and systematically. There was more cohesiveness in the organization, and considerably more delegation of authority at all levels. Cammerer, now the associate director, and Demaray, now the assistant director, assumed larger administrative responsibilities. George A. Moskey, serving as the assistant to the director, demonstrated versatility and competence in a number of different assignments. Conrad L. Wirth, who joined the Park Service about halfway through Albright's directorship, used his considerable executive talents in the bureau's complex land acquisitions program.[27]

In April 1929, a few hours before leaving on his first inspection trip, Albright telephoned a message to Cammerer that succinctly summarized his administrative philosophy. "Clean up everything you can without sending stuff out to me," he ordered, "and don't send anything that doesn't need my attention." The park superintendents were informed that they should "reduce to writing and forward to Washington" all the policy decisions Albright made during his field trips. This was "to facilitate the

27. See *Congressional Directory*, May 1929–Jan. 1933, for information about National Park Service officers; interviews with Lawrence C. Merriam, Sept. 21, 1965, and E. T. Scoyen, Dec. 19, 1965.

work of the director" and to "prevent the failure to carry out his decisions by the Washington office." It was clear that Albright hoped to improve the level of communications between the superintendents and the administrators in Washington.[28]

Getting out from behind his desk and into the parks was more important to Albright than to his predecessor, not only because he preferred to spend his summers in the mountains, but also because his field trips enabled him to take the pulse of the National Park Service. By discussing mutual problems with individual superintendents and by acting as his own trouble shooter, he kept in close touch with both the men in the Service and the problems of the parks. He also had a chance to mingle with the tourists and to win new friends for the national parks. One of his most amusing and newsworthy adventures came in 1930, in the tree-studded Smoky Mountains near Knoxville, Tennessee. Eager to collaborate with D. C. Chapman in generating publicity for the newly opened Great Smoky Mountains National Park, Albright and Cammerer agreed to take a trek through the mountains with a group of influential park boosters from the Knoxville area. Late in the afternoon, while still in the high country, Chapman and the two top officials of the National Park Service got separated from the rest of the party and were soon lost. The sun went down before they could extricate themselves. Drenched to the skin by a thunderstorm, they spent the night in the wilderness, flailing their arms and jumping up and down to keep warm. After dawn they made it safely to Cades Cove, where they were dramatically "rescued" by worried local officials. "Albright Is Lost in Park Area All Night" blazed the headlines in the next edition of the Knoxville *News Sentinel*. It was the most sensational publicity the Smoky Mountains Park ever received. Albright good-naturedly maintained through a long seige of teasing that he had not done it on purpose. After a few hours in bed,

28. "TEB" to Cammerer, Apr. 6, 1929, "Memorandum to all Park Superintendents" (Apr. 1, 1929), NA, Records of NPS, gen., admin., Dir. Albright.

catching up on lost sleep, he kept a speaking engagement that
night at the Smoky Mountain Hiking Club in Gatlinburg.[29]

During his long field trips, Albright spent so much time in remote wilderness areas it was perhaps inevitable that he would
face a number of genuine emergencies. Probably the most dangerous of these came in the Alaskan back country in July 1931,
when he suddenly developed the symptoms of acute appendi-
citis. Acting as tour manager for a party of Congressmen, including members of the all-important House Subcommittee on
Interior Department Appropriations, Albright had led the way
to Mount McKinley National Park for a close-up view of the
tallest mountain in North America. He had planned an extended
horseback trip for the congressmen, who were in a carefree mood
and ready to relax for a few days. When Albright became ill, the
park superintendent, Harry J. Liek, contacted the nearest available physician, A. R. Carter, of Fairbanks, who agreed to fly to
the park to examine the patient. Emergency surgery was not
necessary, but the doctor decided to take Albright to the Fairbanks Hospital at daybreak the next morning. The irrepressible
Albright, armed with topographical maps of the area, managed
to persuade the pilot to make an aerial survey of the Wonder
Lake region of the park and for good measure to circle over the
Nenana Episcopal Indian mission on the way back to Fairbanks. It was an extraordinarily clear day, superb flying weather,
and Albright got a panoramic view of this wonderful wilderness
area, acquiring a "knowledge and conception of it that could
never be obtained from the ground," he recorded. As a result
of his recommendations, nearly three hundred thousand acres
in the vicinity of Wonder Lake were later added to the park.
Dr. Carter, who was painfully susceptible to airsickness, grumbled and cursed throughout the extended flight. The cocky bush
pilot touched his plane down at Fairbanks just before the fuel
tanks ran dry. Two days later, the doctor removed Albright's

29. HMA to M. R. Tillotson, Apr. 1, 1929, "Memorandum for the
Secretary from HMA" (Apr. 3, 1929), NA, Records of NPS, gen.,
admin., Dir. Albright; clippings from Knoxville *News Sentinel*, May
19, 1930, May 20, 1930, and May 24, 1930, scrapbook, HMA Papers.

inflamed appendix, as the navy flashed radio reports of the operation's progress to Park Service headquarters in Washington.[30]

A steady procession of congressmen and senators, including Peter Norbeck, Scott Leavitt, Edward Taylor, William Eaton, Frederick C. Walcott, and Frank Murphy, paraded through Albright's hospital room in Fairbanks, wishing him well. "All your friends hoping for early recovery," Senator Smoot wired. "We cannot afford to lose you." A radio message from President Hoover buoyed Albright's spirits more than anything else: "Exceedingly sorry to learn of your illness," it read. "I trust you will have a speedy recovery." Albright agreed to take "a good rest" after returning from the frontier.[31]

It was clear by the fall of 1931 that Albright's most distinctive contribution to the expanding Park Service program would not come in connection with the national parks, but rather in the specialized field of historic preservation. A long-time history buff, he believed that it was practically as important to preserve historic old buildings, battlefields, and cemeteries—significant parts of the American past—as to protect unique examples of natural beauty. The two tasks were tightly interlocked in his preservationist conservation philosophy. Mather had concentrated almost exclusively on the scenic national parks and had largely ignored the historical aspects of the system, although Mesa Verde National Park, Casa Grande National Monument, and a few other units had intrinsic historical interest. With the assistance of Congressman Cramton, himself an amateur historian, Albright now moved to put the Park Service into the business of restoring and preserving historic sites. He especially cov-

30. Harry J. Liek to Demaray, July 29, 1931, telegram, A. R. Carter to Director of NPS, July 31, 1931, and telegram, HMA to Director of NPS, Aug. 6, 1931, NA, Records of NPS, gen., admin., Dir. Albright; clipping from Fairbanks *Daily News-Miner*, July 27, 1931, scrapbook, HMA Papers; clippings from San Francisco *Chronicle*, July 31, 1931, and Aug. 15, 1931.

31. Telegram, Reed Smoot to HMA, July 31, 1931, NA, Records of NPS, gen., admin., Dir. Albright; interview with HMA, July 24, 1964; telegram, Hoover to HMA, July 30, 1931, and HMA to Hoover, Aug. 12, 1931, Hoover Papers, box 1-G/269.

eted the Civil War battlefields and cemeteries, which were then under the jurisdiction of the War Department, but he sensed that he had little chance of getting control of them in 1929. He decided to concentrate on other facets of historic preservation while waiting for a more opportune time to take up the question of the battlefields. He saw in this enterprise a chance to do something that interested him tremendously, but, more important, he recognized an opportunity to make the Park Service and its program better known in the populous East, thus giving his bureau a truly nationwide appeal. Mather had pushed the idea of establishing national parks in Virginia, Kentucky, Tennessee and North Carolina, for essentially the same reason.[32]

The memory of George Washington and the upcoming bicentennial celebration of his birth gave Albright the entrée he needed. Mrs. H. L. Rust, a resident of the District of Columbia and the great-great-grandniece of George Washington, was the guiding spirit behind the Wakefield Memorial Association, whose members were attempting to raise money to restore Washington's birthplace. The restoration was to be completed by 1932 in time for the two-hundredth anniversary of the great man's birth. The ladies acquired one hundred acres of land at the center of the old Wakefield estate on Pope Creek near the Potomac River, but their fund-raising campaign stalled before they could start on the house, which had to be reconstructed from the foundation up. Mrs. Rust came to Albright for help, although technically the War Department already held jurisdiction over the only government-owned land at Wakefield, a tiny rectangular plot on which a modest granite marker stood identifying the place of Washington's birth. Acting swiftly, Albright got in touch with Cramton and launched the drive that culminated in the establishment of the George Washington Birthplace National Monument. At Albright's urging, John D. Rockefeller, Jr., purchased 254 acres of land for the monument, and the federal government pledged itself to rebuild the old house. Cramton coaxed the necessary legislation through Congress in January

32. HMA candidly discussed his motives for undertaking historic preservation in his "Reminiscences," pp. 391–94.

1930, secure in the knowledge that the members of Congress would find it impossible to turn their backs on the nation's founding father. Albright at last had his foot in the door. He proudly noted in his 1930 annual report that the act placed the George Washington Birthplace National Monument under Park Service administration and marked "the entrance of this Service into the field of preservation of historic places on a more comprehensive scale."[33]

At about the same time, Albright and Cramton started laying the groundwork for the establishment of a proposed Colonial National Monument, which would insure the preservation of the Jamestown-Yorktown-Williamsburg area of Virginia. Rockefeller had already begun the restoration of Williamsburg, but neither Jamestown Island nor the Yorktown battlefield, where Cornwallis surrendered to Washington to end the War of Independence, had received systematic attention. The Association for the Preservation of Virginia Antiquities owned the tip of Jamestown Island and eagerly offered to cooperate with the Park Service. The idea for the Colonial National Monument originated with Cramton, not Albright, but the latter joined enthusiastically in the effort to win approval of the project. Congressional action was necessary because the federal government would have to purchase the land for the monument from private owners. Once again reminding the members of Congress of the glories of the American past, Cramton and Albright got the enabling legislation enacted in July 1930. And in December 1930 Albright secured a presidential proclamation signing over a strip of federally owned land along the York River to the National Park Service for construction of a parkway connecting Yorktown, Williamsburg, and Jamestown. The land had previously belonged to the United States Navy.[34]

33. HMA, "Reminiscences," pp. 396–99; HMA to Ralph L. Phelps, Sept. 26, 1932, NA, Records of NPS, gen. admin., Dir. Albright; *Annual Report, NPS* (1930), p. 6.
34. *Annual Report, NPS* (1931), p. 8; HMA to Harlan P. Kelsey, Apr. 2, 1931, and HMA to Harold P. Fabian, Jan. 4, 1932, NA, Records of NPS, gen., admin., Dir. Albright; HMA, "Reminiscences," pp. 394–96, 399–400.

Establishment of the Colonial National Monument buttressed
the precedent set a few months earlier by the authorization of
the George Washington Birthplace National Monument. The
preservation and protection of historic buildings and locations
now became part of the program of the National Park Service.
Albright's appointment of Verne E. Chatelain as the bureau's
first staff historian further institutionalized the new historical
emphasis in the Park Service.[35]

It was significant that Albright found it necessary to cooperate with groups like the Wakefield Memorial Association, the
Association for the Preservation of Virginia Antiquities, and
the American Scenic and Historic Preservation Society in initi-
ating his program of historic preservation. During the 1920s
the urge to glorify and preserve the American past reached fever
pitch. Congress drastically curtailed immigration. Foreign ideol-
ogies came under heated attack from "100 per cent Americans"
and various patriotic organizations. Groups such as the DAR accelerated their efforts to preserve the traditions and values of
Anglo-Saxon America. By stressing the need to preserve certain
tangible parts of the American heritage—scenic or historic—
for the enjoyment and edification of future generations, Mather
and Albright capitalized on the mood of the times and won the
support of influential old-stock Americans. Madison Grant, one
of the leading spokesmen for the restriction of immigration in
the 1920s, was an enthusiastic supporter of the National Park
Service throughout the Mather-Albright era. One may suspect, in other words, that the nativism and nationalism of the
1920s contributed to the rise of the National Park Service and
helped account for Albright's success in starting a program of
historic preservation. Not a nativist himself, Albright frankly
saw nothing wrong with accepting help from groups that advocated Anglo-Saxon superiority. This, after all, was the kind of
opportunism he had learned from Mather, who made it a practice to cultivate support wherever he could find it, and who will-

35. *Annual Report, NPS* (1931), p. 16.

ingly worked with any and all groups in order to advance the cause of the national parks.[36]

Another area in which Albright exhibited a strong interest was the bureau's educational, or "interpretive," program. Soon after becoming director, he took steps to reorganize and coordinate the interpretive work of the Service. He had inherited from Mather a scant handful of park museums, a vigorous but small nature-guide program, and a feeling for the importance of explaining the outstanding features of the parks to the public. In 1929, following the recommendations of an informal advisory committee headed by John C. Merriam, president of the Carnegie Institution, Albright established a Branch of Education and Research. He then convinced Harold C. Bryant, one of the originators (along with Loye Miller) of the nature-guide program and a member of the advisory committee, to accept an appointment as assistant director in charge of the new branch. Next, he set out to convince the park superintendents of the need for organizing museums and interpreting the parks for the public. In 1930 and 1931 he secured large increases in the appropriations for the bureau's interpretive activities, including research projects in the historical and scientific fields most pertinent to the national parks. Museums, featuring geographic displays and natural exhibits, received unprecedented financial support, and the number of guided hikes, nature trails, and campfire lectures rapidly multiplied. Under Bryant's leadership and with Albright's strong support, the Park Service's educational program became increasingly sophisticated and cohesive. Within two years, it was solidly established as one of the bureau's major functions.[37]

36. Albright stayed in touch with Madison Grant throughout his directorship; see, for example, Grant to HMA, Jan. 25, 1929, HMA to Grant, Jan. 31, 1929, and HMA to W. C. Gregg, July 13, 1932, NA, Records of NPS, gen., admin., Dir. Albright; see also HMA, "Our Scenic and Historic National Parks" (Speech delivered to Virginia chapter of the DAR, Nov. 3, 1931), HMA Papers.

37. *Annual Report, NPS* (1929), pp. 12–18, contains the report of the educational committee, see also (1930), pp. 17–24; John C. Mer-

Albright enjoyed a cordial and gratifying official relationship with both the White House staff and the president during the Hoover administration. He already knew Bill Starling, head of the Secret Service. Within a few weeks, he got to know George E. Akerson and Lawrence Richey, two of Hoover's secretaries. Maurice Latta, the White House legislative clerk, remembered him well from the days of Woodrow Wilson. Albright sometimes went to the president's office, usually at Wilbur's suggestion, to confer with Hoover about national park matters and conservation affairs in general. He confidently assumed that his personal acquaintance with the president would be to his advantage, and it probably was. In budgetary decisions, Hoover often favored the national parks, and he willingly signed a number of executive orders that Albright wanted. In return, the Park Service director evinced a strong loyalty to the Republican chief executive, whose views usually coincided with his own. He found the mood of the Hoover administration, especially in its first two years, both congenial and attractive.[38]

Almost immediately after taking office in 1929, Hoover decided to build a fishing camp and weekend vacation retreat within easy driving distance of Washington. All construction costs were to come out of his own pocket. Albright, as an expert on scenery, found himself appointed to a committee to help select an appropriate site for the camp. Teaming with Starling and Richey, from the White House staff, and Henry O'Malley, commissioner of fisheries, he toured three or four potential campsites, including one in the Catoctin Mountains in Western Maryland that later became Camp David. The committee eventually narrowed its search down to an area along the upper Rapidan River, high in the scenic Blue Ridge Mountains of Virginia. W. E. Carson, Virginia's conservation commissioner, had cham-

---

riam to HMA, June 8, 1929, Merriam to Harold C. Bryant, Mar. 16, 1929, and HMA to Cammerer, Aug. 3, 1929, NA, Records of NPS, Director's Office File, Albright.

38. Albright eventually became a Hoover "fan," collecting pictures and current newspaper articles about the president; see scrapbooks for 1929 and 1930; see also HMA, "Reminiscences," pp. 413–54.

pioned this particular site for partly selfish reasons. Having the president's camp constructed on the Rapidan would publicize the region, which lay at the edge of the much-touted but still not established Shenandoah National Park. There were no roads in the area, so the committee had to make its inspection on horseback. The members agreed unanimously that the possibilities for fishing and hiking were outstanding. Furthermore, the view was superb, and the president could be adequately protected.[39]

A few days after the visit, Carson wrote to Albright requesting him to "put oil in the bearings" when the committee made its decision. Actually, no oil was necessary. The committee reported enthusiastically in favor of the Rapidan site. The state of Virginia readily agreed to construct a gravel road to the Rapidan Valley, and Hoover had his fishing camp ready for use by the fall of 1929. Later, as the problems of the Great Depression became overpowering, the president seldom ventured very far from the White House. The Rapidan camp became his favorite retreat. It was here that he entertained dignitaries from around the world, including Prime Minister Ramsay McDonald of Great Britain, who, according to press reports, sat contentedly on the end of a log to discuss international affairs.[40]

From time to time Hoover also invited groups of his cabinet officers and bureau chiefs to spend the weekend with him at his camp. Albright's turn came in May 1931, just as he was preparing to leave on a junket to Hot Springs National Park. He and Grace hastily joined the other officers of the Interior Department and their wives. Everybody understood that the weekend was not to be entirely social, for the president had announced his intention to take up the matter of how Interior Department expenditures could be reduced in the next fiscal yar. With the depression growing more and more serious every day and the

39. HMA, "Reminiscences," pp. 433–40, 444–45.
40. W. E. Carson to HMA, Mar. 14, 1929, and HMA to Carson, Mar. 27, 1929, NA, Records of NPS, Director's Office File, Albright; *New York Times*, Oct. 4–12, 1929, contains a report of McDonald's visit to the United States.

federal deficit rapidly increasing, he had decided on an all-out attempt to balance the budget.[41]

The group arrived at the camp in time for an early luncheon in the compound's rustic dining hall. No tedious observance of protocol inhibited the group. After luncheon the members of the party scattered "to games, walks, horseback riding, fishing, and other amusements," until about three o'clock, when Hoover called the men to his own cabin for a conference. A friendly debate between Hoover and W. C. Mendenhall, the director of the United States Geological Survey, about which one of them signed on first with the USGS typified the congenial atmosphere of the talks. (Hoover had worked for the Geological Survey as a young geology student, but, as it turned out, Mendenhall had begun his career with the bureau a few weeks earlier.) *The New York Times* later reported that the bureau chiefs voluntarily agreed to lop off about five million dollars from the Interior Department budget for fiscal year 1932 and about seven million dollars in 1933. The president and Mrs. Hoover retired early, after inviting all those interested in horseback riding to meet them at the stables the next morning.[42]

Albright discovered to his utter astonishment that among the leaders of the Interior Department he alone had the stamina and fortitude to roll out of bed early on Sunday morning for a horseback ride with the president and his wife. A Secret Service man and Theodore Joslin, a recent addition to the White House staff, completed the party. "We were out all morning," Albright recalled. "We rode clear to the top of the range and went along . . . the summit, where we could look down into the Shenandoah Valley," which stretched out for fifty miles on the other side of the ridge. "Albright," Hoover remarked after viewing the unusually flat and even contours of the ridge, "there ought to be a highway up here, a parkway. It's just a natural." Albright agreed that the terrain was suitable for a road, and he promised to look

41. HMA to W. W. Thompson, May 13, 1931, NA, Records of NPS, gen., admin., Dir. Albright; Washington *Post*, May 16, 1931.
42. *New York Times*, May 17, 1931; clipping from *Park Service Bulletin* [May 1931], scrapbook, HMA Papers.

into the costs of such a project. The famed Skyline Drive through the heart of Virginia's Blue Ridge country, now one of the most popular attractions in the national park system, grew out of this casual conversation. Albright, Joslin, and the Hoovers cantered back into camp about noon, chiding the others for their slothfulness. The weekend gathering broke up after lunch.[43]

The collapse of the American economy eventually overshadowed everything else during the Hoover administration, especially after the summer of 1931, as the search for ways to restore the nation's economic health became urgent and the congressional budget-slashing drive gained momentum. Fortunately, the National Park Service was in a better position to survive a fiscal crisis than many other federal agencies, not only because of Albright's connections on the Hill, but also because the national parks, like the national forests, provided endless opportunities for public works projects. "Emergency funds," made available by Congress to stimulate the economy, built many miles of roads in the national parks and kept the Park Service organization functioning virtually at full capacity.[44]

43. Clipping from *Park Service Bulletin* [May 1931], scrapbook, HMA Papers; HMA, "Reminiscences," pp. 442–44; "Memorandum for the Secretary from HMA" [about proposed Skyline Drive] (Apr. 21, 1931), and HMA to W. W. Thompson, May 18, 1931, NA, Records of NPS, gen., admin., Dir. Albright.

44. *Annual Report, NPS* (1931), pp. 32–33 (1932), pp. 31–33; Cammerer to W. C. Gregg, June 22, 1932, telegram, HMA to Director of NPS, July 3, 1932, Demaray to HMA, July 9, 1932, and HMA to Gregg, July 13, 1932, NA, Records of NPS, gen., admin. Dir. Albright; interview with George L. Mauger, June 20, 1964.

9

Albright, Ickes, and the Hundred Days

A Ford trimotor plane lumbered down the runway in Albany, New York, and climbed slowly into the gray, stormy sky. Franklin D. Roosevelt sat inside the plane as it bounced through the turbulent air, landing at Buffalo, Cleveland, and at last at Chicago. The day before, the Democrats had nominated him to run for president, and he had unexpectedly announced that he would fly to Chicago to accept the nomination in person. "I pledge you —I pledge myself," he said, "to a new deal for the American people." The hard-fought election campaign of 1932 was now in full swing and its outcome would directly influence both Horace Albright and the National Park Service.[1]

The Republicans also held their convention in Chicago that summer. Albright arrived in the Windy City on the first leg of his annual western inspection trip shortly after the gavel fell opening the proceedings. He attended two long afternoon sessions and was captivated by the ritualistic spectacle. Going through their agenda expeditiously but without much enthusiasm, the Republicans again nominated Hoover to head their ticket. But the president grimly refused to come to Chicago, deciding instead to remain in Washington to concentrate on the problems of the Great Depression. The nation's economy had continued its frightening downward spiral throughout 1931 and 1932. Unemployment figures stood at all-time highs, with mil-

Portions of this chapter appeared, in slightly different form, in *Pacific Historical Review* 34 (Nov. 1965) : 455–65. Reprinted by permission.
1. *New York Times*, July 2–4, 1932.

lions of workers on the relief rolls. By mid-1932 the voters were in a disgruntled mood, and the chances for a Republican victory looked dim.[2]

After three days in Chicago, Albright continued his westward journey, testing and analyzing the political winds at every stop. He inspected the major parks and monuments in the Rocky Mountain region and then proceeded to San Francisco. Not long after he arrived in California, his good friend Ralph Phelps invited him to spend a few days at the Bohemian Grove, a luxurious, redwood-studded campground north of San Francisco, owned by the members of the Bohemian Club. A day or two of camaraderie gave Albright ample opportunity to meet many of the campers. One night, amid loud singing and storytelling around the campfire, he discreetly began questioning his companions about the coming election. At first, most of them asserted their steadfast loyalty to Hoover, who for many years had spent a part of each summer at his cabin in the Bohemian Grove. But as the evening wore on and the gentleman campers slowly drained their hip flasks—standard equipment for gentleman campers during the prohibition era—the incredible truth emerged. Almost all of these men planned to vote against the Republican candidate. A week later, back in San Francisco, Albright revealed the outcome of his informal poll to Secretary Wilbur, who had also been a guest at the Bohemian Grove. The Secretary openly scoffed at him and curtly exclaimed that his own observations made him confident Hoover would win.[3]

Now intensely curious, Albright decided to travel by automobile to Sequoia Park, which was the next stop on his itinerary, pausing to question people all along the way about which candidate they planned to support. By his own reckoning, he talked to 135 persons, including gas station attendants, bank tellers,

2. *New York Times*, June 14–20, 1932; ticket stubs and clippings about the convention are in scrapbook, HMA Papers.

3. Cramton to HMA, Aug. 11, 1932, and HMA to Wilbur, Aug. 23, 1932, NA, Records of NPS, gen., admin., Dir. Albright, reveal Albright's concerted effort to collect political information; interview with HMA, Dec. 19, 1964.

farmers, housewives, businessmen, and waitresses, only two of
whom said they intended to vote for Hoover.[4]

Later that summer, Albright went to Jackson, Wyoming, to
confer with the Senate's Special Committee on Wildlife about the
Jackson Hole–Grand Teton Park project and also about the
problems of preserving the valuable Jackson Hole elk herd.
Senators Frederic C. Walcott, Peter Norbeck, Key Pittman,
Charles L. McNary, and Harry B. Hawes made up the committee. These men, some of the shrewdest politicians in Washington,
unanimously agreed that Hoover would be swamped at the polls.[5]

By the time Albright returned to Washington, it was perfectly
clear to him that Hoover's days in the White House were num-
bered. Yet very few of the president's close associates could
bring themselves to admit that their chief faced almost certain
defeat. Ted Joslin, still a member of Hoover's White House staff,
lived only two doors down the street from the Albrights. One
Indian-summer day, as Joslin and Albright sat on the curb
scuffing their feet in the fallen leaves, their conversation inevitably drifted to the approaching election. Joslin absolutely refused to believe that the voters were as opposed to Hoover as
Albright's impromptu polls showed. In fact, he accused his
neighbor of outright disloyalty and finally shouted, "How do
you expect Hoover to win if even the members of his own administration talk like that?"[6]

Albright sincerely sympathized with Hoover, whom he regarded with great respect and affection. He deeply regretted the
Republicans' impending defeat, but he quickly and pragmatically faced up to the political implications of a probable Democratic triumph.

The National Park Service had always attempted to stand
above partisan politics, and Albright intended for it to continue

4. HMA to I. H. Larom, Nov. 1, 1932, NA, Records of NPS, gen.,
admin., Dir. Albright; interview with HMA, Dec. 19, 1964.

5. HMA to Peter Norbeck, June 13, 1932, NA, Records of NPS, gen.,
admin., Dir. Albright; "Air Views of Dakota Bad Lands," bound scrapbook (Sept. 1932), HMA Papers.

6. Interview with HMA, Dec. 19, 1964; Albright, "Reminiscences,"
p. 605.

its nonpartisan course. There were, however, several questions that needed to be asked. One was—Who would become Secretary of the Interior in the new administration? Albright immediately put out feelers among his Democratic friends in Washington, letting it be known that he wanted to hear about all possibilities for the secretarial post. A second question that had to be faced was whether he himself could expect to be retained as director. To Albright this was much more than a purely personal consideration. The continuity of Park Service policies and the hallowed Mather tradition of Park Service leadership were at stake. A nagging sense of insecurity bothered him more and more. "We are assuming that there will be no change," he confided to a friendly columnist in Los Angeles, "but . . . the situation is dangerous and it may be decided that there will have to be at least a new director." He resolved to concentrate on the dual task of safeguarding his own job and insuring a smooth transition for the Park Service after the Democrats swept to an overwhelming victory in November 1932.[7]

It was almost automatic for Albright to turn to Huston Thompson for information about the Democratic party. In 1925, at the end of a seven-year term on the Federal Trade Commission, Thompson had bowed out of active government service, but like many other retired public officials he chose to stay in Washington to practice law and dabble in politics behind the scenes. As one privy to the highest councils of the Democratic party, he could be, and often was, enormously helpful to Mather, Albright, and the National Park Service. One day, during the third week in February 1933, he telephoned Albright. "Horace, did you ever hear of a man called Ickes?" he asked. When Albright said no, Thompson continued, "Well you'd better find out about him, because he's very likely to be your next secretary." Some fast research in the Park Service files revealed that Mather and Ickes had known each other since the Bull Moose campaign of 1912 and had been on a first-name basis for more than ten years. The Park Service would evidently not be dealing with a com-

7. HMA to Henry Carr, Jan. 17, 1933, NA, Records of NPS, gen., admin., Dir. Albright.

plete stranger if Ickes took over as Secretary. With this com-
forting information in hand, Albright began to relax. The story
of Ickes's selection broke in the newspapers a few days after
Thompson's telephone call.[8]

Albright continued to suspect, however, that his own position
as director was not entirely secure. He had been closely associated with the Hoover administration for the past four years, and
it was conceivable that the Democrats would want to oust him.
Moreover, Senator Kenneth D. McKellar, a powerful Democrat
from Tennessee, seemed to be after his scalp for refusing to
have a road built—the senator had in mind another Skyline
Drive—along the ridge of the Great Smoky Mountains National
Park. Herbert E. Evans, a wealthy New York businessman, assured Albright that "some people very close to Governor Roosevelt have the welfare of your Department at heart." Albright
replied that this was "wonderfully encouraging." But, still worried about his political vulnerability, he asked Raymond T.
Baker, another veteran of the Wilson administration, to help
bolster his personal position.[9]

Ray Baker, formerly director of the Mint, was a remarkable
character, smooth, tough, and versatile. He came from the mining district of Nevada. An inveterate backslapper and big-dealer,
he knew every politician of consequence in Washington, at least
on the Democratic side, and he assiduously maintained his contacts. During World War I, he was reportedly the only man in
America who could walk up to President Wilson, slap him on
the back, and call him "Woody." He moved freely in the highest
Democratic circles, cultivating his well-developed sense of humor and meeting the right people. It seemed only fitting when he
was named chairman of Roosevelt's Inaugural Committee in
1933.[10]

8. HMA, "Reminiscences," pp. 511–15; clipping from Washington
Evening Star, Feb. 23, 1933, scrapbook, HMA Papers.
9. Herbert E. Evans to HMA, Nov. 30, 1932, and HMA to Evans,
Dec. 12, 1932, NA, Records of NPS, gen., admin., Dir. Albright.
10. HMA, "Reminiscences," p. 62.

On official business at the Capitol early in February, Albright accidentally ran into Baker. This was the day the Park Service director had picked for a showdown with Senator McKellar, who had refused his repeated requests for a personal conference. Marching to the Senate chamber, Albright sent in his personal card to request that the senator leave the floor. But McKellar refused. Frustrated and angry, Albright started to walk away when he met Baker. The former director of the Mint listened intently while Albright poured out a description of his feud with McKellar, and then, with a faintly mischievous chuckle, Baker dispatched his own card to the senator. McKellar promptly came out of the Senate chamber, extending his hand for what he thought would be a perfunctory handshake. In the act of returning McKellar's greeting, Baker got a firm purchase on the senator's hand and simply refused to let go. He then invited Albright to step over and have his say. The senator's face flushed and he jerked his head aside, but he could not gracefully extricate himself until Albright had finished explaining why he could not possibly build that road. McKellar may not have appreciated the subtleties of Albright's argument, but he now clearly understood that the Park Service director could summon influential Democrats as well as Republicans to his personal defense. McKellar eased off after that.[11]

Baker had still another artful idea. It had to do with changing Albright's political image. If the main problem was an overly close identification with Hoover, Baker reasoned, would it not be wise now, before the Hoover administration ended, to begin identifying Albright with Roosevelt? There was a legitimate connection to be made. Albright had known the president-elect casually since the early days of the Wilson administration. And in 1930, FDR had prevailed upon Albright to take Franklin Jr. on a tour of Zion, Bryce, and Grand Canyon parks. Later, at the sesquicentennial celebration of the battle of Yorktown, Albright and Roosevelt had renewed their acquaintance, finding

11. Interview with HMA, Dec. 19, 1964.

time for several friendly chats. It would be altogether fitting and politic, Baker decided, to have Albright on the Inaugural Committee. Arranging the appointment would pose no problem, since Baker himself was chairman. Albright readily consented to this scheme and in due course became a working member of the committee to oversee arrangements for the Inauguration Day festivities. His assignment was to see that spectator stands were erected along Pennsylvania Avenue and that decorative flags were posted along the route of the parade. Although his appointment came so late that his name failed to appear on the official printed program, it was widely known around the capital that he had served on the committee.[12]

The number of influential men in Washington, New York, and elsewhere who offered to help Albright in February 1933 demonstrated not only the high esteem in which he was generally held but also how effectively he had maintained his political connections. He could coax, persuade, and maneuver with the best of the politicians. Moreover, he could count on strong editorial support in more than a dozen states from coast to coast. "It is unthinkable," the *Arizona Republic* wrote, "that the great work" of the National Park Service "should be marred by any departure from the civil service system" or that "Mr. Albright and his assistants" should be "succeeded by spoilsmen." The influential Los Angeles *Times* expressed its belief that "even the rapacious Democrats" would "keep their hands off the National Park Department." "Horace Albright," the *Times* continued, has performed his duties "with intelligence and devotion." A Knoxville editor wrote that "East Tennessee is grateful to Horace Albright," who has "impressed everyone with his sincerity of purpose, his ability and his vision in preserving the nation's natural assets for posterity to enjoy." Few bureaucrats in Washington could muster that kind of support. Even before the New

12. An autographed picture of FDR hangs in Albright's study (it was given to Albright in a gesture of gratitude by FDR after his son's trip) ; for mementos of the Sesquicentennial at Yorktown, and Inauguration Day ticket stubs see scrapbook, HMA Papers; interview with HMA, Dec. 19, 1964.

Deal began, predictions had appeared in the press that Albright would survive "the storms of partisanship."[13]

Actually, after the second month of 1933, the question of Albright's retention became mostly academic, at least to Albright himself. Out of concern for the Park Service and personal pride, he wanted to demonstrate that he could weather the change of administration, but he had now decided that his future lay outside of the government service. "I was pleased and happy and proud in what I was doing," he later recalled, "but if a job came along..."[14]

A few days after Hoover's defeat in November 1932, Albright took his family to New York to attend the wedding of John D. Rockefeller III and Miss Blanchette Hooker. He had stayed in close touch with the entire Rockefeller family since first meeting them in Yellowstone. It was on this trip to New York that he received the offer that finally enticed him out of the government service and into the mining business.[15]

Officials of the United States Potash Company had approached him on at least three previous occasions, but he had declined to consider their financially attractive propositions. In the face of Albright's repeated refusals, the company's patience and persistence were more than a little surprising. When the initial offer from United States Potash came in the fall of 1930, Albright explained that he was not ready to quit the directorship, which he had assumed only eighteen months before. About six months later, the potash people made Albright a second offer, which he promptly declined, because by that time he was "engaged in working out the sesquicentennial of the Battle of Yorktown" and the Park Service had moved into the field of historic preservation, which interested him "tremendously." Another offer came late in 1931, and again Albright answered no.

13. Clippings from *Arizona Republic*, Mar. 6, 1933, Los Angeles *Times*, Nov. 29, 1932, and unidentified clipping (probably Knoxville *Courier*), Feb. 14, 1933, scrapbook, HMA Papers.

14. HMA, "Reminiscences," p. 605.

15. Wedding invitation, Nov. 11, 1932, scrapbook, HMA Papers; see also Diary, Nov. 13, 1932, HMA Papers.

But the proposition he received in November 1932, in the wake
of Hoover's stunning defeat, made the three earlier ones look
pale by comparison. The United States Potash Company wanted
him to become its executive vice-president and general manager at an annual salary of $20,000—more than twice as much
as his director's salary. He promised to think it over.[16]

In February 1933 he quietly informed the company that he
would accept its offer, but he insisted that "it might be three
months, it might be six months, it might be a year" before he
could break away from the Park Service. "If you want to stake
out the job for me, all right," he said. "I'll come when I can."
The company agreed.[17]

Possibly the main reason for the potash company's eagerness
to land Albright was Christian Zabriskie, one of its directors,
whose connection with the Albright family dated back to the
days of the Albright and Zabriskie undertaking establishment in
Candelaria. Zabriskie had watched the progress of Albright's
career with intense interest and was convinced that the young
man's background, training, and experience both in Washington
and in the West made him unusually well qualified for an executive position in the mining business. Zabriskie's associates evidently concurred.[18]

It was naturally flattering to Albright to be courted so assiduously by a respectable business concern. Nevertheless, his decision to resign from the Park Service did not come easily. He
had poured his very life into the national parks and had enthusiastically participated in every phase of the organization of
the National Park Service. But the more he thought about it the
more be became convinced that this was the time to make a

16. HMA to Thomas Boles, June 7, 1932, NA, Records of NPS, Director's Office File, Albright, stated that HMA intended to visit the
potash mines at Carlsbad, N.M. and the mine owners were "close
friends of mine"; HMA, "Reminiscences," pp. 603–9; interview with
HMA, Dec. 19, 1964.

17. HMA, "Reminiscences," pp. 608-9.

18. See Zabriskie to HMA, Feb. 13, 1924, HMA Papers; telegram,
Zabriskie to HMA, Jan. 23, 1933, NA, Records of NPS, gen., admin.,
Dir. Albright.

change if he ever intended to make one. After nearly four years as director, he had accomplished most of what he had originally hoped to do. Moreover, he had gone as high as he could go in the Park Service and, while he enjoyed being director, he detested the insecurity that went with the job. Bureau chiefs, like baseball managers, expect to be fired sooner or later, as Albright knew full well. Furthermore, he had the mining business in his blood. Both his father and grandfather had worked in the mines of Nevada and California, and tales of mining adventures had been handed down by word of mouth as part of the Albright-family lore. He had always hoped to specialize in mining law. Steve Mather had made his fortune in mining. From the time of his student days at Berkeley, Albright had intended someday to work in this field.

Two other considerations loomed large in Albright's thinking. One was the fact that an experienced Mather man, Arno Cammerer, was ready to step into the director's shoes. "Cam" was a conscientious administrator and, above all, true to Mather's principles of park management. The Park Service would be in good hands it seemed, at least for the foreseeable future, even without Albright. The other important consideration, one that Albright could not afford to ignore, was money. He had found it impossible to put aside any savings during his years in the Park Service. It was "hard enough to save in the government service," he explained, if a man had no outside social "responsibilities." But as director of the Park Service, he had "an obligation" to do a great deal of entertaining—"entertaining for which I had no expense account." "My children are growing up and must be educated" was his repeated lament. For the sake of his family, he concluded, the move to the business world would be more than justified.[19]

Curiously enough, one of the most persuasive personal reasons for Albright's decision operated essentially on the subconscious level, without ever being clearly articulated. Undoubtedly, he

19. HMA to William Hossley, July 1, 1933, and HMA to Norbeck, July 19, 1933, NA, Records of NPS, gen., admin., Dir. Albright; HMA, "Reminiscences," pp. 603–5.

was reaching for his own particular vision of success. This was, he believed, his "great opportunity," and he felt that he would be foolish to turn it down. "The successful ones," he had written in 1908, "are those who make the best of the occasions that offer."[20]

While considering the offer from United States Potash, Albright confided in only one man in Washington, John H. Edwards, Assistant Secretary of the Interior, whom he had known and trusted for many years. Albright wanted to make certain that he would not open himself to attack on legal or ethical grounds. He knew that since 1925 United States Potash had obtained mineral leases on more than fifteen thousand acres of the public domain through the agencies of the Interior Department. With the Teapot Dome scandal still fresh in mind, Albright wanted to take no chances. He asked Edwards to conduct a quiet but thorough investigation of the mineral leases held by United States Potash to ascertain if they were honest, valid, and aboveboard. When Edwards reported that the leases were entirely clean, he removed the last obstacle to Albright's move. It now became only a matter of picking the right time. Albright told no one except Edwards about his plans, even after his final decision had been made.[21]

The four months between Hoover's defeat and the assumption of power by Roosevelt seemed interminable. With the lame-duck Congress and a repudiated president still in office, the United States slipped and drifted dangerously close to a complete economic collapse. This was surely the nadir of the Great Depression. Hundreds of banks had closed their doors, and a feeling of desperation gripped the nation.

Harassed and besieged as he was, Hoover found the time to think about National Park matters during his last four months in office. "Having just this week explored the entire length of the Blue Ridge Skyline Road," he wrote to Secretary Wilbur, who passed the word to the Park Service, "I am qualified to tell

20. HMA to Joseph M. Dixon, Aug. 5, 1933, NA, Records of NPS, gen., admin., Dir. Albright; *Inyo Register*, May 28, 1908.
21. Interview with HMA, Dec. 20, 1964.

you what I think of it. As one mountaineer to another, it is a good road—and a very beautiful one." Albright was delighted with the president's letter, and he was equally pleased when Hoover offered to give the Rapidan camp to the government for the enjoyment of future presidents; according to Hoover's plan, the land around the camp itself would be added to the proposed Shenandoah National Park. Death Valley National Monument, a project dear to the hearts of both Albright and the residents of the Owens Valley, at last became a reality by virtue of an executive order signed by Hoover on February 11, 1933. As a final friendly gesture toward Albright and the National Park Service, Hoover's grand reorganization scheme, which he proposed in December 1932, placed all of the military parks and cemeteries under Park Service jurisdiction. That Congress refused to approve the plan was a bitter though not unexpected disappointment to Albright.[22]

Late in February 1933 thousands of Democrats flocked into Washington as the capital girded itself for the frantic round of parties and last-minute political caucuses that invariably accompany the beginning of a new administration. On March 4, the New Deal swung into action. Suddenly the city was alive with furious activity. A new boldness permeated nearly every level of the federal establishment, including both the National Park Service and the Department of the Interior, and Albright immediately found himself immersed in enough work to occupy at least three men. The next six months would be the most exciting and exhausting period in his life.

Ickes's appointment to the Roosevelt Cabinet caused many a raised eyebrow in 1933. According to the time-honored pattern of cabinet appointments, he was hardly qualified for the job. As a long-time resident of Chicago, he obviously lacked the credentials of an authentic westerner, that breed of politician to

22. Hoover to Wilbur, Dec. 6, 1932 (copy), clipping (source unidentified), Jan. 12, 1933, scrapbook, HMA Papers; Executive Order no. 2028, Feb. 11, 1933; *Annual Report of the Department of the Interior* (1933), pp. 155–61; memorandum for the Secretary from HMA, Nov. 28, 1932, Hoover Papers, Box 1-E/157; memorandum for the Secretary from HMA, Aug. 24, 1932, NA, Records of NPS, gen., admin., re-org.

whom the Interior portfolio usually passed. By no stretch of the imagination could he be considered a Democrat, although he had ardently supported Roosevelt in 1932 and had the reputation of being a maverick Republican. He was relatively inexperienced in national conservation affairs and astonishingly ignorant of the procedures of the Interior Department. Yet he settled into his new job with marvelous aplomb. By the summer of 1933, only about three months after assuming office, he had taken firm control of his sprawling department and had become one of the best-known figures in the New Deal. He made no effort to hide his sheer delight in being the Secretary of the Interior.[23]

From the beginning, Ickes's explosive personality significantly shaped his administration of the Interior Department. He was a remarkably complex and profoundly suspicious man who thrived on rancorous debate and unending controversy. A self-styled crank, he proudly labeled himself "America's No. 1 Curmudgeon, or Sour Puss," and by design set out to terrorize the employees of the Interior Department and various other governmental agencies. A joke soon made the rounds in Washington that breakfast for Harold Ickes consisted of "half a dozen ten-penny nails and a few buttered brick bats." One tough-minded member of Congress, emerging from an angry confrontation with Ickes, described him as a "prodigious bureaucrat with the soul of a meat ax and the mind of a commissar." Undeniably, the new Secretary made life miserable for hundreds of politicians and bureaucrats in Washington. He sanctioned intramural spying, telephone monitoring, eavesdropping, and professional investigations in an attempt to insure the honesty of his subordinates. He personally roamed the halls of the department looking for loafers and trying to spot inefficiency. He was, as Arthur Krock once observed, a "professional man of wrath," an administrator who often got what he wanted by calculated intimidation and vituperation.[24]

23. Harold L. Ickes, *The Autobiography of a Curmudgeon*, pp. 260–61, 263–66; see also Rexford B. Tugwell, "Reminiscences," pp. 33–34.
24. Ickes, *Autobiography*, p. 4; cartoon labeled "Tough Guy," n.d., Ickes file, HMA Papers; "Re Harold Ickes," Dec. 15, 1955, HMA

Only a few brave and trusted associates ever perceived Ickes's tenderheartedness and the fact that his legendary curmudgeonly personality was essentially contrived. "It was true," Walter Lippmann wrote, "that [Ickes] was the greatest living master of the art of quarreling. But it was not true, as he liked to pretend, that he was quarrelsome because he was bad-tempered. He was a kind and generous and warmhearted man. The Old Curmudgeon business was a false front to protect him against its being generally realized how violently virtuous, how furiously righteous, how angrily unbigoted he was almost all the time." FDR undoubtedly saw through Ickes's crusty facade, for he regarded his fiery Secretary of the Interior with an amused and tolerant eye, overlooking the stream of people who were always "running over to the White House hollering about him." Albright also came to understand that Ickes, despite his monumental outbursts, was capable of thoughtfulness and human kindness. A close friendship between these two conservationists blossomed almost immediately.[25]

Albright met Ickes for the first time in Joseph M. Dixon's office in the Interior Department a few days before FDR's inauguration. A Republican, Dixon was First Assistant Secretary of the Interior during Hoover's administration. He had once been an avid Bull Mooser. Indeed, he had served as Teddy Roosevelt's national chairman in 1912 and in that capacity had worked with Harold Ickes. They were old friends. At Ickes's specific request, Dixon summoned Albright to his office. "There's no reason in the world you should remember me," Ickes said, "but in the early twenties I made a trip out through Yellowstone Park with Howard Eaton . . . and one night you came down and made a speech to us around the campfire. . . . I was impressed with you, and I was also impressed with your administration of the park."

Papers; J. L. Penick, Jr., "Louis Russell Glavis: A Postscript to the Ballinger-Pinchot Controversy," *Pacific Northwest Quarterly* 60 (Apr. 1964): 74–75; Arthur Krock, "Reminiscences," p. 67.

25. Walter Lippmann, "Today and Tomorrow," New York *Herald Tribune*, Feb. 7, 1952, reprinted by permission of the author; Samuel B. Bledsoe, "Reminiscences," p. 186.

He went on to mention that he had a "deep affection" for Steve
Mather, and he concluded by saying that he wanted to arrange
"a talk" as soon as possible. Ickes had already made inquiries
about Albright, both in Chicago and Washington, and was fully
prepared to trust him. Albright's knowledge of Interior Department affairs and his many friends in Congress, Ickes recognized,
would make him a valuable assistant during the next few
months.[26]

The day after the inauguration, Ickes called Albright to his
office for a long talk. First, the Secretary announced that he
wanted Albright to stay on as director of the Park Service. Then
he launched into a discussion of his personal plans. "I have a
feeling there is something awfully wrong with this department,"
he said. "Ever since the days of Ballinger and Fall, I've had the
feeling it wasn't run the way it should be." Albright explained
to the new Secretary that in his opinion the employees of the
Interior Department were honest and that extensive changes
in the department would not really be necessary. Still Ickes persisted, and he specifically asked Albright to help him rebuild the
department. Albright replied that he would "be glad to help."
From that moment on, he became an unofficial Assistant to the
Secretary of the Interior, advising and assisting Ickes in nearly
every facet of Interior Department administration and policy
making. Ickes had apparently not participated in the selection
of his Assistant Secretaries, Oscar L. Chapman and Theodore
A. Walters. He knew and respected Albright and instinctively
turned to him for help.[27]

By personal inclination and conviction Ickes was a conservationist. Moreover, as an old Bull Mooser, he considered himself
a conservationist in the tradition of Theodore Roosevelt and
Gifford Pinchot. "I learned the principles of conservation at
your feet," he proudly wrote to Pinchot in April 1933, "just

26. Ickes quoted in HMA, "Reminiscences," p. 518; Charles E.
Merriam to John C. Merriam, Feb. 23, 1933, John C. Merriam Papers.
27. HMA, "Reminiscences," pp. 519–22; Elmo R. Richardson,
"Western Politics and New Deal Policies: A Study of T. A. Walters of
Idaho," *Pacific Northwest Quarterly* 54 (Jan. 1963): 9–18.

where T. R. learned his." He revealed his progressive conservationist sympathies in many ways during the Hundred Days. Significantly, he selected Harry Slattery as his personal assistant and installed him in a large Interior Department office, an act that had unusual symbolic importance. Slattery had been closely associated with Pinchot since the days of the Ballinger-Pinchot controversy, and he had been one of the small but determined band of investigators who uncovered the Teapot Dome scandal. "Liberals and progressives everywhere," the Washington *Post* observed, hailed Slattery's appointment "as indicative of a 'new deal' in the Interior Department." Later, Ickes selected Louis R. Glavis, whose charges against Ballinger originally touched off the Ballinger-Pinchot fight, to head a new bureau of investigation in the Interior Department.[28]

Ickes further revealed his progressive heritage by his extreme sensitivity to the stigma under which his department rested. He came to Washington determined to rebuild the public image of the Interior Department and to atone for Teapot Dome. "I have one consuming ambition," he told the American Civil Association after about a month in office "so to administer the affairs of the Department of the Interior that it will be restored to the public confidence and at the end of my administration . . . be on a parity in the minds of the people of the United States with any other department of the Government." The theme of expectant renaissance appeared over and over in Ickes's official correspondence and public statements during the Hundred Days. He was counting heavily on Albright to help him rebuild the department. Thus the Park Service director unexpectedly found himself in a position to exert a powerful influence on the new Secretary's emerging ideas and policies.[29]

Ickes and Albright spent many hours talking about legislative and personnel problems and about long-range plans for the In-

28. Ickes to Pinchot, Apr. 20, 1933, and Pinchot to Harry Slattery, May 12, 1932, Gifford Pinchot Papers, box 1905; see M. Nelson McGeary, *Gifford Pinchot: Forester, Politician*, p. 199; Washington *Post*, May 13, 1933; Penick, "Louis Russell Glavis," pp. 74–75.
29. Ickes quoted in Washington *Evening Star*, Apr. 20, 1933.

terior Department. Albright believed that for the sake of efficiency and good administration a department of conservation should be established in the federal government. Ickes leaned in the same direction and was encouraged by Albright to think in terms of making the Interior Department into a department of conservation, if not in name then at least in function. This, of course, would entail transferring the Forest Service from the Agriculture Department to the Interior Department, a move that Albright had favored since the early 1920s as the only way to end the spirited rivalry that existed between the Park Service and the Forest Service. It soon became obvious that Ickes had decided to aim for a department of conservation. Albright was immensely pleased, and he extended his full support to all of Ickes's reorganization schemes.[30]

In personnel matters, Ickes and Albright tended to clash. Ickes generally favored bringing in new men to fill vacancies in the department, while the Park Service director generally stood for continuity of leadership and promotion from within. During their long discussions, Albright discovered that the best way to handle the new Secretary was to stand up to him and argue as long and hard as necessary to win him over. In the case of E. K. Burlew, a career man in the department and administrative assistant to the last three Secretaries, Albright demonstrated how persuasive he could be. Ickes suddenly decided to fire Burlew on grounds that his personal assistants should not be holdovers from Wilbur's regime. Albright took the opposite point of view, explaining to Ickes that as an administrative assistant Burlew would be virtually impossible to replace. It was Burlew, with his vast knowledge of the department, Albright argued, who kept the Secretary's office running from day to day. The argument went on for more than an hour while Ickes fumed and fussed at

30. HMA to P. S. Ridsdale, Aug. 23, 1920, NA, Records of NPS, gen., admin., NPS; HMA to Mather, Oct. 20, 1921, NA, Records of NPS, gen., admin., Dir. Mather; HMA to Frank R. Oastler, Jan. 13, 1933, NA, Records of NPS, gen., admin., Dir. Albright; Harold L. Ickes, *Secret Diary of Harold L. Ickes* 1:21–22; Richard Lieber, HMA, et al. to FDR, Nov. 17, 1937, Franklin D. Roosevelt Papers, OF 177A, reveals Albright's continued support of Ickes' reorganization schemes.

Albright. At the time, Ickes seemed unconvinced, but in the end he kept Burlew on the job and later made him one of his Assistant Secretaries.[31]

At Ickes's request Albright served as one of the Interior Department's representatives at the early meetings of the Public Works Administration council, of which Ickes was chairman. This was an important assignment that required Albright to consult with his fellow bureau chiefs in the department to determine which large construction projects should be undertaken. His primary function was to protect the interests of the resource agencies, making certain that they got a fair share of available PWA money for conservation activities. On more than one occasion, Albright acted on his own initiative at the council meetings to obtain money for various Interior Department bureaus and later informed the bureau chiefs of their good fortune. As Ickes developed and trained his own PWA staff, Albright gladly gave up this job. But for every committee assignment he lost he seemed to gain two new ones.[32]

Perhaps the most important conservation program to come out of the Hundred Days was the Civilian Conservation Corps, an agency proposed by Roosevelt himself for the purpose of putting unemployed young men to work in the national parks and national forests. Albright became one of the central figures in the founding of the CCC by virtue of his appointment as the Interior Department's representative on the CCC council. Albright, R. Y. Stuart of the Forest Service, Frank Persons of the Labor Department, and Colonel Duncan Major of the War Department met almost every day during the early weeks of the New Deal in Louis McHenry Howe's White House office to confer about the CCC. They established the original administrative organization and allocated the original CCC funds. They decided where the first camps should be built, what kind of projects should be undertaken, and what special technicians should be hired. They worked out large transportation, medical, and recreational programs for the boys in the camps. Albright remembers

31. HMA, "Reminiscences," pp. 539–42.
32. HMA, "Reminiscences," p. 521.

with amusement the morning that James A. Farley, the Post-master General, stuck his head into Howe's office and said, "I want to see you boys one of these times, pretty soon." His intentions were so obvious that the council decided then and there to hire their own technicians as soon as possible in order to thwart FDR's patronage boss. By dint of hard work and effective planning, the CCC council had three hundred thousand boys in camp by the middle of June. Without a trace of reluctance, Ickes delegated his authority to Albright even in this project, which was one of the president's pet programs.[33]

Albright continued as director of the Park Service, although he had precious little time to devote exclusively to national park affairs. He let Cammerer take over many of the director's routine administrative chores, but he kept firm control of his bureau's political and legislative programs. Ickes came to think so highly of Albright that he publicly announced his confidence in him; Albright would never be removed from the directorship, the Secretary proclaimed, "except over my prostrate form."[34]

In addition to his many other duties, Albright found that al-most every weekend he received an invitation—actually a com-mand—to go motoring with the Secretary, who enjoyed nothing more than touring the historic and scenic spots in the vicinity of Washington. Albright knew every hill and valley in that part of the country, and he could talk for hours about the Civil War battles that occurred in Virginia and Maryland. His endless fund of anecdotes, his eye for interesting details, and his amiable per-sonality made him a superb tour guide. Together, Ickes and Al-bright visited Manassas, Fredericksburg, Richmond, Gettys-burg, Antietam, the Shenandoah Valley, Jamestown, Williams-

33. "Minutes of the Advisory Council" (Apr.–June, 1933), NA, Records of the CCC; HMA, "Reminiscences," pp. 587–600; for addi-tional evidence of Farley's interest in CCC appointments see "The For-est Service and the ECW," NA, Records of the CCC, Reference Data File, pp. 31–32; see also John A. Salmond, *The Civilian Conservation Corps, 1933–1942: A New Deal Case Study.*

34. Ickes quoted in Washington *Evening Star,* Apr. 20, 1933; for Cammerer's role in NPS affairs, see NA, Records of NPS, gen., admin., Assoc. Dir. Cammerer, Apr.–June, 1933.

burg, and Yorktown. On a number of these outings, Senator Hiram Johnson, Ickes's ally and best friend in Washington, went along. As the weekend trips multiplied, they gave Albright an extraordinary chance to influence Ickes's thinking about important conservation issues and especially about national park affairs. The pragmatic Park Service director consciously strove to make the most of his advantage. Ickes was foot-loose, because his wife, who was a member of the Illinois state legislature, had remained in Chicago to attend to her legislative duties.[35]

In May, Ickes and Albright visited the Colonial National Monument in Virginia. As they returned to Washington, Ickes remembered that he had a dinner engagement at Hiram Johnson's home that evening. It was evident that he would be a few minutes late, so he stopped to telephone the senator. Albright bought a newspaper and stood idly paging through it as he waited for the Secretary. On an inside page, a brief Associated Press article caught his eye. "By special order sent today," the story began, Harold Ickes "renamed" Hoover Dam. The giant concrete structure, the story claimed, would "hereafter" be known as "Boulder Dam." Albright showed the article to Ickes, who muttered that it made him look like a petty politician. Albright concurred and argued strongly against any change in name. It would be a completely pointless gesture, he observed, because the Republicans would surely restore the old name just as soon as they got back in power.[36]

The next morning Ickes called Albright to his office and sheepishly inquired about the proper procedure for officially changing the name of Hoover Dam to Boulder Dam. Apparently

35. Memorandum for the Secretary from HMA, Mar. 27, 1933, HMA to W. P. Kenney, Mar. 28, 1933, and HMA to John D. Rockefeller, Jr., NA, Records of NPS, gen., admin., Dir. Albright; Washington *Post*, Apr. 3, 1933; HMA, "Reminiscences," p. 536; interview with Donald Lee (Ickes' private secretary), Aug. 25, 1964.

36. HMA to Kenneth Chorley, May 19, 1933, NA, Records of NPS, Director's Office File, Albright, contains a full description of the trip; *New York Times*, May 14, 1933; "Secretary Ickes Changes Name of Hoover Dam," (MS), HMA Papers; HMA, "Reminiscences," pp. 542–47.

Senator Johnson had persuaded Ickes to go ahead with the name change. Within a few days a remarkable flood of protesting mail landed on the Secretary's desk. "You miserable dirty pica-yune low down politician," one letter began. "It takes a small democrat to be so low as to try to hurt Hoover. . . . Why not do the whole rotten job and call it after yourself?" The flood of mail continued for the next thirteen years.[37]

During the Hundred Days, Albright also had a chance to exert his persuasive powers on FDR. Early in April, he received a tele-phone call from the White House inviting him to accompany the president on a Sunday outing to the Rapidan Camp. The purpose of the trip was to see whether the campsite would be suitable for Roosevelt's special needs. When Albright arrived at the White House, he found about twenty people waiting and a motor caravan being organized. In the lead car, a sporty Buick roadster, sat the president and his wife. Mrs. Roosevelt was behind the wheel. The rest of the party arranged itself in six trailing vehicles. Henry Morgenthau and his wife were there. Marguerite LeHand, Grace Tully, and Louis McHenry Howe, members of the president's personal staff, were also present. John Roosevelt, Horace Albright, Harold Ickes, and several others, including the ubiquitous Secret Service men, comprised the rest of the group. It was Roosevelt's first full holiday since assum-ing the presidency, and he was enjoying himself enormously.[38]

Albright rode with Ickes during the two-hour drive down to the Rapidan camp. It was a superbly sunny April day. "Peach and apple trees were blooming pink and white," the newspapers reported "and the meadows were green with springtime." Arriv-ing at Rapidan just about noon, Roosevelt climbed out of his car and started to walk on his crutches toward Hoover's cabin, but the rough terrain made this impossibly hard for him. About halfway to the cabin, FDR gave in and let himself be carried

37. "Secretary Ickes Changes Name of Hoover Dam"; anonymous letter to Ickes, received May 16, 1933, NA, Records of the Reclamation Bureau, Colorado River Storage, protests; see Ickes' defense of his position, published in the New York *Herald Tribune*, May 26, 1933; HMA, "Reminiscences," pp. 547–53.

38. *New York Times*, Apr. 10, 1933.

the rest of the way. Albright, as one of the youngest men in the party, helped carry the president to a comfortable chair on the porch. Luxurious white blossoms covered the dogwood trees around the camp, and the swiftly running trout stream sparkled in the sun. It was a magnificent setting, but everyone in the party agreed that FDR would not be able to use the camp. The uneven terrain, the very ruggedness that accounted for its rustic charm, made it unsuitable for a cripple.[39]

After about two hours at the camp, the president decided that it was time to begin the journey back to Washington. He motioned to Albright to join him in his car for the return trip. This time the president preferred to ride in a seven-passenger touring car. The caravan headed north on Skyline Drive to Panorama and then swung back toward Washington by way of Sperryville.[40]

For more than four hours that afternoon, Albright sat with Roosevelt talking about the scenic Skyline Drive, Shenandoah National Park, and other points of interest. It was a made-to-order opportunity for a shrewd salesman like Albright, and he eagerly capitalized on it. Going down the hill by Panorama, he pointed out an abandoned farm as a prime example of destructive soil erosion. Roosevelt immediately stopped the car and examined the scene with great care, ordering a number of pictures to be taken. But Albright had historic preservation on his mind. His specific goal was to arrange the transfer of the Civil War battlefields and cemeteries from the War Department to the National Park Service. As the black limousine crossed the Rappahannock River, Albright casually began talking about the Second Battle of Bull Run, and then shifted the conversation to Williamsburg, Yorktown, and the entire problem of historic preservation. He explained that the famous battlefields of the Civil War should be receiving the specialized care that only the Park Service could give them. FDR enthusiastically agreed and pointed out that he had been trying for years to have the Revolutionary War battlefield at Saratoga, New York, set aside

39. *New York Times*, Apr. 10, 1933; interview with HMA, Dec. 19, 1964.
40. *New York Times*, Apr. 10, 1933; Ickes, *Secret Diary* 1:18–19.

as a park. "I knew before we got to Washington that night," Albright later recalled, "that I had my foot not only in the door for historic preservation, but I had it in the White House." Secretary Ickes provided the one jarring note in an otherwise memorable day. His car, the *New York Times* reported, "bumped another automobile" near Falls Church, Virginia, causing "two bent fenders."[41]

Albright's afternoon conversation with the president came at a highly opportune moment. The director of the National Park Service was not the only one in Washington who had reorganization schemes in mind early in 1933. It was commonly known that Gifford Pinchot's followers had been pushing their old plan to consolidate the Park Service with the Forest Service in the Department of Agriculture. Albright found himself in the forefront of this fight. "I hope you will keep your eyes on the reorganization problem," he wrote to the leaders of the American Civic Association. "If we are not very careful we will wake up some morning and find the National Park Service a subdivision of some other bureau, probably in the Department of Agriculture." Albright's preservationist point of view afforded a timely counterbalance to Pinchot's forceful letters to Roosevelt, all of which were addressed to "Dear Franklin," and most of which preached a militant brand of utilitarian conservation.[42]

The Rapidan outing caused Albright to entertain second thoughts about leaving the Park Service. Having now established close personal relations with the president, he "could see opportunities at every turn," and "money was coming in [for the national parks] in a golden flow." But he decided that his earlier decision—still unannounced—was best. Once he achieved his reorganization objectives, he would feel free to leave. "I have been treated splendidly by the new administration

41. HMA, "Reminiscences," pp. 402–4; interview with HMA, Dec. 19, 1964; *New York Times*, Apr. 10, 1933.

42. Washington *Post*, Nov. 29, 1932; Ickes, *Secret Diary* 1:21–24; HMA to Wallace W. Attwood, Mar. 7, 1933, and William B. Greeley to HMA, Mar. 14, 1933, NA, Records of NPS, Director's Office File, Albright; Pinchot to FDR, Apr. 18, 1933, and FDR to Pinchot, Apr. 21, 1933, Franklin D. Roosevelt Papers, PPF 289.

. . . and I hate to leave," he wrote. "However, I am burning my bridges behind me."[43]

A grand reorganization of the executive branch of the federal government now seemed inevitable. Congress had thwarted Hoover's attempt to carry out a far-reaching federal reorganization just before he left office. But it was generally agreed that changes should be made. A few days after his trip to Rapidan, the president established a committee on reorganization, with Lewis W. Douglas, director of the Budget Bureau, as chairman. Suggestions for remodeling the various departments and bureaus of the executive branch began to flow in, among them many of the same proposals Hoover had made. Albright promptly submitted his plan for shifting the military parks and historic cemeteries to the jurisdiction of the Park Service. In a surprisingly short time, he got a call to meet Douglas at the White House. Albright sensed that he was going to get what he wanted, but he was unprepared for the magnitude of the changes Douglas suggested. Not only did the budget director propose that all military monuments and parks be transferred to the Park Service, but he also planned to give Albright's bureau general jurisdiction over all parks, monuments, and public buildings in the District of Columbia, all national cemeteries in the country, and both the Fine Arts Commission and the National Capital Park and Planning Commission. The Park Service would be renamed the Bureau of National Parks, Public Buildings, and Monuments. Albright's first reaction was to blurt out, "We're in the park business. We don't want the public buildings." Furthermore, he explained, the Park Service had no special competence in burying dead soldiers. He wanted the historic battlefields and the Custis Lee Mansion, but he passionately hoped that the Army Department would fight to retain its own unfilled burial grounds, especially Arlington National Cemetery.[44]

43. HMA, "Reminiscences," pp. 404–8; HMA to Joseph M. Dixon, Aug. 5, 1933, NA, Records of NPS, gen., admin., Dir. Albright.

44. Washington *Evening Star*, Apr. 30, 1933; memorandum for the Secretary, June 9, 1933, NA, Records of NPS, Director's Office File, Albright; Shankland, *Steve Mather*, pp. 300–301; HMA, "Reminiscenses," pp. 404–8.

After consulting with Frederic A. Delano, FDR's uncle, who was the chairman of the National Capital Park and Planning Commission, Albright decided to accept Douglas's proposals, at least for the moment, and work to divest the Park Service of both the public buildings and Arlington Cemetery at some future date. Hopefully, the name "National Park Service" could also be restored eventually. By flatly declaring that he was "not going to be bothered" with army "rigamarole or priority or protocol" and that "if anybody's found to be a deserter after he's dead, we're just going to leave him there in his grave," Albright got the army to reclaim Arlington Cemetery. Of course, he retained jurisdiction over the Civil War battlefields and burial grounds. He also got a supplementary executive order freeing the National Capital Park and Planning Commission and the Fine Arts Commission from Park Service supervision except for purposes of administrative housekeeping.[45]

At last Albright had achieved all of the major goals he had set for himself as director. He decided it would now be proper to submit his resignation and publicly announce his intention to leave the Park Service. He spoke to Secretary Ickes personally about his plans and a few days later sent in a letter of resignation. "It is with the keenest regret," he wrote, "that I leave the Department of the Interior after more than twenty years." His Park Service career had been "filled with hard work," he said, but also with "adventure and excitement." He expressed gratitude for the "efficient aid and support of an extraordinary group of capable, loyal, faithful men and women, my associates in the Service." He thanked Ickes for his "magnificent support" of the national parks and expressed gratitude for the Secretary's kindness to him personally. "I shall always remember with keen delight," he wrote, "the hours we have spent together in our journeys out of Washington. . . ." "If in private life I can serve you at any time," he concluded, "you must not hesitate to command me." Albright's resignation surprised Ickes, who at first

45. *Annual Report of the Department of the Interior* (1933), pp. 154–55; HMA, "Reminiscences," p. 408; Shankland, *Steve Mather*, p. 301; HMA to Cramton, July 11, 1933, NA, Records of NPS, gen., admin., Dir. Albright.

tried to persuade him not to leave. But the Secretary eventually accepted Albright's decision. The resignation, it was agreed, would become effective on August 10, 1933, the same day the reorganization plan was to go into effect.[46]

The delicate business of selecting a new director for the National Park Service still remained. Albright intended to make sure that the Mather tradition would be maintained, and in his own mind there was no question about who should succeed him. He immediately suggested to Ickes that Cammerer would be the logical man. Noisily fulminating against bureaucratic inbreeding, the Secretary opposed Cammerer, stubbornly insisting that a new man should be brought in. Albright then convened a meeting of an informal advisory group, made up of John C. Merriam, J. Horace McFarland, Frank R. Oastler, Herman Bumpus, and a few others, to consider the question of a successor. Just as the session started, Albright was called to the White House for an emergency meeting of the CCC council. In his absence the advisory group decided to recommend Newton B. Drury, executive secretary of the Save-the-Redwoods League. Albright knew full well that Drury would make a first-rate director, but the chances were he would refuse the appointment because of his devotion to the Save-the-Redwoods League, with which he had been associated since 1920. Drury declined the appointment when Ickes offered it to him early in July. Adding Frederic A. Delano and Frederick Law Olmsted to the roster, Albright called a second meeting of his informal advisory group. This time he participated fully in the deliberations, and this time Cammerer received the board's strong endorsement. Grumbling, but not irreconcilably opposed, Ickes offered Cammerer the appointment. The Mather tradition had been preserved, and Albright could now leave Washington with an entirely clear conscience.[47]

Albright's last six months in office had been extremely productive. He had received virtually everything he requested from

46. HMA to Ickes, June 30, 1933, NA, Records of NPS, gen., admin., Dir. Albright.

47. Shankland, *Steve Mather*, p. 302; Ise, *Our National Park Policy*, p. 354; interview with HMA, Dec. 20, 1964.

Hoover. He had guided the Park Service through the chaotic transition to the New Deal. He had influenced Ickes's thinking about conservation matters, nudging him in the direction of aesthetic conservation and away from the Pinchot clique. He had left his mark on the CCC. He had arranged the reorganization and expansion of the Park Service, finally obtaining jurisdiction over the Civil War battlefields and cemeteries and all of the national monuments. In the end, he had decisively influenced the selection of his successor. This was a remarkable record, and Albright was well satisfied.

During his last weeks in the Park Service, Albright received a number of editorial bouquets. "In the resignation of Horace M. Albright," wrote the Washington *Post,* "the Government loses a brilliant and devoted builder and defender of adult playgrounds. . . . A host of friends and associates in government salute him with cordial good wishes." "Utah regrets the retirement of Horace M. Albright," editorialized the Salt Lake City *Tribune.* "The administration of the national parks under Mr. Albright has been all that an exacting public could expect." Moments after Cammerer took the oath of director, Albright accepted the decoration that the king of Sweden had awarded him six years earlier but which he could not accept as long as he remained in government service. He had the distinction of being a "Knight of the Order of the Northern Star" as he returned to private life.[48]

Albright found the outpouring of affection and esteem from his co-workers and long-time friends in Washington intensely rewarding. "I shall continue to keep closely in touch with national park affairs," he promised, "as if we were still together in our beloved Park Service." In breaking away from his colleagues of two decades, he offered one last admonition. "Do not let the Service become 'just another Government bureau,' " he pleaded, "keep it youthful, vigorous, clean and strong."[49]

48. Washington *Post,* July 7, 1933; Salt Lake *Tribune,* July 7, 1933; clipping from Washington *Times,* Aug. 12, 1933, scrapbook, HMA Papers.
49. HMA to Roger B. Toll, July 1, 1933, NA, Records of NPS, gen., admin., Dir. Albright.

10

Potash and Parks

The trees along the Hudson River had taken on the russet look
of autumn by the time Albright got his family completely re-
settled in New York. He and Grace decided to lease a spacious
and comfortable apartment at the Wykagyl Gardens in New Ro-
chelle. Here, on the suburban fringes of the New York metropo-
lis, the Albrights lived for the next twenty-eight years, while
Horace pursued his career as an executive in the mining business.

The most exciting aspect of Albright's job with the United
States Potash Company was that it gave him a chance to pioneer
in the development of a new industry in the United States. Until
the 1930s, no potash mines had existed in this country.

The production of potash had begun in North America in
the seventeenth century when the Jamestown settlers manufac-
tured it by leaching wood ashes and then boiling the residue in
large iron pots to produce "pott ashe," a crude form of potassium carbonate. In colonial America, potash was used primarily
to make gun powder, soap, and glass. Toward the end of the
eighteenth century, however, farmers began using small amounts
of it to fertilize their fields. Wood ashes from the virgin stands
of beech, hickory, ash, and oak along the Atlantic seaboard
produced more than enough potash for domestic consumption.
By 1825, escalating European demand for American potash
created a brisk and profitable, though relatively small, overseas
trade that helped to bolster the unstable American economy
during the Jacksonian era. But total potash output declined
steadily in the middle decades of the nineteenth century, as the

hardwood forests of the East became depleted. After the Civil War, potash production in the United States virtually ceased.[1]

In the meantime, huge subterranean deposits of potash salts were discovered in Germany in the 1840s and 1850s, and enterprising German scientists established the fact that the presence of potassium in the soil, in combination with nitrogen and phosphorus, played an essential role in plant growth. As commercial fertilizers came into wide use during the second half of the nineteenth century, the term "potash" took on a general meaning, referring to any of several naturally occurring potassium salts, especially potassium chloride, that could be used to add potassium to the soil or to produce a high grade of potassium for chemical use. A powerful European cartel gained a virtual monopoly on the mining, refining, and sale of naturally occurring potash salts during the late nineteenth and early twentieth centuries. In 1913, for example, the United States imported approximately one million tons of potash salts, almost all of which came from Germany and France.[2]

The onset of World War I triggered an immediate crisis in American agriculture because the normal supply of imported potash was suddenly cut off. Within a few weeks in 1914 the price jumped from $35 a ton to nearly $500 a ton, and a frantic search began to find new sources of the much-needed mineral. Fortunately, in 1911 Congress had authorized the United States Geological Survey to explore for possible domestic supplies of potash. With considerable ingenuity, the USGS located surface deposits and advised in the establishment of processing plants for salines, brines, minerals, and seaweed from which potash could be produced. By 1918 American operators had an annual output of about two hundred thousand tons of potash salts, approximately 20 percent of normal consumption, almost all of

1. Howard I. Smith, "Potash," in *Industrial Minerals and Rocks,* pp. 684–89; J. Paul Hudson, "Potash and Soap Ashes: Early Jamestown Commodities," reprint by the American Potash Institute, n.d., copy in HMA Papers.
2. Willard L. Thorp and Ernest A. Tupper, "The Potash Industry" (Report submitted to the Department of Justice by the Department of Commerce, May 1, 1940, mimeographed), pp. 24–28; Smith, "Potash."

which came from jerry-built, temporary plants. After the war, as soon as the low-cost European potash came back on the market, all of the American producers went out of business except the American Trona Corporation (later renamed the American Potash and Chemical Corporation), which had developed an efficient and profitable method of extracting potassium chloride and other chemical substances from the brines of Searles Lake in California. The American Potash and Chemical Corporation became an important component of the new potash industry that was to emerge in the United States in the 1930s. But its unique processes drew upon brines that occurred naturally at or near the earth's surface. The company had nothing to do with the mining of potash salts.[3]

With the wartime shortage of potash clearly in mind, a tight-fisted Congress voted to authorize a five-year investigation, beginning in the mid-1920s, to determine the "location and extent of potash deposits in the United States." Handicapped by meager financial support, the USGS and the Bureau of Mines nevertheless drilled twenty-four core tests in the arid wastelands of western Texas and eastern New Mexico, the so-called Permian Basin, which had once been a vast inland sea. The search centered here because the Germans and French had found rich subterranean potash deposits in similar saline strata in Europe. USGS experts soon announced the discovery of potash beds "of possible commercial interest" in New Mexico. Understandably enough, the wildcat oil operators in this region began watching for traces of potash in the debris brought to the surface by their drilling teams.[4]

In the summer of 1925 the Snowden and McSweeney Company, an independent oil-prospecting firm, discovered evidences

3. J. W. Turrentine, *Potash: A Review, Estimate and Forecast*, p. 79; Turrentine, "The Development of the American Potash Industry," pp. 1–3, copy in HMA Papers.

4. *Annual Report of the Director of the U.S. Geological Survey* (1931), pp. 7–8, 13; J. W. Turrentine, *Potash in North America*, American Chemical Society Monograph Series no. 91 (New York: Reinhold Publishing Corporation, 1943), pp. 19–22, all quotations from this work are reprinted by permission.

of potash while wildcatting for oil about twenty-two miles north-east of Carlsbad, New Mexico, then a small settlement devoted mostly to cattle raising and farming, but already well known as the site of the largest and most spectacular underground caverns in the West. V. H. McNutt, a sharp-eyed engineer, first recognized the potassium crystals in the drill leavings. Subsequent test bores sent down in 1926 confirmed the existence of a thick layer of sylvinite, a combination of potassium chloride and common salt, at a depth of approximately one thousand feet. By 1929, after about two dozen additional test cores had been analyzed by government scientists, it was firmly established that this was a potash bed of major commercial proportions, equal in every respect to the best of the European deposits. Snowden and Mc-Sweeney promptly took up leases on fifteen thousand acres of the public domain in the vicinity of Carlsbad. They had already set up a separate company to arrange for the mining and refining of the valuable underground deposits. This was the beginning of the United States Potash Company.[5]

While the Snowden and McSweeney organization had the technical know-how to drill deep wells and produce crude oil, it had practically no experience in mining. The company's board of directors got in touch with a number of large mining firms in an attempt to persuade one of them to take over the technical end of the potash development. Finally, in 1930, the Pacific Coast Borax Company, the firm with which Steve Mather had once been associated and the producers of the famous Twenty Mule Team borax agreed to purchase half of the common stock of United States Potash and to assume responsibility for the sinking of a mine shaft and the design of a refinery near Carlsbad. A subsidiary of Borax Consolidated Limited of London, the Pacific Coast Borax Company had produced a small amount of potash during World War I but had dismantled its experimental plant when potash prices declined in the 1920s. The chief American executive officer of this prosperous borax corporation was

5. "You and USP," copy in HMA Papers; Turrentine, *Potash in North America*, pp. 22–23, 154; Thorp and Tupper, "The Potash Industry," p. 38.

Christian Zabriskie, who now became one of the directors of the United States Potash Company.[6]

By January 1931 a mine shaft had been completed, and by June of that year the company had begun selling potash. Because of its high potassium content, the ore was readily marketable as "manure salts," an unrefined, water soluble form of potash that could be applied directly to the soil. Late in 1932 the refinery went into operation, utilizing a process known as fractional crystallization to remove nearly all of the ore's impurities, the principal one being common salt. The final product was 98 percent pure potash. The refinery boasted an initial capacity of 120 tons of high-grade, processed potash a day. Full production had just been attained when Albright joined the company in August 1933.[7]

While its mining and refining operations were carried on in New Mexico, the United States Potash Company—soon dubbed USP by its employees and stockholders—maintained its home office in New York City. The bulk of the American potash market was in the East and, besides, Henry McSweeney, James H. Snowden, and Zabriskie spent much of their time in or near New York. Albright's main job, once he joined the company, was to build up a competent staff, to expand the sales force, to protect the organizations's vital interests in Washington, and to win a permanent share of the lucrative American potash market, which was still dominated by the cartel.[8]

To do this, Albright needed maximum flexibility and the authority to move quickly and decisively. Without hesitation, the board of directors gave him broad discretionary powers. Henry McSweeney, an energetic octogenarian who lived in Atlantic City, was president of the company and chairman of the board of directors, but he seldom injected himself into the day-to-day affairs of the business. As vice-president and general manager,

6. "You and USP," p. 9–11; HMA, "Reminiscences," pp. 611–16; Thorp and Tupper, "The Potash Industry," pp. 38–40.

7. HMA, "Reminiscences," pp. 611–16; Thorp and Tupper, "The Potash Industry," pp. 30–40.

8. HMA, "Reminiscences," pp. 610–11.

Albright effectively ran USP. He would have been unhappy under any other arrangement, for his years in the National Park
Service had taught him to enjoy the prerogatives of executive
authority and to expect to be top man. His administrative style,
a disarming combination of personal charm and efficiency, remained essentially unchanged. He gave his associates, men like
Paul Speer, vice president and general counsel, Albert W. Davis,
controller, Andrew A. Holmes, vice-president in charge of
sales, Walter Dingley, secretary-treasurer, and Thomas M. Cramer, manager of the mine and refinery, plenty of room to operate on their own, but he made it his job to keep up with every
aspect of the company's affairs, including the technology. He
took charge of all public-relations work and reserved for himself
the slippery political problems that often arose. The company
leased its mineral deposits from the federal government and the
state of New Mexico. Its vital water rights had to be protected.
These two areas, mineral leases and water rights, were unavoidable sources of political intrigue and administrative difficulties.[9]

The next three years, from 1933 to 1936, were crucial in the
development of the American potash industry. The German-
French cartel felt threatened not only by the new American potash mines but also by the expanding Spanish potash industry.
The result was an all-out price war. Wholesale potash prices,
which in 1930 stood at about sixty-four cents per twenty-pound
unit of K_2O, dropped to between thirty-five and forty cents per
unit in 1934 and 1935, a price that meant net losses for USP.
But the company steadily increased its sales. Joining with the
American Potash and Chemical Corporation and the Potash
Company of America (a newly chartered firm that began mining
potash in the Carlsbad area in 1934), the USP initiated a publicity drive against the foreign imports of potash. Undoubtedly,
the strong anti-European sentiment of the 1930s, spawned
largely by the default of the European nations on their war-debt
payments and the increasing distrust of Hitler's Germany, helped

9. HMA, "Reminiscences," pp. 610–11; Mrs. Alice H. Shankland to
the author, Sept. 24, 1965; interview with Thomas M. Cramer, June 29,
1965.

the American potash producers. By 1936 the crisis had ended. Wholesale prices rebounded, stabilizing at about forty-seven cents per unit, and the three American producers laid claim to slightly more than half of the American market. USP declared the first dividend on its common stock in 1936 and geared up for further production increases. The company's net profit in 1937 was $1,432,798, and this rose to $1,642,972 in 1940. By the time of World War II, the mechanized and highly efficient American potash industry, which by then included three large mining operations plus the Searles Lake plant, was in a position to supply all of the nation's needs for agricultural and chemical grades of potash.[10]

After leaving government service in 1933, Albright became increasingly suspicious of New Deal efforts to manage the economy, although he was viewed as an unrepentent New Dealer by many of his associates and competitors. His well-known connection with the CCC and his advocacy of public-works programs earned him a series of gratuitous insults during the decade. But those who knew him well recognized that his Republicanism had reasserted itself. The very fact that he was no longer a government official inevitably changed his point of view. Once a bureaucrat himself, and at times a rather self-certain and determined one, he now resented having government representatives intervene in his affairs. He found, like many old progressives, that he disagreed more and more with Roosevelt's program. A few encounters with New Deal functionaries and reforming politicians hastened his conversion to a mildly anti-New Deal position.

His first contact with the federal government in his new capacity as a business executive came soon after he left Washington. USP and its two main competitors were requested to work out a code of fair practice for the potash industry as provided

10. Turrentine, *Potash in North America*, p. 96; *New York Times*, May 18, 1939, and Apr. 26, 1941; Thorp and Tupper, "The Potash Industry," pp. 18a, 52–62; see also U.S. Bureau of Mines, *Minerals Yearbook* for the years 1932–40, which contain informative annual reports on the potash industry by J. H. Hedges.

under the NRA. Hugh Johnson, the NRA administrator, called
upon Albright, whom he knew, to take a leading role in these
discussions. After protracted talks, the only agreement that could
be reached was about fair-labor practices, including a minimum
wage of twenty cents an hour. In the end, the three potash companies joined the Chemical Code, thus avoiding the necessity
for a separate code in the potash industry. Albright saw to it
that his company cooperated with the NRA, and the Blue Eagle
flew conspicuously above USP's Carlsbad installations. But he
found the time-consuming round of talks and the inefficiency of
Johnson's agency annoying. He breathed easier after the Su-
preme Court declared the NRA unconstitutional in 1935.[11]

In 1934, Antoinette Funk, second in command of the General
Land Office, launched an investigation of the potash leases on
the public domain. By working through his friends in the Interior Department and by dealing directly with Mrs. Funk—"we
had some mutual friends in Winnetka," he wryly recalled—Albright was able to weather the GLO investigation, which confirmed the legality of the USP potash leases.[12]

Albright's most far-reaching and potentially damaging brush
with the New Deal came in 1939, when Thurman Arnold, head
of the antitrust division of the Justice Department, initiated a
trust-busting suit against the four largest potash companies in the
United States. His contention was that the American Potash and
Chemical Corporation, the Potash Company of America, USP,
and the N.V. Potash Export Maatschappy (the cartel organization) had conspired to set prices at artificially high levels. During the mid-1930s, reflecting a shift in Roosevelt's circle of close
advisers, the New Deal turned away from its earlier emphasis
on business cooperation and national economic planning, and
undertook a vigorous trust-busting crusade designed to restore
business competition. Thurman Arnold and the Temporary Na-

---

11. HMA, "Reminiscences," pp. 621–36, quotations from pp. 629 and
631; see Hugh S. Johnson, *The Blue Eagle: From Egg to Earth* for an
amusing and informative account of the NRA.

12. Interview with HMA, July 6, 1965; HMA, "Reminiscences," p.
529.

tional Economic Committee (TNEC) were the bearers of the New Deal's antimonopoly torch.[13]

In the spring of 1939 FBI agents suddenly demanded access to the files of all the potash companies in the United States, announcing tersely than an antitrust investigation was under way. In Albright's view, the timing of this investigation could hardly have been worse, because his company was in the middle of a damage suit involving allegations that it had polluted the waters of the Pecos River by allowing waste salt to pass into the water. He feared that if the investigation led to the company's indictment and if word leaked out that USP had been cited for antitrust violations, the jury in the water case would be adversely influenced. Loss of the suit would mean that USP would be forced to pay damages to hundreds of farmers in west Texas.[14]

As soon as possible, Albright, Speer, and Goldthwaite H. Dorr, the company's consulting attorney, went to Washington for talks with Arnold, a formidable, dark-haired man and a former law professor at Yale University. When Albright and his associates arrived, Arnold called in George Comer, a Justice Department economist, who announced that he intended to launch an investigation of the potash industry, which was notable as one of the newest industrial developments in the United States. Arnold explained that he was particularly interested in broad-gauge studies of this kind, which would give him basic information about the American economy. Albright and his lawyers suggested that USP would cooperate fully and provide all the information the investigators wanted if, in return, Arnold would promise that any antitrust indictment that might be handed down by the federal grand jury would be sealed until the water case had been decided. Arnold agreed, recognizing that if USP promised its cooperation the other potash firms would probably fall into line.[15]

13. For a discussion of New Deal trustbusting see Ellis W. Hawley, *The New Deal and the Problem of Monopoly*, pp. 160, 360–61, 404–38, 440.
14. HMA, "Reminiscences," pp. 761–68.
15. HMA, "Reminiscences," pp. 761–68

USP spent nearly six months collecting and supplying information to the two economists, Willard L. Thorp and E. A. Tupper, of the Department of Commerce, who prepared the potash report. In May 1939, while the company's lawyers argued the water case before a New Mexico jury, Albright received a cryptic telegram: "A baby is born and it is in a bassinette." Decoded and translated, the message ment that the federal grand jury in New York had indicted all the potash companies and that the indictment was sealed. Not until May 16, 1940, well after USP had won its case in New Mexico, did Federal Judge Henry W. Goddard open the sealed indictment. Earlier, Thorp and Tupper had submitted their report to the Justice Department. They stated that their study had "not revealed any circumstances which established the proposition that the [antitrust] laws have been violated." On the contrary, the report concluded, "it appears that the potash industry has demonstrated clearly those factors of pioneering development, technological advance, and responsible management which represent the highest expression of American industry."[16]

Probably because of the Thorp-Tupper Report, Arnold decided not to press criminal antitrust proceedings against the potash companies. But he did file a civil suit asking for an injunction against specific practices attributed to the corporations. "It was intimated," the *New York Times* reported, "that this action . . . would be followed by a consent decree" in which the defendants would agree to refrain from certain pricing practices "without, however, admitting that such practices ever had been followed in the past." It was clear that the industry's CIF (cost, insurance, and freight) pricing system had aroused the suspicions of the Justice Department. USP and all the other American companies quoted their prices as "CIF Atlantic, Gulf, or Pacific ports" because this was the way the cartel had always done it. Thus USP prices were calculated to include freight charges from the refinery at Carlsbad to a port of entry usually on the Atlantic or Gulf coasts, since the potash market was predominantly in

16. HMA, "Reminiscences," pp. 767–69; *New York Times*, May 16, 1940; Thorp and Tupper, "The Potash Industry," p. 95.

the east, plus freight to the final point of destination. The obvious advantage of this pricing system to the American potash producers was that it included a "phantom freight" charge rather similar to the old "Pittsburgh Plus" system in the steel industry. In reality, all New Mexico potash shipments went directly from Carlsbad to the customers without ever going to a port of entry. The extra freight charge included in the CIF prices represented pure profit to the companies. In the early 1930s the CIF prices had probably enabled USP to survive. But by 1940, with World War II raging in Europe and with foreign potash shipments rapidly disappearing from the American market, CIF prices, according to the Justice Department, were nothing more than profiteering devices. By signing the consent decree USP, along with the other American potash firms, agreed to quote an FOB price that would allow its customers to buy potash at the refinery in Carlsbad and pay the freight themselves. USP also agreed to sell its products directly to farmers as well as to fertilizer manufacturers.[17]

But USP and the other potash firms set up an FOB system that forced the customers to pay practically the same total price as before. The companies also refused to sell in less than carload lots so that individual farmers would find it nearly impossible to buy potash directly from the refinery. Albright later admitted that "technically" the Justice Department had "a point" in its case against the potash industry, but he stoutly maintained that USP had not violated the antitrust laws. It was scarcely coincidental, however, that American potash prices eventually reflected the freight savings available to domestic potash producers. Albright had painfully learned the lesson that many business executives had already learned during the 1930s. The New Deal, whether he liked it or not, had drastically altered the relationship between government and business by forcefully interjecting itself into the day-to-day economic affairs of the nation. The potash industry may not have been guilty of antitrust

17. *New York Times*, May 16, 1940; HMA, "Reminiscences," pp. 769–71.

violations in 1939, but by 1940 it was acutely aware of the possibility of federal intervention.[18]

There was no question where Albright's sympathies lay during the 1930s. Making a success of the United States Potash Company became his passion and overwhelming concern. And yet he found the time to continue his participation in numerous conservation organizations and to keep in touch with national conservation affairs. The company's board of directors authorized him to take time off "when necessary" and gave him permission to hire any extra secretarial help he "might need in the office." (He needed none until the 1940s.) The founding fathers of USP were acting not entirely without selfish motives. They wanted to keep their general manager happy, but they recognized the value to the company of helping Albright maintain his connections in conservation circles, especially in the federal conservation agencies; USP leased its potash deposits from the federal government and had to deal with both the Geological Survey and the Bureau of Mines. Because of his own vital interests, then, but also because of the particular concerns of his employers, Albright continued to participate in national conservation affairs. His work as a conservationist provides the unifying link between his pre-1933 and post-1933 careers.[19]

When Albright left the Park Service he vowed that he would keep in touch with the bureau's affairs and make himself available as an informal consultant and lobbyist in behalf of the national parks. Over the years, he more than made good his promise. His letters and memos hit Cammerer's desk in rapid-fire bursts of two and three. Many of them contained advice about organizational problems and appointments in the bureau, advice that Cammerer eagerly solicited. Some of them contained general observations and gratuitous suggestions that Cammerer probably ignored. A few reflected Albright's mild irritation at the changes taking place in the National Park Service, which expanded rapidly during the New Deal era and took on many of the characteristics of a large bureau. In the Petrified Forest and Mesa Verde in 1935, for example, he found it "a bit hard to make

18. Quotations from HMA, "Reminiscences," pp. 771–72.
19. HMA, "Reminiscences," p. 610.

the younger men understand who I am. Fame does not last long," he wistfully observed.[20]

But his loyalty and devotion to the National Park Service never flagged. He kept himself well informed about the bureau's problems. On his frequent trips to Washington he lobbied tirelessly for national park causes, including the establishment of the Everglades National Park, the expansion of Sequoia to include the King's Canyon area, and the completion of the Jackson Hole project. Moreover, he pleaded the case of the National Park Service in the inner councils of the Sierra Club when that influential conservation organization began to have serious qualms about the direction of National Park policies.[21]

Cammerer, Demaray, and Wirth knew that they could always count on Albright's assistance and political influence. Whenever he traveled in the West, Albright sent Cammerer a report on the park areas he saw. On a few occasions he covered up for his old bureau in potentially embarassing circumstances. "I attended the funeral of Dr. W. T. Hornaday [a widely known wildlife conservationist] in Stamford yesterday morning," Albright wrote Cammerer in 1937. "Representatives of all the conservation organizations were there. It would have been fine if there could have been a couple of National Park men in uniform there representing you. However, I took the liberty of saying that I was representing the National Park Service as well as myself."[22]

Throughout the 1930s, Albright remained on close and friendly terms with Cammerer in spite of a few minor differences over policy. "I do hope you are not working so hard in this terribly hot weather," Albright wrote in 1935. "You must conserve yourself, Cam. . . . Should you lose your health, they will take your job and that will be the end of the Mather group [ex-

20. For examples of Albright's extensive correspondence with Cammerer, see HMA to Cammerer, Aug. 27, 1933, Nov. 30, 1933, July 18, 1934, Jan. 11, 1935, July 14, 1935, Feb. 3, 1936, Feb. 28, 1937, Nov. 9, 1937, and Nov. 9, 1939, in NA, Records of NPS, gen., admin., Dir. Albright; quotation from HMA to Cammerer, July 14, 1935.
21. HMA to Joel H. Hildebrand (President, Sierra Club), Oct. 27, 1938, NA, Records of NPS, gen., admin., Dir. Albright.
22. Conrad L. Wirth to HMA, Feb. 17, 1934, and HMA to Cammerer, Mar. 10, 1937, NA, Records of NPS, gen., admin., Dir. Albright.

cept for Demaray] in National Park Service activity." Regrettably, Cammerer suffered a serious heart attack in 1939 and had to resign from the directorship. Within a year he was dead. The burden of carrying on the Mather tradition rested largely on Albright's shoulders.[23]

Meantime, the Park Service directorship fell into friendly hands. Newton B. Drury, who had refused the appointment in 1933, accepted in 1940 when Ickes offered it to him again. Knowledgeable and widely experienced in conservation matters, Drury was devoted to the national parks and to the concept of preserving natural beauty. His appointment came as a result of Ickes's conviction that someone other than a career Park Service man should fill Cammerer's shoes. But, equally important, by appointing Drury, Ickes hoped to mute some of the criticism the wilderness organizations were leveling at the National Park Service. It was clear that the long-time leader of the Save-the-Redwoods League held a somewhat stronger attachment to purely aesthetic goals than his predecessors in the directorship. Albright was delighted when his old friend and classmate accepted the appointment. His intention was to continue his informal connections with the Park Service in the hope of keeping the Mather tradition alive for a while longer.

Albright still preached the virtues of the old-style public relations techniques that he and Mather had used so effectively. This was a crucial matter to him. He became irritated if the Park Service failed to send a letter of congratulations to an old friend of the parks on an appropriate occasion. He became doubly angry when the Park Service failed to keep its political fences mended. "I am terribly sorry about Lou Cramton," he had written to Cammerer, "but I am not surprised. You know he never forgets and rarely forgives. I have written him so much this summer trying to get him to feel better toward his old friends in the National Park Service that he is almost 'off' me now. . . . He may be lost to you." Albright found it difficult to reconcile himself to the inevitable results of the great growth of the parks

23. HMA to Cammerer, July 14, 1935, and Oct. 16, 1934, NA, Records of NPS, gen., admin., Dir. Albright; HMA to Cammerer, June 20, 1940, NA, Records of NPS, gen., admin., Dir. Cammerer.

bureau and to the fact that it was impossible for Cammerer, Demaray, and Drury to continue the personal touches that had become the hallmark of Mather's and Albright's administration.[24]

Above all, Albright refused to change his ideas about making the natural beauty of the parks accessible to the public. In the mid-1930s, he was accused by Bob Yard and others of having softened his attitude toward National Park standards. "I have not changed my views since I entered the National Park Service way back in the days when Steve Mather first came to Washington," he told Yard. "You are the one who has altered yours." In fact, a growing number of old-line Park Service supporters, such as Yard and the leaders of the Sierra Club, had swerved sharply toward the "purist" philosophy of wilderness preservation during the 1930s. A purist may be defined as one who believed that the natural features of the parks should never be disturbed under any circumstances, and that the protection of the parks from commercial utilization and spoilation by the tourists should be the primary job of the National Park Service. The purists held that the parks were "great temples of Nature which people should enter in a spirit somewhat akin to those entering temples of religion." The parks, according to them, existed solely "for those who seek rest and contemplation of nature's highest achievements, for those who want to study nature." On the other hand, Albright maintained that, while the parks must be protected, the public should be allowed to use and enjoy them. "The 'greatest good for the greatest number,' " he wrote in 1935, "has to have a small place even in national park administration." It was ironic but revealing that he should fall back on that particular phrase to defend his position. Gifford Pinchot, the leader of the utilitarian conservationists, used those exact words to define conservation in 1910. Jeremy Bentham, the father of utilitarianism, coined the phrase.[25]

24. HMA to Cammerer, Oct. 12, 1934, and Cammerer to HMA, Oct. 15, 1934, NA, Records of NPS, gen., admin., Dir. Albright.

25. HMA to Cammerer, Jan. 17, 1935, HMA to Robert Sterling Yard, May 24, 1938, and Yard to A.D. Beers, Mar. 21, 1925, NA, Records of NPS, gen., admin., Dir. Albright, in which the complaints of the purists are described.

Albright normally stopped off at the Interior Department when he was in Washington. He always tried to visit with the National Park Service crowd, and he almost always paid his respects to the Assistant Secretary of the Interior, Oscar L. Chapman, whom he first got to know during the Hundred Days in 1933. "Nine times out of ten when Horace was in Washington," Chapman later recalled, "he would come into the Interior Department." The two men became close friends. An affable attorney from Colorado, Chapman combined unusual personal charm with a canny political staying power. He even had the necessary thick skin and quick wit to get along with Harold Ickes. Albright's close ties with Chapman helped him keep track of developments not only in the National Park Service but also in the upper echelons of the Interior Department. Chapman used Albright as an informal adviser and political sounding board. It was a mutually satisfying arrangement. Albright also kept up with E. K. Burlew and Harry Slattery.[26]

Quietly and systematically, Albright remained in touch with Secretary Ickes, whose tempestuous personality and unpredictable outbursts still taxed everybody's patience. Correspondence between the two men traveled between New York and Washington with regularity and general good humor. Ickes occasionally consulted Albright about appointments to be made in the National Park Service, and from time to time talked to him about the department's political problems. Albright made a habit of sending along his unsolicited comments, usually favorable, about Ickes's speeches and public pronouncements. At moments of triumph or sadness, such as the death of Ickes's first wife, the passage of an important piece of legislation, and the Secretary's remarriage, Albright wrote warm human letters of congratulation or condolence that Ickes genuinely appreciated.[27]

26. HMA to Oscar L. Chapman, Apr. 21, 1938, Oscar L. Chapman Papers; interview with Oscar L. Chapman, June 15, 1966; E. K. Burlew to HMA, Apr. 19, 1938, and HMA to Harry Slattery, May 15, 1938, HMA Papers.

27. HMA to Ickes, Sept. 19, 1933, May 3, 1934, Mar. 10, 1935, July 7, 1935, Sept. 24, 1935, Apr. 30, 1937, May 13, 1938, June 21, 1938, and

At various times the two men disagreed—and to clash with the Old Curmudgeon meant being shouted at and insulted—but their friendly relationship always survived. Their worst set-to occurred in 1936 when Ickes tried to disregard the civil service regulations in making a Park Service appointment. The Secretary, ordinarily predisposed to bring in men from outside the bureaucracy, wanted to appoint a University of Chicago professor to take charge of the Park Service's enlarged historical preservation program, following passage of the Historic Sites and Buildings Act of 1935. But the professor had not taken the civil service examination. His name was therefore not on the list of eligibles submitted to Ickes by the Civil Service Commission. Verne Chatelain, already the chief historian of the Park Service, scored well on the test and his name appeared first on the list. Albright favored Chatelain's appointment. When Ickes proposed to put his man in office through irregular administrative procedures, Albright wrote to the Civil Service Commission calling its attention to the situation. A short time afterwards, he got a telephone call to come to see the Secretary at once.[28]

When Albright arrived in the Interior Department he knew immediately that he was in for the full treatment. Pounding the table and shaking his finger at Albright, Ickes demanded that the former director of the Park Service withdraw his letter. But Albright held his ground. "I knew you wouldn't like the letter when I wrote it," he said. Ickes shouted that he had a right to make his own appointments. Albright reminded him that the position they were discussing came under civil service and was not a political appointment. After absorbing considerable abuse and vituperation, Albright got up and shook hands with the Secretary, suggesting that they weren't getting anywhere and that he had better leave. "You know," he said, "this National Park Service is kind of third baby to me . . . and I'm very much interested in seeing that it is protected. . . . [The appointment

Feb. 6, 1939, and Ickes to HMA, Aug. 31, 1933, May 9, 1934, Mar. 12, 1935, July 9, 1935, May 1, 1937, June 24, 1938, and Jan. 16, 1939, Ickes File, HMA Papers.

28. HMA, "Reminiscences," p. 566.

is] nothing to me personally." Admitting defeat, Ickes got up, put his arm around Albright's shoulders, walked to the door with him, and asked him to "talk to Burlew about it." Albright promised that he would, and he did. But he refused to change his position. In the end, as one might have predicted, neither Chatelain nor the professor got the job. While Albright successfully blocked the professor's appointment, Ickes held out stubbornly against Chatelain, who subsequently resigned from the Park Service. After standing vacant for almost two years, the appointment finally went to Ronald F. Lee, an able young man who was fully qualified under the civil service regulations.[29]

Albright had ambivalent feelings about Ickes throughout his long association with him. On the one hand, he characterized the Secretary as "the meanest man who ever sat in a Cabinet office in Washington," and there was abundant evidence to support this opinion. Ickes cruelly browbeat Cammerer, whom he detested, and knowingly insulted many of the finest men in the Interior Department. Moreover, the Secretary suspected everybody, even Albright, who in 1939 was accused of "conspiracy to defraud the government, not for personal profit, but to build up the park system." (Specifically, Albright was charged with arranging the artificially high appraisal of a parcel of land that had been condemned for road-building purposes near General Grant National Park; he immediately dug into the Park Service files and demonstrated conclusively to both Ickes and the General Accounting Office that he was innocent of any wrongdoing.) On the other hand, Albright maintained that Ickes was "the best Secretary of the Interior we ever had." He was "perfectly fearless," Albright observed, and he was a "conservationist at heart." If he "had been allowed to have his way" on the question of reorganization, Albright contended, he would have greatly "advanced" conservation policy in the United States.[30]

29. Verne Chatelain to HMA, Sept. 25, 1936, HMA Papers; HMA, "Reminiscences," pp. 565–68; Ise, *Our National Park Policy*, pp. 357–59.

30. Ickes, *Secret Diary* 2:582–85; HMA, Reminiscences," pp. 337–41, 534–59, quotations on pp. 553, 560. Albright strongly resented the fact that *Secret Diary* included the accusations against him without any reference to his subsequent vindication.

The thing that pulled Albright and Ickes together and kept them working in harmony most of the time in the late 1930s was their strong, mutual desire to convert the Interior Department into a Department of Conservation, which would contain all of the federal conservation agencies. In his headline-hunting and bellicose way, Ickes made the drive to reorganize his department his primary concern. He jousted with Secretary of Agriculture Henry Wallace in an attempt to get the Forest Service transferred to the Interior Department. He mounted a drive to persuade Congress to change the name of his department to the Department of Conservation. He attempted to capture and carry off not only the Forest Service but also the Biological Survey, the Bureau of Fisheries, and the Soil Conservation Service. From his position on the sidelines, Albright gave Ickes consistent support. In November 1937, for example, he helped organize a conference of conservationists at the Palmer House in Chicago "to discuss ways and means of combatting" the "propaganda" and the "misrepresentation" being given out about Ickes's conservation scheme "by several persons, headed by Gifford Pinchot, aided by the United States Forest Service." A letter signed by Albright, Irving Brant, Richard Lieber, and Tom Wallace, all prominent conservationists, went out from the conference to FDR, earnestly requesting "the favor of a personal interview at an early date." Shortly before Christmas the president met the group at the White House. "I wish I had had time yesterday to see you and tell you about the interview with the President," Albright wrote to Demaray. "It was a most remarkable session we had with him, lasting fifty minutes. He is 'on to' the Forest Service more thoroughly than any President I have known."[31]

Both Ickes and Albright were optimistic that the plan to create a Department of Conservation would go through in 1938 or 1939. But they had underestimated the ingenuity of Pinchot and his followers. By 1940 it was obvious that the Forest Service had eluded Ickes's grasp, although the Secretary could take solace in having gained control of the Biological Survey and the

31. Richard Lieber, Horace Albright, et al, to FDR, Nov. 17, 1937, Franklin D. Roosevelt Papers, OF177A; HMA to Demaray, Dec. 22, 1937, NA, Records of NPS, gen., admin., Dir. Albright.

Bureau of Fisheries—soon to be consolidated into the United
States Fish and Wildlife Service—and the Bureau of Mines. Albright anticipated that there would be other chances to promote the idea of a Department of Conservation in future years.[32]

The bitter fight to expand the Grand Teton National Park went
on unabated during the 1930s. Albright, though no longer a public official, was squarely in the middle of the contest, providing
liaison between Rockefeller and the National Park Service, buttonholing members of Congress, and trying to promote a compromise bill that would somehow please the residents of Jackson
Hole without doing violence to the basic plan for preserving the
region. A subcommittee of the Senate Committee on Public
Lands and Surveys held extensive hearings in Jackson in August
1933. Senator Carey of Wyoming spearheaded the opposition to
park extension, while Senators Norbeck and Nye saw to it that
the interests of the Park Service were protected. Fearing that
Carey would "get the hearing into personalities and other side
issues if he can possibly do it," Albright had implored Norbeck
to attend. Out of these hearings came a compromise bill that
would have given the Park Service jurisdiction over Rockefeller's proposed gift of land but which also stipulated that the
Biological Survey and the Forest Service should have jurisdiction over the game lands to the east of the Snake River. Presumably, under this arrangement, the cattlemen and sportsmen
would have access to part of Jackson Hole. The Senate passed the
compromise bill in 1934, but the House killed the measure,
largely because of the negative reaction in Wyoming but also
because of the opposition of the National Parks Association, led
by Bob Yard, and the Izaak Walton League, led by Henry B.
Ward, who insisted that the inclusion of Jackson Lake Reservoir within the park would violate national park standards.
"Ward and his associates are idealists without any respect
whatever for practical problems involved in establishing or
maintaining national parks or other preserves," Albright fumed.
"It is a pity that conservation is always being thwarted by its

32. HMA to Ickes, May 11, 1939, telegram, HMA to Ickes, June 30,
1939, and Ickes to HMA, July 5, 1939, HMA Papers.

own friends." Never again during the 1930s was the Rockefeller-Albright plan for preserving the Jackson Hole region so close to realization.[33]

In cooperation with Harold Fabian, Kenneth Chorley, and Vanderbilt Webb, all associated with Rockefeller, Albright kept lobbying for a Jackson Hole settlement. He established close ties with H. H. Schwartz, who won election to the Senate from Wyoming in 1936, and with Wyoming Congressman Paul R. Greever. But as the controversy dragged on, the local opposition to any extension of the Grand Teton National Park became stronger and stronger. The residents of Jackson Hole strenuously objected to their prospective loss of property-tax revenues. Another Senate investigating committee went to Jackson in 1938 to conduct hearings. After a decidedly bumbling statement by Cammerer, the committee heard nothing but vehement opposition to the proposed park extension, marshaled and led by Milward L. Simpson, who claimed that he represented "the proponents of the proposition to retain this area for the people of Jackson Hole." Albright's confidential correspondence with Rockefeller in 1927 figured prominently in the hearings as Simpson attempted to argue that the local citizens were "being beaten out of their heritage." It became obvious that public opinion in Wyoming was strongly against the proposal for a bigger park. In fact, the main issue in the Wyoming elections of 1938 became "federal intervention" in the state's affairs. A ground swell of opposition to FDR and the New Deal reinforced the campaign against the Jackson Hole project. Governor Miller and Congressman Greever, who had favored enlarging the park, were swept out of office. Frank O. Horton, crusading against the "federal invasion of state lands," easily won a seat in Congress. The

33. HMA to Norbeck, July 19, 1933, NA, Records of NPS, gen., admin., Dir. Albright; U.S., Congress, Senate, Hearings Before a Subcommittee on Public Lands and Surveys, "Investigation of Proposed Enlargement of the Yellowstone and Grand Teton National Parks," 73d Cong., 2d sess. (Aug. 1933), passim; Robert D. Carey to C. R. Van Vleck, Jan. 27, 1934, and HMA to G. H. Lorimer, Jan. 14, 1936, with attached copy of Henry B. Ward to Lorimer, Jan. 11, 1936, HMA Papers; see also Casper (Wyo.) *Tribune-Herald*, Aug. 6–11, 1933.

state legislature then passed a resolution asking Congress to defeat any legislation providing for the "purchase or acceptance as a gift by the United States or any of its agencies, of privately owned lands in Teton County, Wyoming." Later Horton introduced a bill in Congress asking for the Grand Teton National Park to be abolished.[34]

At this point Albright nearly gave up hope. "I must confess that I get pretty discouraged at times in trying to understand what actuates some of the people out there," he wrote to Wyoming's former Congressman Frank Mondell. It almost "makes one weep," he lamented, "not for oneself because after all what difference does it make to an individual what happens to Wyoming, but one weeps for Wyoming itself."[35]

Early in 1939 Albright became so discouraged that he considered recommending to Rockefeller "that he sell his holdings in the Jackson Hole, and let the country go to the dogs, as it certainly will if he ever disposes of his holdings." Albright had already worked for twenty years to bring the Jackson Hole country into the national park system. His discouragement was understandable. Happily, it proved to be a passing phase. A trip to Yellowstone and the Grand Tetons in the fall of 1939, his first since 1932, restored his determination. He "was astounded at the results that have been achieved in cleaning up the Jackson Hole north of Jackson," he delightedly informed the Park Service. "Even though our project has not been fully consummated the controls involved in the program have been effective and results of the greatest significance have been attained." Thanks to the CCC, all the dead timber had been cleared away from the fringes of Jackson Lake. The Snake River Land Company, with Fabian taking the lead, had removed many garish billboards,

34. U.S., Congress, Senate, Hearings Before a Subcommittee of the Committee on Public Lands and Surveys, "Enlarging Grand Teton National Park in Wyoming," 75th Cong., 3d sess. (Aug. 1938), passim, quotations on pp. 56, 222; HMA to Leslie A. Miller, Nov. 16, 1938, HMA to Paul Greever, Nov. 16, 1938, clippings from *Jackson's Hole Courier*, Jan. 26, 1939, and June 22, 1939, and House Joint Memorial no. 2, State of Wyoming, copy in HMA Papers.

35. HMA to Frank W. Mondell, Jan. 21, 1939, HMA Papers.

torn down ramshackle buildings, and turned much of its land back to nature. "The whole region looks more beautiful than I have ever seen it," Albright exclaimed to Struthers Burt, who was still one of his staunchest allies in the Jackson Hole fight. The controversy, now clearly a stalemate, continued into the 1940s. Its most sensational developments were still to come.[36]

Participating unofficially in Park Service affairs and tirelessly crusading in behalf of the Jackson Hole project by no means limited Albright's other conservation activities. He served as a member of the executive board of the American Planning and Civic Association, and in 1938 became its president. He went on the board of the National Association of Audubon Societies. He devoted considerable time to the advisory board of the American Game Association. At the invitation of chairman William B. Greeley, a New York attorney and conservationist, he participated in the affairs of the Conservation Committee of the Camp Fire Club of America. Of course, he continued his long association with the Boone and Crocket Club of New York and the Sierra Club of California.[37]

Probably his most time-consuming conservation involvement during the 1930s—an outgrowth of his intense interest in historical preservation—was the restoration of colonial Williamsburg, a project that Rockefeller and William A. R. Goodwin had initiated in the late 1920s. Colonial Williamsburg was still in its formative stages when Albright became a member of the board of directors. He contributed in many ways, at the policymaking level, to the success of this unprecedented restoration project. "He was helpful in zoning and city planning," recalled Edwin Kendrew, the senior vice-president of Colonial Williamsburg, Incorporated. "He supported the architects and other professionals" and "would tell Mr. Rockefeller that detailed research in the shape and substance of original buildings . . .

36. HMA to Mondell, Jan. 21, 1939, HMA to Demaray, Sept. 30, 1939, HMA to Struthers Burt, Aug. 16, 1939, and clipping from *Jackson's Hole Courier*, Aug. 17, 1939, HMA Papers.

37. See *Who's Who in America*, entries for Albright for the years 1933–39.

was essential." He championed purchase of land "not only for restoration but for protection of the area from encroachment." Perhaps his most important influence on the Williamsburg project resulted from his stout insistence that there be no modern intrusions in the restored area. "Instead of giving the visitor convenience," he said at one board meeting, "we should give him a street map." Linked by parkway to Yorktown and Jamestown, Williamsburg added a new dimension to the Colonial Historical Monument. The simple preservation of Yorktown and Jamestown appealed to the purists; the imaginative recreation of Williamsburg caught the fancy of the less fastidious but equally interested crowds of sightseers. Albright served twenty-four years on the board of directors of Colonial Williamsburg.[38]

By late 1941 the Great Depression had more or less run its course. With war orders pouring in from Europe, American industrial production soared and the national economy bounced back to near normal. The domestic potash industry, and along with it Horace Albright, whose annual salary was now $30,000 a year, had never been so prosperous. Having recognized the political message of the 1938 elections, Roosevelt throttled back the New Deal and focused his attention almost exclusively on foreign affairs. After seven years of crisis, rapid political change, and wide-ranging economic reform, Herbert Hoover's brand of rugged individualism seemed anachronistic to a large majority of Americans, sometimes even to Albright.

38. Kendrew quoted in Frome, "Portrait of a Conserver," pp. 27–28; see also the oral history transcript at Colonial Williamsburg, Inc.

11

Parks and Politics

Albright viewed the events of the early 1940s with weary detachment. To his generation, which had already lived through World War I, it all seemed horribly familiar—international crises, rapid mobilization, casualty lists, slogans, and restrictions. Washington soon bulged with generals, admirals, administrators, politicians, and dollar-a-year-men who somehow, amid swirling confusion, managed to organize and coordinate the war effort. FDR publicly announced his intention not to use the powerful new wartime agencies, such as the War Production Board and the Office of Price Administration, as vehicles for achieving economic reform. "Dr. Win-the-War," he proclaimed, had replaced "Dr. New Deal." A working alliance between big business and big government emerged. It was widely recognized that most of the dollar-a-year men (there were hundreds of them who worked for the government while drawing their usual salaries from business sources) had the interests of their own companies in mind at least part of the time. Albright could hardly have been expected to forego an opportunity to influence the framing of emergency regulations in his own industry.[1]

In 1941 Secretary of Agriculture Claude R. Wickard asked Albright to serve on the Fertilizer Advisory Committee of the Department of Agriculture. As a member of this committee, Albright took part in policy discussions about the procurement,

1. HMA to Harold P. Fabian, Feb. 10, 1941, HMA Papers; for an informative discussion of the wartime agencies see Bruce Catton, *The War Lords of Washington*; HMA, "Reminiscences," pp. 847–48.

stockpiling, and distribution of all types of fertilizers used by American farmers. He stayed on the committee until it was disbanded in 1947. He also sat on the Potash Industry Advisory Committee for both the War Production Board and the Office of Price Administration, thus assuring himself of a voice in many of the pricing and allocation decisions affecting the potash producers.[2]

His executive leadership in the potash industry was more important than his advisory committee work. Once the fighting began in Europe, all potash imports ceased, and American farmers, as during World War I, found themselves wholly dependent on domestic sources. The pressing need for maximum agricultural production created an unprecedented demand for potash fertilizers. At the same time, the manufacture of explosives and other essential war goods increased the need for chemical grades of potassium. Fortunately, no real deficiency ever materialized.[3]

Under Albright's leadership the United States Potash Company expanded rapidly, selling a new block of preferred stock to raise capital, and building new facilities at Carlsbad. Potash prices remained steady throughout the war, but as production soared and sales increased, so did the company's margin of profit. Annual dividend payments rose to $2.75 per share in 1941 and remained at or near this record high level, except in 1944, when $2.25 was paid. Albright settled labor disputes, persuaded federal officials to allocate steel and other scarce materials to USP so that plant expansion could take place, and guided the company through the most prosperous five years in its history. At the request of the government, USP supplied most of the chemical-grade potash needed by the nation's chemical industry during the war. Albright's reward came in 1946, when the USP board of directors named him president and gen-

2. "Prospectus," HMA Papers; HMA to the author, July 27, 1966; for a discussion of the U.S. Department of Agriculture's view of the vital importance of fertilizer see *Report of the Secretary of Agriculture* (1943), pp. 118–20 (1945), pp. 75–77.

3. Smith, "Potash," p. 695.

eral manager of the company, succeeding Henry McSweeney.[4]

At the age of fifty-six, Albright had thus reached the pinnacle of his second career. His salary was $40,000 a year. His level of affluence and style of living far exceeded all of his turn-of-the-century dreams. He had now surely succeeded in terms of the goals he had set for himself early in life. But there remained a warm nostalgia for his years in the Park Service and occasionally a twinge of regret that he ever left it. "While I think I like life in business a good deal better than being Director of the National Park Service," he reminisced in 1942, " I do not think" that anything "could be better than being Superintendent of the Yellowstone in the 1920s."[5]

Albright's interest in the problems of the National Park Service continued. "I thought a week might get by without bothering you with a message of any kind," he wrote Drury in 1941. "However, there are two or three things that have come up that I am passing on to you largely because you are in a public position and cannot help yourself." Because of their long friendship, the two men remained on close personal terms during the 1940s. More often than not they found themselves in agreement, but they also disagreed about certain basic principles of national park management. Not having worshipped at the feet of Steve Mather, Drury had his own ideas about how to operate the parks and his own administrative style. A thoughtful and somewhat retiring man, he disliked politics and disdained promotional gimmicks. While he could be stubborn and courageous in defending national park principles, which he defined from a relatively idealistic, or purist, point of view, he often lacked forcefulness in dealing with specific, day-to-day administrative details. He took a less indulgent attitude toward the tourists and concessioners than had his predecessors. Albright, still preaching the

4. Data on dividend payments compiled from *Moody's Manual of Investments* and *Moody's Industrial Manual;* for a discussion of the potash industry in World War II see Jules Backman, *The Economics of the Potash Industry*, pp. 1–28; *New York Times*, Apr. 9, 1946.

5. Quotation from HMA to Walter V. Sheppard, Mar. 23, 1942, HMA Papers.

Mather gospel, bridled at some of this. "I can not agree with many of the things that are happening in the National Park Service," he commented. Nevertheless, he maintained a harmonious relationship with Drury, and he extended valuable support to his old agency throughout the war years, while Drury fought to protect the parks from emergency-inspired commercial use and wartime neglect. In 1942, Congress slashed the Park Service appropriation by about 50 percent and forced a drastic reduction in the bureau's permanent staff. A few weeks later, Ickes sent Drury and most of the National Park Service packing to Chicago to make room for "essential" wartime operations in Washington, rendering it virtually impossible for the national parks bureau to protect its interests in Congress. "Poor old National Park Service is in a bad way," Albright noted at the height of the war. "It is pitiful to see its situation in Washington with just two or three men, their secretaries, and a couple of rooms."[6]

The war years became a turning point in Albright's relationship with the Park Service. Deeply involved in his own business affairs and increasingly engrossed in national conservation matters, he found less time and had less inclination to enter into the bureau's internal affairs. He maintained his ties with Drury, Demaray, Wirth, and the other top men in the service, assisting them as a political adviser and national park defender, both during the war and in the post-war epoch. But he made fewer and fewer unsolicited suggestions about the bureau's operations. The Mather tradition was quietly buried during World War II, a casualty of time and changing circumstances.[7]

In future years, except on rare occasions when he could not restrain himself, Albright waited for the Park Service to approach

6. HMA to Drury, Feb. 21, 1941, Drury to HMA, Mar. 28, 1941, and Nov. 28, 1942, Hillary A. Tolson to HMA, Dec. 19, 1944, and HMA to Drury, Apr. 8, 1946, NA, Records of NPS, gen., admin., Dir. Albright; Ise, *Our National Park Policy*, pp. 443–53; HMA to Olaus J. Murie, Sept. 12, 1945, and HMA to Charles J. Smith, Sept. 30, 1942, HMA Papers.

7. Albright's correspondence with the Director of the National Park Service decreased markedly after 1946; see NA, Records of NPS, gen., admin., Dir. Albright.

him if it wanted his advice on organizational or political matters. His new stance as the bureau's elder statesman proved workable and satisfying to all concerned. On this basis, then, Albright sustained his interest in the National Park Service and maintained a small but significant influence in the bureau's affairs.

Another important reason for Albright's withdrawal from internal Park Service affairs was his passionate and time-consuming involvement in the politics of the Jackson Hole controversy, a battle that transcended the National Park Service's relatively narrow interests and ultimately became a national political issue. The troublesome stalemate between the opponents and proponents of the proposed extension of Grand Teton National Park threatened to perpetuate itself indefinitely in the 1940s. Congressman Frank A. Barrett, who had replaced Horton, and Senators Joseph O'Mahoney and E. V. Robertson of Wyoming, influential members of the Public Lands Committees, had the power to block congressional action on the proposed park extension. Their price for allowing enabling legislation to go through was the full reimbursement by the federal government of all property-tax revenues that would be lost in Wyoming as a result of the park's enlargement, a matter of about $15,000 a year. The so-called Peterson Bill would have authorized the reimbursement, and both the Rockefeller group and the Park Service men pushed for its adoption. But a solid majority in Congress steadfastly opposed this bill on the grounds that it would establish a costly precedent. To most nonpolitical observers the stubborn refusal of the lawmakers to allow the acceptance of Rockefeller's handsome gift of land, worth more than $1,500,000, seemed utterly preposterous. Rockefeller's one major requirement was that the land he proposed to give to the federal government be administered by the National Park Service, a stipulation reflecting Albright's personal influence on Rockefeller as well as the philanthropist's own commitment to preservationist rather than utilitarian goals.[8]

8. Fosdick, *John D. Rockefeller, Jr.*, pp. 309–15; U.S., Congress, House, Hearings Before a Subcommittee of the Committee on Public

The most dramatic developments of the long Jackson Hole controversy followed swiftly on the heels of a letter Rockefeller wrote to Ickes late in November 1942. "In view of the uncertainty of the times," Rockefeller stated, ". . . I am and have been for some time reducing my obligations and burdens in so far as I wisely can. In line with that policy I have definitely reached the conclusion, although most reluctantly, that I should make permanent disposition of this [Jackson Hole] property before another year has passed. If the Federal Government is not interested in its acquisition, or, being interested, is still unable to arrange to accept it on the general terms long discussed and with which you are familiar, it will be my thought to make some other disposition of it or, failing in that, to sell it in the market to any satisfactory buyers." About three months later, Rockefeller again wrote to Ickes, reiterating his intention to dispose of his Jackson Hole holdings unless Ickes was "successful in persuading the President to bring in as a national monument certain lands . . . in Wyoming." These letters, which Albright helped draft, revealed Rockefeller's impatience rather less than the latest strategem of his advisers, particularly Albright and Chorley. The latter had suggested the idea of creating a Jackson Hole National Monument in 1939, after having given up all hope of getting Congress to approve the enlargement of Grand Teton National Park. The idea was passed along to Ickes in 1940.[9]

Ickes had stoutly supported the Rockefeller-Albright plan during the 1930s because it appealed to his empire-building instincts as well as his conservationist proclivities. Rockefeller's letters catapulted the fiery Secretary into action. Fearing that the Department of the Interior might lose its chance for jurisdiction over the northern Jackson Hole region, including a sizable por-

Lands, "To Abolish Jackson Hole National Monument," 78th Cong., 1st sess. (May–June 1943).

9. Rockefeller to Ickes, Nov. 27, 1942, quoted in Rockefeller to Drury, July 26, 1944, NA, Records of NPS, gen., admin., Dir. Drury; Ickes to Rockefeller, Jan. 7, 1943 (copy), Rockefeller to HMA, Feb. 9, 1943, HMA to Rockefeller, Feb. 10, 1943, and Chorley to HMA, Jan. 23, 1939, HMA Papers; Ickes, *Secret Diary* 3:377–78.

tion of scenic Forest Service land, Ickes coaxed FDR into sign-
ing an executive order, dated March 15, 1943, establishing the
Jackson Hole National Monument immediately adjacent to the
Grand Teton National Park. This was, of course, a transparent
ruse. The president's action, though ostensibly based on the
Lacey Act of 1906, which gave the chief executive authority to
proclaim national monuments of "historic" or "scientific" significance, effectively extended the boundaries of Grand Teton
Park as Congress had repeatedly refused to do. Ickes, Albright,
Chorley, and Drury naturally avoided admitting this in public.
According to FDR's proclamation, which was similar in many
ways to Theodore Roosevelt's proclamation of 1908 establishing
the Grand Canyon National Monument, the Jackson Hole National Monument was to include about one hundred thousand
acres of the Teton National Forest, about forty thousand acres
of withdrawn public lands, approximately thirty-two thousand
acres to be donated by the Snake River Land Company, and
about eighteen thousand acres of other privately owned lands.
Roosevelt's executive order further specified that "the Director
of the National Park Service, under the direction of the Secretary
of the Interior, shall have the supervision, management, and
control of the monument."[10]

Outraged members of Congress thundered their protests from
the floor of the Senate and House as soon as word leaked out
about the president's proclamation. An undercurrent of resentment about executive infringement on legislative prerogatives
had been welling up in Congress for more than two years while
FDR threw his enormous power and influence behind the war
effort. Moreover, many members of Congress disliked the heavy-
handed administrative maneuvers of certain members of the
cabinet. "Congress refused authority for the extension of Grand
Teton National Park," Senator Robertson of Wyoming shouted,
"and Proclamation No. 2578 is a subterfuge to thwart the will of

10. Ickes to FDR, Mar. 5, 1943 (copy), HMA to Rockefeller, Mar.
18, 1943, HMA Papers; proclamation no. 2578, Mar. 15, 1943, in
Congressional Record, 78th Cong., 1st sess. (Mar. 19, 1943), pp. 2235–
36.

Congress by Executive action." Even Carl Hayden, one of Albright's best friends, lost his temper. "One President after another," he proclaimed, "from Theodore Roosevelt down to the present incumbent, has proceeded to exercise in the broadest way an authority [the Lacey Act] which . . . Congress certainly intended to limit." Only a few days later, Congressman Barrett introduced a bill "to abolish the Jackson Hole National Monument . . . and to restore the area . . . to its status as a part of the Teton National Forest." Senator O'Mahoney of Wyoming pledged his full support.[11]

Roosevelt's executive order had touched a raw nerve on Capitol Hill, and the Wyoming delegation moved quickly to take advantage of the anti-Roosevelt, anti-Ickes backlash. The Republican party, hungry for votes after more than a decade out of power, eagerly seized this opportunity to try to discredit the president. Epithets, more than a few aimed at Horace Albright, resounded through Congress in May and June 1943, during the public hearing on the Barrett Bill. At about the same time, Senator O'Mahoney attached a rider to the Interior Department appropriations bill for fiscal 1944 barring the expenditure of any funds for the maintenance of the Jackson Hole National Monument, thus preventing the Park Service from exerting control over the area and effectively blocking the transfer of Rockefeller's holdings to the federal government.[12]

Albright unhesitatingly threw himself into the battle against the Barrett Bill in 1943 and 1944. He had worked too long and dreamed too often of preserving Jackson Hole to give up now. He hired an extra secretary in his New York office. At home on Saturdays and Sundays he sat hunched over his portable typewriter, pounding out long, confidential letters to politicians, conservationists, lobbyists, and friends, arguing against the bill. He spent two weeks in Washington at the beginning of the next session of Congress, working with Senator A. W. Hawkes of

11. *Congressional Record*, 78th Cong., 1st sess. (Mar. 18, 1943), pp. 2234 and 2236 and (Mar. 22, 1943), p. 2278.

12. U.S., Congress, House, Hearings, "To Abolish Jackson Hole National Monument," pp. 275–379; *New York Times*, July 4, 1943.

New Jersey and Congressman Leroy Johnson of California in a hunt for votes against the Barrett Bill. Through Hawkes, he arranged a number of meetings with O'Mahoney in the hope of finding a compromise resolution, but without success. He brought the American Planning and Civic Association, of which he was president, into the pro-monument ranks. And he kept closely in touch with Newton Drury, who, though vitally interested in the Jackson Hole project, suffered the disadvantage of having to spend most of his time at Park Service headquarters in Chicago. In an attempt to silence the political carping of the GOP, Albright got Ray Lyman Wilbur, a staunch Republican and former Secretary of the Interior, to issue a statement vouching for the fact that Coolidge and Hoover had supported the Jackson Hole project in the late 1920s. The "Barrett Bill is dead," Albright confidently predicted to his friends.[13]

But he soon realized that in 1944, a presidential election year, Republican charges of federal intervention and executive tyranny could breathe new life into the dying bill. Recognizing that Governor Thomas E. Dewey, whom he had met casually, was the front-runner for the Republican presidential nomination, he decided to contact Dewey to see if he could convince him to remain silent on the Jackson Hole issue. "I have been thinking about writing you to see whether or not you would like to talk some day with Harold P. Fabian and me," Albright wrote to Dewey. "We do not want any of Mr. Rockefeller's projects involved in politics." Dewey responded cordially, opening the door to future talks on the subject of conservation. When the New York governor got the GOP nomination in 1944, the Jackson Hole project seemed safe enough. Then, as the pressures of the campaign increased, Dewey fell victim to the seductive prospect of winning votes in the mountain states. In Sheridan, Wyoming, he charged that FDR's creation of the Jackson Hole

13. HMA to A. W. Hawkes, Nov. 4, 1943, and Dec. 14, 1943, HMA to D. J. Guy, Jan. 28, 1944, HMA to Drury, May 11, 1944, and Hillary A. Tolson to HMA, Sept. 28, 1944, HMA Papers; HMA, "Third Chapter in the Jackson Hole Story," *Planning and Civic Comment* 9 (Oct. 1943): 18–19.

National Monument was "characteristic of the deviousness of the New Deal and its lack of respect for the rights and opinions of the people affected." He went on to suggest that the land that had been withdrawn should be returned to the people. The incredulous Albright read Dewey's statement in the next morning's *New York Times* and immediately got in touch with the Republican National Committee. "They telephoned the governor at Billings, Montana—so they told me—and asked that he not discuss conservation and land problems any more, or until they could get him further information." Dewey did not bring up the subject again, but the damage had been done. After Roosevelt won the election in November, Albright, who had swallowed his anger long enough to vote for Dewey, noted that "the monuument cannot be undone now. Any bill passed would be vetoed."[14]

In December 1944 the crusade to get the Barrett Bill through Congress once again gathered momentum, with both Democrats and Republicans determined to teach FDR a lesson in the separation of powers. "Do we propose to be rolled back by the Secretary of the Interior," Congressman Everett Dirksen intoned with a grand rhetorical flourish, "or do we propose today . . . to roll him back?" The best any spokesman for the administration could do to counter Dirksen's battle cry was to plead: "Let us not be swept away by prejudices against Mr. Ickes. Let us reason this thing out." Shortly before Christmas, Congress passed the Barrett Bill, which FDR then vetoed, exactly as Albright had predicted. The relentless and bitter Jackson Hole stalemate thus dragged on, with Rockefeller patiently holding his lands along the Snake River and with the Park Service unable to exert complete administrative control over the region even though the lands were now officially a national monument. Many members of Congress still fumed about the effrontery of Roosevelt and Ickes. "I must say this for the Democrats," Albright conceded, ". . . the President and the Secretary went ahead to

14. HMA to Thomas E. Dewey, Mar. 29, 1944, and Apr. 5, 1944, Dewey to HMA, Apr. 1, 1944, HMA to Tom Wallace, Sept. 25, 1944, and HMA to Guy Emerson, Dec. 5, 1944, HMA Papers; *New York Times*, Sept. 15, 1944.

carry out the promises made in the Coolidge Administration regardless of the political repercussions."[15]

Having failed to abolish the Jackson Hole National Monument by legislative action, the political leaders of Wyoming decided to challenge the legality of Roosevelt's proclamation in the federal courts. Their case rested exclusively on the contention that FDR had no right to set aside Jackson Hole as a national monument under the provisions of the Lacey Act, because the area contained very few "historical" relics and had no unique "scientific" value. After a long deliberation, which allowed time for a study of Theodore Roosevelt's proclamation of 1908, the judge dismissed Wyoming's case against the federal government, noting that this was essentially a dispute between the executive and legislative branches of the government and that its resolution would depend upon legislative measures rather than court decisions. Harold Fabian, Paul R. Franke, superintendent of Grand Teton National Park, Drury, and Chorley kept Albright fully informed as the case progressed. While the judge pondered his decision Albright hurried to Washington to confer with Senator O'Mahoney who had begun to angle for a final settlement. "O'Mahoney has really got to get this Monument problem out of the way soon if possible," Albright wrote to Chorley. "Otherwise he has his tail in a vise." Albright tugged at O'Mahoney's ego by telling him that the Jackson Hole project would be "a monument" to him "for all time" if he would only sponsor a bill clearing the way for its completion. "I may see Ickes Monday next," Albright scribbled at the end of his report to Chorley.[16]

After the Barrett Bill failed and the court test went against Wyoming, the prolonged controversy began to peter out. Sensing a new conciliatory mood in Congress, Chorley, Albright,

15. *Congressional Record*, 78th Cong., 2d sess. (Dec. 8, 1944), pp. 9086, 9087–95 (Dec. 11, 1944), pp. 9182–96 (Dec. 19, 1944), p. 9769, and (Dec. 19, 1944), pp. 9807–8; HMA to A. W. Hawkes, Nov. 4, 1943, HMA Papers.

16. Boston *Globe*, Aug. 7, 1944; *New York Times*, Aug. 20, 1944; *Jackson's Hole Courier*, Aug. 25, 1944; State of Wyo. v. Franke, Dist. Court, Feb. 10, 1945, 58F. Supp. 890; HMA to Chorley, Feb. 5, 1945, HMA Papers.

Fabian, Drury, and the others wisely decided to let the political wounds heal and the hot tempers subside. During this brief interlude, Albright vented his activist energies by helping to launch a publicity campaign about the Jackson Hole region, which, one may speculate, was precisely what Steve Mather would have done in similar circumstances. Working through Nicholas Roosevelt, one of his many friends in the New York newspaper establishment, Albright planted a brief article on the Hole in the *New York Times Magazine*. Originally written by Albright himself at the height of the Jackson Hole controversy in 1943, it was pruned and sterilized to fit the calm that set in during 1945. Albright also assisted in placing articles by the faithful Struthers Burt and the talented Freeman Tilden, who had just started writing about the national parks.[17]

In the meantime, Albright kept his finger on the pulse of Wyoming state politics. Characteristic of his political alertness and thoroughness was a note he wrote to William Henry Harrison III, who had served as one of his rangers in Yellowstone in the 1920s, after seeing a news report that the man had recently won a seat in the Wyoming state legislature. "May I ask that when you get to Cheyenne . . . you not make any commitments on the wrong side of conservation until we have had a chance to do some corresponding." Harrison expressed delight in hearing from Albright after nearly twenty years, but he hastened to point out that he opposed the Jackson Hole project. This had become the automatic response of most Wyoming politicians, and for understandable reasons. The voters of the state were "as grumpy as a bear with a sore ear and as immune to reason," Jay ("Ding") Darling, the noted cartoonist, reported to Albright in 1945. Nevertheless, it was now only a matter of time until the Rockefeller-Albright plan for the preservation of Jackson Hole would be brought to a successful conclusion. FDR's veto message, by stating that Congress should pass legislation to reimburse Teton

17. HMA to Drury, Feb. 22, 1945, HMA to Nicholas Roosevelt, Aug. 11, 1944, and HMA to H. I. Brock, Jan. 21, 1945, HMA Papers; HMA, "The Glory of Jackson Hole," *New York Times Magazine*, Jan. 21, 1945, pp. 22–23.

County for lost tax revenues and to protect the grazing rights of the valley's cattlemen, had prepared the way for the compromise that would ultimately end the controversy. Through every tedious delay and heated debate Albright and Chorley reassured Rockefeller that "the project is worth it."[18]

The philanthropist had recently turned over most of his land holdings in Wyoming to Jackson Hole Preserve, Incorporated, a newly chartered corporation (analogous to Colonial Williamsburg, Incorporated), a policy-making body that would control the controversial lands until such time as the National Park Service could accept them. The corporation would take steps to insure the unspoiled character of the lands and to develop tasteful and minimal tourist facilities. Albright was one of the first men named to its board of trustees. Laurance Rockefeller also accepted a seat on the board and began taking an interest in conservation affairs. Albright and Chorley quietly encouraged the young man to continue in the footsteps of his father.[19]

Albright's involvement in national conservation affairs, especially the Jackson Hole controversy, propelled him into big league Republican politics during the 1940s. Although still exasperated by Dewey's outburst against FDR's action in establishing the Jackson Hole National Monument, Albright continued his efforts to "educate" New York's Republican governor, who obviously stood a good chance of being the Republican presidential candidate in 1948. As usual, Albright's persistence and disarming soft sell had the desired effect. Dewey refrained from making any public statements about the Jackson Hole situation in the postwar period, apparently convinced, thanks to Albright's proselytizing, that he would lose more votes in the East than he would gain in the West by opposing the project.

18. Struthers Burt to HMA, Mar. 2, 1945, Drury to HMA, Mar. 12, 1945, HMA to William Henry Harrison III, Dec. 29, 1944, and Jan. 29, 1945, Harrison to HMA, Jan. 22, 1945, and HMA to Rockefeller, Mar. 18, 1943, HMA Papers.
19. HMA, "Prospectus," n.d., HMA Papers; interview with HMA, July 6, 1965; the files entitled "Jackson Hole Preserve, Inc." in HMA Papers contain extensive information about the preserve's affairs.

Late in March 1945 the New York newspapers carried the public announcement of Albright's appointment by Dewey to a position on the Palisades Interstate Park Commission, replacing Alfred E. Smith, whose term had expired. At about the same time Albright established casual, friendly relations with Herbert Brownell, a prosperous New York attorney, who was a member of Dewey's inner circle of political advisers. "This is just a note to tell you how much I enjoyed the visit with you and Nick Roosevelt the other day at our Century Club," Albright wrote in April 1945. "It was worthwhile in every respect and I look forward to seeing you from time to time in the future." He repeatedly disavowed any political ambitions for himself. He wanted mainly to keep Rockefeller's Jackson Hole project out of politics, he said.[20]

In the meantime, of course, the Democrats remained in power in Washington, and Albright, like many successful big-business executives, showed himself adept at working both sides of the political fence. He continued to correspond with Ickes, who seemed likely to stay in office forever, and he visited Chapman nearly every time he went to Washington. But the elevation of Harry S. Truman to the presidency in April 1945, following FDR's death, wrought important changes in the cabinet. For one thing, it brought Clinton P. Anderson, a former congressman from New Mexico, into office as Secretary of Agriculture. Since the USP mine and refinery were located in Carlsbad, Albright had made it a point to get to know the congressmen and senators from New Mexico; he and "Clint" Anderson had been on a first-name basis for more than five years. Another consequence of Truman's succession to the presidency was that it increased the probability that Ickes would quit. Within a year Ickes resigned from the cabinet following a quarrel with Truman over the proposed appointment of oilman Edwin W. Pauley as Undersecretary of the Navy. Albright hurried to Washington to do some behind-the-scenes lobbying in behalf of Oscar Chap-

20. *New York Times*, Mar. 23, 1945; HMA to Herbert B. Brownell, Jr., Apr. 23, 1945, HMA Papers.

man's candidacy for the post vacated by Ickes. Probably because of Truman's interest in public power, Julius A. Krug, who had recently headed the WPB, but had earlier worked for the TVA, got the job. Chapman was promoted to Undersecretary. "I am sorry things did not work out the way we hoped," Albright wrote to Chapman after it was all over.[21]

Chapman saw to it that Albright had an opportunity to meet Krug in the spring of 1946. A hulking, congenial, and informal man, "Cap" to his friends, Krug struck up a friendship with Albright almost immediately after Chapman introduced them. "I thoroughly enjoyed our recent visits," Krug wrote to Albright shortly after taking office, "and I, too, hope, that we will have the opportunity of getting together frequently for further discussions of both potash and our national parks." In the next three years, Albright regularly conferred with Krug about the Jackson Hole project and about the department's minerals policy. In September 1946, following a meeting of the American Mining Congress in Denver, Albright persuaded Krug to tour the Jackson Hole country, and in the process he administered a liberal dose of the Albright charm and the Albright point of view. About a month later, the two men met in Carlsbad, where Albright escorted the Secretary through the USP mine and refinery and gave him a personalized tour of Carlsbad Caverns.[22]

In 1947, at Krug's insistence, Albright became a member of the National Minerals Advisory Council set up by the Secretary "to develop a comprehensive national mineral policy, which would make for a healthy mining industry and at the same time assure our American industries and our American people gen-

21. HMA to Clinton P. Anderson, June 21, 1950, July 26, 1945, Dec. 10, 1945, and Aug. 5, 1947, Anderson to HMA, July 6, 1945, July 31, 1945, and Dec. 28, 1945, and Anderson to Harry S. Truman, Oct. 16, 1947, Clinton P. Anderson Papers; HMA to Chapman, Mar. 15, 1946, in Oscar L. Chapman Papers; Joseph O'Mahoney to HMA, Feb. 27, 1946, NA, Records of NPS, gen., admin., Dir. Albright.

22. HMA to Chapman, Apr. 22, 1946, and Sept. 19, 1946, and HMA to Krug, Oct. 31, 1946, Chapman Papers; Krug to HMA, Apr. 26, 1946, Papers of Julius A. Krug, box 20.

erally a sufficient quantity" of minerals "at a reasonable price."
The council included many of the top executives in the mining
industry. Albright paid the ultimate penalty for missing a meeting of this council in the summer of 1948; he was elected chairman, a fortuitous development that brought him even closer to
Krug and gave him a greater chance to influence the Secretary's
thinking. Krug so esteemed Albright's advice that he wanted him
appointed to the department's Advisory Board on National
Parks, Historic Sites, Buildings,and Monuments, but Albright
declined, preferring to continue as an informal adviser to the
National Park Service. "I think you will see enough of Horace
Albright," he wrote, "in connection with the work" of the National Minerals Advisory Council "without having me active on
the National Parks Advisory Board."[23]

By 1947, then, Albright was in a position to be influential in
the affairs of both the Interior Department and the Agriculture
Department. He counted both Secretaries as personal friends.
He entertained them in New York and in New Mexico. He served
on advisory committees for both departments in areas of vital
concern to the potash industry. He took a generally disinterested
view of his work on these committees, although his biases as a
businessman and conservationist inevitably influenced his decisions. He staunchly advocated the continuation of the mineral
leasing system on the public domain, under which valuable mineral deposits were leased to private developers. This system
dated back to 1920 and was a legacy of the Pinchot conservationists. He argued in favor of tariffs on imported potash to
protect domestic producers.[24]

23. Krug to HMA, Mar. 13, 1947, and Dec. 2, 1947, and Krug to
Drury, Sept. 13, 1947, Krug Papers, box 20; Krug's remarks at the first
meeting of the National Minerals Advisory Council, Dec. 12, 1947, Krug
Papers, box 80; HMA to Krug, Jan. 16, 1948, NA, Records of NPS, gen.,
admin., Dir. Albright.
24. Interview with HMA, July 6, 1965; for evidence that Krug
agreed with Albright's relatively conservative position on mineral
conservation see Krug's remarks at the first meeting of the National
Minerals Advisory Council; HMA to Chapman, Nov. 1, 1946, and HMA
to Krug, Apr. 30, 1947, Chapman Papers.

In the five years following World War II, Albright's increasing conservatism almost perfectly reflected the mood of the American business community. War-weary and tired of government restrictions, most businessmen reacted adversely to continued economic controls, to militant trade unionism, to "radicalism," and to Harry S. Truman, the bespectacled little man in the White House, who inherited the enormously complicated problem of putting the United States back on a peacetime keel. It was "time for a change," Albright contended in both the elections of 1946 and 1948. It was unhealthy for any party "to get the feeling that the Government belongs to it."[25]

Albright's skepticism about Truman stemmed from personal as well as political roots. As president of the American Planning and Civic Association, Albright occasionally wrote to the chief executive in Washington, expressing opinions or offering advice on certain conservation issues. Less than a month after Truman assumed the presidency, Albright sent him a long letter advising him "about certain pending matters of *unfinished business* in which President Roosevelt has been interested or has taken some action." Enclosed with the letter were "paragraphs on separate sheets which may be filed under subject headings for convenient consultation." The first sheet bore the title "Jackson Hole National Monument." Then, in January 1946, the president announced his intention to remodel and expand the White House to provide adequate facilities for his executive assistants and clerical staff. He proposed to convert the east wing into a museum for "furniture, chinaware, papers, and other articles" used by presidents. The west wing would be enlarged to include fifteen thousand square feet of new office space, a cafeteria, and a 375-seat auditorium for press conferences and ceremonial use. The addition, Truman claimed, "will not be visible from Pennsylvania Avenue." Almost immediately, a howl of protest began to rise. The American Institute of Architects severely criticized the proposed changes. Editors from coast to coast objected. And a large amount of protest mail flowed into the White House. Al-

25. HMA to Adolph C. Miller, Nov. 17, 1948, HMA Papers; interview with HMA, July 6, 1965.

bright too sent a letter of protest, one that caused sparks to fly in the chief executive's office.[26]

To a man of Albright's tastes and deep commitments to the concept of historical preservation, Truman's scheme to remodel the White House seemed alarmingly inappropriate. The president should have all the working space he needed, Albright contended, but surely a great national shrine should not be permanently disfigured to provide it. Only a few days after the story broke, Albright found himself at the center of a plan to obstruct Truman's proposed changes. A handful of architects, city planners, and conservationists had collected a formidable array of expert testimony, dating all the way back to 1874, about the nobility and distinction of the White House architecture. They had prepared illustrations of how the expanded White House would look, emphasizing the extent of the changes Truman had proposed. But they needed somebody to sign the covering letter to the president. In a long session at the tap room of the Cosmos Club, they persuaded Albright, as president of the American Planning and Civic Association, to sign the letter and send it to the White House. They then persuaded the publisher of the Washington *Star* to publish the letter and its documentation in the next Sunday edition of the paper, a move designed to prevent Truman from simply ignoring the communiqué. The letter called for a "thorough consideration" of alternative plans, such as using the old State Department Building— now the Executive Office Building—to house the bulk of the president's staff. "The general public, including the planning and civic groups," it stated, "have a right to know what is being done with their historic monuments by those temporarily in authority." In a conciliatory gesture, Truman dropped plans for a museum and cafeteria, but it was too late. The Senate and the House voted to rescind all funds authorized in the previous ses-

26. HMA to Truman, May 5, 1945, Charles G. Ross to HMA, June 9, 1945, Papers of Harry S. Truman, PPF 9A; *New York Times*, Jan. 12, 1946, and Jan. 25, 1946; Mrs. G. Bullick-Willes to Truman, Jan. 27, 1946, and Resolution of Virginia Chapter of the AIA, Truman Papers, OF 50.

sion for use in the proposed extension. When this occurred, Truman's still unheralded temper suddenly came into play. He wrote Albright a furious letter, accusing him of grossly misrepresenting the facts and of pridefully obstructing a much needed project.[27]

In spite of his personal and political disagreements with the president, Albright continued to collaborate with both Democrats and Republicans in Washington and New York. His maneuvering became more and more subtle as the 1948 elections approached. He maintained his connections with Dewey in New York, although the ties between the two men were never very close. As a registered Republican, he favored Dewey's candidacy for president. In June 1948, to practically nobody's surprise, the New York governor received the GOP nomination. So glum were the Democrats that most of the cabinet officers began looking for alternate sources of livelihood. Anderson resigned from his post as Secretary of Agriculture to run for the Senate from New Mexico, and Krug elected to sit on the sidelines during the campaign, not wanting to embarrass himself in a losing cause. Chapman, too, began casting about for a nonpolitical position, but he was uncertain about what he should do.

In the spring of 1948, Chapman telephoned Albright at the Hay Adams Hotel in Washington and invited him to lunch, confiding that he had something he wanted to talk over. The two men drove across the Potomac to Alexandria, Virginia, to a small restaurant where they would be assured of privacy. Chapman explained that he was considering leaving the Interior Department. He had a chance to establish a law practice in Washington, but he had serious qualms about the propriety of abandoning Truman just then. He asked Albright's advice. "If I were you," Albright replied, "I would stay on the burning deck." There was an outside chance that Truman might win, he pointed

27. *New York Times*, Jan. 12, Jan. 25, Jan. 27, Jan. 30, 1946, and Feb. 3, Feb. 10, Feb. 16, 1946; Washington *Star*, Jan. 27, 1946; HMA to Truman, Jan. 26, 1946, and Truman to HMA, Jan. 26, 1946, Truman Papers, OF 50 (a cross reference sheet summarizes these letters; the originals have been transferred to the permanent White House file); interview with HMA, July 24, 1964.

out, in spite of the polls that had Dewey in the lead. If Chapman stayed with the president and made himself politically useful, Albright reasoned, he would probably be in line to replace Krug as Secretary of the Interior. In the end, Chapman decided to stick it out in the Interior Department. He put Truman in his debt by helping to mastermind the president's successful whistle-stop tour in the fall of 1948, and on election day, the voters swept Truman back into the White House in the greatest political upset of the twentieth century. The morning after the election, the jubilant Truman reportedly promised to name Chapman Secretary of the Interior as soon as Krug retired. Within a year, Chapman took over the job.[28]

The irony of this situation was quite apparent to insiders who knew both Chapman and Albright. There had been persistent preelection rumors in New York and Washington that Dewey would probably nominate Albright as his Secretary of the Interior. Amused by these speculations, Chapman had startled his old friend one day shortly before the election by greeting him with a cheerful: "Good morning, Mr. Secretary." Albright laughed at the joke and demurred. He was well satisfied with the knowledge that Chapman, a man who would respond sympathetically to the needs of the national parks and to the problems of the potash industry, stood next in line for the Secretarial appointment.[29]

While the political campaign of 1948 built toward its surprising climax, Albright devoted much of his time to the Hoover Commission's Task Force on Natural Resources. The commission had a broad mandate to recommend organizational changes in the executive branch of the federal government; the Task Force on Natural Resources was to concentrate on the federal conservation agencies. Leslie A. Miller, former governor of Wyoming, John Dempsey, former governor of New Mexico, Ralph

28. Interview with Oscar L. Chapman, June 15, 1966; interview with HMA, July 6, 1965.
29. Details from interview with Chapman, June 15, 1966; Cabell Phillips, *The Truman Presidency*, pp. 212–13, 232–33.

Carr, former governor of Colorado, Donald H. McLaughlin, president of Homestake Mining Corporation, Isaiah Bowman, president of Johns Hopkins University, Gilbert White, president of Haverford College, and Samuel T. Dana, dean of the School of Forestry and Conservation at the University of Michigan, were the other members of the task force. This assignment gave Albright an opportunity to be associated with Herbert Hoover once again, and it afforded him a new chance to push for the establishment of a Department of Conservation. "I think my twenty years in the Interior Department probably qualify me to play a useful part in the work of this conservation subcommittee," he modestly allowed in a letter to Krug early in 1948.[30]

In the fifteen years from 1933 to 1948, Albright had built an enduring personal friendship with Hoover. The former president enjoyed talking to Albright, and the two men saw each other periodically in New York. They agreed on the urgent need for governmental reorganization.[31]

The job of the task force narrowed down mainly to a search for a formula to increase the efficiency of the government's vast conservation establishment. Some of Hoover's ideas on reorganization, originally proposed in 1932 and 1933, and some of Ickes's ideas, dating from 1937 and 1938, were resurrected and thoroughly discussed. Albright and the other members of the subcommittee prepared position papers on specific areas of conservation organization. Albright was in constant touch with Drury, Krug, and Chapman during the year-long deliberations. He also wrote to Ickes to keep him informed about the general thinking of the task force. "Under the terms of the law it is not possible to discuss what has been done," Albright wrote the former Secretary in September 1948, "but I can say to you that if you could see our program you would be pleased with it. I can

30. Quotation from HMA to Krug, Jan. 16, 1948, NA, Records of NPS, gen., admin., Dir. Albright.
31. HMA to Hoover, Oct. 22, 1942, May 25, 1944, Sept. 17, 1946, and Mar. 12, 1947, and Hoover to HMA, June 8, 1945, Sept. 27, 1946, and Mar. 15, 1947, Hoover Papers, boxes 1–41.

tell you that your reorganization plans of the late 30's received the utmost consideration." In fact, the task force had already recommended the establishment of a "Department of Natural Resources," almost exactly as Ickes had advocated. "The Department of the Interior," the task force report stated, "would cease to exist." Albright was frankly elated.[32]

He anticipated, however, that the plan would encounter serious opposition once it passed out of the hands of the task force. The obvious stumbling blocks were the Forest Service and the Army Engineers, whose supporters immediately opposed the suggested changes. The Forest Service was passionately attached to the Department of Agriculture, and the Army Engineers did not want to turn over its rivers and harbors work to the Bureau of Reclamation. A long delay ensued while Hoover and the members of his commission deliberated. "Our Committee did a job that would have received your wholehearted approval," Albright explained to Ickes in January 1949. "Of that I am sure. However, the report seems to be under wraps . . . [and] it is likely to suffer the same fate that your plan of 1939 suffered." The committee had "tried to combine the administrative functions of the Bureau of Land Management and the Forest Service," Albright explained "which we thought would be a powerful inducement to get the Forest Service to move in with the other natural resources agencies." The committee's strategy, though sound, ultimately failed. The Hoover Commission's concluding report recommended a compromise, namely, that the nondefense functions of the Army Engineers be transferred to the Bureau of Reclamation and that the Forest Service should remain in the Agriculture Department. "I do not know what was the cause of the failure," Albright lamented. "At any rate, a good conservation department plan has been wrecked." Disappointed but not surprised by the final outcome, Albright put away the Hoover Commission's concluding report and turned his attention to another matter that

32. HMA to Ickes, Sept. 16, 1948, HMA Papers; Commission on Organization of the Executive Branch of Government, *Organization and Policy in Field of Natural Resources: Report with Recommendations*, pp. 6–7.

held promise of a happier ending. After nearly thirty years, the fight over Jackson Hole was on the verge of an amicable settlement.[33]

33. HMA to Ickes, Jan. 14, 1949 and Mar. 21, 1949, HMA Papers; Commission on Organization of the Executive Branch of the Government, *Concluding Report*, pp. 65–67; HMA to Robert Moses, Nov. 12, 1948, with attached memorandum, and HMA to Hoover, Nov. 26, 1948, Hoover Papers, box 1-Q/37.

12

Resources for the Future

During the 1930s and 1940s, the Jackson Hole controversy affected every level of Wyoming politics. There were many men in public office whose careers had been built almost exclusively on their opposition to the National Park Service taking control of Jackson Hole. One of the most promising developments of the postwar years, one that augered well for a final settlement of the long dispute, was the gradual dying down of political passions in Jackson, Cheyenne, Laramie, and Cody. A flood of free-spending tourists, most of whom came to see the famous Yellowstone Park and the Grand Teton–Jackson Hole preserve, engulfed the state in 1946 and 1947, helping to convince the doubters that in the long run Wyoming had much to gain by insuring national park status for Jackson Hole. The stock growers still maintained their control of the state legislature, but the voters and most of their elected representatives were growing weary of the dispute. "My God, how I'd like to see this constant controversy stop," the governor groaned to Struthers Burt in 1948. Both time and the tides of politics were running strongly in favor of a settlement after World War II.[1]

One more crisis had to be overcome before the controversy finally died. In November 1946 the Republicans made sweeping gains in both the House and Senate. When the first session of the Eightieth Congress convened in January 1947, the Republicans

1. Quotation from Lester C. Hunt to Burt, Mar. 20, 1948, copy in HMA Papers; for a report on the political power of the Wyoming stock-growers, see Lester Velie, "They Kicked Us Off Our Land," *Collier's* 120 (July 26, 1947): 20, and 120 (Aug. 9, 1947): 72.

assumed control. In the House, Representative Barrett of Wyoming fell heir to the chairmanship of the permanent subcommittee on public lands, and in the Senate, E. V. Robertson of Wyoming stepped up to a powerful position on the Committee on Public Lands and Surveys. It was a perfect setup, the opponents of the Jackson Hole project recognized, for an all-out drive to destroy the national monument once and for all. There were those in the West, especially the cattle and sheep men, who saw in this situation an opportunity to undermine not only the National Park Service but also the Bureau of Land Management and the grazing division of the Forest Service. Spouting slogans about the "communist-minded bureaucrats" in Washington, these men, a notably small minority of westerners, mounted a campaign to prevent the effective regulation of the public domain and ultimately, it was said, to gain title to 145 million acres of public grazing lands. Barrett reintroduced his bill to abolish the Jackson Hole National Monument. With Robertson lending strong support in the Senate, he appeared confident that it would get through both houses without much trouble. Senator O'Mahoney though treading cautiously, took a position in favor of compromise.[2]

The conservationists were not long in sounding the alarm. The Sierra Club, the Boone and Crockett Club, the American Planning and Civic Association, the Izaak Walton League, the Camp Fire Club of America, the National Parks Association, and the Wilderness Society moved to oppose the emasculation of the federal conservation program. Once again, as in 1943 and 1944, Albright became one of the leaders of the small but influential group of conservationists who battled the Barrett Bill. The National Park Service, still headquartered in Chicago, also opposed the Barrett Bill but with only marginal effectiveness. There were serious administrative problems confronting the Park Service that drained off most of Drury's energy. Besides, the director had little stomach for tough political infighting. More and more

2. Velie, "They Kicked Us Off Our Land," pp. 72–73, 80; HMA to Dewey, July 3, 1947, HMA Papers.

he delegated the bureau's political troubleshooting to Demaray and Wirth, who seemed to enjoy it.[3]

Albright advocated the simple, hard-hitting strategy of opposing the Barrett Bill strenuously at every stage of the legislative process. "If the bill can be definitely stopped in either the House or Senate," he advised, "it should be defeated there in Congress," rather than by a presidential veto. Moreover, he counseled against any significant territorial compromises. "Dealing with Wyoming is like dealing with the Russians," he bristled to Laurance Rockefeller. "You never get anywhere by trying to cooperate or in other directions be helpful." "I have found in my many years of conservation work that as a general rule one must fight uncompromisingly."[4]

Working mostly through Congressmen J. Hardin Peterson of Florida and Leroy Johnson of California, Albright concentrated his efforts on the House. He cooperated closely with Chorley and Fabian. A number of other conservationists, including Kenneth Reid of the Izaak Walton League, and Arthur Carhart, a freelance writer from Colorado, lent their aid. Albright asked Governor Dewey to intervene with Speaker Joe Martin, GOP floor leader Charles Halleck, and New York Congressmen Dean Taylor and Jay Le Fevre, both members of the Public Lands Committee, requesting that they "move slowly in acting on any measures that would detrimentally affect sound conservation policy." He persuaded Hoover to talk to Halleck and Martin and Richard Welch, chairman of the House Public Lands Committee, which had jurisdiction over Barrett's subcommittee. He obtained the help of R. R. M. Carpenter, a member of the Boone and

3. Richard M. Leonard, circular letter to the members of the Sierra Club, Apr. 1947, Harlean James to HMA, Apr. 15, 1947, and Olaus J. Murie to Harry S. Truman, July 18, 1947, HMA Papers; see U.S., Congress, House, Hearings Before a Subcommittee of the Committee on Public Lands, "To Abolish the Jackson Hole National Monument," 80th Cong., 1st sess. (Apr. 1947) for positions of various groups opposing the Barrett Bill.

4. HMA, memorandum re Jackson Hole National Monument, July 29, 1947, and HMA to Laurance S. Rockefeller, May 7, 1947, HMA Papers.

Crockett Club and the vice-president of DuPont, and Lionel Weil, an influential North Carolina businessman, in lining up opposition to the bill. He acted as coordinator and middleman between H. E. Anthony of the Boone and Crockett Club, John Baker of the National Audubon Society, and Marshall McLeon of the Camp Fire Club, who rounded up congressmen willing to object to the Barrett Bill when it came up on the consent calendar. Every possible contact was explored. Albright even called upon his old friend and classmate Earl Warren, now governor of California, to join the fight.[5]

By painstaking effort and fast footwork the Rockefeller group bottled up the Barrett Bill. It was repeatedly objected to on the consent calendar during the first session of the Eightieth Congress. Barrett's only hope then rested with the Rules Committee, which had the power to call the bill up at any time during the second session for final consideration by the House. In August 1947 Albright focused his attention almost exclusively on the members of that committee, earnestly urging them "to deny a rule for this bill." He wrote to all the members of the committee and talked personally to most of them. He again invoked the aid of Hoover and Dewey. Other conservationists, essentially the same group that worked with Chorley, Albright, and Fabian in the first session, brought great pressure to bear on Leo E. Allen, the chairman of the Rules Committee. By the spring of 1948, it was clear that the Barrett Bill would never reach the House floor. Unmourned and virtually unnoticed, the bill to abolish the Jackson Hole National Monument languished and finally died. Earlier in the session, when Barrett approached the Park Service about a possible "compromise" (which would have markedly reduced the dimensions of the monument), Albright denounced the scheme. "I personally dislike a 'face-saving' plan of this

5. HMA to J. Hardin Peterson, May 1, 1947, and July 17, 1947, HMA to Leroy Johnson, Apr. 24, 1947, HMA to Dewey, Apr. 9, 1947, Dewey to HMA, Apr. 14, 1947, HMA to Hoover, Mar. 21 and Apr. 29, 1947, memorandum for the files, Mar. 17, 1947, HMA to Earl Warren, Apr. 28, 1947, and July 3, 1947, and Warren to HMA, May 8, 1947, and Aug. 7, 1947, HMA Papers.

kind," he informed Drury. He pointed out that neither the Park
Service nor the Rockefeller group needed to compromise now.
Although the O'Mahoney rider, denying the National Park Service funds to administer the monument, still encumbered the
Interior Department's annual appropriations bill, the situation
in Congress as well as in Wyoming was such that a satisfactory
settlement would soon be possible.[6]

In 1948, Lester C. Hunt, Wyoming's moderate governor, was
elected senator, replacing the lackluster Robertson. Hunt joined
O'Mahoney in favoring a settlement of the Jackson Hole controversy, while Barrett, having reassessed the political climate in
his home state, ceased his obstructionist tactics. Peace talks between Wyoming's congressional delegation and representatives
of the National Park Service, the Jackson Hole Preserve, Incorporated, and the state of Wyoming got underway in February
1949. Wirth handled most of the negotiations for the Park
Service, and Fabian represented the Jackson Hole Preserve,
Incorporated. Oscar Chapman, acting as spokesman for the
Secretary of the Interior, played an essential role in these discussions. Albright stayed away from the formal negotiating sessions, most of which took place in O'Mahoney's office, on the
theory that his presence might rekindle old animosities. But he
labored effectively behind the scenes, soothing tender egos and
pouring balm on old wounds. Through the good offices of J. Hardin Peterson, he effected a rapprochement with Barrett. "I am
particularly indebted to Congressman Peterson for what he did
in bringing Mr. Barrett and me together," Albright wrote to
Wirth early in 1949. "He did it in such a way that Mr. Barrett
and I were personal friends on a first name basis within 15 minutes. My hat is off to 'Pete' as a superb public relations man."[7]

6. HMA, memorandum re Jackson Hole National Monument; Peterson to HMA, July 24, 1947, Richard Welch to HMA, July 22, 1947, and
June 17, 1948, HMA to Leo E. Allen, Feb. 24, 1948, HMA to Johnson,
Mar. 11, 1948, James W. Wadsworth to HMA, June 1, 1948, A. J. Sabath
to HMA, June 23, 1948, and HMA, memorandum [to the file], June
16, 1948, HMA Papers.
7. Drury to HMA, Apr. 27, 1949, with enclosure reporting on the
progress of negotiations, HMA Papers; quotation from HMA to Wirth,
Feb. 7, 1949, HMA Papers.

The era of good feelings that had now clearly emerged in Congress on the issue of Jackson Hole was made possible partly because of the political know-how of the Rockefeller group. Albright and his colleagues had waged a hard fight to block the Barrett Bill, but their methods had never violated the gentlemanly code that governs most congressional combat. It was therefore relatively easy to patch things up with the opposition when the contest ended. Albright's long years in Washington had taught him the inevitability of disagreement and the practical benefits of tolerance.[8]

Gradually the pieces of a Jackson Hole agreement fell together. About nine thousand acres in the southeast section of the Jackson Hole National Monument were to be transferred to the National Elk Refuge and the Teton National Forest, but the remaining two hundred thousand acres were to be added to Grand Teton National Park, with picturesque Jackson Lake and the rolling Jackson Hole flatlands providing the perfect foreground for the superb beauty of the Teton range. This part of the agreement assured the realization of the Rockefeller-Albright dream, still a noble vision in spite of its advanced age. Other provisions in the agreement established a descending schedule of tax reimbursements for Teton County over a twenty-five-year period and the continuation of existing grazing rights within the park for the lifetime of the leaseholder and his heirs. The question of who would have jurisdiction over the elk herd that wintered in Jackson Hole proved the thorniest issue. Wyoming game officials held out against the elimination of hunting rights, and the National Park Service balked at permitting hunting within the confines of a national park. Finally a compromise was reached, stipulating that the Wyoming Game and Fish Commission would administer the elk herd in cooperation with the National Park Service and that whenever the herd became overpopulated, Wyoming hunters would be deputized as temporary park rangers and empowered to kill surplus animals inside the park boundaries. The latter provision, though angrily denounced by many park purists, removed the last objection to a settlement.

8. HMA to Wirth, Feb. 7, 1949, HMA Papers.

The O'Mahoney-Hunt Bill to establish "A New Grand Teton National Park" passed Congress practically without debate and received President Truman's signature in September 1950. Buried in the bill's preamble was a provision, designed to satisfy Barrett's crowd, that "no further extension or establishment of national parks or monuments in Wyoming may be undertaken except by express authorization of the Congress." Since the Park Service had no interest in acquiring other scenic regions in Wyoming, this was a harmless concession.[9]

As in many another hard-fought political dispute, the Jackson Hole controversy ended in a crashing anticlimax. The careful negotiating sessions settled all of the substantive issues, and a refreshing mood of accommodation had superseded the petty bickering long before the O'Mahoney-Hunt Bill slipped through Congress. Actually and symbolically, the end of the long controversy came on December 16, 1949, at a simple ceremony in the office of the Secretary of the Interior when the federal government at last accepted title to the Rockefeller lands in Jackson Hole. Laurance Rockefeller, representing his aging father, handed the deed to Oscar Chapman, whom Truman had named Secretary of the Interior only a few days before. Throughout 1949 Chapman had taken a close personal interest in the negotiations with O'Mahoney. The Secretary spoke admiringly of Albright's "pioneering efforts in behalf of the Jackson Hole project" and expressed appreciation to John D. Rockefeller, Jr., for his generosity. Laurance Rockefeller then made a "gracious statement in behalf of his father." Harold Fabian, Newton Drury, Leslie Miller, Conrad Wirth, and a handful of Park Service officials watched the ceremony. Curiously, Albright failed to show up that day in Washington. "I fully intended to go down Friday morning," he explained to Laurance Rockefeller,

9. Drury to HMA, Apr. 27, 1949, Chorley to Leslie A. Miller, Apr. 28, 1949, HMA to Olaus J. Murie, May 16, 1950, HMA to Drury, June 16, 1950, Drury to HMA, July 14, 1950, and HMA to O'Mahoney, July 18, 1950, HMA Papers; *Congressional Record*, 81st Cong., 2d sess. (July 26, 1950), pp. 11043–45 (Aug. 24, 1950), pp. 13381–82, and (Aug. 31, 1950), pp. 13965, 13982.

"but I had a little sinus condition annoying me and [a labor dispute at] Carlsbad was keeping me on the long distance telephone to such an extent that I felt I had better not leave here, so I did not go. I shall probably always regret it." About two weeks after the ceremony the elder Rockefeller wrote to Albright: "The recent transfer of property in Washington must have brought you hardly less satisfaction than it brought me. What a pleasure it has been to work with you in this matter over the years, as well as in so many other park matters!"[10]

The establishment of the expanded Grand Teton National Park in 1950 did not end Albright's association with the problems of Jackson Hole. He continued as a trustee of the Jackson Hole Preserve, Incorporated, which now undertook to purchase private holdings in the park for donation to the National Park Service. He also accepted a position on the board of directors of the Grand Teton Lodge Company, another Rockefeller enterprise, which poured millions of dollars into the construction and operation of a much needed hotel and other tourist facilities.

Albright originally interested Rockefeller in the idea of preserving the most scenic part of Jackson Hole. He took a leading part in the long and ultimately successful political fight to win congressional approval of Rockefeller's proposed gift. And he participated at the policy-making level in the development of the area, which soon included some of the most impeccable and unobtrusive tourist accommodations in the national park system. His constancy, imagination, energy, and political skill accounted for the project's success quite as much as Rockefeller's millions. The spectacularly beautiful Grand Teton National Park, unblemished by commercial exploitation and unparalleled in its scenic integrity, stands today as Albright's single most important achievement in the field of conservation.

10. Chapman to Arthur Carhart, Aug. 31, 1949, Chapman Papers; Chorley to Chapman, Apr. 28, 1949, Drury to HMA, Dec. 16, 1949, Laurance S. Rockefeller to HMA, Dec. 19, 1949, HMA to L. S. Rockefeller, Dec. 21, 1949, and John D. Rockefeller, Jr., to HMA, Jan. 10, 1950, HMA Papers; Drury to HMA, Apr. 7, 1949, and Apr. 11, 1949, NA, Records of NPS, gen., admin., dir.; New York *Herald Tribune*, Dec. 17, 1949; *New York Times*, Dec. 18, 1949.

Once assured that the O'Mahoney-Hunt Bill would pass through Congress without opposition, Albright and his wife left for Europe in August 1950 on a combination business and pleasure trip. Suddenly, in Rome, the news reached them that their son Bob had suffered a severe attack of ileitis. He died in a Los Angeles hospital late in November, about two weeks after the Albrights returned home.[11]

After a period of brooding and deep anguish, Albright plunged into a seemingly perpetual round of board meetings, business and conservation conferences, and civic affairs. The pace of his conservation activities steadily accelerated as at least half a dozen organizations and agencies vied for his time. He took a more and more discerning interest in the affairs of the Palisades Interstate Park Commission to which Dewey reappointed him in 1950. He continued to play a leading role in the American Planning and Civic Association, although he relinquished the organization's presidency to U. S. Grant III and took on the less demanding position of board chairman. The American Pioneer Trails Association, of which he was vice-president, the Conservation Committee of the Camp Fire Club, the American Scenic and Historic Preservation Society, and the Boone and Crockett Club each laid claim to his energies.[12]

His newest organizational interest during these years was the National Trust for Historic Preservation, authorized by Congress in 1949 to "coordinate efforts to preserve the nation's landmarks and shrines." The February 27, 1950, issue of the *New York Times* carried a story announcing the selection of Albright, George C. Marshall, Herbert Hoover, U. S. Grant III, Winthrop W. Aldrich, and Mrs. Francis B. Crowninshield, as trustees. This was in recognition of Albright's experience and preeminence in the field of historic preservation. But it was also an outgrowth

11. HMA to Fabian, Aug. 11, 1950, HMA Papers; Drury to whom it may concern, Aug. 7, 1950 (letter of introduction for HMA's use in European parks), Drury to HMA, Oct. 4, 1950, and HMA to Drury, Oct. 23, 1950, and Dec. 4, 1950, Papers of Newton B. Drury.

12. Information on HMA's organizational affiliations compiled from *Who's Who in America* (1950–67).

of his letter to Truman during the squabble over the proposed White House remodeling. The ad hoc committee of architects and conservationists who put together the letter Albright signed, and the Council on Historic Preservation had obtained the legislation that authorized the National Trust. The idea was to establish an organization to guard the White House and other historic buildings from defacement or destruction. Albright was an active member of the board for the next twelve years.[13]

Albright took pains to remain on personal, friendly terms with Drury during the late 1940s and early 1950s. The two men met now and then in New York or Washington to "make some medicine together." They also consumed a little "medicine" at these get-togethers, for Albright had now quietly abandoned the theory and practice of total abstinence. Drury's main concern was to regain some of the appropriations the Park Service had lost during the war, and he wanted Albright's help. By 1949, the bureau's budget had been partially restored. Later, Albright tried to help Drury avoid a drastic cut in Park Service funds during the early stages of the Korean War, which began in June 1950. Drury was exceedingly grateful for his old friend's efforts.[14]

On the subject of concessions policy, however, Albright and Drury disagreed. When Drury and Demaray moved to scrap the old pattern of privately owned, regulated park concessions in favor of operations by a single nonprofit, government-controlled corporation, National Park Concessions, Incorporated, Albright opposed the plan, although he conceded that in the long run government ownership of tourist facilities in the parks would eliminate many administrative problems. The new corporation eventually took over concessions at Isle Royale, Mammoth Cave,

13. *New York Times*, Feb. 19, 1950, Feb. 27, 1950, Apr. 4, 1947, and May 21, 1954; HMA to Mrs. Charles D. Missar (of the National Trust for Historic Preservation), Sept. 8, 1962, HMA to Gordon Gray, Nov. 19, 1962, and Gray to HMA, Nov. 28, 1962, HMA Papers.

14. HMA to Hillary A. Tolson, Jan. 14, 1946, HMA to Drury, Apr. 8, 1946, and Drury to HMA, Mar. 4, 1947, NA, Records of NPS, gen., admin., Dir. Albright; information about appropriations compiled from *Annual Report, NPS* (1941–51).

Olympic National Park, and a few other places. But concessions in all of the major parks remained in private hands because of congressional hostility to the idea of keeping private investors out and because of the momentum of the "old way," that is, Albright's way. No one had worked harder on concessions policy in the early days of the Park Service than Albright, and therefore it was anticipated that he would raise objections to any change. Drury responded moderately and affectionately to Albright's rather defensive letters.[15]

It was probably unavoidable that Albright, because of his close connections with both men, would become involved when trouble erupted between Chapman and Drury late in 1950. As Undersecretary, Chapman had always found it difficult to communicate with Drury, but during the early 1940s the two men could easily avoid each other. From 1942 to 1947, while the National Park Service served out its inglorious exile in Chicago, there were few chances for a feud to develop. After 1947, when the two were thrown into close contact with each other, the sparks began to fly. Chapman indignantly contended that Drury's lack of political savvy had become a serious impediment not only to the Park Service but to the department as a whole. More than once after taking over as Secretary, Chapman made disparaging remarks about Drury in Albright's presence. In his turn, Drury treated Chapman with thinly veiled contempt. The public controversy over Dinosaur National Monument, in which Chapman initially favored the construction of two high dams inside the monument and Drury opposed them, further separated the two men. Under the circumstances, Albright was not surprised when Assistant Secretary Dale Doty telephoned in December 1950 to say that Chapman intended to dismiss Drury and make Arthur Demaray director. Albright immediately came to Drury's defense, arguing that it would be unwise for Chapman to take such precipitous action. But in the course of the conver-

15. HMA to Drury, July 24, 1950, Drury to J. K. van der Hoagen, Aug. 7, 1950, and HMA to Mrs. Nattie N. Benson, Apr. 21, 1950, with attached copy of HMA to Clinton P. Anderson, Feb. 12, 1950, Drury Papers; Ise, *Our National Park Policy*, pp. 459–64; for an entertaining and informative exchange of views between HMA and Drury see Amelia Roberts Fry, "Comments on Conservation, 1900 to 1960."

sation it became abundantly clear that the Secretary had already made up his mind. Albright then suggested that since Demaray would soon reach retirement age a younger man should be groomed as his successor. Chapman had previously intimated that Conrad Wirth might eventually be in line for the director-ship. Albright stated that Wirth's background, professional training, and personality would qualify him for the job.[16]

A few days later Drury told Albright the other side of the argument and asked his advice. Chapman, it seemed, had de-manded that Drury vacate the directorship and, as a face-saver, either accept appointment as governor of Samoa or become a special assistant to the Secretary at a somewhat reduced salary. Rumors of Drury's impending dismissal were widespread in Washington. A number of conservation organizations were poised to come to his defense. He wanted to know whether to make a fight of it. Albright's response was pragmatic. Always averse to bad publicity, he hoped Drury would avoid a fight. He suggested that it might be appropriate for the Park Service direc-tor to spend the Christmas holidays in California and, while there, seek the advice of both Governor Earl Warren and the leading members of the Save-the-Redwoods League. Drury went back to California. On his return to Washington he and Albright had a long talk at the Cosmos Club. Drury decided to resign and asked Albright to convey his decision to Chapman, whose anger had been thoroughly aroused by the long delay. Albright got permission for his old friend to stay on for sixty days, during which time Warren named him chief of the Division of Beaches and Parks in California. Demaray assumed the Park Service directorship in April 1951. Less than a year later, Conrad L. Wirth, whom Albright had recruited into the Service in 1931, became director.[17]

16. Interview with Drury, Sept. 21, 1965; interview with Chapman, June 15, 1966; interview with HMA, July 6, 1965; Ise, *Our National Park Policy*, pp. 479–80, 517.

17. Interview with Drury, Sept. 21, 1965; interview with HMA, July 6, 1965; interview with Chapman, June 15, 1966; Drury to HMA, Feb. 14, 1951, Drury Papers; *Annual Report, NPS* (1951), p. 343 (1952), p. 381.

Albright held the highest respect for Wirth's abilities as a politician and public relations man. Moreover, he felt confident that Wirth would reflect the traditional Park Service values. A personable, outgoing, practical man, a landscape architect by profession, Wirth believed profoundly in the national parks, although he perceived no deep mysticism in nature. He held, as Albright did, that while the Park Service had the responsibility for protecting the parks, it also had the obligation to serve the needs of the ordinary citizens, many of whom were out for "fun and excitement as well as inspiration." The leaders of the Wilderness Society and Sierra Club cringed, but Albright cheered Wirth's appointment, which represented a reversal of the trend toward uncompromising aestheticism, a trend that Drury had personified. The new director was clearly in the Albright mold if not quite in the Mather tradition.[18]

Under Wirth's leadership, the Park Service weathered the Korean War and moved out of the doldrums into which it had fallen—through no fault of Drury's—during World War II. The bureau rebuilt its strength in Congress and faced up to the long-range implications of the vast popularity of the national park system. Nearly fifty million tourists visited the national parks and monuments in 1953, although the roads, campgrounds, and living accommodations were woefully inadequate. Mission 66, an ambitious ten-year program designed to upgrade and expand the facilities of the national park system to cope with a projected 60 percent increase in visitors by 1966, the fiftieth anniversary of the National Park Service, was the new director's brainchild. The program's "whole purpose," Wirth wrote in his annual report for 1956, "is to make possible the best and wisest use of America's scenic and historic heritage." The Mission 66 program, he said, would enable the Park Service to give the parks "maximum protection" while at the same time allowing the tourists "maximum enjoyment" and providing services "adequate

18. Quotation from the 1947 edition of HMA and Taylor, *"Oh Ranger,"* p. 206, in which Albright criticized the National Park Service for ignoring the needs of the tourists.

in kind and quality to meet the legitimate requirements of 80 million or more visitors in 1966."[19]

This sort of rhetoric would have warmed the cockles of Mather's heart. Launched with great ballyhoo and fanfare, Mission 66 caught the fancy of congress, the president, and the public, and sent National Park Service appropriations skyrocketing. Albright could scarcely have been happier. Mission 66 embodied almost to the letter his own national park values. Succumbing to Chapman's importunings and to his own enthusiasm for Wirth's style, Albright agreed in June 1952 to accept a six-year appointment to the Advisory Board on National Parks, Historic Sites, Buildings, and Monuments. From this vantage point he gave Wirth his unqualified support during the mid-1950s when the Mission 66 idea was aborning.[20]

Helping to found Resources for the Future (RFF), an independent organization devoted to the study of natural-resource problems and to the critical evaluation of federal conservation policies, was Albright's most ambitious conservation venture in the 1950s. Backed by the Ford Foundation, RFF developed into a lively social-science study center and into one of the respected conservation institutions of the United States.

The Ford Foundation, notwithstanding its enormous initial endowment of more than half a billion dollars, was a struggling, ungainly infant in 1951. Its highest-level officials made their headquarters in a mansion on the grounds of the Huntington Hotel in Pasadena, California, although the foundation also maintained offices in New York. The first uncertain efforts of the Ford people attracted more criticism than praise from the American intellectual community, which was disappointed at the distinctly middle-brow pitch of the entire program. One writer, for example, called the Ford Foundation a "great lumber-

19. *Annual Report, NPS* (1953), p. 289 (1954), p. 333 (1955), pp. 334–36, quotation from (1956), pp. 299–300.
20. Ibid. (1951), p. 345 (1953), pp. 288–89; for a sample of HMA's enthusiasm for the Mission 66 program, see U.S., Congress, House, Hearings Before a Subcommittee of the Committee on Government Operations, "Death Valley National Monument," 88th Cong., 2d sess. (Jan.–Apr. 1964), p. 286.

ing beast with its brains in Pasadena, its vital organs in Detroit, and its legs in New York. . . . The vital organs do the thinking, the brains do the traveling, and the legs digest all the information." In 1951, Chester C. Davis, the associate director of the foundation, and Rowan Gaither, the future president of the foundation, then the director of studies, began groping toward a program in the general area of natural resources.[21]

At about the same time, Albright and Fairfield Osborn, of the Conservation Foundation, Waters Davis, of the National Association of Soil Conservation Districts, and Edward Condon, representing a conservation organization called Friends of the Land, began talking about the possibility of interesting the Ford Foundation in the establishment of a "Ford Conservation Fund," which would provide financial assistance to the nation's relatively impoverished conservation organizations. Albright contacted Chester Davis, whom he had known since the 1920s, and laid the plan informally before the foundation.[22]

Busy with other matters, Davis pigeonholed the idea until March 1952, when he invited Albright, Osborn, and Condon to Pasadena for exploratory talks. Robert M. Hutchins, the former president of the University of Chicago now employed by the Ford Foundation, and Charles W. Eliot II, the former director of the Natural Resources Planning Board of New Deal fame, sat in on most of the discussions, which were congenial and noncommital. Albright agreed to help work up a formal proposal for submission to the foundation later in the year. Eliot subsequently went on the Ford Foundation payroll and supplied many of the ideas that were embodied in the final proposal, which was submitted to Davis in June 1952. Albright's main contribution was to persuade twenty-five nationally recognized conservationists to join him as cosponsors. On July 15, the trustees of the Ford

21. Quotation from Holmes Welch, "Philanthropy Uninhibited: The Ford Foundation," *The Reporter* 8 (March 17, 1953) : 22, reprinted by permission.
22. Conservation Foundation, Friends of the Land, and National Association of Soil Conservation Districts, "Preliminary Proposal" [1951], HMA to Davis, Feb. 15, 1952, and Feb. 29, 1952, HMA Papers.

Foundation earmarked $100,000 for use in starting a conservation program.[23]

In September, the Ford Foundation set up a "program development committee" on natural resources and called it together in New York. William S. Paley, head of CBS and chairman of the President's Materials Policy Commission, Stanley Ruttenberg, of the CIO, M. L. Wilson, director of Agricultural Extension in the Department of Agriculture, and Charles Eliot, of the Foundation's staff, joined Albright, Osborn, Condon, and a few others at these meetings. The committee made a series of specific proposals. Its key recommendation was that an independent "Resources Center" be set up immediately, with its own board of directors, its own budget, and a "small but highly trained staff." The center would provide up-to-date information about the "current situation and outlook" in conservation and would continuously reevaluate the "long-range programs" of the federal government. The committee also recommended that a "National Resources Conference" be called in Washington in 1953 and stated that it was prepared "to organize a nonprofit corporation to make the necessary arrangements for the conference." As the informal head of the program committee, Albright was asked to write to the presidential candidates, Dwight D. Eisenhower and Adlai E. Stevenson, and to President Truman, asking them to pledge their support for a national conservation conference to be held a few months after the new president took office. It was a well-devised ploy. Neither Eisenhower nor Stevenson could afford to turn his back on this lofty suggestion with the election barely a month away. Truman, of course, had nothing to lose. Albright received assurances of cooperation from all three men.[24]

23. HMA to Davis, Mar. 21, 1952, and Mar. 26, 1952, Davis to HMA, Feb. 19, 1952, Mar. 24, 1952, and Mar. 31, 1952, William Voight, Jr., to HMA, June 17, 1952, and July 1, 1952, Tom Wallace to HMA, June 16, 1952, Donald H. McLaughlin to HMA, June 9, 1952, S. T. Dana to HMA, July 7, 1952, HMA to Voight, July 7, 1952, and HMA to Chester C. Davis, June 19, 1952, with attached proposal, HMA Papers.

24. Minutes of the Program Development Committee, Sept. 18–19, 1952, Recommendations to the Ford Foundation Resources Program

At a second meeting of the Program Development Committee, in November 1952, it was decided to assume control of a small nonprofit corporation named Resources for the Future, Incorporated. Paley had originally set up RFF to publicize the recommendations of the President's Materials Policy Commission and to keep the commission's statistical data up to date. Now he placed the corporation, which had been dormant, at the disposal of the Ford Foundation committee, the members of which quickly transformed themselves into the board of directors and elected Albright president of the corporation. Charles Eliot, still as full of ideas and enthusiasm as in the halcyon days of the New Deal, was appointed executive director and was sent to Washington to arrange for offices and staff. Albright looked forward eagerly to his role in planning the Washington meetings, which he envisioned as a full-blown White House conference, "the first such conference since the one called by President Theodore Roosevelt in 1908." A news release went out within a week proclaiming that RFF would sponsor a "citizens conference on the conservation and development of the nation's natural resources." The release identified RFF as "an advisory group" for the Ford Foundation.[25]

Albright confidently assumed that the conference would be easily arranged. In this he was sadly mistaken. Through the good offices of Milton Eisenhower, he got John A. Hannah, president of Michigan State College, to accept the position of conference chairman. On December 30, 1952, he and Hannah went to see Eisenhower in New York, arrangements for the interview having been taken care of by Paul G. Hoffman, president of the Ford Foundation. Ike, florid-faced and friendly, "agreed with what we were planning to do," Albright reported, "except that

by the Program Development Committee, Sept. 1952, HMA to Truman, HMA to Eisenhower, HMA to Stevenson, Sept. 26, 1952, Eisenhower to HMA, Oct. 2, 1952, Stevenson to HMA, Oct. 14, 1952, and Truman to HMA, Oct. 24, 1952, HMA Papers.

25. HMA to Davis, Feb. 20, 1953, HMA Papers; interview with HMA, Dec. 19, 1964; *New York Times*, Nov. 17, 1952.

he hoped we would not expect him to attend a cocktail party, reception, or dinner." At the end of the conversation, Eisenhower pulled Hannah aside and offered him the position of Assistant Secretary of Defense; Albright thus lost a capable and politically acceptable conference chairman. During that same visit, Albright met Sherman Adams, the former Vermont governor who was slated to become Ike's chief assistant, and Gabriel Hauge, whom the president-elect had named as administrative assistant for economic affairs. Hauge was designated as the White House liaison man for the conference.[26]

Trouble came almost immediately from Sherman Adams, who thought he detected the strong odor of "ex-New Dealers," "idealists," and "planners" on the RFF's staff and board of directors. Eliot, because of his long association with Ickes and the NRPB, was immediately suspect. Albright too may have aroused Adams's anti-New Deal sensitivities, at least at first. Adams "seemed to feel," Albright reported, "that there were not enough businessmen among us." Albright decided that Eliot would have to be replaced as executive director.[27]

Adams still remained suspicious and in spite of Albright's efforts came to the conclusion that it would be a mistake for Eisenhower to associate himself with a crowd of New Dealers and planners. Albright spent ten days in Washington at the time of Ike's inauguration, trying to satisfy the White House staff about the propriety of the conference. Finally, after Albright and Paley persuaded Lewis W. Douglas, former director of the Budget Bureau and a conservative critic of the New Deal, to serve as conference chairman, Adams relented slightly. According to his final edict, the conference would receive a general endorsement from the president, but it could not be held at the White House. Albright and the RFF staff, now temporarily headed by Norvell W. Page, began planning for a "Mid-Century

26. Progress report for Board of Directors, RFF, Dec. 31, 1952, by Charles Eliot, HMA to Davis, Feb. 20, 1953, HMA Papers.

27. HMA to Davis, Feb. 20, 1953, "Status of Conference Arrangements" [Feb. 1953], and Norvell W. Page to HMA, Jan. 11, 1953, HMA Papers.

Conference on Resources for the Future" to be held at the Shoreham Hotel in December 1953.[28]

Albright realized by this time that he "had a bear by the tail and couldn't let go." Many of the sponsors of the original proposal had now lost interest or had spun off in other directions. RFF had to find a permanent replacement for Eliot as executive director, and, if it planned to hold a citizens conference rather than one at the White House, the base of support for the proposed meetings would have to be broadened to include business, labor, professional, agricultural, scientific, and political groups.[29]

Finding an executive director who would be politically innocuous but still capable of vigorous leadership posed no small problem for Albright. After sifting through a long list of names, the RFF board voted to hire Reuben Gustavson, then chancellor of the University of Nebraska, as the new director. At Albright's insistence, Gustavson was also named president of RFF; Albright became chairman of the board of directors.[30]

In April 1953, RFF called a meeting of its expanded "Council of Sponsors," which included about seventy-five representatives from trade associations, chambers of commerce, scientific groups, conservation organizations, labor unions, and professional societies. It was expected that the sponsors would return to their individual organizations and whip up enthusiasm for the forthcoming Mid-Century conference. At this meeting Albright sketched in the general objectives of the conference. The delegates, he said, would be expected to "identify" and "call attention to" the leading conservation issues of the 1950s. But the utimate aim of the conference, as he saw it, "would be not policy, but [providing] the basis for policy."[31]

28. HMA to E. B. McNaughton, Apr. 3, 1953, HMA to Davis, Feb. 20, 1953, William S. Paley to HMA, Mar. 24, 1953, HMA to Gabriel Hauge, Mar. 9, 1953, and Hauge to HMA, Mar. 11, 1953, HMA Papers.

29. Interview with HMA, Dec. 19, 1964.

30. Leslie A. Miller to HMA, Mar. 19, 1953, E. B. MacNaughton to HMA, Apr. 6, 1953, Davis to HMA, Apr. 17, 1953, and Reuben Gustavson to Davis, Apr. 16, 1953, HMA Papers; HMA to Drury, May 31, 1953, Drury Papers.

31. Norvell W. Page to RFF Board of Directors, Apr. 29, 1953, with attached proceedings of the Council of Sponsors meeting, HMA Papers.

Late winter and early spring of 1953 was the crucial time for RFF. It could easily have collapsed, and the proposed Mid-Century conservation conference might have become fatally entangled in partisan politics. Largely because of Albright's efforts, plans for the conference proceeded. Late in April the outspoken Fairfield Osborn expressed to Albright "the great admiration we all have of you for the immense amount of work, in the face of many other pressures, that you have done and how much it has meant in building up and carrying forward the purposes of RFF." The nation's conservationists now had a "virtual guarantee," Osborn added, of a "great national conference."[32]

More than sixteen hundred persons crowded into the Shoreham Hotel in Washington during the first week in December to attend the much heralded Mid-Century Conference on Resources for the Future. Virtually every prominent conservationist in the country put in an appearance, although a few avid public-power advocates refused to come because of the convention's alleged anti-public-power bias. As if to balance the scale, a few businessmen stayed at home because of the refusal of the United States Chamber of Commerce and the National Association of Manufacturers to endorse the conference. By coincidence, the meetings took place at the very height of the extreme reaction against radicalism and political dissent that swept the United States during the early 1950s. Senator Joseph McCarthy of Wisconsin, playing upon the Cold War anxieties of many Americans, indiscriminately pointed the finger of suspicion at individuals who happened to arouse his ire. Almost inevitably, the Mid-Century conference encountered charges of radicalism, the absurdity of which became apparent to anyone who troubled himself to investigate.[33]

The delegates divided themselves into eight study sections and spent three days discussing such topics as "Problems in Re-

32. Osborn to HMA, Apr. 24, 1953, see also Paul G. Hoffman to HMA, Feb. 27, 1953, HMA Papers.
33. *The Nation Looks at Its Resources* (Report of the Mid-Century Conference on Resources for the Future), Washington, D.C., Dec. 2–4, 1953, pp. 1–6; "Resources: The Plot Thickens," *Business Week*, (Dec. 12, 1953), pp. 126–29.

sources Research," "Competing Demands for Use of Land," and "Patterns of Cooperation." A battery of stenographers preserved nearly every syllable uttered. According to the preannounced plan, however, the participants endorsed no legislative or political proposals. There were those who contended that the conference produced nothing but a frothy confection of words.[34]

This criticism had some validity. Most of the ideas brought forth at the Mid-Century conference would have sounded familiar to Theodore Roosevelt. The old shibboleths about trees, land, water, minerals, grazing, and wildlife rang through the discussion rooms. The obvious lack of fresh approaches was disappointing but probably unavoidable. Many of the leading advocates of conservation in the United States, including Albright, were nearing retirement. Their suggestions plainly reflected their age. Moreover, the conference occurred during a period of domestic crisis, when many Americans felt troubled and insecure. The United States in the early 1950s, wracked by the Korean War and McCarthyism, produced few new ideas in any field. Irrevocably and inescapably a prisoner of the times, the Mid-Century conference could scarcely have avoided becoming, as one reporter tartly described it, a "middle of the road" affair.[35]

The conference, nevertheless, had considerable significance. Like its illustrious predecessor of 1908, its primary importance lay in the publicity it received. It sparked a new public awareness of natural resource problems. It created a mood of mutual cooperation among the nation's often cantankerous conservation organizations. And it called attention to the need for research in certain major areas of natural resources management, such as the conservation of minerals, recreational planning, land utilization, and wilderness preservation. Albright and the RFF staff, all of whom participated energetically in the discussions, felt elated at the conclusion of the conference, and so did the Ford

34. *The Nation Looks at Its Resources*, passim.
35. James B. Craig, "A Look at the Future of Resources," *American Forests* 60 (Jan. 1954) : 10–13, quotation on p. 10, reprinted by permission; "Resources for the Future," *Business Week* (Dec. 12, 1953), p. 188.

Foundation, although President Eisenhower's refusal to offer more than a few perfunctory welcoming words at the opening luncheon was a disappointment.[36]

Probably the most important thing the Mid-Century conference accomplished was to assure the future of RFF. With the Ford Foundation's bountiful support, the new organization flourished. It hired a staff of specialists, mostly economists, to make specific studies of resource problems. It began awarding research grants to stimulate scholarly interest in conservation subjects. A constant stream of books appeared under its imprint. RFF's youthful social scientists, happily jettisoning the Malthusian guidelines and doomsday rhetoric so evident at the Mid-Century conference, made a habit of questioning the sacrosanct assumptions of the past. Albright served as chairman of RFF's board of directors until 1962, contributing creatively to the organization's stability during its first decade.[37]

In the months immediately before and after the conference, Albright entertained serious doubts about the Eisenhower administration's attitude toward conservation. "I am very much afraid," he wrote to Hauge shortly before the Mid-Century conference, "that . . . a general impression has spread over the country that this administration is somehow or other, somewhere or other going to weaken the conservation policies that have been built up to control our renewable and nonrenewable resources." Legislation granting tidelands oil rights to the states, he claimed, "was not popular with the conservationists who are

36. *The Nation Looks at Its Resources*, pp. 1–6; "Resources for the Future"; *New York Times*, Dec. 6, 1953.

37. *Resources for the Future, Annual Report* (1956–65); see the following as examples of RFF publications: Henry Jarrett, ed., *Perspectives on Conservation: Essays in American Natural Resources*; Bruce C. Netschert et al., *Energy in the American Economy, 1850–1975* (Baltimore: John Hopkins Press, 1960); Ise, *Our National Park Policy*; Lowdon Wingo, Jr., ed., *Cities and Space: The Future Use of Urban Land* (Baltimore: Johns Hopkins Press, 1963); Vernon W. Ruttan, *The Economic Demand for Irrigated Acreage: New Methodology and Some Preliminary Projections, 1954–1980* (Baltimore: Johns Hopkins Press, 1965); R. Burnell Held and Marion Clawson, *Soil Conservation in Perspective* (Baltimore: Johns Hopkins Press, 1966).

unable to see the difference between the Tidelands and any other public lands." There were also "apprehensions" growing out of the "efforts of certain lumber interests of the northwest" to reduce the size of Olympic National Park, and of certain irrigationists to win authorization for "Glacier View Dam" in Glacier National Park. "Add to these things, and I am not naming them all," Albright continued, "the removal of a good many technical and scientific positions from the Civil Service Rules . . . thus affecting the morale of the Scientific Bureaus and [the agencies] concerned with resource conservation, and we have a situation which needs to be noted."[38]

Albright might also have added to his list the proposed dams —Echo Park and Split Mountain—in Dinosaur National Monument, which for a time seemed certain to win approval. He repeatedly remonstrated with Eisenhower's Secretary of the Interior, Douglas McKay, about these dams. McKay had told Albright that he intended to call on him for advice. A friendly Chevrolet dealer from Oregon, McKay had little understanding of complex conservation issues. Albright often chuckled at the Secretary's habit of saying, "Well, you know, I'm just a Chevrolet salesman," when he sensed that he was losing a conservation battle. The statement was heard fairly often during Ike's first term.[39]

With the Echo Park dam defeated and the Mission 66 program approved, Albright found his faith in the GOP returning. In the midst of the 1956 presidential campaign, when Eisenhower came under attack for his alleged anticonservation record, Gabriel Hauge and Sherman Adams prevailed upon Albright to issue a statement countering these charges. On November 3, 1956, the White House released an exchange of letters between Albright and the president in which Albright deplored "the ill-conceived movement to persuade conservationists that their cause is linked with the political fortunes of Mr. Stevenson." He declared, for

38. HMA, "Notes for Mr. Gabriel Hauge" (Nov. 27, 1953), HMA Papers.

39. *New York Times*, May 3, 1955; HMA, "Reminiscences," pp. 837–40; interview with HMA, July 24, 1964.

good measure, that the national park system, the national forests, wildlife refuges, and public lands were "better protected than ever before." This may very well have been true, but there were areas of conservation, such as range management, air and water pollution, and river-basin planning, that were badly neglected. Albright justified his partisan statement on grounds that conservation should be kept out of partisan politics. This was a curious kind of logic.[40]

During the 1950s, Albright probably got as much satisfaction out of his extramural conservation activities as he did from his job with USP, although he continued to be proud of his achievements as a business executive. He had been running the potash company for twenty years, and he knew exactly what to do under most conditions. After a period of expansion and wrenching labor troubles during the late 1940s he and USP enjoyed comparatively smooth sailing. This accounts to a large extent for his deep involvement in Resources for the Future and other conservation activities. Self-confident and well organized, he could find the time to head RFF and advise the National Park Service without really slighting his executive duties. He was in the fortunate position of not having to choose between his business interests and his conservation affiliations. It was his willingness to give his time to nonbusiness, nonprofit enterprises that set him apart from most other business executives. He rarely devoted himself exclusively to the task of making money.

Nevertheless, both Albright and USP prospered in the 1950s. Between 1945 and 1955 the company's annual sales nearly doubled and its net income increased by more than 70 percent. Albright's own salary climbed into the sixty-thousand-dollar bracket. By 1956 the USP mines had a capacity of six thousand tons of ore per day, and the refinery was equipped to produce sixteen hundred tons of high-grade muriate every twenty-four hours. The company had been forced to reduce dividend payments to stockholders in the late 1940s, but both profits and dividends rebounded sharply in the 1950s as increased mechani-

40. HMA's letter to Ike, quoted in *New York Times*, Nov. 3, 1956.

zation of the Carlsbad operations improved efficiency. Under Albright's leadership, USP's operations were aggressive, efficient, and profitable. But by the spring of 1956, after twenty-three years as the company's general manager, Albright was almost ready to call it quits. "I am thinking of retiring from the company this year," he confided to a close friend in April 1956. "I would probably still remain as Chairman of the Board and have some sideline activity, but I ought to get more time to travel and do other things I have had in mind for a long time."[41]

Merger talks had already begun between USP and the Pacific Coast Borax Company, the British-owned firm that had helped USP get started in 1930 and, in fact, still owned about 31 percent of the outstanding shares of USP common stock. The British company wanted to remold itself into an "American" firm so it could qualify for the generous depletion allowance, a tax benefit given to American companies. On the other hand, USP's impulse was to diversify. On May 31 the boards of directors of both companies agreed to merge, and by the end of June the stockholders had ratified the agreement. A new company, the United States Borax and Chemical Corporation, combining the assets of the two parent organizations, would come into existence on July 1, 1956, with headquarters in Los Angeles. Albright decided that the time had come for him to bow out. He retired on August 1, 1956, only a month after the new corporation swallowed up United States Potash. He agreed to accept a retainer as a consultant for the United States Borax and Chemical Corporation and to go on its board of directors, but his active business career had now essentially ended. "I am not only an ex-director of the National Park Service," he lightheartedly informed Drury a few days after retiring, "but I am now ex-president of the United States Potash Company."[42]

41. Information about USP's financial and business affairs compiled from *Moody's Industrial Manual* (1955), p. 808, and (1956), p. 1591; HMA to Drury, Apr. 5, 1956, Drury Papers.

42. *New York Times*, May 1, 1956, and May 31, 1956; HMA to Drury, Aug. 13, 1956, Drury Papers.

13

Retirement

Albright adjusted readily to the slow pace of retirement; he had few regrets about ending his long stint as general manager of USP. He commuted into his New York office frequently at first, but he deliberately stayed out of the problems of day-to-day management, leaving the operational details and decisions to his younger successor. In his capacity as a consultant he handled an occasional legal or political matter, and as a member of the corporation's board of directors he kept himself abreast of the major developments in Carlsbad as well as in Los Angeles and New York. But he become less and less personally involved in the potash industry as time went on. Within a few years his attachment was mostly sentimental. By 1962, when Horace and Grace returned permanently to California, to the beauty of its mountains and warmth of its deserts, he had terminated all of his business activities.

After 1956, Albright also began scaling down his participation in conservation affairs, although he had no intention of entirely ending his career as a conservationist. From 1956 to about 1961 his schedule remained nearly as cluttered with meetings and conservation conferences as before his retirement. By the time of his move to California, he had extricated himself from most of his elected or appointed offices. He remained an active member, however, of more than a dozen national and regional conservation organizations.[1]

1. HMA to Laurance S. Rockefeller, Mar. 12, 1959, A. Edwin Kendrew to HMA, Aug. 20, 1958, and D. W. Bailey to HMA, June 15, 1959, and June 20, 1960, HMA Papers; *Who's Who in America* (1956–62).

There were times after 1956 when Albright simply could not avoid making new and time-consuming commitments to conservation enterprises. Toward the end of the 1950s, for example, Newton Drury, who had taken over once again as executive secretary of the Save-the-Redwoods League, pressed him into service as an unpaid consultant in the campaign for a Redwoods National Park in northern California. Earlier, Frederick A. Seaton, who had succeeded McKay as Secretary of the Interior, urged Albright to accept an appointment on the United States Geological Survey Advisory Board. In 1958, in spite of his genuine reluctance, Albright found himself involved in the work of the Outdoor Recreation Resources Review Commission (ORRRC), which Congress had authorized to undertake a grand survey of the nation's recreational resources, including parks, wilderness areas, reservoirs, campgrounds, forests, lakes, and seashores.[2]

Conrad Wirth had at first argued that the Park Service should coordinate the survey under existing legislation, but the National Recreation Association, the Sierra Club, and the Wilderness Society coaxed Congress into establishing ORRRC. Once the commission's establishment became a certainity, a scramble occurred over the selection of a chairman, whose appointment would be made by the president. Wirth immediately thought of Albright, who could be counted upon to be friendly toward the National Park Service. "I know it is asking you to do additional work, Horace," Wirth wrote in July 1958, "and that it is time you had a little fun, rest, and relaxation, but I think it would be a fine thing if you could . . . take on the Chairmanship of this new Recreation Commission." The "conservation people" had already sent a list of names to the White House, he added, "and I happen to know that your name is on it." Senator Anderson of

2. Donald R. Brower to Wirth, Apr. 11, 1957, telegram, Wirth to Alexander Hildebrand (Sierra Club board chairman), May 2, 1957, telegram, Hildebrand to Wirth, May 3, 1957, and Wirth to HMA, May 9, 1957, HMA Papers; U.S., Congress, House, Hearings Before the Committee on Interior and Insular Affairs, "Establishment of National Outdoor Recreation Resources Review Commission," 85th Cong., 1st sess. (May 13–14, 1957).

New Mexico and Secretary Seaton also suggested Albright for the chairmanship. But the retired potash executive withdrew his name from consideration. "Five years ago, I would have welcomed an assignment like this if it had come to me," he confided to a conservationist friend, "but now I am too old and lazy."[3]

Albright's view was that Laurance Rockefeller, who had now emerged as a leading conservationist in his own right, would make an excellent chairman, one who would bring to bear a broad viewpoint and who would take pains to be fair to the Park Service. Eventually, Rockefeller accepted the appointment— most observers agreed he was the logical choice. One of the first things he did was to insist that Albright become a member of ORRRC's twenty-five man Advisory Council. Albright could hardly refuse. "I would remind you, my old friend," he replied, "that if you have need of this position now or later to secure the services of some other individual, you can count on me to be available to help you whether I hold any official place or not. You always have that assurance."[4]

In the next three years, ORRRC compiled a large amount of information about outdoor recreation facilities in the United States. It commissioned a series of specialized studies on such topics as "Wilderness and Recreation," "The Future of Outdoor Recreation in Metropolitan Regions of the United States," and "Federal Agencies and Outdoor Recreation." Its own staff inventoried the existing recreational facilities of the country and projected the demands for outdoor recreation opportunities up to the year 2000. The commission's final report, entitled *Outdoor Recreation for America,* advocated a sweeping national com-

3. Wirth to HMA, July 31, 1958, Fred Smith to HMA, June 27, 1958, and July 17, 1958, HMA to Smith, July 1, 1958, HMA to Clinton P. Anderson, Aug. 25, 1958, Anderson to HMA, Sept. 10, 1958, and E. B. MacNaughton to HMA, July 25, 1958, HMA Papers; *Congressional Record* (June 16, 1958), p. 11367 (June 17, 1958), p. 11431, and (July 10, 1958), p. 13310.

4. Outdoor Recreation Resources Review Commission, *Outdoor Recreation for America* (Report to the President and Congress) pp. iv–viii; *New York Times,* Apr. 6, 1959; HMA to Frederick A. Seaton, Aug. 22, 1958, Laurance S. Rockefeller to HMA, Mar. 6, 1959, and HMA to Rockefeller, Mar. 12, 1959, HMA Papers.

mitment to the goal of making "accessible to all American people such quantity and quality of outdoor recreation as will be necessary and desirable for individual enjoyment," and it suggested the establishment of a new agency, the Bureau of Outdoor Recreation, in the Department of the Interior, to have "over-all responsibility for . . . coordinating the various Federal programs and assisting other levels of government to meet the demands for outdoor recreation." Albright and a handful of other conservationists acted as Rockefeller's sounding board throughout this project.[5]

Beneficial results began to flow from the ORRRC report almost immediately. One of the most significant aspects of the report, especially from Albright's point of view, was its indirect reinforcement of the Mission 66 program. But even more important was the proposal for a Bureau of Outdoor Recreation. With its territorial jurisdiction carefully circumscribed, the new bureau would pose no real threat to the existing resource agencies. Its purpose would be to promote cooperation among the older bureaus, particularly the Forest Service, the Park Service, the Army Engineers, and the Bureau of Reclamation, whose plans and programs increasingly overlapped in the area of recreation. Stewart L. Udall, who became Secretary of the Interior in 1961, organized a Bureau of Outdoor Recreation in the Interior Department in April 1962. He immediately underscored the nonpartisan objectives of the new agency by appointing Edward C. Crafts, formerly a high-ranking Forest Service officer, as its first director. By this appointment, Udall hoped to bring the

5. Wildland Research Center, University of California, *Wilderness and Recreation*, Report on Resources, Values, and Problems (Washington, D.C.: Government Printing Office, 1962) ; *Future of Outdoor Recreation in Metropolitan Regions of U.S.*, 3 vols. (Washington, D.C.: Government Printing Office, 1962) ; Frederick Burk Foundation for Education, San Francisco State College, *Federal Agencies and Outdoor Recreation*, report to ORRRC (Washington, D.C.: Government Printing Office, 1962) ; *Outdoor Recreation for America*, pp. 5–10; Rockefeller to HMA, Apr. 2, 1959, May 1, 1959, July 2, 1959, Feb. 10, 1960, Apr. 21, 1960, and Jan. 21, 1961, HMA to Rockefeller, July 2, 1959, Jan. 13, 1961, and miscellaneous reports and speeches by Rockefeller, HMA Papers.

Forest Service closer to the Interior Department, an objective that Albright wholeheartedly supported. In fact, the creation of the proposed bureau shoved the Department of the Interior a step further in the direction of becoming a department of conservation, as Ickes, Albright, and others had earlier envisaged.[6]

Albright reaped a rich harvest of high honors after his retirement. Honorary doctorates came to him from three universities, including the University of California at Berkeley, each citing his pioneering work in the National Park Service and his leadership in the potash industry. He received the Francis K. Hutchinson Medal of the Garden Club of America and the rarely bestowed Gold Medal of the Camp Fire Club of America. In 1959, at a posh New York banquet, the Theodore Roosevelt Association awarded him its Distinguished Service Medal for "almost half a century" of creative leadership in "the preservation and development of the Nation's natural and human resources." The Department of the Interior presented him its highest conservation award, and, a few months later, the National Park Service paid him a fitting tribute by naming its new ranger training school in the Grand Canyon National Park the "Horace M. Albright Training Center."[7]

Albright's most gratifying honor came in December 1959, on the eve of his seventieth birthday, when nearly eight hundred friends and admirers gave him a rousing testimonial dinner in the grand ballroom of the Sheraton Park Hotel in Washington. Politicians, cabinet members, scientists, conservationists, businessmen, bureaucrats, publishers, architects, and journalists joined in the warmhearted tribute. Chapman and Seaton gave brief, good-humored talks about the guest of honor. President

6. *Outdoor Recreation for America*, pp. 5–10; *Annual Report of the Secretary of the Interior* (1963), pp. 125–26; interview with HMA, Nov. 13, 1966.

7. Citations for honorary doctor of law degrees, University of Montana, June 8, 1956, University of California, Mar. 20, 1961, and University of New Mexico, June 15, 1962, citation for T. R. Association Distinguished Service Medal, Oct. 27, 1959, U.S. Dept. of the Interior, news release, Aug. 6, 1963, HMA Papers; *Who's Who in America* (1966–67), p. 32.

Eisenhower dispatched a message of "congratulations and best wishes." In a wry tribute to Albright's own inimitable style of entertaining, there was a showing of amusingly candid slides and photographs of him at various stages in his career. The high point of the evening came with the announcement of the establishment of the "Horace M. Albright Lectureship in Conservation" on the Berkeley campus of the University of California. The permanent endowment for this lectureship, a fund of $60,000, had been contributed, the program explained, "by hundreds of generous friends and ardent admirers of Mr. Albright throughout the United States." No other award so clearly revealed the large amount of good will Albright had accrued over the past five decades.[8]

While Albright collected many laurels after his retirement, he also found himself entangled in a conflict of interest investigation that grew out of the fact that for a few years in the 1950s he served concurrently on the board of directors of the United States Borax and Chemical Corporation and the Advisory Board on National Parks, Historic Sites, Buildings, and Monuments. The conflict of interest charges, which Albright strenuously denied, were perhaps the inescapable outgrowth of his dual career as a businessman and conservationist. They resulted partly from his characteristic style of political and administrative behavior. They reflected a certain tightening up of the conflict of interest rules in Washington. And, ironically enough, they arose out of a political fight in which Albright was not directly involved.

Congress and the executive branch of the federal government

8. "Man from Inyo County," tape recording, Dec. 4, 1959 (used at testimonial dinner), clipping, Drew Pearson, "Conservationists Honor National Parks Director," De Land (Fla.) *Sun News*, Jan. 24, 1960, and Eisenhower to HMA, Dec. 3, 1959, HMA Papers; invitation to the Albright testimonial dinner, and Mrs. Le Roy Clark to Drury, Oct. 13, 1959, Drury Papers; quotation from Robert Gordon Sproul, "Horace Marden Albright," in HMA, "Great American Conservationists," First Horace M. Albright Conservation Lectureship, Mar. 13, 1961 (Berkeley: University of California, School of Forestry, 1961), p. 29.

became embroiled in a controversy late in the Eisenhower administration over the right of cabinet officers to deny Congressmen access to the current files of government bureaus. Congressman John E. Moss of California, a respected member of the House Committee on Government Operations, squared off publicly against Secretary Seaton, accusing him of a "conspiracy of silence" and of improperly denying Moss permission to examine the files of the National Park Service. Moss claimed he had information that indicated a failure of the Park Service to protect the government's water rights in Death Valley National Monument. Seaton asserted that Moss had seriously distorted the evidence and, in any case, the charges should be investigated by the Interior Department rather than Congress. After an acrimonious exchange of statements in the newspapers, Seaton and Moss reached an understanding and, in 1960, the Park Service files were thrown open to congressional scrutiny. The events on which Moss chose to concentrate occurred between November 1956 and July 1958. The issue was whether he could prove his charges against the Department of the Interior, thus making his point that Congress needed to have unrestricted access to information about the executive agencies.[9]

It was no secret that Albright had an intense interest in Death Valley. He had come to admire its scorched contours and arid landscape during his boyhood in the Owens Valley, which was only about one hundred miles away. In 1933, as director of the National Park Service, he had persuaded Hoover to set aside this unique desert region as a national monument. After leaving the Park Service, Albright often visited Death Valley, sometimes for personal reasons and sometimes for business purposes; it happened that the British firm which controlled the United States Borax and Chemical Corporation (and had once owned a large block of common stock in USP) also owned the Furnace

9. *New York Times*, Apr. 11, Apr. 13, Apr. 30, 1960; U.S., Congress, House, Hearings Before a Subcommittee of the Committee on Government Operations, "Death Valley National Monument," 88th Cong., 2d sess. (Jan.–Apr. 1964), pp. 215–16.

Creek Inn and ranch lands in Death Valley. Albright represented the British firm from time to time in the 1930s and 1940s in its dealings with the National Park Service.[10]

The Furnace Creek Inn, which stood adjacent to, but not directly on, the federal preserve, antedated the establishment of Death Valley National Monument by more than five years. Its operations were wholly dependent upon water appropriated for use by the owners of the Furnace Creek ranch lands early in the twentieth century. Efficiently managed and popular with the tourists, the Inn provided the only hotel and cabin accommodations at the monument.[11]

From 1933 to 1956, few federal dollars were available for improvements in Death Valley National Monument. Campgrounds and other government-built accommodations were totally inadequate. Acutely aware of the shortage of tourist facilities at the monument, the National Park Service had no intention of jeopardizing the operation of the Furnace Creek Inn, which Wirth's administration tended to regard as a national park concession, although, as a matter of fact, it was entirely exempt from government regulation. Because Congress refused to appropriate funds for the construction of government-owned tourist accommodations in the monument, an unspoken gentleman's agreement developed between the Park Service and the owners of the Inn, which called for the government to take a benevolent attitude toward the resort in return for maintenance and expansion of much needed tourist services in Death Valley.

With the onset of the Mission 66 program in 1956, however, the National Park Service had the funds to build new roads, to construct a large visitor center, and to double the number of campsites in Death Valley. Landscape architects drew up an elaborate plan for improving the monument. When the Park Service

10. U.S., Congress, House, report no. 193, "Death Valley National Monument," 89th Cong., 1st sess. (Mar. 22, 1965), pp. 51–54; U.S., Congress, House, Hearings, "Death Valley National Monument," pp. 285–91.

11. U.S., Congress, House, report no. 193, "Death Valley National Monument," pp. 52–53; interview with Newton B. Drury, Sept. 21, 1965.

indicated its desire to erect a visitor center and some new campgrounds on property then owned by the lodge company, an exchange of land was proposed. As part of the exchange agreement, the company suggested that the water rights in Death Valley be clearly specified (at roughly the current consumption rates), thus reducing the possibility of a future legal dispute. The Park Service stood ready to reach a compromise agreement on water use on the assumption that there would be enough water for both the hotel and the enlarged national monument facilities. In the interim, Albright persuaded the company to deed ninety acres of land to the government so that construction of the new visitor center would not be delayed. Later, working with Wirth and Congressman Clair Engle of California, he helped obtain legislation authorizing both an exchange of land and an agreement on water rights in Death Valley. As Wirth later testified, he recognized and appreciated the fact that Albright "was trying to hit a compromise" that would protect the legitimate interests of both the Furnace Creek Inn and the National Park Service. The enabling legislation became law in July 1958.[12]

At the invitation of the National Park Service, Albright also reviewed the Mission 66 plan for developing Death Valley. In a long letter to Wirth, he suggested a number of changes in the plan (for example, the relocation of proposed campgrounds and monument headquarters and a recommendation that the employees' village should remain where it was in the Cow Creek watershed). There was no mention of water rights. Wirth subsequently made a personal inspection of Death Valley and found himself in agreement with most of Albright's suggestions. On the spot he ordered the Mission 66 plan to be changed.[13]

12. U.S., Congress, House, Hearings, "Death Valley National Monument," pp. 350–51; U.S., Congress, House, report no. 193, "Death Valley National Monument," pp. 60, 67–78; *Congressional Record*, 85th Cong., 2d sess. (Jan. 29, 1958), p. 1305 (May 19, 1958), p. 9001 (June 23, 1958), p. 11906, and (July 3, 1958), p. 13014; HMA to Wirth, Nov. 1, 1956, in U.S., Congress, House, Hearings, "Death Valley National Monument," p. 183.

13. HMA to Wirth, Nov. 1, 1956, dir. NPS to supt. Death Valley, Nov. 6, 1956, Wirth to HMA, Nov. 6, 1956, supt. of Death Valley to dir.

Moss's painstaking investigation of the management and development of Death Valley National Monument culminated in public hearings before a subcommittee of the Committee on Government Operations early in 1964. Moss introduced testimony to the effect that the hotel company held legal rights to no more than two or three cubic feet of water per second, somewhat less than its current consumption rate. He produced letters from the files of the Park Service documenting Albright's involvement in Death Valley policy decisions, implying that the former director had used his influence to protect the interests of the Furnace Creek Inn. Albright's suggested modifications in the preliminary Mission 66 plan, according to Moss's interpretation of the circumstantial evidence, were designed to bring the plan into conformity with the hotel company's wishes. Moss emphasized that this was accomplished while Albright served as a member of the Advisory Board on National Parks, Historic Sites, Buildings, and Monuments.[14]

The officers of the National Park Service closed ranks in Albright's defense, unanimously expressing their high regard for his integrity and judgment. Lawrence C. Merriam, for example, then the San Francisco Regional Director, stated flatly: "Mr. Horace Albright is a man that everybody in the Park Service reveres." Conrad Wirth, having recently retired as director, also attempted to defend his old friend, although he succeeded mainly in getting himself into hot water because of his faulty memory. As a last resort, Albright took the stand in his own defense, but he could only assert his innocence. "If, in spite of my testimony . . .," he later wrote to Moss, "the committee concludes that there was a technical 'conflict,' I can only say that I appear to be helpless to overcome such a view. However, I

NPS, Nov. 23, 1956, telegram, Wirth to regional dir., Region 4, Nov. 26, 1956, Wirth to HMA, Dec. 28, 1956, HMA to Wirth, Feb. 4, 1957, dir. NPS to acting regional dir., Region 4, Feb. 21, 1957, supt. Death Valley to regional dir., Region 4, Mar. 25, 1957, in U.S., Congress, House, Hearings, "Death Valley National Monument," pp. 183–204; for Bennewies's testimony see pp. 152–90.

14. For an example of Moss's probing style see U.S., Congress, House, Hearings, "Death Valley National Monument," pp. 318–436.

can insist that whatever I did was in the public interest and it was beneficial to taxpayers and to all tourists who visit Death Valley now or in the future."[15]

In its concluding report, the House Committee decided that Albright had indeed been guilty of a conflict of interest. From 1933 to 1951, the committee conceded, he had acted "within his legal rights" in attempting to influence Park Service decisions on Death Valley. "However," the report continued, "Mr. Albright's position changed in 1952" when he accepted appointment to the Advisory Board on National Parks, Historic Sites, Buildings, and Monuments. "The committee believes that the Government was entitled to expect from Mr. Albright, and especially from Mr. Wirth because of his position as director, the conscientiousness and circumspection to cause them to recognize at the outset the duality and ambivalence of Mr. Albright's role." The report also reprimanded the officers of the National Park Service for accepting gratuities from the Furnace Creek Inn and the officers of the Interior Department for failure to safeguard the government's water rights. The proposed land exchange and water agreement between the Park Service and the hotel company, as authorized by the legislation of 1958, collapsed in the face of the committee's wrath.[16]

Moss had made his point. A few months later he and his cohorts on the Government Operations subcommittee persuaded Congress to pass a precedent-setting "Freedom of Information Act" that gave congressmen and senators the right to examine the files of all executive agencies except those dealing in highly sensitive matters of national defense. It was Albright's misfortune, after nearly fifty years of high-minded service to the National Park Service and the Department of the Interior, to have become a whipping boy. The Moss committee's assertions about the distribution of water rights in Death Valley and the

15. Quotation from Merriam, ibid., p. 248, Wirth's testimony, pp. 381–90, Albright's testimony, pp. 285–302, quotation from HMA to Moss, Mar. 3, 1964, pp. 302-4.

16. U.S., Congress, House report no. 193, "Death Valley National Monument," pp. 54, 61, 62, 13–21; for news coverage of the Moss committee's findings see Sacramento *Bee*, Mar. 25, 1965.

propriety of Albright's activities were in no sense legally binding. Formal charges were never filed.[17]

Albright's Death Valley difficulties may be traced directly to his administrative assumptions and personal style. A mediator by nature, he was trying to frame a compromise between the National Park Service and the hotel company that would have served the interests of both parties. This was how he had ordinarily resolved concessions problems in his years as superintendent and director. This was, one suspects, exactly what Steve Mather would have done. To Albright, conciliation and compromise were creative administrative devices. His style, his methods, and his administrative values had not changed appreciably since 1917.

What had changed to some extent were the ground rules in Washington. The conflict of interest regulations, though seldom invoked, had become steadily more stringent since the 1920s. Congressman Moss, in pursuit of a legitimate goal but for essentially political reasons, chose to invoke these rules against Albright, who was powerless to prove his innocence. At the 1964 hearings, he became the symbol and personification of the Mather tradition, the Park Service of yesteryear, whose prime concern was to build good will and seek cooperation. To Moss, the Mather tradition was obviously an anachronism.

17. For Moss's charge of a "million dollar land deal" see *New York Times*, Apr. 11, 1960; for debate on the "Freedom of Information Bill" see *Congressional Record*, 89th Cong., 2d sess. (June 20, 1966), pp. 13007–27.

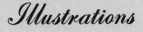

Illustrations

1900

Mary Albright and her sons

1915

The Mather mountain party

1916

Mather, Albright, and visitors
on summit of Mount Washburn in Yellowstone.
Courtesy of The Haynes Foundation.

1919

Albright and party of governors in Yellowstone

1921

Albert B. Fall camping with Mather and Albright

1924

Albright and Mather

1925

Opening ceremonies at West Yellowstone.
Left to right: Gov. J. E. Erickson of Montana,
Gov. C. C. Moore of Idaho, Gov. G. H. Dern of Utah,
Gov. Nellie Ross of Wyoming, and Albright.

1932

National Park Service staff.
Left to right: C. L. Wirth, A. B. Cammerer,
R. Holmes, Albright, H. C. Bryant, A. E. Demaray,
G. A. Moskey, Isabelle F. Story.
Courtesy of the National Park Service.

14

Half-Century of Conservation

Throughout his long and active career as a conservationist, Albright prided himself on his ability to stay in touch with the times. To a rather marked degree his attitudes and assumptions —particularly about economics and politics—exemplified the ideas and values of the leaders of the conservation movement in the United States. He combined the zeal of a reformer with the orthodoxy of a relatively contented conservative. Genuinely reverent toward Nature, he resented the kind of blatant commercialism that paid no heed to aesthetic considerations. He abhorred wastefulness and was sometimes disheartened by the resistance of vested interest groups to farsighted conservation programs. Yet he never seriously questioned the basic assumptions underlying the nation's economic system, and, like most of his conservationist colleagues, he never seriously doubted the long-run inevitability of progress. Moreover, he almost always tried to avoid dogmatic or doctrinaire commitments. His characteristic response, if not his automatic reaction, was to opt for a flexible middle position where he could compromise and maneuver. One may argue that his optimistic viewpoint, his unabashed pragmatism, and his relatively uncritical frame of reference provided the foundations for his success as a conservationist and national park pioneer.

From about 1900 to 1920, a remarkable group of government administrators, led by the aggressive Gifford Pinchot, dominated the national conservation scene. Their ambitious and expansive natural resources program embodied the utilitarian values of George Perkins Marsh, a nineteenth-century ecologist, and John

Wesley Powell, a scientist who shaped the early destinies of the United States Geological Survey. Their conservation plans revolved around the concept of multiple-purpose planning and the idea that the federal government should regulate the development of natural resources on the public domain. President Theodore Roosevelt wholeheartedly supported these utilitarian-minded conservationists, for he sympathized with their values and approved of their goals. Geared to a rapidly expanding industrial economy, the Pinchot-Roosevelt conservation program was designed to rationalize and regulate the exploitation of the remaining resources of the public domain.[1]

While Pinchot and his followers grabbed most of the headlines and exerted a powerful influence on national conservation policies during the first decade of the twentieth century, a small but articulate group of conservationists and nature lovers repudiated the assumption that aesthetic values should be subordinate to utilitarian values. Holding high the precepts of Henry David Thoreau and John Muir, the aesthetic conservationists, or preservationists as they sometimes called themselves, mustered surprising political strength. An increasing number of Americans found emotional and intellectual satisfaction in the idea of protecting and preserving the wild, unspoiled regions of the country. A so-called cult of the primitive, which glorified the wilderness (or the frontier) and associated it with the rise of certain desirable national traits, was rapidly emerging. There were those, too, who championed the wilderness in protest against the crassness they observed in their urban-industrial environment. The cultists joined the aesthetic conservationists in attempting to defeat certain resource projects, such as the Hetch Hetchy reservoir, that would seriously impinge upon or destroy unusual examples of natural beauty. The clash between the utili-

1. The best general discussion of the Roosevelt-Pinchot conservation program is in Hays, *Conservation and the Gospel of Efficiency;* Penick, *Progressive Politics and Conservation* contains an informative discussion of Pinchot's conservation values; for a discussion of Powell's ideas see Wallace Stegner, *Beyond the Hundredth Meridian;* see also George Perkins Marsh, *Man and Nature.*

tarians and the preservationists reached its peak in 1913, about the time Albright arrived in Washington.[2]

Albright's boyhood in the Owens Valley had conditioned him to cherish the symbols and folklore of the frontier and to appreciate the wilderness, although he lived in a comfortable town and took for granted the trappings of civilization. Moreover, he reached adulthood at the very time Muir and the aesthetic conservationists undertook their battle to "save" Hetch Hetchy. His youthful ideas were significantly influenced by both Muir and the cult of the primitive. His early work in the national parks tended to reinforce his intuitive hostility toward the utilitarian point of view and to confirm his suspicions about the Forest Service, the agency that had institutionalized Pinchot's ideas. Mather and Albright took pains to inculcate the aesthetic point of view in the National Park Service program. The first two decades of National Park Service history—the Mather-Albright era—may be viewed as a perpetual contest between the Park Service and the Forest Service and as a continuation of the old rivalry between the utilitarians and the aesthetic conservationists.[3]

The real thrust of Albright's position as a mature conservationist, however, was toward the middle ground of compromise and accommodation between the warring factions in the conservation movement. Albright jousted vigorously with the Forest Service over the years, and he always considered himself a preservationist, but it became apparent at an early stage in his career that he was willing to compromise in the direction of utilitarianism. Albright realized above all that congressmen and senators liked to vote for practical, "useful" programs. His main operating assumption, therefore, was that the national parks should be used—and used conspicuously—by the voters. Moreover, he became adept at the rhetoric of utilitarianism. On

2. Roderick Nash, "The American Cult of the Primitive," *American Quarterly* 18 (Fall 1966) : 517–37; see also Nash, *Wilderness and the American Mind*, pp. 84–181; for a discussion of the rise of aesthetic conservation see Huth, *Nature and the American*, pp. 148–212.

3. Swain, *Federal Conservation Policy*, pp. 123–43.

his numerous western swings, he whipped up local support for the parks by pointing out the economic advantages of tourism rather than the pristine beauty of the parks. He rationalized Park Service road-building programs in terms of "the greatest good for the greatest number." At the same time, he advocated the maintenance of large wilderness areas in each park.

In the late 1920s and 1930s Albright's pragmatic views came under attack from avid wilderness disciples, such as Robert Sterling Yard, of the National Parks Association, and to a lesser extent, Robert Marshall, founder of the Wilderness Society. But Albright staunchly defended the efficacy of compromise—in this case, a compromise between the militant utilitarianism of Pinchot and the prideful aestheticism of Yard, whose uncompromising stance and stylized view of the wilderness, while emotionally rewarding, had practically no political appeal. Albright was sympathetic to the goals of the purists, but he was too much of a pragmatist and too skillful a politician to be locked into a narrow and doctrinaire position. While consistently defending the national parks, he also defended the right of the tourists to have access to nature's splendors, and he opposed all schemes that would have effectively reserved the parks for the exclusive pleasure of a few mystics and nature worshippers.

After World War II it became clear that Albright's position accurately reflected one of the major trends of the American conservation movement. The federal resource agencies, which had traditionally represented the extremes of utilitarianism and aestheticism, moved toward the middle, adopting broad-based, nondoctrinaire, noncontroversial programs that held out the hope of compromise and accommodation. The National Park Service, for example, established dozens of National Recreational Areas (similar to the separate class of parks that Secretary

4. For an example of Yard's animosity toward Albright in the 1930s see Yard to Donald Peattie, Mar. 8, 1938, Papers of Donald Peattie, University of California, Santa Barbara; for an informative treatment of Robert Marshall's career see Roderick Nash, "The Strenuous Life of Bob Marshall," *Forest History* 10 (Oct. 1966) : 18–25.

Fall had proposed in 1922) where mining, reclamation, oil prospecting, grazing, lumbering, and the production of hydroelectric power were allowable. The Forest Service, in its turn,
materially enlarged its system of wilderness preserves in the national forests and began to show signs that the "cult of the primitive" had penetrated its ranks. The conflict between powerful
conservation agencies, though still noticeable, was becoming
somewhat less abrasive.

For fifty years Albright had been in the thick of National
Park Service affairs. He had begun campaigning against billboards and for the preservation of natural beauty at a time when
the goals of aesthetic conservation commanded neither widespread popular support nor clear-cut governmental endorsement. He played a key role in getting the epoch-making National
Park Service Act of 1916 through Congress. He stepped into
Mather's shoes in 1917 and 1918, at a crucial stage in the early
history of the Park Service, successfully organizing the new bureau. Later, as superintendent of Yellowstone, he established the
pattern of administration for the major national parks. During
his tenure as director, he moved the Park Service into large-
scale historical preservation. His persistence and political skill
insured that the matchless Teton–Jackson Hole country would
eventually win national park status. Indeed, the national park
system, which Albright was instrumental in establishing, expanding, and protecting, has become one of the most remarkable conservation institutions of the twentieth century. In 1966
its 220 scenic, historic, and recreational units, attracted more
than 130 million visitors. Fifty years earlier, only about 350,000
tourists visited the national parks.[5]

Albright's creative political efforts in behalf of the National
Park Service and general aesthetic conservation goals never
flagged. He enthusiastically buttonholed congressmen and senators in every session of Congress from the time of Woodrow
Wilson to the time of John F. Kennedy. He worked with and to
some degree influenced every Secretary of the Interior from

5. Statistics compiled from *Annual Report of the Superintendent
of National Parks* (1916) and *Annual Report, NPS* (1966).

Lane to Udall, demonstrating a rare ability to carry into action the ideas and conservation plans he espoused. As Struthers Burt once observed, Albright was "practically unbeatable" in an extended political contest. No other man, not even the redoubtable Steve Mather, defended the national parks more faithfully and contributed more creatively to the institutional strength of the National Park Service during its first fifty years.[6]

Although Albright's most significant achievements in conservation were made in connection with the national parks and the preservation of natural beauty, his activities and interests were never confined solely to these fields. He held high office and participated in the affairs of many national conservation organizations. He helped establish the Civilian Conservation Corps, which became one of the most widely acclaimed conservation agencies in America, and he left his stamp on Resources for the Future. He helped restore Colonial Williamsburg. Even his business career had certain conservation overtones, for the mining of potash in New Mexico occurred on lands leased from the federal government and was carried on under the scrutiny of the United States Geological Survey in accordance with accepted mineral conservation practices. Through dozens of political fights and conservation battles, his integrity and personal dignity remained intact.

Albright was not a major historical figure. Neither was he a great theoretician or philosopher of conservation. But his accomplishments as an expert administrator and pragmatic politician, operating within the limitations of a complex, pluralistic governmental system, were altogether extraordinary. His persistent efforts and concrete achievements, especially in the realm of national park administration and policy making, earned him a place in the front rank of American conservationists.

6. Burt, "A Certain Mountain Chief," p. 623.

Bibliography

The Papers of Horace M. Albright, a large and valuable collection of private correspondence, diaries, scrapbooks, government reports, photographs, and miscellaneous personal papers
dating from 1908 to the present, provided the major source of
biographical and historical information for this book. The Records of the National Park Service (Record Group 79, National
Archives) were indispensable for the years 1916–33. Other
manuscript collections at the National Archives, the Library of
Congress, the Harry S. Truman Library, the Franklin D. Roosevelt Library, and the Herbert Hoover Library yielded much
valuable information. Oral history transcripts, correspondence,
and personal interviews with individuals who knew Albright at
various stages in his career added background and dimension to
my research. Pertinent newspapers, books, government documents, and periodicals were also consulted. The following is a
selected list of primary and secondary source materials used in
this study. No attempt has been made to be exhaustive. One
should consult the footnotes for more complete information on
the sources.

MANUSCRIPTS

Albright, Horace M. Personal Papers. In storage at 427 Landfair Ave.,
    Los Angeles, Calif.
Anderson, Clinton P. Personal Papers. Harry S. Truman Library, In-
    dependence, Mo.
Boyd, James. Personal Papers. Harry S. Truman Library.
Chapman, Oscar L. Personal Papers. Harry S. Truman Library.

Drury, Newton B. Personal Papers. Save-the-Redwoods League, Office of the Secretary, 114 Sansome St., San Francisco, Calif.

Hoover, Herbert. Presidential Papers, Official File and Personal File. Herbert Hoover Library, West Branch, Iowa.

Krug, Julius A. Personal Papers. Library of Congress.

Merriam, John C. Personal Papers. Library of Congress.

Pinchot, Gifford. Personal Papers. Library of Congress.

Records of the Bureau of Reclamation. R. G. 115, National Archives.

Records of the Civilian Conservation Corps. R. G. 35, National Archives.

Records of the Forest Service. R. G. 95, National Archives.

Records of the National Park Service. R. G. 79, National Archives.

Records of the Office of the Secretary of the Interior. R. G. 48, National Archives.

Roosevelt, Franklin D. Presidential Papers, Official File and Personal File. Franklin D. Roosevelt Library, Hyde Park, N.Y.

Save-the-Redwoods League: Official Files. Office of the Secretary, 114 Sansome St., San Francisco, Calif.

Truman, Harry S. Presidential Papers, Official File and Personal File. Harry S. Truman Library.

Wolfsohn, Joel D. Personal Papers. Harry S. Truman Library.

Wilbur, Ray Lyman. The Wilbur Collection. Herbert Hoover Library.

PERSONAL INTERVIEWS

Albright, Grace
Albright, Horace M.
Andrews, Russell
Baer, Ethyl McConnel
Boles, Thomas
Brierly, A. A.
Brooks, Fred
Brooks, Stella
Bulpitt, Ernest
Cashbough, Gus
Chapman, Oscar L.
Cramer, Thomas M.
Davis, John M.
Drury, Newton B.
Gorman, Mary Watterson
Hadley, Lawrence
Horne, J. C.
Jackson, A. S.

Jewett, Gladys Jones
Kern, Joe
Lee, Donald
Mauger, George L.
Merriam, Lawrence C.
Miller, Loye
Partridge, Hazel
Partridge, Wallace
Price, Jackson T.
Quinn, John
Rowan, Mabel Matlick
Scoyen, E. T.
Scoyen, Mrs. E. T.
Sitton, Jack
Webb, Paul
Wheeler, Blanche Chalfant
Yandell, Birdie

ORAL HISTORY TRANSCRIPTS

Albright, Horace M. "Reminiscences." Oral History Research Office, Columbia University.

Bledsoe, Samuel B. "Reminiscences." Oral History Research Office, Columbia University.

Fry, Amelia Roberts. "Comments on Conservation, 1900 to 1960." Interviews with Horace M. Albright and Newton B. Drury, Mar. 21 and Mar. 23, 1961. Oral History Office, Bancroft Library, University of California, Berkeley, Calif.

Krock, Arthur. "Reminiscences." Oral History Research Office, Columbia University.

Tugwell, Rexford B. "Reminiscences." Oral History Research Office, Columbia University.

GOVERNMENT DOCUMENTS

Annual Report of the Department of the Interior.

Annual Report of the Director of the National Park Service.

Annual Report of the Director of the United States Geological Survey.

Annual Report of the National Capital Park and Planning Commission.

Annual Report of the Secretary of the Interior.

Annual Report of the Superintendent of National Parks (1916).

Commission on Organization of the Executive Branch of Government. *Concluding Report.* Washington D.C.: Government Printing Office, 1949.

———. *Organization and Policy in Field of Natural Resources: Report with Recommendations.* Washington, D.C.: Government Printing Office, 1949.

Congressional Directory.

National Parks Conference in New National Museum, Washington, D.C., Jan. 2–6, 1917. Washington, D.C.: Government Printing Office, 1917.

Outdoor Recreation Resources Review Commission, *Outdoor Recreation for America: A Report to the President and Congress.* Washington, D.C.: Government Printing Office, 1962.

Proceedings, Third National Parks Conference, Berkeley, Mar. 11–13, 1915. Washington, D.C.: Government Printing Office, 1915.

Proceedings of a Conference of Governors in the White House, Washington, D.C., May 13–15, 1908. Washington, D.C.: Government Printing Office, 1909.

Report of the Secretary of Agriculture.

Thorp, Willard L., and Ernest A. Tupper. "The Potash Industry." Report submitted to the Department of Justice by the Department of Commerce, May 1, 1940. Mimeographed.

U.S., Bureau of Mines. *Minerals Yearbook.*

U.S., Congress. *Congressional Record.*

———, House. Hearings Before the Committee on Interior and Insular Affairs. "Establishment of National Outdoor Recreation Resources Review Commission." 85th Congress, 1st session, May 13–14, 1957.

———, House. Hearings Before the Public Lands Committee on H.R. 434 and H.R. 8668. "To Establish a National Park Service." 64th Congress, 1st session, Apr. 5–6, 1916.

———, House. Hearings Before a Subcommittee of the Committee on Government Operations. "Death Valley National Monument." 88th Congress, 2d session, Jan. 27–29, Mar. 23, and Apr. 21, 1964.

———, House. Hearings Before the Subcommittee of the House Appropriations Committee in Charge of Sundry Civil Appropriations Bill for 1918. "Sundry Civil Bill, 1918." 64th Congress, 2d session, Jan.–Feb. 1917.

———, House. Hearings Before a Subcommittee of the Public Lands Committee. "To Abolish Jackson Hole National Monument." 78th Congress, 1st session, May–June, 1943.

———, House. Hearings Before a Subcommittee of the Public Lands Committee. "To Abolish Jackson Hole National Monument." 80th Congress, 1st session, Apr. 14–18, 1947.

———, House. Report no. 193. "Death Valley National Monument." Fifth report by the Committee on Government Operations. 89th Congress, 1st session, Mar. 22, 1965.

———, Senate. Hearings Before a Subcommittee of the Committee on Public Lands and Surveys. "Enlarging Grand Teton National Park in Wyoming." 75th Congress, 3d session, Aug. 1938.

———, Senate. Hearings Before a Subcommittee of the Committee on Public Lands and Surveys. "Investigation of Proposed Enlargement of the Yellowstone and Grand Teton National Parks." 73d Congress, 2d session, Aug. 1933.

———, Senate. Hearings Before a Subcommittee of the Committee on Public Lands and Surveys. "National Forests and Public Domain." 69th Congress, 1st session, Aug. 29, 1925.

NEWSPAPERS

Berkeley *Gazette*
Boston *Globe*
Boston *Transcript*
Casper *Tribune-Herald*
Daily Californian

Grand Teton
Inyo Register
Jackson's Hole *Courier*
Livingston *Enterprise*
Los Angeles *Times*

New York *Herald Tribune*
New York Times
Rocky Mountain News
Sacramento *Bee*
Salt Lake *Tribune*
San Francisco *Call*
San Francisco *Chronicle*

San Francisco *Examiner*
Tulare County Times
Visalia *Morning Delta*
Visalia *Times*
Washington *Post*
Washington *Star*

ARTICLES AND PAMPHLETS

Albright, Grace. "Horace Marden Albright: Man with a Sense of History." *The Aglaia* 52 (Winter 1958) : 20–23.

Albright, Horace M. "For a Young Man, A Reluctant Trip to Columbus Marsh: A Profile of Christian Brevoort Zabriskie. . . ." *Pioneer* 4 (Sept. 1963) : 20–23.

———. "The Glory of Jackson Hole." *The New York Times Magazine* (Jan. 21, 1945), pp. 22–23.

———. "John D. Rockefeller, Jr." *National Parks Magazine* 35 (Apr. 1961) : 8–10.

———. "Mather, Maker of National Parks." *The Survey* 64 (July 1, 1930) : 293.

———. "The Mather Mountain Party." *Westways* 56 (June 1964) : 24–25.

———. "Mt. McKinley, Park of the Far North." *Home Geographic Monthly* 2 (Oct. 1932) : 43–48.

———. "Reminiscing." *The Deller* [official publication of the Del Rey Club] 3 (July 1929) : 26–28.

———. "Report on the Proposed Mount Evans Addition to Rocky Mountain National Park." *Municipal Facts Monthly* 2 (Aug. 1919) : 3–17.

———. "Says the NPS to the NEA. . . ." *School Life* 16 (May 1931) : 165–66.

———. "Third Chapter in the Jackson Hole Story." *Planning and Civic Comment* 9 (Oct. 1943) : 18–19.

Albright, Horace M., and Frank J. Taylor. "How We Saved the Big Trees." *Saturday Evening Post* 225 (Feb. 7, 1953) : 31.

———. "The Everlasting Wilderness." *Saturday Evening Post* 201 (Sept. 29, 1928) : 28.

Boyd, Katherine. "Heard About Jackson Hole?" *Atlantic* 175 (Apr. 1945) : 102–6.

Brant, Irving. "Fight Over Jackson Hole." *The Nation* 161 (July 7, 1945) : 13–14.

Burt, Struthers. "A Certain Mountain Chief." *Scribner's Magazine* 35 (June 1929) : 621–26.

Craig, James B. "A Look at the Future of Resources." *American Forests* 60 (Jan. 1954) : 10–13.

"Does the Public Want It?" *Saturday Evening Post* 198 (Jan. 9, 1926): 42.

Frome, Michael. "Portrait of a Conserver." *Westways* 56 (Oct. 1964): 26–28.

"Grand Duke Horace of Yellowstone." *Saturday Evening Post* 197 (Apr. 18, 1925) : 58.

Graves, Henry S. "A Crisis in National Recreation." *American Forestry* 26 (July 1920) : 391–400.

Grosvenor, G. H. "The Land of the Best." *National Geographic* 29 (Apr. 1916) : 327–430.

Hough, Emerson. "Maw's Vacation." *Saturday Evening Post* 193 (Oct. 16, 1920) : 14.

Hunkins, Hazen H. "Department of Tours—1917, Bureau of Service, National Parks and Resorts—1920," Mar. 1, 1963. Mimeographed.
———. "The Organization and Wartime Activities of the Chicago Bureau of Service National Parks and Monuments of the U.S. Railroad Administration, 1918–1920," Mar. 1, 1962. Mimeographed.

"*Look* Applauds Horace M. Albright." *Look* 17 (Oct. 6, 1953) : 18.

Mills, Enos A. "Warden of the Nation's Mountain Scenery." *Review of Reviews* 51 (Apr. 1915) : 428.

Nash, Roderick. "The American Cult of the Primitive." *American Quarterly* 18 (Fall 1966) : 517–37.
———. "The Strenuous Life of Bob Marshall." *Forest History* 10 (Oct. 1966) : 18–25.

"National Park Service." *Saturday Evening Post* 188 (Mar. 18, 1916): 26.

"New Boundaries for Yellowstone." *Saturday Evening Post* 198 (Feb. 6, 1926) : 32.

Penick, J. L., Jr. "Louis Russell Glavis: A Postscript to the Ballinger-Pinchot Controversy." *Pacific Northwest Quarterly* 60 (Apr. 1964): 67–75.

Quick, Herbert. "Handling the Parks." *Saturday Evening Post* 188 (June 24, 1916) : 16.

"Resources for the Future." *Business Week*, Dec. 12, 1953, p. 188.

"Resources: The Plot Thickens." *Business Week*, Dec. 12, 1953, pp. 126–29.

Richardson, Elmo R. "The Struggle for the Valley: California's Hetch Hetchy Controversy, 1905–1913." *California Historical Society Quarterly* 38 (Sept. 1959) : 249–58.
———. "Western Politics and New Deal Policies: A Study of T. A. Walters of Idaho." *Pacific Northwest Quarterly* 54 (Jan. 1963) : 9–18.

"S. 4 Urged by Horace M. Albright." *Living Wilderness* 83 (Spring to Summer 1963) : 30.

"Shall Our Game Join the Dodo?" *Saturday Evening Post* 194 (Jan. 21, 1922) : 22.

Smith, Howard I. "Potash." In *Industrial Minerals and Rocks*, New York: American Institute of Mining and Metallurgical Engineering, 1949. pp. 684–89.

"The Owens Valley Controversy." *The Outlook* 146 (July 13, 1927) : 341–43.

Turrentine, J. W. "The Development of the American Potash Industry." Pamphlet, American Potash Institute, n.d.

Velie, Lester. "They Kicked Us Off Our Land." *Collier's* 120 (July 26, 1947) : 20; 120 (Aug. 9, 1947) : 72.

Welch, Holmes. "Philanthropy Uninhibited: The Ford Foundation." *The Reporter* 8 (Mar. 17, 1953) : 22.

"You and USP." Pamphlet, United States Potash Company, n.d.

BOOKS

Albright, Horace M., and Frank J. Taylor. *"Oh Ranger!" A Book About the National Parks*. New York: Dodd, Mead, 1947.

Backman, Jules. *The Economics of the Potash Industry*. Washington, D.C.: American Potash Institute, 1946.

Baker, R. S., and W. E. Dodd, eds. *The Public Papers of Woodrow Wilson*. New York: Harper, 1926.

Bates, J. Leonard. *The Origins of Teapot Dome: Progressives, Parties, and Petroleum, 1909–1921*. Urbana: University of Illinois Press, 1963.

Bean, Walton E. *Boss Ruef's San Francisco*. Berkeley and Los Angeles: University of California Press, 1952.

Burnham, W. P. *Three Roads to a Commission*. New York: D. Appleton, 1900.

Cameron, Jenks. *The National Park Service: Its History, Activities, and Organization*. Service monographs of the U.S. Government, no. 11. New York: Brookings Institution, 1922.

Catton, Bruce. *The War Lords of Washington*. New York: Harcourt, Brace, 1948.

Cowie, G. A. *Potash, Its Production and Place in Crop Nutrition*. London: Edward Arnold, 1951.

Fosdick, Raymond B. *John D. Rockefeller, Jr.: A Portrait*. New York: Harper, 1956.

Graham, Otis L., Jr. *An Encore for Reform: The Old Progressives and the New Deal*. New York: Oxford University Press, 1967.

Green, Constance McLaughlin. *Washington: Capital City 1879–1950*. Princeton: Princeton University Press, 1963.

Harding, Warren G. *Speeches and Addresses of Warren G. Harding . . . Delivered During the Course of His Tour from Washington, D.C., to Alaska. . . .* Washington, D.C.: published under the patronage of Calvin Coolidge, 1923.

Hawley, Ellis W. *The New Deal and the Problem of Monopoly.* Princeton: Princeton University Press, 1966.

Hays, Samuel P. *Conservation and the Gospel of Efficiency: The Progressive Conservation Movement, 1890–1920.* Cambridge, Mass.: Harvard University Press, 1959.

Hoover, Herbert. *The Memoirs of Herbert Hoover: The Cabinet and the Presidency, 1920–1933.* New York: Macmillan, 1952.

Hunt, D. Rockwell. *History of the College of the Pacific, 1851–1951.* Stockton, Calif.: College of the Pacific, 1951.

Huth, Hans. *Nature and the American.* Berkeley: University of California Press, 1957.

Ickes, Harold L. *The Autobiography of a Curmudgeon.* New York: Reynal and Hitchcock, 1943.

———. *Secret Diary of Harold L. Ickes.* Vol. 1, *The First Thousand Days, 1933–1936.* New York: Simon and Schuster, 1953. Vol. 2, *The Inside Struggle, 1936–1939.* New York: Simon and Schuster, 1954. Vol. 3, *The Lowering Clouds, 1939–1941.* New York: Simon and Schuster, 1954.

Industrial Minerals and Rocks. New York: American Institute of Mining and Metallurgical Engineers, 1949.

Ise, John. *Our National Park Policy: A Critical History.* Baltimore: Johns Hopkins Press, 1961.

Jarrett, Henry, ed. *Perspectives on Conservation: Essays in American Natural Resources.* Baltimore: Johns Hopkins Press, 1958.

Johnson, Hugh S. *The Blue Eagle: From Egg to Earth.* Garden City, N.Y.: Doubleday, 1935.

Kaltenborn, H. V. *Fifty Fabulous Years, 1900–1950: A Personal Review.* New York: Putnam, 1950.

King, Clarence. *Mountaineering in the Sierra Nevada.* New York: Scribner's, 1926.

Leuchtenburg, William E. *Franklin D. Roosevelt and the New Deal, 1932–1940.* New York: Harper & Row, 1963.

Link, Arthur S. *Wilson: The New Freedom.* Princeton: Princeton University Press, 1956.

Marsh, George Perkins. *Man and Nature.* Cambridge, Mass.: John Harvard Library, 1965.

McGeary, M. Nelson. *Gifford Pinchot: Forester, Politician.* Princeton: Princeton University Press, 1960.

Mementos of Bishop, California. Bishop: Chamber of Commerce, 1961.

Mr. John D. Rockefeller, Jr.'s Proposed Gift of Land for the National Park System in Wyoming. Privately published, 1933.

Muir, John. *Steep Trails.* Boston and New York: Houghton Mifflin, 1918.

Nash, Roderick. *Wilderness and the American Mind.* New Haven: Yale University Press, 1967.

Nadeau, Remi A. *The Water Seekers.* Garden City, N.Y.: Doubleday, 1950.

Nation Looks at Its Resources. Report of the Mid-Century Conference on Resources for the Future. Washington, D.C.: Resources for the Future, 1954.

Nixon, Edgar B., ed. *Franklin D. Roosevelt and Conservation, 1911–1945.* Hyde Park, N.Y.: Government Printing Office, 1957.

Noggle, Burl. *Teapot Dome: Oil and Politics in the 1920's.* Baton Rouge: Louisiana State University Press, 1962.

Penick, James L., Jr. *Progressive Politics and Conservation: The Ballinger-Pinchot Affair.* Chicago: University of Chicago Press, 1968.

Phillips, Cabell. *The Truman Presidency.* New York: Macmillan, 1966.

Resources for the Future, Annual Report. Washington, D.C.: Resources for the Future, 1956–65.

Rosenman, Samuel I., ed. *The Public Papers and Addresses of Franklin D. Roosevelt.* New York: Random House, 1938.

Salmond, John A. *The Civilian Conservation Corps, 1933–1942: A New Deal Case Study.* Durham: Duke University Press, 1967.

Schlesinger, Arthur M., Jr. *The Age of Roosevelt.* Vol. 1, *Crisis of the Old Order.* Boston: Houghton Mifflin, 1956. Vol. 2, *The Coming of the New Deal.* Boston: Houghton Mifflin, 1957.

Shankland, Robert. *Steve Mather of the National Parks.* New York: Alfred A. Knopf, 1954.

Starling, Edmund William. *Starling of the White House.* New York: Simon and Schuster, 1946.

Stegner, Wallace. *Beyond the Hundredth Meridian.* Boston: Houghton Mifflin, 1953.

Swain, Donald C. *Federal Conservation Policy, 1921–1933.* Berkeley: University of California Press, 1963.

Teeple, John E. *The Industrial Development of Searles Lake Brines.* The American Chemical Society Monograph Series. New York: The Chemical Catalog Co., 1929.

Tilden, Freeman. *The National Parks: What They Mean to You and Me.* New York: Alfred A. Knopf, 1951.

Turrentine, J. W. *Potash: A Review, Estimate, and Forecast.* New York: John Wiley, 1926.

―――. *Potash in North America.* American Chemical Society Monograph Series no. 91. New York: Reinhold, 1943.

Udall, Stewart L. *The Conservation Challenge of the Sixties.* The Horace M. Albright Conservation Lectureship. Berkeley: University of California, School of Forestry, 1963.

———. *The Quiet Crisis.* New York: Holt, Rinehart & Winston, 1963.

Warren, Harris G. *Herbert Hoover and the Great Depression.* New York: Oxford University Press, 1959.

Wilbur, Ray Lyman. *The Memoirs of Ray Lyman Wilbur, 1875–1949.* Edited by Edgar E. Robinson and Paul C. Edwards. Stanford, Calif.: Stanford University Press, 1960.

Index